T0299383

Java Programming Exercises

Take the next step in raising your coding skills and dive into the intricacies of Java Standard Libraries. You will continue to raise your coding skills, and test your Java knowledge on tricky programming tasks, with the help of the pirate *Captain CiaoCiao*. This is the second of two volumes which provide you with everything you need to excel in your Java journey, including tricks that you should know in detail as a professional, as well as intensive training for clean code and thoughtful design that carries even complex software.

Features:

- 149 tasks with commented solutions on different levels
- For all paradigms: object-oriented, imperative, and functional
- Clean code, reading foreign code, and object-oriented modeling

With numerous best practices and extensively commented solutions to the tasks, these books provide the perfect workout for professional software development with Java.

Java Programming Exercises
Volume Two: Java Standard Library

Christian Ullenboom

CRC Press
Taylor & Francis Group
Boca Raton London New York

CRC Press is an imprint of the
Taylor & Francis Group, an **informa** business
A CHAPMAN & HALL BOOK

Designed cover image: Mai Loan Nguyen Duy, Rheinwerk Verlag GmbH

First edition published 2025
by CRC Press
2385 NW Executive Center Drive, Suite 320, Boca Raton FL 33431

and by CRC Press
4 Park Square, Milton Park, Abingdon, Oxon, OX14 4RN

CRC Press is an imprint of Taylor & Francis Group, LLC

ISBN: 978-1-032-80117-9 (hbk)
ISBN: 978-1-032-79801-1 (pbk)
ISBN: 978-1-003-49555-0 (ebk)

DOI: 10.1201/9781003495550

Typeset in Times
by codeMantra

Access the Support Material: https://routledge.com/9781032798011

Contents

About the Author

Christian Ullenboom started his programming journey at the tender age of ten, typing his first lines of code into a C64. After mastering assembler programming and early BASIC extensions, he found his calling on the island of Java, following his studies in computer science and psychology. Despite indulging in Python, JavaScript, TypeScript, and Kotlin vacations, he remains a savant of all things Java.

For over 20 years, Ullenboom has been a passionate software architect, Java trainer (check out http://www.tutego.com), and IT specialist instructor. His expertise has resulted in a number of online video courses and reference books:

- *Java: The Comprehensive Guide* (ISBN-13: 978-1493222957)
- *Java ist auch eine Insel: Java programmieren lernen mit dem umfassenden Standardwerk für Java-Entwickler* (ISBN-13: 978-3836287456)
- *Java SE 9 Standard-Bibliothek: Das Handbuch für Java-Entwickler* (ISBN-13: 978-3836258746)
- *Captain CiaoCiao erobert Java: Das Trainingsbuch für besseres Java* (ISBN-13: 978-3836284271)
- *Spring Boot 3 und Spring Framework 6: Professionelle Enterprise-Anwendungen mit Java* (ISBN-13: 978-3836290494)

Christian Ullenboom has been spreading Java love through his books for years, earning him the coveted title of Java Champion from Sun (now Oracle) way back in 2005. Only a select few—about 300 worldwide—have achieved this status, making him a true Java superstar.

As an instructor, Ullenboom understands that learning by doing is the most effective way to master a skill. So, he has compiled a comprehensive catalog of exercises that accompany his training courses. This book features a selection of those exercises, complete with documented solutions.

His roots are in Sonsbeck, a small town in the Lower Rhine region of Germany.

Introduction

Many beginners in programming often ask themselves, "How can I strengthen my skills as a developer? How can I become a better programmer?" The answer is simple: study, attend webinars, learn, repeat, practice, and discuss your work with others. Many aspects of programming are similar to learning new skills. Just as a book can't teach you how to play a musical instrument, watching the *Fast and the Furious* movie series won't teach you how to drive. The brain develops patterns and structures through repeated practice. Learning a programming language and a natural language have many similarities. Consistent use of the language, and the desire and need to express and communicate in it (just as you need to do so to order a burger or a beer), leads to gradual improvement in skills.

Books and webinars on learning a programming language are available, but reading, learning, practicing, and repeating are just one aspect of becoming a successful software developer. To create effective software solutions, you need to creatively combine your knowledge, just as a musician regularly practices finger exercises and maintains their repertoire. The more effective your exercises are, the faster you will become a master. This book aims to help you progress and gain more hands-on experience.

Java 21 declares more than 2300 classes, about 1400 interfaces, around 140 enumerations, approximately 500 exceptions, and a few annotation types and records are added to this. However, in practical terms, only a small subset of these types proves to be relevant. This book selects the most important types and methods for tasks, making them motivating, and following Java conventions. Alternative solutions and approaches are also presented repeatedly. The goal is to make non-functional requirements clear because the quality of programs is not just about "doing what it should." Issues such as correct indentation, following naming conventions, proper use of modifiers, best practices, and design patterns are essential. The proposed solutions aim to demonstrate these principles, with the keyword being *Clean Code*.

PREVIOUS KNOWLEDGE AND TARGET AUDIENCE

The book is aimed at Java developers who are either new to Java or are already advanced and wish to learn more about the Java SE standard libraries. The intended audience includes:

- Computer science students
- IT specialists
- Java programmers
- Software developers
- Job applicants

The book is centered around tasks and fully documented solutions, with detailed explanations of Java peculiarities, good object-oriented programming practices, best practices, and design patterns. The exercises are best solved with a textbook, as this exercise book is not a traditional textbook. A useful approach is to work through a topic with a preferred textbook before attempting the exercises that correspond to it.

DOI: 10.1201/9781003495550-1

The first set of tasks are designed for programming beginners who are new to Java. As you gain more experience with Java, the tasks become more challenging. Therefore, there are tasks for both beginners and advanced developers.

The Java Standard Edition is augmented by numerous frameworks and libraries. However, this exercise book does not cover specific libraries or Java Enterprise frameworks like Jakarta EE or Spring (Boot). There are separate exercise books available for these environments. Additionally, the book does not require the use of tools like profiling tools, as these are beyond the scope of the book.

WORKING WITH THE BOOK

The task book is organized into different sections. The first section covers the Java language, followed by selected areas of the Java standard library, such as data structures or file processing. Each area is accompanied by programming tasks and "quiz" questions that contain surprises. Each section starts with a small motivation and characterization of the topic, followed by the exercises. Additional tips and hints are provided for particularly challenging assignments, while other exercises offer optional extensions for further exploration.

The majority of exercises are independent of each other, making it easy for readers to dive in anywhere. However, in the chapter on imperative programming, some tasks build on each other to develop a larger program, and the same goes for the chapter on object-oriented programming. The problem definitions make this clear, and more complex programs help to provide context for understanding different language characteristics. Furthermore, a more complex program can motivate readers to continue.

The exercises are rated with one, two, or three stars to indicate their complexity, although this rating is subjective to the author.

1 star ★: Simple exercises, suitable for beginners. They should be easy to solve without much effort. Often only transfer of knowledge is required, for example, by writing down things that are in a textbook differently.

2 stars ★★: The effort is higher here. Different techniques have to be combined. Greater creativity is required.

3 stars ★★★: Assignments with three stars are more complex, require recourse to more prior knowledge, and sometimes require research. Frequently, the tasks can no longer be solved with a single method, but require multiple classes that must work together.

THE SUGGESTED SOLUTIONS

The task book provides at least one suggested solution for each problem. The term "sample solution" is not used to avoid implying that the given solution is the best one and that all other solutions are useless. Readers are encouraged to compare their solutions with the proposed solution and can be satisfied if their solution is more elegant. All proposed solutions are commented, making it possible to follow all steps well.

The suggested solutions are compiled at the end of each chapter to reduce the temptation to look into a solution directly after the task, which takes the fun out of solving the task. The suggested solutions can also be found on the website https://github.com/ullenboom/captain-ciaociao. Some solutions contain comments of the type //tag::solution[], which marks the parts of the solutions printed in the book.

USE OF THE BOOK

To become a software developer, you must master the art of turning problems into code, and that's where practice and role models come in. While there are plenty of exercises available online, they're often disorganized, poorly documented, and outdated. That's where this book shines, by offering a systematic approach to tasks and well-thought-out solutions. Studying these solutions and reading code in general helps the brain develop patterns and solutions that can be applied to future coding challenges. It's like reading the Bible; you need to read to understand and learn. Surprisingly, many software developers write code without bothering to read others' code, which can lead to confusion and misunderstanding. Reading good code elevates our writing skills by building patterns and solutions that our brains unconsciously transfer to our own code. Our brains form neuronal structures independently based on templates, and the quality of the input we receive matters greatly. Therefore, we should only feed our brains with good code, as bad solutions make for bad models. The book covers important topics such as exception handling or error handling, discussing the correct input values, identifying erroneous states, and how to handle them. In software, things can and will go wrong, and we must be prepared to deal with the less-than-perfect world.

It's easy for developers to get stuck in their ways of writing code, which is why it's important to explore new approaches and "expand our vocabulary", so to speak. For Java developers, libraries are their vocabulary, but too many enterprise Java developers write massive, non-object-oriented code. The solution is to continuously improve object-oriented modeling, which is precisely what this book demonstrates. It introduces new methods, creates new data types, and minimizes complexity. Additionally, functional programming is becoming increasingly important in Java development, and all solutions in this book take advantage of modern language features.

While some solutions may appear overly complex, the tasks and proposed solutions in this book can help developers improve their ability to concentrate and follow through with steps. In practice, the ability to concentrate and quickly comprehend code is crucial for developers. Often, developers must join a new team and be able to understand and modify unfamiliar source code, and possibly fix bugs. Those who wish to expand upon existing open-source solutions can also benefit from honing their concentration skills through these exercises.

In addition to its emphasis on the Java programming language, syntax, libraries, and object orientation, this book provides numerous side notes on topics such as algorithms, the historical evolution of programming, comparisons to other programming languages, and data formats. These additional insights and perspectives offer readers a more well-rounded understanding of software development beyond just the technical aspects.

If you're looking for one more reason to add this book to your collection, it doubles as a fantastic sleep aid!

REQUIRED SOFTWARE

While solving a task with just a pen and paper is possible in theory, modern software development requires the proper use of tools. Knowing programming language syntax, object-oriented modeling, and libraries is just the tip of the iceberg. Understanding the JVM, using tools like Maven and Git for version management, and becoming proficient in an IDE are all crucial aspects of professional software development. Some developers can even perform magic in their IDE, generating code and fixing bugs automatically.

USED JAVA VERSION IN THE BOOK

While Java 8 remains prevalent in enterprise settings, it's crucial for learners to become acquainted with the latest language features. Accordingly, whenever feasible, the suggested solutions in this book leverage Java 17. Not only is this version equipped with Long-term Support (LTS), but runtime environment providers also offer extensive support, ensuring that the release retains its relevance for an extended period.

JVM

If we want to run Java programs, we need a JVM. In the early days, this was easy. The runtime environment first came from Sun Microsystems, later from Oracle, which took over Sun. Today, it is much more confusing. Although a runtime environment can still be obtained from Oracle, the licensing terms have changed, at least for Java 8 up to Java 16. Testing and development are possible with the Oracle JDK, but not in production. In this case, Oracle charges license fees. As a consequence, various institutions compile their own runtime environments from the OpenJDK, the original sources. The best known are *Eclipse Adoptium* (https://adoptium.net/), *Amazon Corretto* (https://aws.amazon.com/de/corretto), *Red Hat OpenJDK* (https://developers.redhat.com/products/openjdk/overview) and others such as those from *Azul Systems* or *Bellsoft*. There is no specific distribution that readers are required to follow.

Development Environment

Java source code is just plain text, so technically a simple text editor is all you need. However, relying solely on Notepad or vi for productivity is like trying to win a race on a tricycle. Modern integrated development environments support us with many tasks: color highlighting of keywords, automatic code completion, intelligent error correction, insertion of code blocks, visualization of states in the debugger, and much more. It is therefore advisable to use a full development environment. Four popular IDEs are: *IntelliJ*, *Eclipse*, *Visual Studio Code*, and *(Apache) NetBeans*. Just like with Java runtime environments, the choice of IDE is left to the reader. Eclipse, NetBeans, and Visual Studio Code are all free and open-source, while IntelliJ Community Edition is also free, but the more advanced IntelliJ Ultimate Edition will cost you some cash.

Halfway through the book, we delve into implementing project dependencies using Maven in a few places.

CONVENTIONS

Code is written in `fix width font`, filenames are *italicized*. To distinguish methods from attributes, methods always have a pair of parentheses, such as in "the variable `max` contains the maximum" or "it returns `max()` the maximum". Since methods can be overloaded, either the parameter list is named, as in `equals(Object)`, or an ellipsis abbreviates it, such as in "various `println(…)` methods". If a group of identifiers is addressed, * is written, like `print*(…)` prints something on the screen.

In the suggested solutions, there are usually only the relevant code snippets, so as not to blow up the book volume. The name of the file is mentioned in the listing caption, like this:

VanillaJava.java

```
class VanillaJava { }
```

Sometimes, we need to flex our terminal muscles and execute programs from the command line (also known as console or shell). Since each command-line program has its own prompt sequence, it is symbolized here in the book with a $. The user's input is set in bold. Example:

```
$ java -version
java version "17.0.5" 2022-10-18 LTS
Java(TM) SE Runtime Environment (build 17.0.5+9-LTS-191)
Java HotSpot(TM) 64-Bit Server VM (build 17.0.5+9-LTS-191, mixed mode,
sharing)
```

If the Windows command line is explicitly meant, the prompt character > is set:

```
> netstat -e
Interface Statistics

                         Received            Sent

Bytes                    218927776        9941980
Unicast packets             162620          64828
Non-unicast packets            276            668
Discards                         0              0
Errors                           0              0
Unknown protocols                0
```

HELPING CAPTAIN CIAOCIAO AND BONNY BRAIN

Ahoy there! Once upon a time, Captain CiaoCiao and Bonny Brain lent ye a hand with a certain matter we won't speak of. And now, ye owe them a favor. But fear not, for it will be worth yer while to assist them on their latest venture. Join the daring duo and their loyal crew as they sail the seven seas, striking deals with unsavory characters across the globe. Their secret hideout is on the island of Baloo, where the currency of choice is Liretta. With a crew hailing from all corners of the world, all program outputs be in English, me hearties.

Advanced String Processing

1

After dealing with basic data types around characters and strings in another chapter, we will now discuss advanced string processing. The topics are formatted output, regular expressions, and string splitting.

Prerequisites

- Be able to format strings.
- Be able to match, search, and replace with regular expressions.
- Be able to split strings.
- Understand character encodings and UTF-8.

Data types used in this chapter:

- `java.util.Formatter`
- `java.lang.String`
- `java.util.regex.Pattern`
- `java.util.regex.Matcher`
- `java.util.Scanner`

FORMAT STRINGS

There are different ways in Java to format strings, numbers, and temporal data as a string. In the package `java.text`, you can find the classes `MessageFormat`, `DateFormat`, and `DecimalFormat` as well as the class `Formatter` and in `String` the method `String.format(...)`. The next tasks can be solved using the formatting strings from `Formatter` in a rather easy way.

Build ASCII Table ★

Bonny Brain has installed a new app on her Aye Phone that shows her the ASCII alphabet:

```
$ ascii
Usage: ascii [-adxohv] [-t] [char-alias...]
   -t=one-line output  -a=vertical format
   -d=Decimal table  -o=octal table  -x=hex table  -b binary table
   -h=This help screen -v=version information
Prints all aliases of an ASCII character. Args may be chars, C \-escapes,
English names, ^-escapes, ASCII mnemonics, or numerics in decimal/octal/hex.
```

DOI: 10.1201/9781003495550-2

Dec	Hex		Dec	Hex		Dec	Hex		Dec	Hex		Dec	Hex		Dec	Hex		Dec	Hex		Dec	Hex	
0	00	NUL	16	10	DLE	32	20		48	30	0	64	40	@	80	50	P	96	60	'	112	70	p
1	01	SOH	17	11	DC1	33	21	!	49	31	1	65	41	A	81	51	Q	97	61	a	113	71	q
2	02	STX	18	12	DC2	34	22	"	50	32	2	66	42	B	82	52	R	98	62	b	114	72	r
3	03	ETX	19	13	DC3	35	23	#	51	33	3	67	43	C	83	53	S	99	63	c	115	73	s
4	04	EOT	20	14	DC4	36	24	$	52	34	4	68	44	D	84	54	T	100	64	d	116	74	t
5	05	ENQ	21	15	NAK	37	25	%	53	35	5	69	45	E	85	55	U	101	65	e	117	75	u
6	06	ACK	22	16	SYN	38	26	&	54	36	6	70	46	F	86	56	V	102	66	f	118	76	v
7	07	BEL	23	17	ETB	39	27	'	55	37	7	71	47	G	87	57	W	103	67	g	119	77	w
8	08	BS	24	18	CAN	40	28	(	56	38	8	72	48	H	88	58	X	104	68	h	120	78	x
9	09	HT	25	19	EM	41	29	)	57	39	9	73	49	I	89	59	Y	105	69	i	121	79	y
10	0A	LF	26	1A	SUB	42	2A	*	58	3A	:	74	4A	J	90	5A	Z	106	6A	j	122	7A	z
11	0B	VT	27	1B	ESC	43	2B	+	59	3B	;	75	4B	K	91	5B	[	107	6B	k	123	7B	{
12	0C	FF	28	1C	FS	44	2C	,	60	3C	<	76	4C	L	92	5C	\	108	6C	l	124	7C	|
13	0D	CR	29	1D	GS	45	2D	-	61	3D	=	77	4D	M	93	5D	]	109	6D	m	125	7D	}
14	0E	SO	30	1E	RS	46	2E	.	62	3E	>	78	4E	N	94	5E	^	110	6E	n	126	7E	~
15	0F	SI	31	1F	US	47	2F	/	63	3F	?	79	4F	O	95	5F	_	111	6F	o	127	7F	DEL

However, their Aye Phone doesn't have such a widescreen, and the first two blocks are not visible characters anyway.

Task:

- Write a program that prints all ASCII characters from position 32 to 127 in the same formatting as the Unix program `ascii` does.
- At position 127, write DEL.

Aligned Outputs ★

Captain CiaoCiao needs a table of the following type for a listing:

```
Dory Dab    paid
Bob Banjo   paid
Cod Buri    paid
Bugsy       not paid
```

Task:

- Write a method `printList(String[] names, boolean[] paid)` that prints a collection on the screen. The first string array contains all names, the second array contains information whether the person has paid or not.
- All names can be of different lengths, but the texts in the second column should be aligned.
- The longest string in the first column has a distance of four spaces to the second column.
- If passed arrays are `null`, a `NullPointerException` must be thrown.

REGULAR EXPRESSIONS AND PATTERN RECOGNITION

Regular expressions are a curse and a blessing for many. Used incorrectly, they lead to programs that are impossible to read later, used correctly, they shorten the program massively and contribute to clarity.

The next exercises will show that we can use regular expressions to test whether

1. A string completely matches a regular expression.
2. A partial string exists and if so, find out where, and then replace it.

Later, we will also use regular expressions to specify separators and decompose strings.

Quiz: Define Regex ★

What does the regex look like to match or find the following?

- A string of exactly 10 digits.
- A string of 5–10 digits and letters.
- A string ending in ., ! or ? like a sentence.
- A nonempty string that does not contain digits.
- An official title or a name title: `Prof.`, `Dr.`, `Dr. med.`, `Dr. h.c.` in the string.

Determine Popularity in Social Media ★

Of course Captain CiaoCiao is active on social media; his identifier is `#CaptainCiaoCiao` or `@CaptainCiaoCiao`.

Now Captain CiaoCiao wants to know how popular he is.

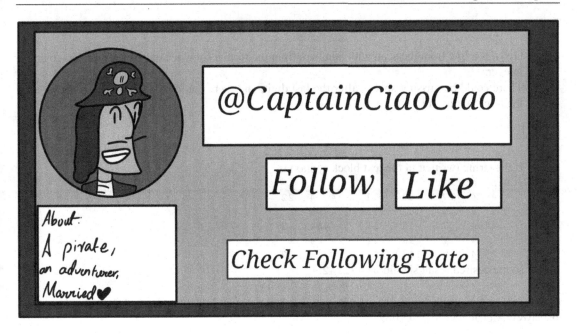

Task:

- Given an aggregated text with messages; how often does #CaptainCiaoCiao or @ CaptainCiaoCiao occur there?

Example:

- For the following input, the result is 2.
```
Make me a baby #CaptainCiaoCiao
Hey @CaptainCiaoCiao, where is the recruitment test?
What is a hacker's favorite pop group? The Black IP's.
```

Detect Scanned Values ★

Bonny Brain receives scanned lists of numbers that need to be processed electronically. In the first step, it sends the scans through an OCR recognizer, and the result is ASCII text. The numbers from the OCR recognition always look like this:

Representation of the numbers 0 to 9

```
 000    11    22   333   4   4 5555    6     77777  888    9999
0   00 111   2  2     3  4   4 5      6         7   8    8 9    9
0  0  0  11     2    33  4444 555  6666       7     888    9999
00   0  11     2     3   4     5 6   6       7      8    8      9
 000   1111 2222 333      4 555    666       7      888       9
```

Task:

- Given is a line from the scan with numbers from the format shown. Convert the numbers to an integer.
- There could be missing spaces after the last digit, and there could be several spaces between the large characters.

Example:

- If the string (written in the text block syntax) is
  ```
  String ocr = """
       4   4 77777  11     11      4   4   22
       4   4      7 111   111      4   4 2   2
      4444     7    11     11     4444     2
         4     7    11     11         4   2
         4     7  1111  1111         4 2222""";
  ```
  so the desired result should be 471142.

If you want to play around with the strings, you can find a way at https://patorjk.com/software/taag/#p=display&f=Alphabet&t=0123456789.

Quiet Please! Defuse Shouting Texts ★

Captain CiaoCiao often gets letters, and the senders often SCREAM in capital letters—how nasty for his eyes.

Task:

- Write a method String silentShoutingWords(String) that converts all capitalized words over three letters in length to lowercase.

Example:

- `silentShoutingWords("AY Captain! Smutje MUST GO!")` → `"AY Captain! Smutje must GO!"`

Converting Time from AM/PM Format to 24-Hour Format ★★

Bonny Brain frequently gets messages where the time is given in AM and PM.

`We raid the harbor at 11:00 PM and meet on the amusement mile at 1:30 AM.`

Bonny Brain doesn't like that; she wants only the 24-hour count of Military Time.

Task:

- Write a converter that converts strings with AM/PM (case-insensitive, even with periods) to Military Time. As a reminder, 12:00 AM is 00:00, and 12:00 PM is 12:00.

Examples:

- `"Harbour: 11:00 PM, entertainment districts: 1:30 a.m.!"` → `Harbour: 2300, entertainment districts: 0130!"`
- `"Get out of bed: 12:00AM, bake a cake: 12 PM."` → `"Get out of bed: 0000, bake a cake: 1200"`

DECOMPOSE STRINGS INTO TOKENS

Tokenizing is the opposite of constructing and formatting a string. A string is split into substrings, with separators determining the separation points. Java provides various classes for tokenizing strings and input. The separators can be symbols or strings described by regular expressions. The split(...) method of the String class works with regular expressions just like the Scanner, and the StringTokenizer class does not.

Split Address Lines with the StringTokenizer ★

The software of Captain CiaoCiao has to evaluate addresses consisting of three or four lines.
The meaning of the lines

LINE	CONTENT	OPTIONAL
1	name	no
2	street	no
3	city	no
4	country	yes

The lines are separated with a line break. There are four valid separator symbols or sequences:
LF is the abbreviation for "line feed" and CR for "carriage return"; in old teleprinters, CR moved the carriage to the first column, and LF pushed the paper up.
Traditionally, DOS and Microsoft Windows use the combination \r\n, while Unix systems use \n.
Task:

- Break a newline-separated string into four lines, and assign the lines to the variables name, street, city, and country.
- If a fourth line with the country name is not given, let country be "Drusselstein".
- Reassemble the line as a CSV line separated by semicolons.

Examples:

- "Boots and Bootles\n21 Pickle Street\n424242 Douglas\nArendelle" →
  Boots and Bootles;21 Pickle street;424242 Douglas;Arendelle
- "Doofenshmirtz   Evil   Inc.\nStrudelkuschel   4427\nDanville" →
  Doofenshmirtz   Evil   Inc.;Strudelkuschel   4427;Gimmelshtump;
  Drusselstein

TABLE 1.1 Line break

CHARACTER (ABBREVIATION)	DECIMAL	HEXADECIMAL	ESCAPE SEQUENCE
LF	10	0A	\n
CR	13	0D	\r
CR LF	13 10	0D 0A	\r\n
LF CR	10 13	0A 0D	\n\r

Split Sentences into Words and Reverse Them ★

Bonny Brain is waiting for a message, but something went wrong with the transmission—all the words are reversed!

`erehW did eht etarip esahcrup sih kooh? tA eht dnah-dnoces pohs!`

Task:

1. Break the string into words. Separators of words are spaces and punctuation marks.
2. Turn over all the words one by one.
3. Output the words one after the other, separated by a space. The punctuation marks and other separators are not critical.

Example:

- `"erehW did eht etarip esahcrup sih kooh? tA eht dnah-dnoces pohs!"`
  → `"Where did the pirate purchase his hook At the hand second shop"`

Check Relations between Numbers ★

Captain CiaoCiao practices archery, and he records the scores from 0 to 10 in a list. He also notes if he got better, worse, or if the score stays the same. It may look like this:

`1<2>1<10=10>2`

Goldy Goldfish has the task of checking the relation signs <,> and =.
Task:

- Write a program that gets a string like the one in the example and returns `true` if all relation signs are correct, and `false` otherwise.

Examples:

- `1<2>1<10=10>2` → `true`
- `1<1` → `false`
- `1<` → `false`
- `1` → `true`

Convert A1 Notation to Columns and Rows ★★

Captain CiaoCiao keeps records of his loot and uses spreadsheets. With his staff, he discusses the figures, and to address the cells he uses the column and row index; for example, he says 4–16 to refer to the 4th column and the 16th row. Now he has heard of a whole new way to name cells, *A1 notation*, which uses a new kind of software called ECKSEL. This involves coding the column with letters from A to Z, according to the following scheme:

`A, B, ..., Z, AA, ..., AZ, BA, ..., ZZ, AAA, AAB, ...`

The lines are still described with numbers. Thus, A2 stands for cell 1–2.

Since Captain CiaoCiao has its difficulties with A1 notation, the specification is to be converted back to numeric columns and rows.

Task:

- Write a method `parseA1Notation(String)` that gets a `string` in A1 notation and returns an array with two elements, in which at position 0 is the column and at position 1 is the row.

Examples:

- `parseA1Notation("A1") → [1, 1]`
- `parseA1Notation("Z2") → [26, 2]`
- `parseA1Notation("AA34") → [27, 34]`
- `parseA1Notation("BZ") → [0, 0]`
- `parseA1Notation("34") → [0, 0]`
- `parseA1Notation(" ") → [0, 0]`
- `parseA1Notation("") → [0, 0]`

Parse Simple CSV Files with Coordinates ★

Bonny Brain notes the locations with loot in a CSV file *coordinates.csv*, where the coordinates are floating-point numbers separated by commas.

For example, the file looks like this:

com/tutego/exercise/string/coordinates.csv

```
20.091612,-155.676695
23.087301,-73.643472
21.305452,-71.690421
```

Task:

- Create a CSV file manually. It should contain several lines with coordinates; a comma separates the coordinates.
- A Java program should read the CSV file and output an HTML file with SVG for the polygon course on the screen.
- Use the class `Scanner` to parse the file. Make sure to initialize the `Scanner` with `useLocale(Locale.ENGLISH)` if your locale is not English by default.

Example: For the upper block, we want to create

```
<svg height="210" width="500">
<polygon points="20.091612,-155.676695 23.087301,-73.643472 21.305452,-
71.690421 " style="fill:lime;stroke:purple;stroke-width:1" />
</svg>
```

Compress Strings Lossless by Runlength Encoding ★★★

To reduce the volume of data, files are often compressed. There are different compression algorithms; some are lossy like vowel removal, others work without loss like ZIP. Lossy compression is found in images, JPEG is a good example. Depending on the degree of compression, the image quality degrades. In JPEG, very high compression results in an image with strong artifacts.

A simple lossless compression is *run-length* encoding. The idea is to combine a sequence of identical symbols so that only the number and the symbol are written. The graphic format GIF, for example, uses this form of compression. Therefore, images with many monochrome lines are also smaller than, for example, images in which each pixel has a different color.

The next task is about run-length encoding. Suppose a string consists of a sequence of . (dot) and - (minus sign), such as:

```
--...----------..-
```

To shorten the length of strings, we can first write the symbol followed by the number of symbols. The string with 17 characters could be shortened to the following string with 9 characters:

```
-2.4-8.2-
```

Task:

1. Create a new class `SimpleStringCompressor`.
2. Write a static method `String compress(String)` that encodes sequences of . and - according to the described algorithm: First comes the character, then the number.
3. Write a decoder `String decompress(String)` that unpacks the compressed string. Let `decompress(compress(input))` be equal to `input`.

Extensions:

• The program shall be able to handle all nondigits.
• Refine the program so that the number is omitted if the character occurs only exactly once.

CHARACTER ENCODINGS AND UNICODE COLLATION ALGORITHM

Over the network and in the file system, everything is stored as a byte. One byte can have 256 different values, but this is not enough for all the characters in the world. Therefore, there are *character encodings*, which can encode all characters in the world in a certain way. The character encodings differ thereby. Sometimes characters are mapped to a fixed number of bytes, sometimes characters are mapped to a different number of bytes, or perhaps some characters are just not recognized at all. Java supports all kinds of character encodings, but the most important character encoding today is the UTF-8 encoding.

Quiz: Encoding for Unicode Characters ★

What characterizes an *UTF-8 encoding*?

Quiz: Order of Strings with and without Collator ★

After comparing with the Comparator, are the outputs positive, negative, or 0?

```
Comparator<String> comparator = Comparator.naturalOrder();
System.out.println( comparator.compare( "a", "ä" ) );
System.out.println( comparator.compare( "ä", "z" ) );
System.out.println( comparator.compare( "n", "ñ" ) );
System.out.println( comparator.compare( "ñ", "o" ) );

Comparator<Object> collatorDE = Collator.getInstance( Locale.GERMAN );
System.out.println( collatorDE.compare( "a", "ä" ) );
System.out.println( collatorDE.compare( "ä", "z" ) );
System.out.println( collatorDE.compare( "n", "ñ" ) );
System.out.println( collatorDE.compare( "ñ", "o" ) );
```

SUGGESTED SOLUTIONS

Build ASCII Table

com/tutego/exercise/string/PrintAsciiTable.java

```
System.out.println( "Dec Hex    ".repeat( 6 ) );

for ( int row = 0; row < 16; row++ ) {
  for ( int asciiCode = 32 + row; asciiCode <= 127; asciiCode += 16 ) {
    System.out.printf(
        "%1$3d %1$X %2$s  ", asciiCode,
        asciiCode == 127 ? "DEL" : Character.toString( asciiCode ) );
  }
  System.out.println();
}
```

First, the program writes the table header, in which the string "Dec Hex" for the six columns is set six times in a row with spacing.

The generated table has 16 rows, which generates a loop. In principle, we could also dynamically calculate the number of rows from the start and end values and the number of columns (six in our case). However, we know that if we start at position 32, and end at 127, with 6 columns we need 16 rows.

The inner loop writes all columns for a given row. At the top left is the first element, the space character. To the right, the character increases not by one, but by 16, which is, therefore, the loop counter. In the next line, we don't start at 32 but at 33, the pattern here is the following: the start value of the inner loop is 32 + row, so 32 plus the row number. Altogether, the loop ends when the ASCII code has reached 127.

Within the inner loop's body, the character is required to be displayed as a string. Essentially, each character is outputted as a string. The conditional operator verifies whether the character at positions 127 is the DEL character; all other characters are converted to a string of length 1 through the Character method. The format string consists of three components: the first two parts access the first format argument and begin by displaying the character's position as a decimal number, followed by its number in hexadecimal format. The integer is left-padded with white space, while the hexadecimal number doesn't require any width information, as it always contains two digits when starting with 32. The third block contains the character as a string and the second format argument. Finally, a line feed is added at the end of the line.

Output of PrintAsciiTable

Dec Hex	Dec Hex	Dec Hex	Dec Hex	Dec Hex	Dec Hex
32 20	48 30 0	64 40 @	80 50 P	96 60 '	112 70 p
33 21 !	49 31 1	65 41 A	81 51 Q	97 61 a	113 71 q
34 22 "	50 32 2	66 42 B	82 52 R	98 62 b	114 72 r
35 23 #	51 33 3	67 43 C	83 53 S	99 63 c	115 73 s
36 24 $	52 34 4	68 44 D	84 54 T	100 64 d	116 74 t
37 25 %	53 35 5	69 45 E	85 55 U	101 65 e	117 75 u
38 26 &	54 36 6	70 46 F	86 56 V	102 66 f	118 76 v
39 27 '	55 37 7	71 47 G	87 57 W	103 67 g	119 77 w
40 28 (	56 38 8	72 48 H	88 58 X	104 68 h	120 78 x
41 29)	57 39 9	73 49 I	89 59 Y	105 69 i	121 79 y
42 2A *	58 3A :	74 4A J	90 5A Z	106 6A j	122 7A z
43 2B +	59 3B ;	75 4B K	91 5B [	107 6B k	123 7B {
44 2C ,	60 3C <	76 4C L	92 5C \	108 6C l	124 7C |
45 2D -	61 3D =	77 4D M	93 5D]	109 6D m	125 7D }
46 2E .	62 3E >	78 4E N	94 5E ^	110 6E n	126 7E ~
47 2F /	63 3F ?	79 4F O	95 5F _	111 6F o	127 7F DEL

Aligned Outputs

com/tutego/exercise/string/PaidOrNotPaid.java

```java
public static void printList( String[] names, boolean[] paid ) {

  if ( names.length != paid.length )
    throw new IllegalArgumentException(
        "Number of names and paid entries are not the same, but "
        +names.length+" and "+paid.length );

  int maxColumnLength=0;
  for ( String name : names )
    maxColumnLength=Math.max( maxColumnLength, name.length() );

  String format="%-"+maxColumnLength+"s    %spaid%n";

  for ( int i=0; i<names.length; i++ )
    System.out.printf( format, names[ i ], paid[ i ] ? "" : "not " );
}
```

First, the method checks if the two arrays have an equal number of elements, and if not, an IllegalArgumentException is thrown. Accessing length generates the desired NullPointerException if the arrays are null.

Since it is unknown in advance how wide the first left column will be, we have to go over all the strings and determine the maximum length. Using this maximum maxColumnLength we can build a format string. The format string gets a format specifier that determines the width of a string, padded with spaces. The format string has a leading minus sign, so this gives a left-aligned string that is padded on the right with spaces up to the maximum length maxColumnLength. In addition, the format string contains a space to the right column of four spaces.

The right column contains either "paid" or "not paid". That is, the string "paid" always occurs, and only the word "not" is to be set dependent on a boolean value. This is done by the condition operator, which either returns an empty string or the string "not" as a format argument for the format string.

Quiz: Define Regex

com/tutego/exercise/string/RegexExamples.java

```
// A string of exactly 10 digits

var p1 = Pattern.compile( "\\d{10}" );
out.println( p1.matcher( "0123456789" ).matches() );      // true
out.println( p1.matcher( "1" ).matches() );               // false
out.println( p1.matcher( "sauma ovo" ).matches() );       // false


// A string of 5 to 10 numbers and letters.

var p2 = Pattern.compile( "\\w{5,10}" );
out.println( p2.matcher( "01234567" ).matches() );        // true
out.println( p2.matcher( "0" ).matches() );               // false
out.println( p2.matcher( "01234567890123" ).matches() ); // false


// A string that ends with `.`, `!` or `?`, like a sentence.

var p3 = Pattern.compile( ".*[.!?]$" );
out.println( p3.matcher( "jes? jes!" ).matches() );       // true
out.println( p3.matcher( "ne?" ).matches() );             // true
out.println( p3.matcher( "okej." ).matches() );           // true
out.println( p3.matcher( "se vi diras tion" ).matches() );// false


// A string that contains no digits.

var p4 = Pattern.compile( "\\D*" );
out.println( p4.matcher( "Ciao" ).matches() );            // true
out.println( p4.matcher( "Cia0" ).matches() );            // false
out.println( p4.matcher( "" ).matches() );                // true


// Contains an official title, Prof., Dr., Dr. med., Dr. h.c.

var p5 = Pattern.compile( "(Prof\\.|Dr\\. med\\.|Dr\\. h\\.c\\.|Dr\\.)\\s" );
out.println( p5.matcher( "Saluton Sinjoro Dr. Miles" ).find() ); // true
out.println( p5.matcher( "ne korekta Dr. h.c. Thai med." ).find() );// true
out.println( p5.matcher( "Megan Dr.Thai" ).find() );             // false
```

In the last example, it is about finding and not about a complete match, so the find() method of Matcher is used. In principle, tests of existence can also be formulated by .*FIND.* and matches(...), but matching makes a little more work for the regex engine than just providing the first find and not having to look to the end.

Determine Popularity in Social Media

com/tutego/exercise/string/Popularity.java

```
String text = """
    Make me a baby #CaptainCiaoCiao
    Hey @CaptainCiaoCiao, where is the recruitment test?
    What is a hacker's favorite pop group? The Black IP's.""";

var pattern = Pattern.compile( "[#@]CaptainCiaoCiao" );
System.out.println( pattern.matcher( text ).results().count() );
```

The task can be solved with a one-liner because the `Matcher` method `results()` returns a `Stream<MatchResult>`, and for `Stream` objects the `count()` method determines the number of occurrences.

Detect Scanned Values

com/tutego/exercise/string/OcrNumbers.java

```
private final static String[] searches = {
    "000", "11", "22", "333", "44", "55555", "6", "77777", "888", "9999" };

private static int parseOcrNumbers( String string ) {
  String line = new Scanner( string ).nextLine().replaceAll( "\\s+", "" );

  for ( int i = 0; i < searches.length; i++ )
    line = line.replaceAll( searches[ i ], "" + i );

  return Integer.parseInt( line );
}
```

If we take a closer look at the big numbers, we quickly realize that each large number contains the actual number itself. The large zero contains 0, the large one contains 1, and so on. So, we don't have to evaluate several lines, it's enough to take any line. We just take the first one.

After extracting the first line, we can search for the substring that makes up the single digits. The blanks interfere a bit, so they are removed in the first step. A new `String` is created from the first line, in which all spaces have been removed, and then the digits of each major character are aligned. For example, if the line starts with 000, we know that the first digit in the result must be 0. We can simply use `replaceAll(...)` to replace the sequence 000 with 0. For example, if there are two zeros in a row, 0000 correctly becomes 00.

Since not only three zeros have to be replaced by zero, but also two ones by a one, and there are ten different replacements, we store the individual strings in an array beforehand. A loop runs through the array, and in the body, there are repeated calls to `replaceAll(...)`, which replaces all partial strings from the search with the loop index, so that, for example, 000 becomes `""` + 0, i.e., `"0"`. At the end, we convert the number to an integer and return the result.

If the incoming string is `null`, empty, or contains foreign characters, there will be exceptions in the following. This behavior is fine.

Quiet Please! Defuse Shouting Texts

com/tutego/exercise/string/DoNotShout.java

```java
public static String silentShoutingWords( String string ) {
  return Pattern.compile( "\\p{javaUpperCase}{3,}" )
             .matcher( string )
             .replaceAll( matchResult -> matchResult.group().toLowerCase() );
}
```

The proposed solution proceeds in three steps: Building the pattern object, matching the string, and replacing the match group with lowercase strings. The regex string must describe a sequence of uppercase letters. Upper case letters, over the entire Unicode alphabet, determine \p{javaUpperCase}. We want to have at least three uppercase letters in a row, which {3,} takes care of. Whether to keep the pattern precompiled in a static variable depends entirely on how often the method is called. In general, it is a good strategy to keep the `Pattern` objects in memory because translation always costs a little execution time. On the other hand, you reference an object, and if you rarely need it, you don't have to.

The method `compile(…)` gives us a `Pattern` object, and the `matcher(…)` method gives us a `Matcher` object. We can well use the `replaceAll(Function<MatchResult, String>)` method, which can perform a transformation of the found strings. The argument passed is a function that maps a `MatchResult` to a string. Our function accesses the group, converts the string to lowercase, and returns it. `replaceAll(…)` finds all places with the selected uppercase letters and calls this `function` multiple times.

Converting Time from AM/PM Format to 24-Hour Format

com/tutego/exercise/string/AmPmToMilitaryTime.java

```java
private static final Pattern AM_PM_PATTERN =
    Pattern.compile( "(?<hours>\\d\\d?)" +          // hours
                     "(?::(?<minutes>\\d\\d))?" +// minutes
                     "\\s?" +                        // optional whitespace
                     "(?<ampm>[ap])[.]?m[.]?",       // AM/PM
                  Pattern.CASE_INSENSITIVE );

public static String convertToMilitaryTime( String string ) {
  Matcher matcher = AM_PM_PATTERN.matcher( string );
  return matcher.replaceAll( matchResult -> {
    int hours   = Integer.parseInt( matcher.group( "hours" ) );
    int minutes = matcher.group( "minutes" ) == null ?
                  0 :
                  Integer.parseInt( matcher.group( "minutes" ) );
    boolean isTimeInPm = "pP".contains( matcher.group( "ampm" ) );
    if ( isTimeInPm && hours < 12 ) hours += 12;
    else if ( !isTimeInPm && hours == 12 ) hours -= 12;
    return String.format("%02d%02d", hours, minutes);
  } );
}
```

At the heart of the program is a regular expression that captures times. This regular expression consists of four parts, which are also split into four lines in the code. The first part captures the hours, the part captures the minutes, the third part is an optional white space between the time, and the last part, AM/PM.

1. The hours consist of at least one integer, the second integer being optional if, for example, 1 AM is written. In principle, we could write the expression a bit more precisely so that something like 99 AM is not recognized, but we do not make that check here. The hours themselves are in round brackets, a group named ?<hours>. All regular expression groups can be named so that we can access them more easily later by that name and not have to use a group index.
2. The minute's part is optional, that is, it is enclosed in round brackets altogether, and there is a question mark at the end. The inside starts with a ?:, which is a small regular expression optimization so that this group is inaccessible via the API later. If hours and minutes are specified at the same time, a colon separates them. The minutes themselves are also a named group, and they consist of two decimal numbers. Again, we do not make any checks about possible ranges of validity.
3. The third part is a white space, which is optional.
4. The last part must capture different notations of AM/PM. A dot could be placed between the two symbols, perhaps even mistakenly just after a letter, so say A.M or AM. So that we don't have to specify case, we include a special pattern flag that checks case independently, so it doesn't matter whether we write AM, am, Am, or pM.

The `convertToMilitaryTime(String)` method gets the `string` with the time information as a parameter. The `Pattern` object was stored as a constant, and the `matcher(…)` method connects the `Pattern` with the `string` method parameter. The result is a `Matcher`. This type can do all the work with `replaceAll(Function<MatchResult, String> replacer)`: the method runs over all the matches for us, calls our `Function`, and we can access the match from the `MatchResult` and replace it with a string.

Regarding the `Function`: first, we access the group for the hours and convert it to an integer. Converting an integer will not throw an exception because our regular expression ensures that only digits occur. The peculiarity with minutes is that they can be missing. So, we have to go back to the group `minute` and ask if it exists at all. If it does not exist, we assign the variable `minutes` with 0; otherwise, we convert the string with the minutes into an integer and set the variable `minutes` with it.

Now we evaluate the group ampm and declare a variable `isTimeInPm`, which becomes `true` if the time is given in PM. For AM, the variable remains `false`. This variable helps with the conversion. If `isTimeInPm` is `true`, then the time is "post meridiem", i.e., afternoon, and 12 hours must be added. It may happen that the text mistakenly enters 23 PM, for example; in this case, we want to correct the error and do not add 12. Moreover, if the time of the hours is equal to 12 o'clock, we also do not correct. The next check is specifically for 12:xx, which becomes 00xx clock. So, if `isTimeInPm` equals `false`, then it is the time "ante meridiem", that is, the morning, and we subtract 12.

After the two variables `hours` and `minutes` are set, we generate a string with the hours and minutes and use `String.format(…)` so that we get the times with only one digit padded with a 0. This is the return of the `Function`.

Split Address Lines with the StringTokenizer

com/tutego/exercise/string/SplitAddressLines.java

```
// String address="Boots and Bootles\n21 Pickle Street\r\n424242 Douglas\
rArendelle";
String address="Doofenshmirtz Evil Inc.\nStrudelkuschel 4427\nGimmelshtump";
```

```
StringTokenizer lines=new StringTokenizer( address, "\n\r" );
String name=lines.nextToken();
String street=lines.nextToken();
String city=lines.nextToken();
final String DEFAULT_COUNTRY="Drusselstein";
String country=lines.hasMoreTokens() ? lines.nextToken() : DEFAULT_COUNTRY;

System.out.println( name+";"+street+";"+city+";"+country );
```

In the center of the job is the class `StringTokenizer`, which is useful whenever.

1. Not (all) tokens are to be extracted in advance like with `split(...)`, but step by step.
2. The separators consist of single characters, but no strings.

Similarly, we create an instance of `StringTokenizer`, but it's important to note that the two specified characters are not treated as a combined separator; instead, they are considered as individual characters that can serve as a separator for the tokens in any combination.

With the method `nextToken()` we ask for the lines three times, and since we don't know if there is a fourth line, we look ahead with `hasMoreTokens()`. If there is a token, we consume it. Otherwise, we choose the desired default country.

Since `StringTokenizer` is an `Enumeration<Object>`, in principle we could have used `hasMoreElements()` and `nextElement()`, but the latter method has the awkward `Object` return type.

Split Sentences into Words and Reverse Them

Let's start with a small helper method that prints words reversed:
   com/tutego/exercise/string/PrintReverseWords.java

```
private static void printWordReversed( String word ) {
  System.out.print( new StringBuilder( word ).reverse() );
  System.out.print( ' ' );
}
```

The reversing of the string is done by the `reverse(...)`- method of the `StringBuilder`. We then output the result to the screen, separated by a space at the end.

Now we have to split the sentence and recognize the words.
   com/tutego/exercise/string/PrintReverseWords.java

```
String string="erehW did eht etarip esahcrup sih kooh? tA eht dnah-dnoces pohs!";

String pattern="[\\p{Punct}\\s]+";

new Scanner( string )
    .useDelimiter( pattern )
    .forEachRemaining( PrintReverseWords::printWordReversed );

System.out.println();

for ( String word : string.split( pattern ) )
  printWordReversed( word );
```

At the center is the regular expression [\p{punct}\s]+. It captures a sequence of punctuation marks, parentheses, etc., and white space separating words. We make use of predefined character classes. It uses \p{punct} for a character out of

```
!"#$%&'()*+,-./:;<=>?@[\]^_'{|}~
```

and \s for the white space; it is the character class [\t\n\x0B\f\r]. For a connection, we put both into a new character class, and since characters can occur any number of times in a row, we add a plus.

Java supports splitting with regular expressions via the Pattern-Matcher combination, and two well-known facades are the Scanner and the split(...) method. Both variants are shown in the proposed solution. The Scanner is always good if the number of matches can be large because with the split(...) method the answer is always an array with all words. The Scanner implements Iterable and at forEachRemaining(...) we put a method reference to the helper method printWordReversed(...) for the Consumer, which writes each word reversed on the screen.

Check Relations between Numbers

com/tutego/exercise/string/RelationChecker.java

```java
private static boolean isValidRelation( int number1, String operator,
int number2 ) {
  return switch ( operator ) {
    case ">" -> number1 > number2;
    case "<" -> number1 < number2;
    case "=" -> number1 == number2;
    default  -> false;
  };
}

public static boolean isValidRelation( String string ) {
  Scanner scanner = new Scanner( string );
  int number1 = scanner.nextInt();

  while ( scanner.hasNext() ) {
    String operator = scanner.next();
    int number2 = scanner.nextInt();
    if ( isValidRelation( number1, operator, number2 ) )
      number1 = number2;
    else
      return false;
  }

  return true;
}
```

The actual method checkRelation(String) gets the string and checks the relations. However, the method falls back on its own private method isValidRelation(int, String, int) so we want to start with that. isValidRelation(...) gets a number, a comparison operator, and another number. It checks if the comparison operator with the two numbers returns a true result. If so, the answer is true; if the comparison is false, the answer is false just as in the case of a misplaced symbol because we evaluate only <, > and =.

The method `checkRelation(…)` builds a `Scanner` with the passed `String` and now uses a combination of `nextInt()`, `hasNext()`, and `next()` to process tokens from the `Scanner`. At the beginning, there must always be a number, which means we can initialize a variable `number1` with the first number. The data stream could be empty now, but if the `Scanner` has the next symbols, this will be a comparison operator, which we will refer to. After the comparison operator comes to a second integer, which we also read in and store in `number2`. Now we call our method `isValidRelation(…)`, and this method returns `true` if the comparison was fine. Then `number2` will become the new `number1`, so in the next loop pass, `number2` will be assigned the following number. If `isValidRelation(…)` returns `false`, then we can abort the method because at this point the comparison is false. If there was no break-out from the loop, all comparisons were correct, and the method ends with `return true`.

Convert A1 Notation to Columns and Rows

com/tutego/exercise/string/A1Notation.java

```java
private static final int NUMBER_OF_LETTERS = 26;

private static int parseColumnIndex( String string ) {
  int result = 0;
  for ( int i = 0; i < string.length(); i++ ) {
    // Map A..Z to 1..26
    int val = Character.getNumericValue( string.charAt( i ) ) - 9;
    result = NUMBER_OF_LETTERS * result + val;
  }
  return result;
}

public static int[] parseA1Notation( String cell ) {
  Matcher matcher = Pattern.compile( "([A-Z]+)(\\d+)" ).matcher( cell );
  if ( ! matcher.find() || matcher.groupCount() != 2 )
    return new int[]{ 0, 0 };
  int column = parseColumnIndex( matcher.group( 1 ) );
  int row    = Integer.parseInt( matcher.group( 2 ) );
  return new int[]{ column, row };
}
```

Let us consider the cell AA34 mentioned in the task as an example. In the first step, we need to separate the column from the row. The column here would be AA, the row 34. We then need to convert the column AA to the numeric representation, 27. Two separate methods handle these two steps. The main method `parseA1Notation(String)` first extracts the row and column, and then calls an internal method `parseColumnIndex(String)`, which converts the column to a numeric value for us after the A1 notation.

Let's start with the `parseColumnIndex(String)` method. We'll take a few examples to make it easier to read the calculation pattern.

What we can read is the following:

- Each letter is transferred to a number—A to 1, B to 2 until finally Z to 26.
- The example is a place value system. It is similar to our decimal system, but here the factor 26 is used as a multiplier.

TABLE 1.2   Calculation of A1 notation

SYMBOL SEQUENCE	CALCULATION	RESULT
A	1×26^0	1
Z	26×26^0	26
AA	$1 \times 26^1 + 1 \times 26^0$	27
IV	$9 \times 26^1 + 22 \times 26^0$	256
AAA	$1 \times 26^2 + 1 \times 26^1 + 1 \times 26^0$	703

To convert the whole thing now into an algorithm, we use the *Horner scheme*. Let us illustrate this with an example:

$$\text{WDE} = 23 \times 26^2 + 4 \times 26^1 + 5 \times 26^0 = ((23 \times 26) + 4) \times 26 + 5$$

The Horner scheme is important for us because we don't need to calculate powers anymore. If we go one place further to the right, we multiply the old result by 26 and repeat the scheme for the other places. This is precisely what the method `parseColumnIndex(String)` does. A loop runs over all characters, extracts them, and queries the numeric representation with `Character.getNumericValue(char)`. This is defined not only for digits but also for letters. For the letter `'a'` the result is 10, the same as for `'A'`. For `'Z'` it is 35. If we subtract 9 from this, we get the range of values 1–26. We take the old result, multiply it by 26, and add the numeric representation of the letter. The next step is to calculate the new numeric value of the next character, multiply the last result by 26, and again add the value of the last letter. This performs the calculation exactly as we planned it.

The method `parseA1Notation(String)` has little work to do. First, we compile a `Pattern` that extracts the column and row—since the column is all letters and the row is all digits, we can easily capture that via the groups in the regular expression. If the string is wrong, and if we don't have two matches, we return an array of $\{0, 0\}$, signaling incorrect input. If there are two match groups, we take the column information from the first one and convert it to an integer using our own `parseColumnIndex(String)` method. The second string, according to the regular expression, is a valid string of digits, which `Integer.parseInt(String)` converts to an `int`. The numeric column and row go into a small array, and that goes back to the caller.

Parse Simple CSV Files with Coordinates

com/tutego/exercise/string/GenerateSvgFromCsvCoordinates.java

```java
String filename = "coordinates.csv";
try ( InputStream is =
        GenerateSvgFromCsvCoordinates.class.getResourceAsStream( filename );
      Scanner scanner = new Scanner( is, StandardCharsets.ISO_8859_1 ) ) {
  scanner.useDelimiter( ",|\\s+" ).useLocale( Locale.ENGLISH );

  StringBuilder svg = new StringBuilder( 1024 );
  svg.append( "<svg height=\"210\" width=\"500\">\n<polygon points=\"" );

  while ( scanner.hasNextDouble() ) {
    double x = scanner.nextDouble();

    if ( ! scanner.hasNextDouble() )
      throw new IllegalStateException( "Missing second coordinate" );
```

```
    double y = scanner.nextDouble();
    svg.append( x ).append( "," ).append( y ).append( " " );
  }

  svg.append( "\" style=\"fill:lime;stroke:purple;stroke-width:1\" />\n</svg>" );
  System.out.println( svg );
}
```

The file consists of sequences of integers separated by either a semicolon or a newline, generally speaking by arbitrary white space. We need to find a tokenizer that we can feed with a regular expression that stands for just these separators. Since we want to read from a file and process that with regular expressions, the class Scanner is a good choice. This is also how the proposed solution does it.

The Scanner is connected to an input stream, the file we would like to read. The character encoding is explicitly set to UTF-8.

Then the Scanner is initialized with a regular expression for the delimiters. These delimiters are set by the Scanner method useDelimiter(...). It is important to set the Locale.ENGLISH because by default the Scanner is preconfigured with the Locale by the operating system, and if that is, for example, German, the Scanner expects floating-point numbers with a comma as separator. But the source always has English formatted numbers.

After the Scanner is prepared, the program can produce the output. It starts with the SVG container and the polygon start tag. The Scanner method hasNext() helps to iterate through the file. When the hasNext() method returns a token, we always expect pairs. We can read the first integer, and now there must be a second integer. But if the Scanner cannot give a new token, this is an error, and we raise an exception. If the second number exists, it will also be read in. The pair can then be placed in the SVG container.

At the end of the loop, we close the polygon tag and print the SVG element to the screen. For the output, we don't need to pay attention to the language for append(double) because the formatting of the double is automatically in English.

Compress Strings Lossless by Runlength Encoding

com/tutego/exercise/string/SimpleStringCompressor.java

```
public static String compress( String string ) {

  if ( string.isEmpty() )

    return "";

  char lastChar = string.charAt( 0 );
  int   count = 1;
  StringBuilder result = new StringBuilder( string.length() );

  for ( int i = 1; i < string.length(); i++ ) {
    char currentChar = string.charAt( i );
    if ( currentChar == lastChar )
      count++;
    else {
      result.append( lastChar );
      if ( count > 1 )
        result.append( count );
      count = 1;
```

```
        lastChar = currentChar;
      }
  }

  result.append( lastChar );
  if ( count > 1 )
    result.append( count );

  return result.toString();
}

private static CharSequence decodeToken( String token ) {

  if ( token.isEmpty() )
    return "";

  if ( token.length() == 1 )
    return token;

  int length = Integer.parseInt( token.substring( 1 ) );
  return String.valueOf( token.charAt( 0 ) ).repeat( Math.max( 0, length ) );
}

public static String decompress( String string ) {
  StringBuilder result = new StringBuilder( string.length() * 2 );
  Matcher pattern = Pattern.compile( "[.-](\\d*)" ).matcher( string );

  while ( pattern.find() )
    result.append( decodeToken( pattern.group() ) );

  return result.toString();
}
```

In the first step, we want to compress the string. To achieve this, we first query whether the string contains any text at all; if not, we are quickly done with the task.

To see how many of the same characters occur in the text in a row, we use a variable `lastChar` for the last character seen so that we can compare a new character with the last character. In addition, we note the number of same characters in `count`. Since this result is freshly built, we add a variable `result` of the data type `StringBuilder`.

The `for` loop goes over each character and stores it in the auxiliary variable `currentChar`. Now, two things can happen: The character `currentChar` just read can be the same as the previous character in `lastChar`, or it can be a different character. We have to handle this difference.

The initial check determines if the previously observed character matches the currently read character. If it's a match, we simply increase the counter and continue the loop. However, if the newly read character differs from the previous one, the local compression process concludes. We begin by writing this character to the buffer. Then, we address the count: if more than one identical character was previously counted, we input that count into the data stream. But if there was just one character, we don't add 1 to the buffer, in accordance with the task's instructions. After finalizing the character-counter pair, it's essential to reset the counter to 1. We are almost done with the loop. The moment a new character is found, we set `lastChar` to exactly the current character `currentChar`.

When we are done with the loop, we still have a character in `lastChar` and `count`. We therefore perform the same query as before in the case distinction, and append the counter to the string if the counter is greater than 1.

In the method for unpacking, we fall back on the pattern that results from the compression. There are always pairs of a string and a number, with the special case that the pair is single, and the number is missing. Using a regular expression, we run the entire string and look at all the pairs. To keep the method from getting too big, we use a helper method called decodeToken(String) that takes a pair and expands it.

First, the method must find out whether the token consists of only one character or of several characters. If the string consists of only one character, then it must have been our symbol, and it comes into the output. If the string is longer than 1, then there is a length encoding from the second position upward. With substring(1) we extract the string and convert it to an integer, so that the repeat(int) method of String can generate us exactly this number of characters token.charAt(0). With substring(1) we extract the string and convert it to an integer, so that the repeat(int) method of String can generate us exactly this number of characters token.charAt(0).

Quiz: Encoding for Unicode Characters

When we write a string in source code, we don't worry much about encoding because we can write numerous characters directly in quotes. But when these strings are written to a file, for example, the encoding is relevant because other parties will naturally want to read that file again.

Unicode's characters require four bytes in their full extent. However, this is a waste if the character can only be encoded in one byte, such as a simple ASCII character. Therefore, one encodes Unicode characters to get the shortest possible representation. Common encodings are UTF-8 and UTF-16; they can represent all Unicode characters. This is not true for Latin-1, for example, because Latin-1 is only eight bytes, and hundreds of thousands of characters cannot be represented in Latin-1. UTF-8 encoding will use one byte if possible, then use two bytes if possible, otherwise use three or four.

Quiz: Order of Strings with and without Collator

The outputs are:
com/tutego/exercise/string/CollatorDemo.java

```
Comparator<String> comparator = Comparator.naturalOrder();
System.out.println( comparator.compare( "a", "ä" ) ); //< 0
System.out.println( comparator.compare( "ä", "z" ) ); //> 0 !!
System.out.println( comparator.compare( "n", "ñ" ) ); //< 0
System.out.println( comparator.compare( "ñ", "o" ) ); //> 0 !!

Comparator<Object> collatorDE = Collator.getInstance( Locale.GERMAN );
System.out.println( collatorDE.compare( "a", "ä" ) ); //< 0
System.out.println( collatorDE.compare( "ä", "z" ) ); //< 0
System.out.println( collatorDE.compare( "n", "ñ" ) ); //< 0
System.out.println( collatorDE.compare( "ñ", "o" ) ); //< 0
```

TABLE 1.3 Bit assignments of UTF8 encoding

NUMBER OF BYTES	BITS	FIRST CODE POINT	LAST CODE POINT	BYTE 1	BYTE 2	BYTE 3	BYTE 4
1	7	U+0000	U+007F	0*******			
2	11	U+0080	U+07FF	110*****	10******		
3	16	U+0800	U+FFFF	1110****	10******	10******	

TABLE 1.4   Some characters with their positions in the Unicode standard

CHARACTER	θ	A	a	Ä	ß	ä	ñ
Code point (decimal)	48	65	97	196	223	228	241

The natural ordering of strings is lexicographic, meaning that the position of the character in the Unicode alphabet counts. Let's illustrate this with some characters.

From the table, you can see that the digits are first, followed by the uppercase letters and then the lowercase letters. The umlauts are far behind the capital letters and not sorted between the upper and lower case letters.

Umlauts are regular letters in German, which do not come after "Z" in the order. The standard DIN 5007-1 describes under "Ordering of character sequences (ABC rules)" two sorting procedures:

DIN 5007, variant 1 (used for words, for example, in dictionaries)

- "ä" and "a" are the same.
- "ö" and "o" are the same.
- "ü" and "u" are the same.
- "ß" and "ss" are the same,

DIN 5007, variant 2 (special sorting for lists of names, such as in telephone directories)

- "ä" and "ae" are the same.
- "ö" and "oe" are the same.
- "ü" and "ue" are the same.
- "ß" and "ss" are the same.

There are similar rules for other languages. The lexicographical order does not support this. Therefore, the *Unicode Collation Algorithm* describes how the sorting looks like in different national languages. For an introduction, see also https://en.wikipedia.org/wiki/Unicode_collation_algorithm.

In Java `Collator` objects are available. They are initialized with a `Locale` object. In addition to the language, so-called levels can be passed; the Javadoc gives further examples under the heading "Collator strength value".

Mathematics

2

Integers and floating-point numbers already appeared in the first exercises; we were using the common mathematical operators to crunch numbers. But Java does not have an operator for everything, and so the class Math offers further methods and constants; early on we used Math.random(), for example. Throughout this chapter's upcoming tasks, our focus will be on various rounding techniques, particularly exploring the methods offered by the Math class. In addition, the java.math package provides two classes that can be used to represent arbitrarily large numbers—there are tasks for these as well.

Prerequisites

- Know rounding methods of the class Math.
- Know BigInteger and BigDecimal.

Data types used in this chapter:

- java.lang.Math
- java.math.BigInteger
- java.math.BigDecimal

THE CLASS MATH

The class Math contains numerous mathematical functions. It is also important to look at wrapper classes, for example, or at the Scanner or Formatter when it comes to converting a number to a string or parsing a string so that there is a primitive type at the end again.

Quiz: Rule of Thumb ★

There are different approaches and different kinds of problems for rounding numerical values:

- On the one hand, a floating-point number can be converted to an integer.
- On the other hand, the number of decimal places can be reduced for a floating-point number.

The Java library supports different possibilities for conversion and rounding, among other things with

- The explicit type conversion (int) double → int.
- Math.floor(double) → double.
- Math.ceil(double) → double.
- Math.round(double) → long.

DOI: 10.1201/9781003495550-3

- `Math.rint(double) → double`.
- `BigDecimal` and `setScale(..) → BigDecimal`.
- `NumberFormat`, configured with `setMaximumFractionDigits(…)`, then `format(…) → String`.
- `DecimalFormat`, configured with `setRoundingMode(…)`, then `format(…) → String`.
- `Formatter` with a format string, then `format(…) → String`.

Four of the methods originate from `Math`, but when it comes to gigantic and precise floating-point numbers or string representation, other classes are involved. Since the methods differ slightly in the result, the following task should make these differences clear once again.
Task:

- Fill in the following table with the results of the roundings:

DOUBLE VALUE D	(INT) D	(INT) FLOOR(D)	(INT) CEIL(D)	ROUND(D)	(INT) RINT(D)
-2.5					
-1.9					
-1.6					
-1.5					
-1.1					
1.1					
1.5					
1.6					
1.9					
2.5					

Check If Tin Tin Cheated on Rounding ★

The accountant Tin Tin does the accounting for Captain CiaoCiao of income and expenses. She gets *positive and negative floating-point values* and writes down the total as a *rounded integer* for a summary at the end. Captain CiaoCiao suspects that Tin Tin is not being completely honest and is pocketing the penny amounts when she should use commercially rounding. As a reminder, if the number at the first omitted decimal place is a 0, 1, 2, 3, or 4, round down; if it is 5, 6, 7, 8, or 9, round up.

To test his guess, Captain CiaoCiao needs a program that can sum and check different rounding modes.
Task:

- Given an array of floating-point numbers (positive and negative) and the sum converted to an integer by Tin Tin.
- Captain CiaoCiao wants to find out which rounding was used to form the integer of the sum. Therefore, the elements in the array are to be summed and compared to Tin Tin's sum. The rounding is done after the numbers are added.
- Implement a method `RoundingMode detectRoundingMode(double[] numbers, int sum)` that gets a `double` array of numbers and the sum of Tin Tin and checks which rounding mode was used.
  - To allow the rounding mode to be represented, introduce an enumeration type:
    ```
    enum RoundingMode {
        CAST, ROUND, FLOOR, CEIL, RINT, UNKNOWN;
    }
    ```

- • The enumeration elements represent different rounding modes:
- • (int), that is, a type conversion.
- • (int) Math.floor(double).
- • (int) Math.ceil(double).
- • (int) Math.rint(double).
- • (int) Math.round(double).

- • Which rounding is bad for Captain CiaoCiao and good for Tin Tin? Which variation could Tin Tin use to cheat?

Example:

- • The call might look like this:
```
double[] numbers = { 199.99 };
System.out.println( detectRoundingMode( numbers, 200 ) );
```

Notes:

- • There is an enumeration type RoundingMode in the java.math package, but for our case, it does not fit the task.
- • It may well happen that more than one rounding mode fits—such as when the sum of the floating-point values itself gives an integer—then the method is free to choose one of the rounding modes.

HUGE AND VERY PRECISE NUMBERS

The classes java.math.BigInteger and java.math.BigDecimal can be used to represent arbitrarily large integer and floating-point numbers.

Calculate Arithmetic Mean of a Large Integer ★

To calculate the arithmetic mean of two numbers, they are added together and divided by two. This works well if the sum of the two values does not exceed the largest number that can be represented. If there is an overflow, the result is wrong. Some algorithms in computer science can handle this problem as well, but we can make it a little easier and take the higher data type in each case. For example, if we want to calculate the mean value of two int variables, we convert the two int to a long, add the numbers, divide, and convert back to the int. With the long data type, there is no larger primitive data type, but the BigInteger type can be used well for the case.
Task:

- • Calculate the arithmetic mean of two long values so that there is *no* overflow and wrong results. The result should be a long again.

Number by Number over the Phone ★

A new deal has made Bonny Brain a lot of money. The number is so big that you can't just announce it over the phone at all; it has to be conveyed in chunks.

Task:

- Write a new method `BigInteger completeNumber(int... parts)` that gets a variable number of numbers and returns the big total number at the end.

Example:

- `completeNumber(123, 22, 989, 77, 9)` returns a `BigInteger` with the value `12322989779`.

Develop Class for Fractions and Truncate Fractions ★★

Bonny Brain is trying a new recipe for a rum punch. Fractions like "1/4 liter grape juice" or "1/2 liter rum" keep appearing in the directions for making it. For the party, she prepares 100 servings, and fractions like "100/4 liters" occur. The fractions can be shortened so that Bonny Brain knows, for example, that 25 liters of grape juice must be purchased.

Task:

1. Create a new class `Fraction`.
2. Let there be a constructor `Fraction(int numerator, int denominator)` that stores numerator and denominator in `public final` variables.
    - Consider whether there can be faulty arguments, which we should report through exceptions.
    - Every created fraction should be simplified automatically. Use the `gcd(…)` method of `BigInteger`, which calculates the *greatest common divisor* (gcd)_. Remember: the gcd of numerator and denominator is the largest number by which both are divisible. You can simplify the fraction by dividing both the numerator and denominator by this number.
    - Both numerator and denominator can be negative, but then you can flip the sign so that both values become positive.
    - The objects are all supposed to be immutable, and therefore the variables can be `public` since they are not supposed to be changed after initialization via the constructor. In other words, the class `Fraction` does not contain any setters.
3. Add the constructor `Fraction(int value)`, where the denominator automatically becomes 1.
4. Implement a method to multiply fractions and detect overflows.
5. Implement a method `reciprocal()` that returns the inverse of a fraction, that is, swaps the numerator and denominator. Thanks to this method, the division of fractions can be implemented.
6. `Fraction` shall extend `java.lang.Number` and implement all mandatory methods.
7. `Fraction` shall implement `Comparable` because fractions can be converted to a decimal number, and decimal numbers have a natural order.
8. `Fraction` shall implement `equals(…)` and `hashCode()` correctly.
9. Implement a `toString()` method that returns a string as bare as possible.

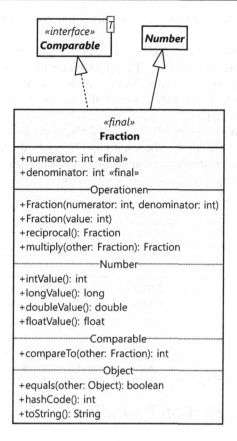

FIGURE 2.1   UML diagram of `Fraction`.

SUGGESTED SOLUTIONS

Quiz: Rule of Thumb

TABLE 2.1   Different roundings of a floating-point number `d` in comparison

VALUE `d`	`(INT) d`	`(INT) FLOOR(d)`	`(INT) CEILING(d)`	`ROUND(d)`	`(INT) RINT(d)`
-2.5	-2	-3	-2	-2	-2
-1.9	-1	-2	-1	-2	-2
-1.6	-1	-2	-1	-2	-2
-1.5	-1	-2	-1	-1	-2
-1.1	-1	-2	-1	-1	-1
1.1	1	1	2	1	1
1.5	1	1	2	2	2
1.6	1	1	2	2	2
1.9	1	1	2	2	2
2.5	2	2	3	3	2

`Math.round(double)` and `Math.rint(double)` differ for .5 numbers "on the edge":

- `round(double)` rounds *commercially*. As can be seen in the table, `round(-2.5)`, `round(-1.5)`, `round(1.5)`, and `round(2.5)` round up; the numbers always become larger. If one always rounds up only commercially, this produces small errors because the procedure is not symmetrical. To be fair, some .5 would also have to be rounded down; this is where another method comes into play.
- `rint(double)` behaves like `round(double)` for numbers not ending in .5, but when ending in .5 the following rule applies: the last digit to be retained becomes even. This behavior is called *symmetric (also mathematical, scientific) rounding* because it rounds up or down in half the cases, respectively.

In summary:

TABLE 2.2 Rounding method

PROCEDURE	RESULT
type conversion `(int) d`	Truncates decimal places of a floating-point number.
`floor(d)`	Rounds to the next smaller number against $-\infty$.
`ceil(d)`	Rounds to the next larger number against $+\infty$.
`round(d)`	Rounds the value according to commercial rules.
`rint(d)`	Rounds `double` values. symmetrically/ mathematically/scientifically.

Check If Tin Tin Cheated on Rounding

Now we come to the question of which rounding is bad for Captain CiaoCiao and good for Tin Tin. The difference between the rounded value and the sum is the difference Tin Tin can pocket. Example: If the total is 222.22 and Tin Tin rounds to 222, there is a difference of 0.22 that Captain CiaoCiao misses and goes into Tin Tin's pocket. What do the differences look like for the example numbers?

TABLE 2.3 Difference from rounding, sum in foot

VALUE d	d - (INT) d	d - FLOOR(d)	d - CEIL(d)	d - ROUND(d)	d - RINT(d)
−2.5	−0.5	0.5	−0.5	−0.5	−0.5
−1.9	−0.9	0.1	−0.9	0.1	0.1
−1.6	−0.6	0.4	−0.6	0.4	0.4
−1.5	−0.5	0.5	−0.5	−0.5	0.5
−1.1	−0.1	0.9	−0.1	−0.1	−0.1
1.1	0.1	0.1	−0.9	0.1	0.1
1.5	0.5	0.5	−0.5	−0.5	−0.5
1.6	0.6	0.6	−0.4	−0.4	−0.4
1.9	0.9	0.9	−0.1	−0.1	−0.1
2.5	0.5	0.5	−0.5	−0.5	0.5

We can read that for the numbers Tin Tin chose, she gets the most out of rounding off all the sums. Rounding off makes the numbers smaller, and she gets the difference in each case, whether the numbers are negative or positive.

To the proposed solution:
com/tutego/exercise/math/RoundingModeDetector.java

```java
public enum RoundingMode {
  CAST, ROUND, FLOOR, CEIL, RINT, UNKNOWN
}

private static RoundingMode detectRoundingMode( double value, int rounded ) {
  return rounded == (int) value          ? RoundingMode.CAST :
         rounded == Math.round( value )  ? RoundingMode.ROUND :
         rounded == Math.floor( value )  ? RoundingMode.FLOOR :
         rounded == Math.ceil( value )   ? RoundingMode.CEIL :
         rounded == Math.rint( value )   ? RoundingMode.RINT :
         RoundingMode.UNKNOWN;
}

public static RoundingMode detectRoundingMode( double[] numbers, int sum ) {
  double realSum = 0;
  for ( double number : numbers )
    realSum += number;
  return detectRoundingMode( realSum, sum );
}
```

The proposed solution is composed of two methods. The public method `detectRoundingMode(…)` sums the elements of the array and calls the private method `detectRoundingMode(double, int)` to determine the actual rounding mode. The method sequentially compares the integer value with the different rounded variants, and if there is a match, the enumeration element is returned. If the totals and the rounded value do not match at all, the return is `RoundingMode.UNKNOWN`.

Calculate Arithmetic Mean of a Large Integer

com/tutego/exercise/math/BigIntegerMean.java

```java
private final static BigDecimal TWO = BigDecimal.valueOf( 2 );

public static long meanExact( long x, long y ) {
  BigInteger bigSum  = BigInteger.valueOf( x ).add( BigInteger.valueOf( y ) );
  BigInteger bigMean = bigSum.divide( BigInteger.TWO );
  return bigMean.longValue();
}
```

In the first step, we build a new object of type `BigInteger` for the parameters x and y using the factory method `valueOf(long)`. In the second step, the sum is built and in the third step, the sum is divided by 2. For the division, we also have to use a `BigInteger` object for the divisor. Since the divisor is constant, the solution defines a constant—the class `BigInteger` has constants for 0, 1, and 10, but not for 2.

When averaging integers, there is always the question of rounding. The addition of two even or two odd numbers always results in an even number, but the sum of an even number with an odd number is odd. If odd numbers are divided by two, there is a remainder, and the question is whether to round up or down, round the result to 0, or round to plus or minus infinity—there are quite a few possibilities. The `BigInteger` method `divide(…)` behaves like the division of two integers, it is rounded toward 0.

A result is a number, not greater than `Long.MAX _ VALUE` and not smaller than `Long.MIN _ VALUE`, so converting the number from the `BigInteger` with `longValue()` gives no loss.

Number by Number over the Phone

com/tutego/exercise/math/SequentialNumbersToOneNumber.java

```
static BigInteger completeNumber( int... parts ) {
  StringBuilder bigNumber = new StringBuilder( parts.length * 2 );
  for ( int part : parts )
    bigNumber.append( part );

  return new BigInteger( bigNumber.toString() );
}
```

We can solve the task using strings or math. Using a temporary string, the task is easy to solve.

In the first step, we run the array, take all the numbers one by one, and append them to a `StringBuilder`. If we assume that each number consists on average of two digits, we can estimate approximately how big the result will be; therefore, we use the parameterized constructor of `StringBuilder` with a capacity.

After appending all the digits, `StringBuilder` is converted to a `String` and this feeds the constructor of `BigInteger`. Here, the actual conversion of the string into a `BigInteger` begins.

Of course, the task can also be solved without a temporary `StringBuilder`. Let us take the call as an example

```
completeNumber(123, 22, 989, 77, 9);
```

If at the end we want to create the `BigInteger` with `12322989779`, we could first build the `BigInteger` with `123`, then multiply the number with `100`, and add `22`, resulting in `12322`. In the next step, we take the result, multiply it by `1000` and add `989`. Then we multiply again by `100`, add `77`, multiply the result by `10` and add `9`. That is, we always multiply the old value by 10^n, where n is the number of digits in the coming number.

Develop Class for Fractions and Truncate Fractions

com/tutego/exercise/math/Fraction.java

```
import java.math.BigInteger;

public final class Fraction extends Number implements Comparable<Fraction> {
  public final int numerator;
  public final int denominator;
  public Fraction( int numerator, int denominator ) {
    if ( denominator == 0 )
      throw new ArithmeticException( "denominator of a fraction can't be 0" );
    // denominator always positive
    if ( denominator < 0 ) {
      numerator   = -numerator;
      denominator = -denominator;
    }

    // shortcut if denominator == 1
    if ( denominator == 1 ) {
      this.numerator   = numerator;
      this.denominator = 1;
    }
```

```
    else {
      // try to simplify every fraction
      int gcd=gcd( numerator, denominator );
      // might be 1, but divide anyway
      this.numerator   =numerator / gcd;
      this.denominator=denominator / gcd;
    }
  }
  private static int gcd( int a, int b ) {
    return BigInteger.valueOf( a )
                     .gcd( BigInteger.valueOf( b ) )
                     .intValue();
  }
  public Fraction( int value ) {
    this( value, 1 );
  }
  public Fraction reciprocal() {
    return new Fraction( denominator, numerator );
  }
  public Fraction multiply( Fraction other ) {
    return new Fraction( Math.multiplyExact( numerator, other.numerator ),
                         Math.multiplyExact( denominator, other.denominator )
);
  }
  @Override
  public int intValue() {
    return numerator / denominator;
  }
  @Override
  public long longValue() {
    return (long) numerator / denominator;
  }
  @Override
  public double doubleValue() {
    return (double) numerator / denominator;
  }
  @Override
  public float floatValue() {
    return (float) numerator / denominator;
  }
  @Override
  public int compareTo( Fraction other ) {
    return Double.compare( doubleValue(), other.doubleValue() );
  }
  @Override
  public boolean equals( Object other ) {
    if ( other == this )
      return true;
    return    other instanceof Fraction otherFraction
         && numerator   == otherFraction.numerator
         && denominator == otherFraction.denominator;
  }
  @Override
  public int hashCode() {
    return numerator+Integer.reverse( denominator );
  }
  @Override
```

```
  public String toString() {
    return numerator   == 0 ? "0" :
           denominator == 1 ? ""+numerator :
           numerator+" / "+denominator;
  }
}
```

Let's start with the constructor `Fraction`, which takes the numerator and denominator. The denominator must never be 0; this is punished with an exception. We could in principle build our own `Exception` class, but an `ArithmeticException` fits perfectly.

The numerator and denominator can be negative or positive, there are four cases:

- numerator > 0, denominator > 0.
- numerator < 0, denominator > 0.
- numerator > 0, denominator < 0.
- numerator < 0, denominator < 0.

Let us consider two cases:

- If the numerator and denominator are both negative, we can reverse the sign so that both values become positive.
- If the denominator is negative and the numerator is positive, we can shift the sign to the numerator.

Both cases can be dealt with a control flow statement: if the denominator is negative, we flip both signs. A negative denominator then becomes positive. If the numerator was also negative, the numerator becomes positive, so a negative numerator and negative denominator thus both become positive. If the denominator was negative and the numerator was positive, we thus shift the sign to the numerator because the numerator becomes negative.

The numerator and denominator are now prepared, and if the denominator is 1, then the fraction does not need to be truncated, and we save the following work and leave the constructor. Otherwise, we continue in the `else` block.

The last part of the constructor deals with the reduction of the fraction. The task briefly explained how to proceed here: we need the greatest common divisor. The constructor delegates here to its method `gcd(int, int)`, which first builds a `BigInteger` for two numbers, then lets it calculate the greatest common divisor, and then returns it as an integer. In our scenario, the parameter types are `int` so the divisor will be smaller in any case, with `intValue()` we read from the `BigInteger`. After the constructor asks for the greatest common divisor, we divide the numerator and denominator by it, initializing our instance variables. In principle, gcd could also be 1, so we don't need a division, but we save this special case distinction here because a division by 1 is not expensive.

The second constructor takes only one numerator, and in that case, the denominator is 1. We delegate to our constructor, but in general, we can do the storing ourselves, since we don't need the special treatment for a negative denominator, and the denominator is not 0 either.

The first of the two methods, `reciprocal()`, creates a new `Fraction` object by turning the denominator into the numerator and the numerator into the denominator. The method `multiply(...)` multiplies its numerator with the numerator of the passed object and symmetrically does the same for the denominator. Multiplication quickly produces large numbers and the value range of `int` could be blown up, so `Math.multiplyExact(...)` makes sure that the product fits into an `int`; otherwise, an exception follows.

The next category of methods comes from the base type `Number`. We divide the numerator by the denominator and return the result at the different methods.

The next method `compareTo(...)` comes from the `Comparable` interface. We make it simple and calculate the quotient and compare our quotient with the passed fraction.

In the next step, we override the method `equals(...)` and `hashCode()`. A good hash code will return a different hash code if the numerator or denominator changes. The realization of `hashCode()` does this by flipping the bits of the denominator. If the number of required bits of the numerator and denominator together does not exceed 32 (the number of bits of an `int`), we can detect each change by a different hash code.

The last method is `toString()`. If the numerator is 0, we don't even have to look at the denominator and return the string 0. If the denominator is 1, we can return only the numerator. Otherwise, we return the numerator and denominator separated by a fraction bar.

Locale, Date, and Time

3

In almost all exercises we have screen outputs, and whoever writes in everyday life, for example, Chinese, Spanish, or Arabic, will probably prefer program outputs in this language as well. However, in some places, a wrong format might appear, e.g., when decimal places in floating-point numbers are not separated correctly. The decimal separator is only one of many examples of how different the standards are in the countries: currencies sometimes precede and then follow the number; for dates, the format is year-month-day in some countries, day-month-year in others, and then month-day-year again.

This chapter focuses on exercises around internationalization (how to make programs language-independent in principle) and localization (adaptation to a specific language). After all, if our software is to be successful, it must, of course, run anywhere on the planet at any time of day. Java can easily accommodate many language specifics, and we'll look at that in the exercises, so that Captain CiaoCiao and Bonny Brain can also do their business anywhere and everyone understands their "language".

Prerequisites

- Know `Locale` class and constants, like `Locale.US`.
- Be able to recognize the need for country-specific formatting.
- Know temporal data types `LocalDate`, `LocalDateTime`, Duration.

Data types used in this chapter:

- `java.util.Locale`
- `java.time.LocalDate`
- `java.time.LocalDateTime`
- `java.time.format.DateTimeFormatter`
- `java.time.format.FormatStyle`
- `java.time.format.DateTimeFormatter`
- `java.time.Duration`

LANGUAGES AND COUNTRIES

For the Java library to parse and format floating-point numbers and dates, as well as translate text, there is a data type called `Locale` that represents a language with an optional region. We want to use this data type to solve some exercises that show well where `Locale` occurs everywhere.

DOI: 10.1201/9781003495550-4

Apply Country-/Language-Specific Formatting for Random Number ★

Bonny Brain is preparing a new email scam: bitcoins are to be "sold" well below their price. It prepares subject lines for this, which look like this, for example:

Buy **Bitcoin** for just $11,937.70 🪙

Of course, the crew is planning a worldwide scam, and that's where it's important to format the number according to the rules of the different countries.

The printf(…) method is overloaded, as is String.format(…):

- With Locale as the first parameter.
- Without Locale. If no Locale object is passed, the default locale applies. This leads to the fact that the Java Virtual Machine under let's say an operating system language Spanish; this language adopts and with the output with System.out.printf(…) and a floating-point number by default a comma as a decimal separator is used. If you have an English-language operating system, the point is used as a separator by default because decimal places are separated with a point in English-speaking countries.

Exercise:

- Create a random number of type double between 10 000 (inclusive) and 12 000 (exclusive); decimal places are desired.
- To format a floating-point number with two decimal places and a thousand separator, employ the String.format(String format, Object... args) method.
- Get all Locale objects of the system, and use them as arguments to the String.format(Locale l, String format, Object... args) method, so that the floating-point number is formatted "locally" in each case. Output the string.

As a general rule, it can be stated that all methods implementing language-dependent formatting, or parsing strings, usually accept a `Locale` object as a parameter. There may be language-dependent methods without parameters in addition, but these are often overloaded methods that internally query the default language, and then pass to the method with the explicit `Locale` parameter.

DATE AND TIME CLASSES

At first glance, it looks like the date consists only of year, month, and day. However, you would expect an application programming interface (API) to be able to answer more questions: is a day a Wednesday? If a party goes for three days on February 27, when does it end? When does week 12 start? If I leave Beijing at 09:30 on December 31, 2024, and arrive in Miami after 11 hours, what time is it when I get there?

The Java library has evolved over the years, and so there are various types for date and time calculation:

- `java.util.Date` since Java 1.0
- `java.util.Calendar`, `java.util.GregorianCalendar`, `java.util.TimeZone` since Java 1.1
- package `java.time` since Java 8 with classes like `LocalDate`, `LocalTime`, `LocalDateTime`, `Duration`.

For a date with time part, there are three possibilities at once; however, `Date` and `Calendar` are no longer popular since Java 8 because they are causing several problems. However, these data types can still be found in many written examples, especially online. We should stay away from these "old" types, and therefore this section specifically trains how to use the current data types from `java.time`.

Formatting Date Output in Different Languages ★

September 19 marks the return of International Talk Like a Pirate Day. Bonny Brain is planning a party and preparing invitations, and the date is to be formatted for the languages `Locale.CHINESE`, `Locale.ITALIAN` and `Locale.of("th")`; Germans, for example, write `Day.Month.Year`, but what about in the other languages?

Exercise:

- Create a `LocalDate` object for September 19:
  `LocalDate now=LocalDate.of( Year.now().getValue(), Month.SEPTEMBER, 19 );`
- Call the `toString()` method; what is the output?
- Call `format(DateTimeFormatter.ofLocalizedDate(FormatStyle.MEDIUM))` on the `LocalDate`; what is the output?
- There are four `FormatStyle` styles in total—try them all. Which pattern is shown?
- On the `DateTimeFormatter` object, you can call `withLocale(Locale)` and change the language; try this for different languages.

On Which Day Does Sir Francis Beaufort Celebrate His Birthday? ★

Captain CiaoCiao celebrates the birthday of Sir Francis Beaufort every year, who was born on May 27, 1774.

Exercise:

- Given a `LocalDate` with Francis' birthday:
  `LocalDate beaufortBday = LocalDate.of( 1774, Month.MAY, 27 );`
- Starting from `beaufortBday`, develop a new `LocalDate` object with the current year, where the current year should not be hard-coded but dynamically obtained from the system.
- Create an output on which day of the week Francis celebrates his birthday this year. In which form the weekday is output, i.e., number or string or which language, is not relevant.

Example:

- For the year 2026, the output could be:
  ```
  WEDNESDAY
  3
  Wednesday
  ```

Find All Friday the 13th ★

Every Friday the 13th, Captain CiaoCiao feels uncomfortable sailing. On such days, he does not set sail and sends Bravius Gritty instead.
Task:

- Write a program that lists all Fridays that fall on the 13th for a given year.
- Bonus: for this, write a `TemporalAdjuster` that returns the next Friday the 13th for a `Temporal` object.

Examples:

- For the year 1925, the output may look like this:
  ```
  1925-02-13
  1925-03-13
  1925-11-13
  ```
- For 2024:
  ```
  2024-09-13
  2024-12-13
  ```

Get Average Duration of Karaoke Nights ★

Karaoke nights with rum, dancing, and singing are popular among the crew. Often the parties go on until dawn, and this disturbs Bonny Brain because the crew is dozy the next day.

To find out how many hours the excesses go on average, Bonny Brain wants to keep a record of statistics. She writes down the start and end times and can calculate the average later. For example, the note sheets say "2025-03-12, 20:20 - 2025-03-12, 23:50".

Exercise:

- Write a program that evaluates a string in the format above, finds the average party duration, and prints it out.
- The program does not need to consider time zones, leap seconds, or other special cases—a day can be exactly 24 hours long.

Example:

- For the string
  ```
  2025-03-12, 20:20 - 2025-03-12, 23:50
  2025-04-01, 21:30 - 2025-04-02, 01:20
  ```
  the output should look like this:
  ```
  3h 40m
  ```

For time differences, the class `Duration` helps.

Parse Different Date Formats ★★★

A date can be specified as absolute or relative, and there are several ways to specify dates. A few examples:

```
2025-10-10
2025-12-2
1/3/1976
1/3/25
Tomorrow
Today
Yesterday
1 day ago
2234 days ago
```

Exercise:

- Write a method `Optional<LocalDate> parseDate(String string)` that recognizes the above formats.
- If the string is in one of the formats, the method should parse the string, convert it to a `LocalDate`, and return it in `Optional`.
- If no format could be parsed, the return is `Optional.empty()`.

SUGGESTED SOLUTIONS

Apply Country-/Language-Specific Formatting for Random Number

com/tutego/exercise/util/RandomInEveryLocalePrinter.java

```
double random = ThreadLocalRandom.current().nextDouble( 10_000, 12_000 );
Locale[] locales = Locale.getAvailableLocales();
for ( Locale locale : locales )
  System.out.printf( locale, "%,.2f (%s)%n", random, locale.getDisplayName() );
```

The solution consists of four steps: in the first part, we generate a random number. In the second part, we query all registered `Locale` objects as an array containing all supported languages of the Java library. We can traverse this array in the third step and output it in the fourth step.

`System.out.printf(…)` expects a formatting string that puts the random number as a floating-point number, just like the language name. The part in the formatting string for the number is `%,.2f`—the comma indicates the desire for a thousand separator, `.2` indicates the two decimal places.

The important parameter in `printf(…)` is the first one, which says that a `Locale` instance can be passed, which determines the formatting of the floating-point number in the following.

Formatting Date Output in Different Languages

com/tutego/exercise/time/DateTimeFormatterDemo.java

```
LocalDate date = LocalDate.of( Year.now().getValue(), Month.SEPTEMBER, 19 );
System.out.println( date );
DateTimeFormatter formatterShort =
    DateTimeFormatter.ofLocalizedDate( FormatStyle.SHORT );
DateTimeFormatter formatterMedium =
    DateTimeFormatter.ofLocalizedDate( FormatStyle.MEDIUM );
DateTimeFormatter formatterLong =
    DateTimeFormatter.ofLocalizedDate( FormatStyle.LONG );
DateTimeFormatter formatterFull =
    DateTimeFormatter.ofLocalizedDate( FormatStyle.FULL );
```

```
DateTimeFormatter[] dateTimeFormatter = {
    formatterShort,
    formatterMedium,
    formatterLong,
    formatterFull,
    formatterShort.withLocale( Locale.CANADA_FRENCH ),
    formatterMedium.withLocale( Locale.CHINESE ),
    formatterLong.withLocale( Locale.ITALIAN ),
    formatterFull.withLocale( Locale.of( "th" ) )
};
for ( DateTimeFormatter formatter : dateTimeFormatter )
  System.out.println( date.format( formatter ) );
```

Assuming the current Locale is US, the program's output for the year 2023 would be:

```
2023-09-19
9/19/23
Sep 19, 2023
September 19, 2023
Tuesday, September 19, 2023
2023-09-19
2023年9月19日
19 settembre 2023
วันอังคารที่ 19 กันยายน ค.ศ. 2023
```

The temporal data types override the `toString(…)` method, but it cannot be parameterized with a formatting type. Instead, `LocalDate` has the `format(…)` method, which can be passed a `DateTimeFormatter`. There are three common ways to get a `DateTimeFormatter`:

- You select a constant, like `DateTimeFormatter.ISO_LOCAL_DATE`.
- You specify via a pattern precisely where, e.g., the day or the month is placed and which separator symbols are used.
- You choose language-independent standard formatting, which is very practical for screen outputs. It returns `DateTimeFormatter.ofLocalizedDate(…)`.

The `ofLocalizedDate(…)` method expects a parameter of type `FormatStyle` and the proposed solution builds four of these `DateTimeFormatter` instances and then calls the `format(…)` method with just these formats.

The method name `ofLocalizedDate(…)` already contains a hint about the localization. With `withLocale(…)` any `DateTimeFormatter` can be associated with a `Locale`. All temporal data types are immutable; the return of the method is a new object with a `Locale` set.

On Which Day Does Sir Francis Beaufort Celebrate His Birthday?

In the solution, we proceed in two steps:

1. Starting from `beaufortBday` we have to build a `LocalDate` with May 27th of this year.
2. The day of the week must be retrieved.

To the first part:
com/tutego/exercise/time/SirFrancisBeaufortBirthday.java

```
LocalDate beaufortBday = LocalDate.of( 1774, Month.MAY, 27 );
// 1.
LocalDate beaufortBdayThisYear = beaufortBday.withYear( Year.now().getValue()
);
// 2.
LocalDate beaufortBdayThisYear2 = LocalDate.of( LocalDate.now().getYear(),
                                      beaufortBday.getMonth(),
                                      beaufortBday.getDayOfMonth()
);
// 3.
LocalDate beaufortBdayThisYear3 = LocalDate.now()
                                    .withMonth( beaufortBday.
getMonthValue() )
                                    .withDayOfMonth( beaufortBday.
getDayOfMonth() );
```

For the construction of a `LocalDate` object, the proposed solution shows three variants:

1. In the first variant, we use a wither, i.e., a method with the prefix `with` instead of `set`, which returns a new object with a changed value. Java's temporal data types are immutable, so there are no setters. `withYear(int)` returns a new `LocalDate` object with a changed year. For the current year, we can use the `Year` data type. The static method `now()` returns the current year, and since `withYear(int)` needs an integer, `getValue()` is needed on the `Year` object.
2. Instead of using a wither method (a method with a prefix `with` that returns new object), we can use the static factory method `of(...)` to compose a new `LocalDate` object by taking the current year and retrieving the month and day from `beaufortBday`.
3. In the third variant, we query `LocalDate.now()` for the current date with day, month, year, but get a new `LocalDate` object with the month set first and then a new `LocalDate` object with the day of the month using the two wither methods. This variant is not optimal because two temporary `LocalDate` objects are created, which then end up in the automatic garbage collection again.

To the second part:
com/tutego/exercise/time/SirFrancisBeaufortBirthday.java

```
DayOfWeek dayOfWeek = beaufortBdayThisYear.getDayOfWeek();
System.out.println( dayOfWeek );
System.out.println( dayOfWeek.getValue() );
System.out.println( dayOfWeek.getDisplayName( TextStyle.FULL, Locale.GERMANY
) );

DateTimeFormatter formatter =
    DateTimeFormatter.ofPattern( "EEEE" /*, Locale.GERMANY */ );
System.out.println( beaufortBdayThisYear.format( formatter ) );
```

The proposed solution shows different variants of how to output the day of the week.

1. A `LocalDate` object provides various getters. `getDayOfWeek()` returns the enumeration `DayOfWeek`, and we get the day in the week. `DayOfWeek` is an enumeration type, and since all enumerations have a `toString()` method, the output is, for example, WEDNESDAY. If a numeric value is desired, `getValue()` from `DayOfWeek` will return a number such as 3 for Wednesday.
2. `DayOfWeek` provides the convenient method `getDisplayName(TextStyle style, Locale locale)`; it returns a string formatted in the local language for the day of the week.

3. Another variant does not work via DayOfWeek, but uses the format(...) method provided by LocalDate. This must be passed a DateTimeFormatter, and if we use the pattern EEEE, then that stands for the day of the week. A language for the day of the week can be specified optionally, if it is missing, the default language of the operating system is taken as default.

Find All Friday the 13th

Let us break the solution into two parts. At the beginning, there should be the implementation of the interface TemporalAdjuster. Reminder:

```
package java.time.temporal;
import java.time.DateTimeException;

@FunctionalInterface
public interface TemporalAdjuster {
  Temporal adjustInto( Temporal temporal );
}
```

By implementing the TemporalAdjuster interface, we can well increase the reusability of code. Firstly, the implementations are applied to a variety of date or time objects, and secondly we can well collect the implementations, just as Java SE provides useful implementations in TemporalAdjusters. The implementation gets a temporal object (e.g., LocalDate or LocalDateTime) and also returns a Temporal object; it may look like this:

com/tutego/exercise/time/NextFridayThe13th.java

```
TemporalAdjuster nextFriday13th = date -> {
  while ( true ) {
    date = date.with( TemporalAdjusters.next( DayOfWeek.FRIDAY ) );
    if ( date.get( ChronoField.DAY_OF_MONTH ) == 13 )
      return date;
  }
};
```

The functional interface is implemented by a lambda expression, so at the end there is a reference in the variable nextFriday13th. The basic idea is to move from Friday to Friday via TemporalAdjusters.next(...) and check if the day of the month is then 13. If it is, the date is returned. The usage can look like this:

com/tutego/exercise/time/NextFridayThe13th.java

```
Year thisYear = Year.of( 2017 );
for ( LocalDate nextDate = thisYear.atDay( 1 ).with( nextFriday13th );
      thisYear.equals( Year.from( nextDate ) );
      nextDate = nextDate.with( nextFriday13th ) ) {
  System.out.println( nextDate );
}
```

The main program works by looping until the current year is exited. In detail:

- Since the input is always a year (the type Year is appropriate here), atDay(1) upgrades the Year to a LocalDate object, resulting in the 1/1 of the year. With with(TemporalAdjuster) our TemporalAdjuster can be used directly, so that nextDate is initialized with the first 13th day of the month, which falls on a Friday.

- The loop is terminated when the year of `thisYear` and `nextYear` is no longer the same.
- The for-update returns the next 13th day of the month that falls on a Friday.
- In the body, the date is printed.

Get Average Duration of Karaoke Nights

com/tutego/exercise/time/AverageDuration.java

```
String input = "2024-03-12, 20:20 - 2024-03-12, 23:50\n" +
               "2024-04-01, 21:30 - 2024-04-02, 01:20";

var formatter =
    DateTimeFormatter.ofPattern( "yyyy-MM-dd, HH:mm" );
var scanner = new Scanner( input ).useDelimiter( " - |\\n" );
var totalDuration = Duration.ZERO;

int lines;
for ( lines = 0; scanner.hasNext(); lines++ ) {
  String start = scanner.next();
  String end   = scanner.next();   // potential NoSuchElementException

  // potential DateTimeParseException
  var startDateTime = LocalDateTime.parse( start, formatter );
  var endDateTime   = LocalDateTime.parse( end, formatter );

  var duration = Duration.between( startDateTime, endDateTime );
  totalDuration = totalDuration.plus( duration );
}
Duration averageDuration = totalDuration.dividedBy( lines );
System.out.printf( "%d h %02d m", averageDuration.toHours(),
                                  averageDuration.toMinutesPart() );
```

Several steps are necessary to solve the task. Firstly, the program has to extract all start and end values from the large string. Then the strings have to be transferred to the corresponding temporal data types. Then, the differences between these start and end times must be calculated and summed. Finally, we divide the sum by the number of entries, and the task is solved.

The detection of the start and end time points can be done by the `Scanner`. The `Scanner` is initialized with white space as a separator by default. We change this and set a minus sign and a newline as separators. Repeated calls to the `next()` method will return the start and end values, succeeding.

Once we have extracted the string, we pass it to the `parse(...)` method of the `LocalDateTime` class. Since our string does not follow an ISO standard (International Organization for Standardization), we must pass a `DateTimeFormatter` to `parse(...)`. We built this before with the method `ofPattern(...)`, where the passed string corresponds exactly to the pattern we used to format the date with the time information. The symbol strings `YYYY`, `MM`, `dd`, etc., can be taken from the Javadoc.

With two `LocalDateTime` objects, we can determine the difference—we do not do this manually but resort to the `Duration` class. There are two classes in the Java Date–Time API that are used for the difference of temporal data types: the `Duration` class stores the intervals of two-time values in fractions of seconds, while `Period` is used for date values and works based on days. `Period` can be used well if, for example, leap days are to be considered in the difference; with `Duration` a day is exactly 24 hours long, which corresponds to 86 400 seconds. For our calculation, `Duration` is just right.

Conveniently, a `Duration` object can be built directly with the `between(...)` method, and you pass the start and end values. Like all temporal data types, `Duration` is immutable. To add the differences, we access the plus(…) method and store the result back in the totalDuration variable. Finally, we count up one more variable for the total number of date–time pairs, and it goes back to the loop test to see if any more dates follow.

Two runtime errors can occur in the program: once because there is an odd number of date–times in String, and of course because the formatting of the date–time specification is wrong. We do not catch these exceptions; they cause the program to abort.

If all values are correct, the program ends with the calculation of the average duration. The method dividedBy(…) helps to divide the total summed duration by the number of occurring date–time pairs. The resulting object of type Duration is then asked for the number of hours and minutes, and the whole result is formatted.

Parse Different Date Formats

The challenge with the task is that there is not one format given in which each date is formatted, but rather we have different formats. For a certain number of different formats, the Java library provides support, with the DateTimeFormatterBuilder. With the method appendPattern(…) a pattern can be specified to determine a format. You put the format in square brackets to express that it is optional. Example:

```
DateTimeFormatter formatter = new DateTimeFormatterBuilder()
    .appendPattern( "[d/M/yyy]" )
    .appendPattern( "[yyyy-MM-dd]" )
    .parseDefaulting( ChronoField.MONTH_OF_YEAR, YearMonth.now().getMonthValue() )
    .parseDefaulting( ChronoField.DAY_OF_MONTH, LocalDate.now().getDayOfMonth() )
    .toFormatter();
```

In our case, such a configured DateTimeFormatter cannot be used because relative information like "yesterday", "today", or "tomorrow" cannot be expressed. We could in principle produce a part via such a configured DateTimeFormatter, but the proposed solution proceeds differently.

com/tutego/exercise/time/ParseDatePattern.java

```
public static Optional<LocalDate> parseDate( String string ) {
  LocalDate now = LocalDate.now();

  Collection<Function<String, LocalDate>> parsers = List.of(
    input -> LocalDate.parse( input, DateTimeFormatter.ofPattern
( "yyyy-M-d" ) ),
      input -> LocalDate.parse( input, DateTimeFormatter.ofPattern
( "d/M/yyyy" ) ),
      input -> LocalDate.parse( input, DateTimeFormatter.ofPattern
( "d/M/yy" ) ),
      input -> input.equalsIgnoreCase( "yesterday" ) ? now.minusDays
( 1 ) : null,
      input -> input.equalsIgnoreCase( "today" ) ? now : null,
      input -> input.equalsIgnoreCase( "tomorrow" ) ? now.plusDays
( 1 ) : null,
      input -> new Scanner( input ).findAll( "(\\d+) days? ago" )
                                    .map( matchResult -> matchResult.group
( 1 ) )
                                    .mapToInt( Integer::parseInt )
                                    .mapToObj( now::minusDays )
                                    .findFirst().orElse( null ) );
```

```
for ( Function<String, LocalDate> parser : parsers ) {
  try { return Optional.of( parser.apply( string ) ); }
  catch ( Exception e ) { /* Ignore */ }
}
return Optional.empty();
}
```

Ultimately, our task is to transform a `String` into a `LocalDate`. But this is nothing else than a mapping, which we can express in Java by the data type `Function`. We can write a `Function` that tries to recognize a certain format. In the best case, the mapping works, and we can map a `String` to a `LocalDate`; in the worst case, there is an `Exception`, or we program this `Function` to return `null`. The reason for this generalization, which may seem unusual at first glance, is that it allows us to collect all `function` objects later and try them out one by one. In programming, we should always consider whether we can generalize things—from the specific to the general.

We can identify three different types of mappings:

- The first three mappings try to recognize a pattern directly and make use of the `DateTimeFormatter`.
- The second type of function detects whether today, yesterday, or tomorrow was in question. We fall back on the local variable `now`, which is initialized when the method is called. For testing this is inconvenient, so in practice, one would write an internal method for test cases where one can introduce a `LocalDate` as a reference point.
- The third `Function` is the most complex because it has to detect a relative reference with a given number of days. Several methods work together here. The `Scanner` can recognize a string and can simply return the place of discovery for the number of days. The result is in a `MatchResult`: we extract the specification of the days, convert it to an integer, get a new `LocalDate` object where this number of days has been reduced, and return the result. If the pattern did not match, we get the return `null`.

For each possible format, there is now a `Function`, and we add new mappings if more formats are to be recognized—this is busywork. The actual recognition works by traversing all mappings; the functions are applied to the string in order until a `function` returns a valid result. To accomplish this, the functions are first added to a list. If the application fails and there is an exception, the `catch` block catches the exception and selects the next function from the list. The relative references all answer `null`, which through the `Optional.of(...)` leads to a `NullPointerException`, which is caught so that the next function can be used.

In the end, there are only two outputs: either a function responded with a valid `LocalDate`, and we get out of the `try` block with `return`, or there were only exceptions, and the `for` loop could not detect a candidate—in which case the method is exited with an `Optional.empty()`.a

Concurrent Programming with Threads

4

Programs often utilize threads as a programming aid, and operating systems provide them as a feature. If you are using Windows and check the task manager, you'll see that there are roughly 3000 running threads. In this chapter, we aim to increase this number further to execute our own threads. However, the exercises should not solely focus on creating threads; concurrency requires careful attention to ensure proper access to shared resources, necessitating coordination among the threads.

Prerequisites

- Be able to use `main` thread.
- Be able to create own threads; know the difference between `Thread` and `Runnable`.
- Be able to put threads to sleep.
- Be able to interrupt threads.
- Be able to submit tasks to the thread pool for processing.
- Be able to use concurrent operations with returns.
- Understand the difference between `Runnable` and `Callable`.
- Synchronize threads with `Lock` objects.
- Be able to notify other threads with `Condition` objects.
- Know synchronization helpers like `Semaphore`.

Data types used in this chapter:

- `java.lang.Thread`
- `java.lang.Runnable`
- `java.util.concurrent.TimeUnit`
- `java.util.concurrent.Callable`
- `java.util.concurrent.Executor`
- `java.util.concurrent.Executors`
- `java.util.concurrent.Future`
- `java.util.concurrent.locks.Lock`
- `java.util.concurrent.lock.ReentrantLock`
- `java.util.concurrent.Semaphore`
- `java.util.concurrent.locks.Condition`
- `java.util.concurrent.CyclicBarrier`
- `java.util.concurrent.CountDownLatch`

DOI: 10.1201/9781003495550-5

CREATE THREADS

When the Java virtual machine (JVM) starts, it creates a thread named `main`. This thread executes the `main(...)` method, and it has executed our programs in all previous exercises. We want to change that in the next exercises. We want to create more threads and let them execute program code.

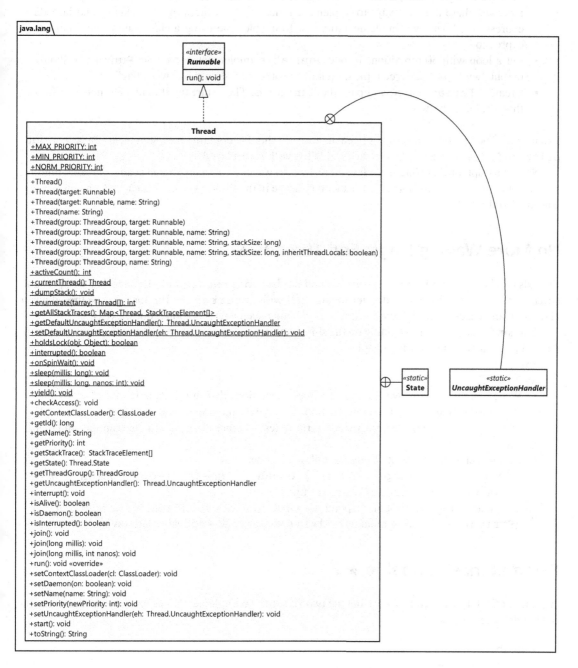

FIGURE 4.1   UML diagram of the class Thread.

Create Threads for Waving and Flag Waving ★

There is a parade in honor of Captain CiaoCiao. He stands at the ramp of his ship, waves with one hand, and waves a flag with the other.

Exercise:

- Threads always execute code of type `Runnable` in Java. `Runnable` is a functional interface, and there are two ways to implement functional interfaces in Java: classes and lambda expressions. Write two implementations of Runnable; one using a class, one using a lambda expression.
- Put a loop with 50 repetitions in both `Runnable` implementations. One `Runnable` should output "wink" on the screen, the output of the other one should be "wave flag".
- Create a `Thread` object, and pass the `Runnable`. Then start the threads. Do not start fifty threads, but only two!

Extension: The `run()` method of each thread should contain the statement `System.out.println(Thread.currentThread());`. What will be displayed?

Suppose Captain CiaoCiao has a few more arms to wave. How many threads can be created until the system comes to a standstill? Observe the memory usage in the Windows Task Manager. Can you estimate how much a thread "costs"?

No More Waving Flags: End Threads ★

Threads can be killed with `stop()`—the method has been `deprecated` for decades, but will probably never be deleted—or kindly asked to terminate itself with `interrupt()`. But for this, the thread has to play along and check with `isInterrupted()` whether such a termination request exists.

Captain CiaoCiao is still standing on the ship, winking and waving flags. When things get serious, he must stop this amusement for the people.

Exercise:

- Write a program with two `Runnable` implementations that in principle wink-and-wave flags indefinitely, unless there is an interruption. The `run()` method should therefore use `Thread.currentThread().isInterrupted()` to test whether there was an interruption, and then exit the loop.
- Build a delay into the loop. Copy the following code:
  `try { Thread.sleep( 2000 ); } catch ( InterruptedException e ) { Thread.currentThread().interrupt(); }`
- The main program should respond to input with `JOptionPane.showInputDialog (String)` so that the commands `endw` stop winking and `endf` stop flag waving.

Parameterize Runnable ★★

A glance at the following code shows that the two `Runnable` implementations are very similar, differing only in the screen output:

```java
// Runnable 1
class Wink implements Runnable {
  @Override public void run() {
    for ( int i = 0; i < 50; i++ )
```

```
        System.out.printf( "Wink; %s%n", Thread.currentThread() );
        //                  ^^^^
    }
  }
}
Runnable winker = new Wink();

// Runnable 2
Runnable flagWaver = () -> {
  for ( int i = 0; i < 50; i++ )
    System.out.printf( "Wave flag; %s%n", Thread.currentThread() );
    //                  ^^^^^^^^^^
};
```

Code duplication is rarely good, though this should be changed.
Exercise:

- Think about how to pass data to a Runnable.
- Implement a parameterized Runnable so that in the above loop:
- the screen outputs and
- the number of repetitions can be freely determined.
- Rewrite the waving-and-flag-waving program so that the parameterized Runnable is passed to a thread for execution.

EXECUTE AND IDLE

A thread can be in several states, these include *running*, *waiting*, *sleeping*, *blocked*, or *terminated*. In the previous exercises, we started the thread so that it is in the running state, and we ended the run() method by completing the loop, which also ends the thread. In this section, the exercises are about the sleeping state, and in the sections "Protect Critical Sections" and "Thread Cooperation and Synchronization Helpers", there are exercises about the waiting/blocked states.

Delay Execution by Sleeping Threads ★★

The *sleep* program (http://man7.org/linux/man-pages/man1/sleep.1.html), known on Unix, can be invoked from the command line and then sleeps for a while, thus delaying subsequent programs in scripts.
Exercise:

- Re-implement the sleep program in Java so that one can write comparable to the example on the command line:
  ```
  $ java Sleep 22
  ```
  The Java program should then sleep for 22 seconds and if there are subsequent program invocations in a script, for example, they will be delayed.
- The Java program should be able to be given the sleep time in various formats on the command line. If only an integer is passed, then the waiting time is in seconds. Suffixes behind the integer should be allowed for different durations:
  - s for seconds (default).
  - m for minutes.
  - h for hours.

- d for days.

  If more than one value is passed, they are summed up to give the total waiting time.
- Various things can go wrong with the call, for example, if no number is passed or the number is too large. Check if the values, ranges, and suffixes are correct. Optional: in case of an error, exit the program with an individual exit code via `System.exit(int)`.

Example:

- Valid call examples:
  ```
  $ java Sleep 1m
  $ java Sleep 1m 2s
  $ java Sleep 1h 3h 999999s
  ```
- Invalid calls leading to termination:
  ```
  $ java Sleep
  $ java Sleep three
  $ java Sleep 1y
  $ java Sleep 99999999999999999
  ```

Tip: structure the program so that the three essential parts are recognizable:

1. Running the command line and analyzing the arguments.
2. Converting the units to seconds.
3. The actual sleeping, for the accumulated seconds.

Watch File Changes by Threads ★

After successful looting, all new treasures are systematically added to an inventory list. This is saved in a simple file. Bonny Brain wants to be notified when the file changes.

Exercise:

1. Write a class `FileChangeWatcher` with a constructor `FileChangeWatcher(String filename)`.
2. Implement `Runnable`.
3. Output the filename, file size, and `Files.getLastModifiedTime(path)` at half second intervals.
4. Check with `getLastModifiedTime(…)` if the file has changed. Print a message if the file changes. All this should happen endlessly; every new change should be reported.
5. Extension: we now want to react more flexibly to changes. Therefore, we want to be able to pass a `java.util.function.Consumer` object in the constructor. The consumer should be stored by `FileChangeWatcher` and always call the `accept(Path)` method when something changes. This way, we can register an object that will be informed when a file change occurs.

Catch Exceptions ★

The distinction between checked exceptions and unchecked exceptions is important because if unchecked exceptions are not caught, this can escalate to the point where they end up at the executing thread, which is then terminated by the virtual machine. This is done automatically by the runtime environment, and we kindly get a message on the standard error channel, but we can't revive the thread anymore.

On a local thread or globally for all threads, an UncaughtExceptionHandler can be installed, which is informed when an exception terminates the thread. It can be used in four scenarios:

1. An UncaughtExceptionHandler can be set on an individual thread. Whenever this thread gets an unhandled exception, the thread is terminated and the set UncaughtExceptionHandler is informed.
2. An UncaughtExceptionHandler can be set on a thread group.
3. An UncaughtExceptionHandler can be set globally for all threads.
4. The main thread is special in the sense that the JVM automatically creates it and executes the main program. Of course, there can be unchecked exceptions in the main thread as well, which can be reported by an UncaughtExceptionHandler. However, there is an interesting feature to this: at the main(...) method there can be throws, and checked exceptions can thus go back to the JVM. In case of a checked exception, a set UncaughtExceptionHandler is also notified.

The processing takes place in a cascade: if there is an unchecked exception, the JVM first looks to see if an UncaughtExceptionHandler is set on the individual thread. If not, it looks for an UncaughtExceptionHandler in the thread group and then looks for a global handler to inform.
Exercise:

- Run a thread that is terminated by division by 0. Use your own global UncaughtExceptionHandler to document this exception.
- Start a second thread that has a local UncaughtExceptionHandler that ignores the exception, so no message appears either.
- If the main(...) method says throws Exception and the body says URI. create("captain").toURL(), is the global UncaughtExceptionHandler also called?

THREAD POOLS AND RESULTS

It is not always the best way for Java developers to create threads themselves and associate these with program code; it is often more sensible to separate the program code from the physical execution. This is done in Java by an Executor. This makes it possible to separate the program code from the current thread, and also to use the same thread several times for different program codes.

In the Java library, there are three central Executor implementations: ThreadPoolExecutor, ScheduledThreadPoolExecutor, and ForkJoinPool. The ThreadPoolExecutor and ForkJoinPool types implement thread pools that manage a collection of existing threads so that exercises can be passed to existing free threads.

Each operation running in the background in Java is performed by a thread. These threads are either explicitly created and started or indirectly utilized through an Executor or an internal thread pool. There are two important interfaces to encapsulate concurrent code: Runnable and Callable. A Runnable can be directly passed to the Thread constructor, a Callable cannot be passed to Thread; for Callable you need an Executor. A Callable also returns a result, as does a Supplier, but it has no parameter to pass. With a Runnable nothing can be returned and also not passed. The run() method does not throw an exception, call() has throws Exception in the method signature, so it can pass on any exceptions.

UML diagram of the Runnable and Callable interfaces

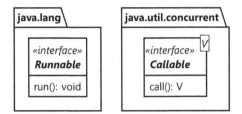

So far, we have always built threads ourselves and used only `Runnable`. The following exercises will be about thread pools and also about `Callable`.

Using Thread Pools ★★

Easter is coming up, and Bonny Brain goes to an orphanage dressed as a Wookiee with her crew members to deliver gifts.

Exercise:

- Create an `ExecutorService` with `Executors.newCachedThreadPool()`, which is the thread pool.
- Create a string array with presents.
- Bonny Brain processes each gift in the `main` thread and passes it to a crew member, which is a thread in the thread pool, at 1–2 second intervals.
- The crew members are threads in the thread pool. They execute Bonny Brain's commands to distribute a gift. It takes them between 1 and 4 seconds to do this.
- The flow is as follows: the gift distribution is implemented by a `Runnable`, the actual action. A free thread from the thread pool (the crew member) is selected and executes the `Runnable`. The `Runnable` needs a way to receive the gift from Bonny Brain.

Get Last Modification of Web Pages ★★

The following class implements a method that returns a timestamp in which a web page was last modified (the data may not be available, in which case the time is set to 1/1/1970). The server should send in zone time UTC±0.

```java
import java.io.IOException;
import java.net.HttpURLConnection;
import java.net.URL;
import java.time.Instant;
import java.time.ZoneId;
import java.time.ZonedDateTime;

public class WebChecker {

    public static void main(String[] args) throws IOException {
      ZonedDateTime urlLastModified = getLastModified(URI.create("http://www.
tutego.com/index.html").toURL());
      System.out.println(urlLastModified);
      ZonedDateTime urlLastModified2 = getLastModified(new URI.create("https://
en.wikipedia.org/wiki/Main_Page").toURL());
      System.out.println(urlLastModified2);
```

```
  }

  private static ZonedDateTime getLastModified(URL url) {
    try {
       HttpURLConnection con = (HttpURLConnection) url.openConnection();
       long dateTime = con.getLastModified();
       con.disconnect();
       return ZonedDateTime.ofInstant( Instant.ofEpochMilli( dateTime ),
ZoneId.of( "UTC" ) );
    } catch ( IOException e ) {
       throw new IllegalStateException(e);
    }
  }
 }
}
```

Exercise:

- Create a record WebResourceLastModifiedCallable with a record component URL url.
- Let WebResourceLastModifiedCallable implement the Callable <ZonedDateTime> interface. Put the implementation of getLastModified(URL) from the example into the call() method. Does call() need to catch the checked exception itself?
- Build WebResourceLastModifiedCallable objects, and let the thread pool execute them.
  - Let the Callable execute once with no time limit.
  - Give the Callable only one microsecond to execute; what is the result?
  - Optional: convert the time since how many minutes relative to the current time the web page has changed.

PROTECT CRITICAL SECTIONS

When multiple parts of a program run simultaneously, they may access shared resources or memory areas. To avoid faulty states, these accesses must be synchronized, allowing one thread to finish its work before another thread accesses the same resource. Failing to coordinate access to shared resources can lead to errors.

Programs must protect *critical sections*, so that only one other thread may be in a section. Java provides two mechanisms:

1. The keyword synchronized.
2. Lock objects.

synchronized is a convenient keyword, but limited in capability. The *Java Concurrency Utilities* provide more powerful data types. For "locking" exclusively executed program parts, the interface java. util.concurrent.locks.Lock and various implementations exist, such as ReentrantLock, ReentrantReadWriteLock.ReadLock, ReentrantReadWriteLock.WriteLock.

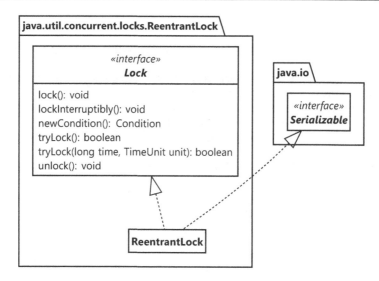

FIGURE 4.2   UML diagram of the `Lock` and `ReentrantLock` types.

Writing Memories into a Poetry Album ★

Once a cargo ship carrying valuable nepenthe has changed hands successfully, the pirates are chronicling their memories in a poetry album. The Captain CiaoCiao later adorns the album with stickers.

Given is the following program code in the `main(...)` method of a class:

```java
class FriendshipBook {
  private final StringBuilder text = new StringBuilder();

  public void appendChar( char character ) {
    text.append( character );
  }
```

```java
  public void appendDivider() {
    text.append(
        "\n_,.-'~'-.,__,.-'~'-.,__,.-'~'-.,__,.-'~'-.,__,.-'~'-.,_\n" );
  }

  @Override public String toString() {
    return text.toString();
  }
}

class Autor implements Runnable {
  private final String text;
  private final FriendshipBook book;

  public Autor( String text, FriendshipBook book ) {
    this.text = text;
    this.book = book;
  }

  @Override public void run() {
    for ( int i = 0; i < text.length(); i++ ) {
      book.appendChar( text.charAt( i ) );
      try { Thread.sleep( 1 ); }
      catch ( InterruptedException e ) { /* Ignore */ }
    }
    book.appendDivider();
  }
}

FriendshipBook book = new FriendshipBook();

String q1 = "The flowers need sunshine and " +
            "I need Captain CiaoCiao to be happy";
new Thread( new Author( q1, book ) ).start();

String q2 = "When you laugh, they all laugh. " +
            "When you cry, you cry alone.";
new Thread( new Author( q2, book ) ).start();

TimeUnit.SECONDS.sleep( 1 );

System.out.println( book );
```

Exercise:

- Before running the program, figure out the expected result.
- Put the code in its own class and main(...) method, and check the assumption.
- The flaw in the code is the unrestrained access to the FriendshipBook. Improve the program with a Lock object so that the FriendshipBook can only be written to by one pirate at a time.

THREAD COOPERATION AND SYNCHRONIZATION HELPER

It is important to synchronize program code so that two threads do not overwrite each other's data. We've learned that this can be done with Lock objects. However, Lock objects only lock a critical area, and the runtime environment will automatically make a thread wait when a critical area is locked. An enhancement of this is to have a thread—or multiple threads—not only wait for entry into a critical section, but be informed via signals that it has something to do. Java provides different synchronization helpers with the internal states that cause other threads to wait or start executing when certain conditions are met.

- Semaphore: Whereas a lock only allows a single thread to be in a critical section, a Semaphore allows a user-defined number of threads to be in a block. The method names are also slightly different: Lock declares the lock() method and Semaphore declares the acquire() method. If acquire() reaches the maximum number, a thread must wait for access, just as with a lock. A semaphore with a maximum count of 1 is like a Lock.
- Condition: With a Condition a thread can wait and be woken up again by another thread. Using Condition objects, consumer-producer relationships can be programmed, but in practice, there is little need for this data type because there are Java types based on it, which are often simpler and more flexible. Condition is an interface, and the Lock object provides factory methods that return Condition instances.
- CountDownLatch: Objects of type CountDownLatch are initialized with an integer, and various threads count down this CountDownLatch, which puts them in a waiting state. Finally, when the CountDownLatch reaches 0, all threads are released. A CountDownLatch is a way to bring different threads together at a common point. Once a CountDownLatch is consumed, it cannot be reset.
- CyclicBarrier: The class is an implementation of a so-called barrier. With a barrier, several threads can meet at one point. If, e.g., work orders are parallelized and have to be rejoined later, this can be realized by a barrier. After all threads have met this barrier, they continue to run. The constructor of CyclicBarrier can be passed a Runnable, which is called at the time of the coincidence. Unlike a CountDownLatch, a CyclicBarrier can be reset and reused.
- Exchanger: Producer–consumer relationships occur frequently in programs, and the producer transmits data to the consumer. Exactly for this case, there is the class Exchanger. This allows two threads to meet at a point and exchange data.

Attending the Banquet with the Captains—Semaphore ★★

Bonny Brain and Captain CiaoCiao are planning a banquet with many companions. They both sit at a table with six seats and receive different guests. The guests come, stay a little, tell and eat, and leave the table again.

Exercise:

- Create a `Semaphore` with as many seats as there can be guests at the table with the captains at the same time.
- Model a guest as record `Guest`, which implements `Runnable`. All guests have a name.
- Guests are waiting for a seat. It does not have to be `fair`, so the guest who has been waiting for the longest is not necessarily next to the table.
- The program should do a screen output for a guest who would like to come to the table, for a guest who has been seated, and for a guest who is leaving the table.

Swearing and Insulting—Condition ★★

Pirates don't duel with cutlasses these days, they duel with curses.
   Exercise:

- Start two threads, each representing two pirates; give each thread a name.
- A random pirate starts cursing and gets an endless insult contest going.
- The curses should be random from a given collection of curses.
- Before the actual curse, a pirate may take a "pause for thought" of up to one second.

Take Pens Out of Paintbox—Condition ★★

In kindergarten, the little pirates regularly get together and paint pictures. Unfortunately, there is only one box with 12 pencils. When one child has taken pens from the box, another child has to wait whenever he wants more pens than are available in the box.
   The scenario can be well implemented with threads.
   Exercise:

- Create a class `Paintbox`. This class should get a constructor and accept the maximum number of free pens.

- In the class `Paintbox` place a method `acquirePens(int numberOfPens)`, by which the children can request several pens. The requested number of pens may be greater than the available number, in which case the method shall block until the number of requested pens is available again.
- The class `Paintbox` additionally has the method `releasePens(int numberOfPens)` for putting the pens back. This method signals that pens are available again.
- Create a class `Child`.
- Give the class `Child` a constructor so that each child has a name and can get a reference to a paintbox.
- The class `Child` shall implement the interface `Runnable`. The method shall determine a random number between 1 and 10, representing the number of pencils desired. Then the child requests this number of pens from the paintbox. The child uses the pencils for between 1 and 3 seconds and then puts all the pencils back into the paintbox—no more and no less. Subsequently, the child waits between 1 and 5 seconds and starts again, claiming a random number of pencils.

Painting can be started with the following children:

```java
public static void main( String[] args ) {
  Paintbox paintbox = new Paintbox( 12 );
  ExecutorService executor = Executors.newCachedThreadPool();
  executor.submit( new Child( "Mirjam", paintbox ) );
  executor.submit( new Child( "Susanne", paintbox ) );
  executor.submit( new Child( "Serena", paintbox ) );
  executor.submit( new Child( "Elm", paintbox ) );
}
```

Play Rock, Paper, Scissors—CyclicBarrier ★★★

Rock, Paper, Scissors is an old game that was played as early as the 17th century. After a start signal, the two players form a shape for scissors, stone, or paper with one hand. Which player wins is determined by the following rules:

- Scissors cuts the paper (scissors wins).
- Paper wraps the stone (paper wins).
- Rock blunts the scissors (rock wins).

So, each hand sign can win or lose.

We want to write a simulation for the game and take the following enumeration for hand signs as a base:

```java
enum HandSign {
  SCISSORS, ROCK, PAPER;

  static HandSign random() {
    return values()[ ThreadLocalRandom.current().nextInt( 3 ) ];
  }

  int beats( HandSign other ) {
    return (this == other) ? 0 :
           (this == HandSign.ROCK && other == HandSign.SCISSORS
```

```
      || this == HandSign.PAPER && other == HandSign.ROCK
      || this == HandSign.SCISSORS && other == HandSign.PAPER) ? +1 :
-1;
  }
}
```

The enum HandSign declares three enumeration elements for scissors, stone, paper. The static method random() returns a random hand sign. The beats(HandSign) method is similar to a comparator method: it compares the current hand sign with the passed hand sign and returns 0 if both hand signs are equal, +1 if the own hand sign is higher than the passed sign, and -1 otherwise.

Rock   Paper   Scissors

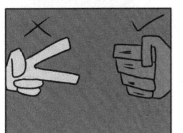 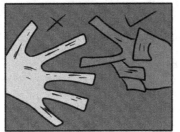 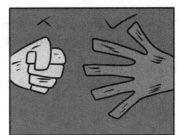

Exercise:

- Run a starter thread that triggers a snick-snack game every second. For repeated execution, a ScheduledExecutorService can be used.
- A player is represented by a Runnable that chooses a random hand signal and puts the choice into a data structure of type ArrayBlockingQueue with add(…).
- After a player picks a hand sign, the await() method is to be called on a previously constructed CyclicBarrier.
- The constructor of CyclicBarrier shall get a Runnable which determines the winner at the end of the game. The Runnable takes out of the ArrayBlockingQueue the two hand signs with poll(), compares them, and evaluates the winner and loser. At the first position of the data structure is player 1, at the second position is player 2.

Find the Fastest Runner—CountDownLatch ★★

For the next heist, Bonny Brain needs fast runners. For this, she hosts a competition and lets the best runners compete. With a starting gun, Bonny Brain stands at the track, and everyone waits for the starting gun.

Exercise:

- Create ten threads that wait for Bonny Brain's signal. Thereafter, the threads start and take between a freely chosen number of 10 and 20 seconds to run. In the end, the threads *should* write their time into a common data structure, so that the name of the thread (runner name) is noted with the runtime.
- Bonny Brain starts the runners in the main thread and at the end outputs all run times sorted in ascending order with the runner names.

If several threads are to come together in one place, a `CountDownLatch` can be used well for this. The `CountDownLatch` is initialized with an integer (a counter) and provides two central methods:

- `countDown()` decrements the counter.
- `await()` blocks until the counter becomes 0.

SUGGESTED SOLUTIONS

Create Threads for Waving and Flag Waving

The following is part of the `main(...)` method:

com/tutego/exercise/thread/CaptainsParade.java

```java
class Wink implements Runnable {
  @Override public void run() {
    for ( int i=0; i<50; i++ )
      System.out.printf( "Wink; %s%n", Thread.currentThread() );
  }
}

Runnable winker=new Wink();
Runnable flagWaver=() -> {
  for ( int i=0; i<50; i++ )
    System.out.printf( "Wave flag; %s%n", Thread.currentThread() );
};

Thread winkerThread    =new Thread( winker );
Thread flagWaverThread=new Thread( flagWaver, "flag waver" );

winkerThread.start();
flagWaverThread.start();
```

In the body of the `run()` method and the lambda expression, we find a simple loop with the desired outputs. After building the `Runnable` instances, they need to be connected to the thread. To achieve this, the `Runnable` objects are passed to the constructor of `Thread`. The constructor is overloaded several times; one variant allows setting a name, which we do for the flag wavers. Building the thread instances does not start a thread; this requires a call to the `Thread` method `start()`.

```
Wink; Thread[Thread-0,5,main]
Wave flag; Thread[flag waver,5,main]
Wave flag; Thread[flag waver,5,main]
Wave flag; Thread[flag waver,5,main]
Wink; Thread[Thread-0,5,main]
Wink; Thread[Thread-0,5,main]
Wink; Thread[Thread-0,5,main]
Wink; Thread[Thread-0,5,main]
...
```

The output shows the `toString()` representation of `Thread`, which consists of the thread name, thread priority, and thread group. From the output, you can see that `thread-0` (which is the automatically assigned name) and `flag waver` alternate. Each time they are called, the output will look slightly different—concurrent programs are typically nondeterministic.

No More Waving Flags: End Threads

com/tutego/exercise/thread/CaptainsParadeIsInterrupted.java

```java
Runnable winker = () -> {
  while ( ! Thread.currentThread().isInterrupted() ) {
    System.out.printf( "Wink; %s%n", Thread.currentThread() );
    try { TimeUnit.SECONDS.sleep( 2 ); }
    catch ( InterruptedException e ) { Thread.currentThread().interrupt(); }
  }
};

Runnable flagWaver = () -> {
  while ( ! Thread.currentThread().isInterrupted() ) {
    System.out.printf( "Wave flag; %s%n", Thread.currentThread() );
    try { TimeUnit.SECONDS.sleep( 2 ); }
    catch ( InterruptedException e ) { Thread.currentThread().interrupt(); }
  }
};

Thread winkerThread    = new Thread( winker );
Thread flagWaverThread = new Thread( flagWaver );

winkerThread.start();
flagWaverThread.start();

String message = "Submit 'endw' or 'endf' to end the threads or cancel to end
main thread";
for ( String input;
      (input = JOptionPane.showInputDialog( message )) != null; ) {
  if ( input.equalsIgnoreCase( "endw" ) )
    winkerThread.interrupt();
  else if ( input.equalsIgnoreCase( "endf" ) )
    flagWaverThread.interrupt();
}
```

For a thread to respond to an interrupt, the interrupt flag must be deliberately polled in the `Runnable`. This query is handled by the `isInterrupted()` method. We put the query in a `while` loop because we want to execute our operation as long as the flag is not yet set. In the body of both loops is a console output and a waiting time of 2 seconds. There is a special feature to note when sleeping: if we sleep and then get interrupted, the `sleep(...)` method first throws an `InterruptedException`, and second, it resets the interrupt flag. So, we have to set the interrupt flag again in the `catch` block and fall back to the `interrupt()` method. This is also exactly the method we use in the `main(...)` method to signal a selected thread to terminate itself.

There is a significant difference between killing a thread with `stop()` and setting a flag: when calling the `stop()` method, the thread is killed hard, and it can be in any state. Setting an interrupt flag requires the active cooperation of the thread. The thread must independently request the flag and exit the `run()` method without any exception.

Parameterize Runnable

The run() method has no return and no parameter list. Therefore, the run() method must take parameters in some other way. This can be done by using variables that the run() method can access.

Two suggested solutions:

com/tutego/exercise/thread/ParameterizedRunnable.java

```java
class PrintingRunnable implements Runnable {
  private final String text;
  private final int repetitions;

  PrintingRunnable( String text, int repetitions ) {
    this.text = text;
    this.repetitions = repetitions;
  }

  @Override public void run() {
    for ( int i = 0; i < repetitions; i++ )
      System.out.printf( "%s; %s%n", text, Thread.currentThread() );
  }
}
```

If we write a new class that implements Runnable, we can give it a constructor that takes states. We can store these states in instance variables. If we then call the constructor, the values are set when the Runnable object is built, and if the thread later calls the run() method, the implementation of run() can access the values.

com/tutego/exercise/thread/ParameterizedRunnable.java

```java
public static Runnable getPrintingRunnable( String text, int repetitions ) {
  return () -> {
    for ( int i = 0; i < repetitions; i++ )
      System.out.printf( "%s; %s%n", text, Thread.currentThread() );

  };
}
```

The second proposed solution uses a factory method. As a reminder, factories are object creators and alternatives to the constructor, and in that case, the parameterization is not done by a constructor, but by the method. Lambda expressions can access local variables, and parameter variables are one of them. A method can return a lambda expression in the body, and since this can fall back on the parameters, we have thus also created a parameterized Runnable.

Delay Execution by Sleeping Threads

com/tutego/exercise/thread/Sleep.java

```java
public class Sleep {
  static long parseSleepArgument( String arg ) {
    Matcher matcher = Pattern.compile( "(\\d+)(\\D)?" ).matcher( arg );
    boolean anyMatch = matcher.find();

    // Check if any match at all or gibberish
    if ( ! anyMatch ) {
```

```
      System.err.printf( "sleep: invalid time interval '%s'%n", arg );
      System.exit( 2 );
    }

    // Found at least a number, but maybe too huge to parse
    long seconds = 0;
    try { seconds = Long.parseLong( matcher.group( 1 ) ); }
    catch ( NumberFormatException e ) {
      System.err.printf( "sleep: interval to huge '%s'%n", arg );
      System.exit( 3 );
    }

    // Also a unit?
    String unit = matcher.group( 2 );
    if ( unit == null )
      return seconds;

    switch ( unit ) {
      case "s": break;
      case "m": seconds = TimeUnit.MINUTES.toSeconds( seconds ); break;
      case "h": seconds = TimeUnit.HOURS.toSeconds( seconds ); break;
      case "d": seconds = TimeUnit.DAYS.toSeconds( seconds ); break;
      default:
        System.err.printf( "sleep: invalid interval unit '%s'%n", arg );
        System.exit( 4 );
    }

    return seconds;
  }

  public static void main( String... args ) {
    if ( args.length == 0 ) {
      System.err.println( "sleep: missing operand" );
      System.exit( 1 );
    }

    long seconds = 0;
    for ( String arg : args )
      seconds += parseSleepArgument( arg );

    try { TimeUnit.SECONDS.sleep( seconds ); }
    catch ( InterruptedException e ) { /* intentionally empty */ }
  }
}
```

Parsing the arguments takes up the most space. We move the parsing out to a parseSleepArgument(String) method, which returns the wait time in seconds. A regular expression helps to recognize a decimal number of any length followed by a nondecimal character. Both parts are enclosed in round brackets so that we can later access exactly this number and unit via the groups.

If the regular expression does not match, we print an error message and exit the program with System.exit(int). With a return not equal to 0 we express an error. Error-free programs generally return 0.

If there were two groups in the string, we continue. We convert the first match group to the number of seconds. This can lead to an exception if the number is too large and does not fit into a long. We have excluded letters in a number by choosing the regular expression, but a regular expression cannot restrict the size. A `NumberFormatException` will alert us if an error occurs; then there will also be an output, and the program will terminate.

The number has been recognized, but does a unit follow? We extract the second match group, and if it is `null`, we can exit the method because no unit was specified. If it is not `null`, we have a character and check which character it is. When the answer was `s`, we abort the `switch-case` and do not need to do any conversion. If it was an `m`, `h`, or `d`, the constants in the `TimeUnit` enumeration help to convert it to seconds. When none of the four characters were used, an error message is also displayed, and the application is ended. In the best case, the seconds are returned.

The `main(...)` method also first performs a test to see if any arguments were supplied before continuing. If not, an error message is shown and `System.exit(...)` terminates the program with an error code. This is more correct than using `return` to exit the `main(...)` method because that would result in an exit code of 0, which signals something wrong to a calling program on the shell.

The extended `for` loop runs all arguments from the command line, we don't need an index. We transfer each string to our `parseSleepArgument(...)` method and sum up the result in the `seconds` variable. Finally, the `sleep(long)` method puts the main thread to sleep for the specified number of seconds. The `sleep(...)` method throws an `InterruptedException`, a checked exception that we must handle; however, we don't have to put anything in `catch` because there is no outside thread to interfere with us.

Watch File Changes by Threads

com/tutego/exercise/thread/FileChangeWatcher.java

```java
public class FileChangeWatcher implements Runnable {

  private final Path path;
  private final Consumer<Path> callback;

  public FileChangeWatcher( String filename, Consumer<Path> callback ) {
    this.callback = Objects.requireNonNull( callback );
    path = Paths.get( filename );
  }

  @Override
  public void run() {
    try {
      FileTime oldLastModified = Files.getLastModifiedTime( path );

      while ( true ) {
        TimeUnit.MILLISECONDS.sleep( 500 );

        FileTime lastModified = Files.getLastModifiedTime( path );
        if ( ! oldLastModified.equals( lastModified ) ) {
          callback.accept( path );
          oldLastModified = lastModified;
        }
      }
    }
    catch ( Exception e ) {
      // Catch any exception and wrap in a runtime exception
      throw new RuntimeException( e );
    }
  }
}
```

```
public static void main( String[] args ) {
  Consumer<Path> callback =
      path -> System.out.println( "File changed "+path );
  new Thread( new FileChangeWatcher( "c:/file.txt", callback ) ).start();
  }
}
```

Since the run() method of the Runnable interface has no parameter list, we have to transfer possible values or return values differently. The solution is simple: if we have a class that implements the Runnable interface, then we can use a parameterized constructor so that we can introduce the state from outside. This is precisely what the constructor of FileChangeWatcher does—it takes a file name and a consumer. The constructor performs a test to check if null is passed accidentally, and then throws an exception; otherwise, the constructor stores the states in private instance variables. The factory method of the Paths class automatically throws a NullPointerException, so we can save ourselves a separate null test on the filename.

The central method run() is called by the thread. The first thing we do is get the time when the file was last modified. This is the first reference point we will later compare to. All this happens in an infinite loop because we don't stop after one check or one detected change.

The body of the loop starts with a wait. We let the thread rest for 30 seconds so as not to put a performance bottleneck because of the tight loop. Then the time of the last change is polled again and compared with the old time. If the time is not the same, then the file has changed. We have to inform our consumer in that case, call the accept(...) method on the passed callback object and hand over the path. One should be aware that the call is synchronous and blocking. That is, if the callback method works for a very long time, our thread will not be able to continue watching the file either.

After calling the consumer, we set the old date to the current date and start comparing again in the loop.

The try-catch block surrounds both the loop and the initial time query to handle exceptions that may occur in several places. Exceptions can be thrown by input/output methods and sleep. All exceptions are caught outside the loop as a design decision. Alternatively, one could catch exceptions inside the infinite loop, allowing the file change check to continue even if exceptions are thrown. However, if the file is deleted, the thread should stop running. In case of exceptions, they are encapsulated in a RuntimeException and thrown, causing the thread to abort. Threads terminated by RuntimeException can be detected using a Thread.UncaughtExceptionHandler. The next exercise will cover this topic.

A somewhat invisible place for an exception is the callback operation, which can also throw a RuntimeException. If left unhandled, it would lead to the death of the thread; however, we don't do anything else either ... We could also consider separating our exceptions from the exceptions in the Consumer, or reporting them with a second callback object.

Catch Exceptions

com/tutego/exercise/thread/GlobalExceptionHandlerDemo.java

```
enum GlobalExceptionHandler implements Thread.UncaughtExceptionHandler {
  INSTANCE;

  @Override public void uncaughtException( Thread thread,
                                           Throwable uncaughtException ) {
    Logger logger = Logger.getLogger( getClass().getSimpleName() );
    logger.log( Level.SEVERE, uncaughtException.getMessage()
                           +" from thread "+thread, thread );
  }
}
```

```
public class GlobalExceptionHandlerDemo {
  public static void main( String[] args ) throws Exception {
    Locale.setDefault( Locale.US );
    Thread.setDefaultUncaughtExceptionHandler( GlobalExceptionHandler.
INSTANCE );

    Thread zeroDivisor=new Thread( () -> System.out.println( 1 / 0 ) );
    zeroDivisor.start();

    Thread indexOutOfBound =
        new Thread( () -> System.out.println( (new int[0])[1] ) );
    indexOutOfBound.setUncaughtExceptionHandler( ( t, e ) -> {} );
    indexOutOfBound.start();

    URI.create( "captain" ).toURL();
  }
}
```

The output is:

```
Sep 25, 2023 11:03:31 AM com.tutego.exercise.thread.GlobalExceptionHandler
uncaughtException
SEVERE: / by zero from thread Thread[#22,Thread-0,5,main]
Sep 25, 2023 11:03:31 AM com.tutego.exercise.thread.GlobalExceptionHandler
uncaughtException
SEVERE: URI is not absolute from thread Thread[#1,main,5,main]
```

An enum implements an UncaughtExceptionHandler, which together with the single static variable INSTANCE results in a singleton. The enumeration element implements the uncaughtException(...) method from the functional interface. When activated, the JVM passes the method a reference to the dying thread and the unhandled exception. The type is throwable, which means that an error can also be reported.

The main(...) method globally sets the UncaughtExceptionHandler, which consequently gives for all threads. The first thread will throw an ArithmeticException by dividing by 0, which our globally set UncaughtExceptionHandler will report directly.

The second thread will also be aborted by an exception, but here we have set a local UncaughtExceptionHandler via a lambda expression, which reports nothing.

The main thread also causes trouble because the constructor of the URI class will throw an exception with this argument. We did not catch and handle this by a try-catch block, but the main(...) method forwards it to the JVM. This also activates the set UncaughtExceptionHandler.

Using Thread Pools

The following is part of the main(...) method; it declares a local record DistributeGift and accesses it in the code:

com/tutego/exercise/thread/GiftsInTheOrphanage.java

```
record DistributeGift( String gift ) implements Runnable {
  @Override public void run() {
    try {
      System.out.println( Thread.currentThread().getName()
                      +" gives "+gift );
      Thread.sleep( ThreadLocalRandom.current().nextInt( 1000, 4000 ) );
    }
```

```
       catch ( InterruptedException e ) { /* Ignore */ }
    }
  }

  Iterator<String> names =
      Arrays.asList( "Polly Zist", "Jo Ghurt", "Lisa Bonn" ).iterator();

  ExecutorService crew=Executors.newCachedThreadPool( runnable -> {
    ThreadFactory threadFactory=Executors.defaultThreadFactory();
    Thread thread=threadFactory.newThread( runnable );
    thread.setName( names.next() );
    return thread;
  } );

  String[] gifs={
      "Dragon", "Pomsies", "Coat", "Tablet", "Doll", "Art Station",
      "Bike", "Card Game", "Slime", "Nerf Blaster" };
  for ( String gift : gifs ) {
    Thread.sleep( ThreadLocalRandom.current().nextInt( 1000, 2000 ) );
    crew.submit( new DistributeGift( gift ) );
  }
}
```

The Runnable is the action that is executed by the threads. Java provides two interfaces in the framework for program code to be executed: Runnable and Callable, where Callable is only used when programs want to return something in the background, this is not necessary in our case.

We can implement the Runnable using a lambda expression. However, in this case, it's not possible because each Runnable needs to be uniquely associated with a String, which is the gift. If the lambda expression could access the data through a variable, it would be a different scenario. We use a record that implements Runnable and accepts the gift to distribute through its constructor. The Runnable displays an output on the screen, pauses for a moment, and then completes its execution.

In the next step, we build a thread pool. Whether the Runnable is run by a brand-new or existing thread is insignificant. The creation of threads costs significantly more compared to normal object creation. To build a thread pool, we can use the parameterless method Executors.newCachedThread-Pool() or a special variant that allows us to build and parameterize the thread of the pool itself. This is not required by the task, and it has more cosmetic reasons because this way we can set the name of the thread. To be able to adapt as much of the infrastructure as possible, we query the defaultThreadFactory(), create a thread via newThread(...), and can then set the name of the thread with the familiar Thread method setName(...). The crew member name is obtained from the Iterator via the next() method, and since the task does not require more than three threads in the thread pool, no exception occurs.

The last part is the bumping of the work packages. The program runs through the array and always creates new Runnable objects with the submitted gifts. submit(...) passes the Runnable to the thread pool, which selects a free thread or creates one at the beginning and thus distributes the gift.

Get Last Modification of Web Pages

com/tutego/exercise/thread/PageLastModifiedCallableDemo.java

```
record WebResourceLastModifiedCallable(URL url) implements
Callable<ZonedDateTime> {
  @Override public ZonedDateTime call() throws IOException {
    HttpURLConnection con=(HttpURLConnection) url.openConnection();
```

```
      long dateTime = con.getLastModified();
      con.disconnect();
      return ZonedDateTime.ofInstant( Instant.ofEpochMilli( dateTime ),
                                      ZoneId.of( "UTC" ) );
  }
}
```

The implementation of the `Callable` interface offers no surprises. The parameterized constructor takes a `URL` object and stores it in a private variable, making the URL accessible later in the `call()` method. The implementation of the `call(…)` method is not much different from the template, except for the difference that we do not catch exceptions, but can easily pass them up from the `call()` method. Then, if an exception occurs, `get(…)` is interrupted by an `ExecutionException`.

A usage could look like this:

com/tutego/exercise/thread/PageLastModifiedCallableDemo.java

```
ExecutorService executor = Executors.newCachedThreadPool();
URL url = URI.create("https://en.wikipedia.org/wiki/Main_Page").toURL();
Callable<ZonedDateTime> callable = new WebResourceLastModifiedCallable( url );

Future<ZonedDateTime> dateTimeFuture = executor.submit( callable );

try {
  System.out.println(
      executor.submit( callable ).get( 1, TimeUnit.MICROSECONDS )
  );
}
catch ( InterruptedException | ExecutionException | TimeoutException e ) {
  e.printStackTrace();
}

try {
  ZonedDateTime wikiChangedDateTime = dateTimeFuture.get();
  System.out.println( wikiChangedDateTime );
  System.out.println(
      Duration.between( wikiChangedDateTime,
                        ZonedDateTime.now( ZoneId.of( "UTC" ) ) )
          .toMinutes()
  );
}
catch ( InterruptedException | ExecutionException e ) {
  e.printStackTrace();
}

executor.shutdown();
```

To dispatch `Callable` instances, we access a thread pool obtained via `newCachedThread-Pool()`. The `URL` object denotes the Wikipedia home page, and after building a `WebResourceLastModifiedCallable` with this URL, we can call the `submit(..)` method with the `Callable` object. This alone does not throw any exceptions (apart from the parameterized URL constructor), exception handling is only needed by retrieving the result with `get(…)`.

The example implements two scenarios: the first `submit(…)` lets a `Callable` be executed by the thread pool, and it then works in the background. The second `submit(…)` also puts a `Callable` into the thread pool, but only gives `get(…)` a microsecond to complete; this is not enough, and there is a `TimeoutException`.

The second `try-catch` block is for the first `Callable` sent. The `dateTimeFuture` is queried for the result with a blocking `get()`, call, and it's likely that a few milliseconds have already elapsed, used by the runtime environment for managing the prior requests. When we examine the `catch` blocks, we see that when there's a time constraint, we must address an additional `TimeoutException`. However, when using the `get()` method without parameters, we only need to handle `InterruptedException` and `ExecutionException`.

For the calculation of the difference, we use the method `between(…)` of the class `Duration`. The static method gets two arguments: once the time from the `Future` and the current time. We must remember not to just ask for the current time with `now()`, but we must ask for the current time in the UTC time zone. Otherwise, unless coincidentally, the program itself runs in a UTC±0 environment, the difference would be incorrect.

Writing Memories into a Poetry Album

The problem is two threads accessing a shared resource. Both access the resource concurrently and mess up the output. The output might look like this:

```
TWhheen  fyloou wlearugsh ,ne tehd eysu nalshli nlea uganhd .I  Wnheeend
Cyaoput acirny ,C iyaoouC icaroy  taloo nbee .h
_,.-'~'-.,__,.-'~'-.,__,.-'~'-.,__,.-'~'-.,__,.-'~'-.,_
appy
_,.-'~'-.,__,.-'~'-.,__,.-'~'-.,__,.-'~'-.,__,.-'~'-.,_
```

Appending letters is a critical section that must be protected. `synchronized` blocks are somewhat outdated, and we want to use `Lock` objects. For our use case, the `ReentrantLock` implementation is suitable.

com/tutego/exercise/thread/WriteInFriendshipBook.java

```java
Lock lock = new ReentrantLock( true );

class Author implements Runnable {
  private final String text;
  private final FriendshipBook book;

  public Author( String text, FriendshipBook book ) {
    this.text = text;
    this.book = book;
  }

  @Override public void run() {
//      lock.lock();
    try {
      for ( int i=0; i<text.length(); i++ ) {
        book.appendChar( text.charAt( i ) );
        Thread.sleep( 1 );
      }
      book.appendDivider();
    }
    catch ( InterruptedException e ) { /* Ignore */ }
    finally {
//      lock.unlock();
    }
  }
}
```

Threads coordinate with each other via the `Lock` objects. When one thread enters the critical section, another thread will have to wait until the critical section is unlocked. To enter and exit the block, there are two central methods in `Lock`: `lock()` and `unlock()`. The constructor of `ReentrantLock` is overloaded, and the parameterized variant uses a `boolean` parameter to determine whether the `Lock` is fair or not. Fair in this context means that the threads that wait for the longest are allowed to enter the released block first. Otherwise, the behavior is nondeterministic. This is also one of the differences from the `synchronized` keyword, where the virtual machine can choose any thread. Whether the allocation is fair or not depends on the implementation of the JVM, and the fairness in `synchronized` is not controllable.

The proposed solution has adapted the source code a bit. One place is outside the `Author` class declaration because the `Lock` object must be available to all threads, since that is what the threads coordinate against. The second change is inside the `run()` method because the operation to be saved is writing to the journal. Before the loop the block is closed with `lock()`, all characters are appended, the separator is written, and finally `unlock()` is called again, which releases the block for the next thread. An `unlock()` should always be in a `finally` block because if a `Lock` is requested, it should always be released, even if there is a `return` or an exception that exits the method. `finally` blocks are always processed, regardless of whether there was an exception or not.

Besides the `lock()` method, there is a second method `lockInterruptibly()` which can be interrupted by an interrupt from outside. `lock()` does not react to an interrupt from outside, which means the `catch` of the `InterruptedException` is only valid for the `sleep(...)` method.

Attending the Banquet with the Captains—Semaphore

The following is part of the `main(...)` method:
   com/tutego/exercise/thread/Banquet.java

```
record Guest( String name, Semaphore seats ) implements Runnable {
  @Override
  public void run() {
    try {
      System.out.printf( "%s is waiting for a free place%n", name );
      seats.acquire();
      System.out.printf( "%s has a seat at the table%n", name );
      Thread.sleep( ThreadLocalRandom.current().nextInt( 2000, 5000 ) );
    }
    catch ( InterruptedException e ) { /* Ignore */ }
    finally {
      System.out.printf( "%s leaves the table%n", name );
      seats.release();
    }
  }
}
List<String> names = new ArrayList<>( Arrays.asList(
    "Balronoe", "Xidrora", "Zobetera", "Kuecarro", "Bendover",
    "Bane", "Cody", "Djarin", "Enfy"
) );
for ( int i = 0, len = names.size(); i < len; i++ )
  Collections.addAll( names, "Admiral " + names.get( i ),
                             "Commander " + names.get( i ) );
ExecutorService executors = Executors.newCachedThreadPool();
Semaphore seats = new Semaphore( 6 - 2 );
for ( String name : names )
  executors.execute( new Guest( name, seats ) );
executors.shutdown();
```

The class `Banquet` consists in its core of four parts:

1. The declaration of the record, which implements `Runnable` and accesses the `Semaphore`.
2. The construction of names.
3. The construction of the `Semaphore`.
4. The creation of the `Runnable` instances and execution over a thread pool.

Since there are six seats at the table and two seats are already occupied by Bonny Brain and Captain CiaoCiao, it leaves four seats that different guests can switch between.

All guests have a name, which is stored in the object. The name appears three times in the output:

1. At first, the name of the guest is printed because the guest is waiting and may not have a place yet. A thread must first get permission from the `Semaphore` using `acquire()`; the method blocks if the maximum number of four free seats has already been reached. Everyone waits for a free seat before taking one, and the first four people are given seats right away, as can be seen in the console output.
2. If `acquire()` is unblocked, the thread can spend time at the table with the captains together with the other four threads.
3. After a waiting period, the `finally` block is processed and the name of the guest is printed again because the guest now leaves the table. It is important to call the `release()` method on the `Semaphore`, so that other waiting guests can come to the table.

A simple algorithm generates the demo data. A list is pre-populated with some strings. This list is now run with the original length, and new strings are generated starting with `Admiral` in the front, and more strings starting with `Commander`.

Now only the `Runnable` instances have to be created and the `ExecutorService` can start them.

Swearing and Insulting—Condition

The code is part of the `main(...)` method:
com/tutego/exercise/thread/InsultSwordFighting.java

```
record Insulter(
    String[] insults,
    Lock lock,
    Condition condition
) implements Runnable {
  @Override public void run() {
    while ( ! Thread.currentThread().isInterrupted() ) {
      lock.lock();
      try {
        Thread.sleep( ThreadLocalRandom.current().nextInt( 1000 ) );
        String name = Thread.currentThread().getName();
        int rndInsult = ThreadLocalRandom.current().nextInt( insults.length );
        System.out.println( name+": "+insults[ rndInsult ]+'!' );
        condition.signal();
        condition.await();
      }
      catch ( InterruptedException e ) { Thread.currentThread().interrupt();
      finally {
        lock.unlock();
```

```
            }
        }
    }
}

String[] insults1 = {
    "Trollop", "You have the manners of a trump",
    "You fight like a cow cocky", "Prat",
    "Your face makes onions cry",
    "You are so full of s**t, the toilet's jealous"
};

String[] insults2 = {
    "Wazzock", "I've spoken with rats more polite than you",
    "Chuffer", "You make me want to spew",
    "Check your lipstick before you come for me",
    "You are more disappointing than an unsalted pretzel"
};

Lock lock = new ReentrantLock();
Condition condition = lock.newCondition();
new Thread( new Insulter( insults1, lock, condition ), "pirate-1" ).start();
new Thread( new Insulter( insults2, lock, condition ), "pirate-2" ).start();
```

The solution relies on `Condition`, and that has two critical methods: for notifying other waiting threads and for waiting for a notification.

The `Insulter` record in our scenario is a `Runnable` that receives various curses, a `Lock` object, and a `Condition` object through its canonical constructor. The `run()` method has an infinite loop that can be ended using an interrupt since insulting never ceases, and every action prompts a reaction. To use a `Condition` object, `lock()` must mark a critical section because `Condition` objects originate from a `Lock` object.

After the time of thinking, a random curse word is selected and output, and then `signal()` is used to inform the other thread. With the following `await()` we wait again in the thread for the signal of the other thread.

The flow will be as follows: `main(…)` will start two `Insulter` threads, and one of the two threads will enter the area first via the `Lock` object, then lock and claim the block exclusively for itself. The second thread will come in a little later, and hang in the `Lock` and get no further. The first thread then starts cursing and finally signals the other waiting thread that it is done. After signaling, the first thread also waits for a signal. It is important to understand that the associated lock is temporarily released so that the other thread can run into the protected block, receive the signal, and then in turn perform the action. While one thread waits in `await()`, the other thread performs its operation and later sets a signal again. This wakes up the waiting thread again, it gets the lock back and continues its operation while the other side waits.

Take Pens Out of Paintbox—Condition

Let's start with the `Paintbox` class. The maximum number of pens initializes the instance variable `freeNumberOfPens`, which is decreased or increased below.

com/tutego/exercise/thread/Kindergarten.java

```
class Paintbox {

    private int freeNumberOfPens;
    private final Lock lock = new ReentrantLock();
    private final Condition condition = lock.newCondition();

    public Paintbox( int maximumNumberOfPens ) {
```

```
      freeNumberOfPens = maximumNumberOfPens;
      System.out.printf( "Paintbox equipped with %s pens%n", freeNumberOfPens
);
  }

  public void acquirePens( int numberOfPens ) {
    lock.lock();
    try {
      while ( freeNumberOfPens < numberOfPens ) {
        System.out.printf( "%d pens from paintbox requested, available only %d,"
                         + " someone has to wait :(%n",
                           numberOfPens, freeNumberOfPens );

        condition.await();

      }

      freeNumberOfPens -= numberOfPens;
    }
    catch ( InterruptedException e ) { Thread.currentThread().interrupt(); }
    finally {
      lock.unlock();
    }
  }

  public void releasePens( int numberOfPens ) {
    lock.lock();
    try {
      freeNumberOfPens += numberOfPens;
      condition.signalAll();
    }
    finally {
      lock.unlock();
    }
  }
}
```

acquirePens(int numberOfPens) is called by the children who want to take a certain number of pens from the paintbox. The operation takes place in a critical section, so Lock is used to lock the section for other threads. A loop condition checks if the number of free pens is less than the number of desired pens, and if it is, then it must wait. If a signal comes later, it must be asked repeatedly whether this condition still applies. It is a programming error if an if statement is used instead of a loop. After the end of the while loop, the number of free pins is reduced and the critical section is released again. Consider: when waiting for a signal, the lock is temporarily released.

releasePens(int numberOfPens) is easier: it increases the number of free pens and then signals other waiting threads that pens are available again. signalAll() signals all waiting threads. Signaling, just like waiting, must occur in a locked section, which is terminated in a finally block with unlock() as usual.

The record Child implements Runnable and takes the name of the child and the paintbox in the constructor.

com/tutego/exercise/thread/Kindergarten.java

```
record Child( String name, Paintbox paintbox ) implements Runnable {
  @Override
  public void run() {
    while ( ! Thread.currentThread().isInterrupted() ) {
      ThreadLocalRandom random = ThreadLocalRandom.current();
```

```
      int requiredPens = random.nextInt ( 1, 10+1 );
      paintbox.acquirePens ( requiredPens );
      System.out.printf ( "%s got %d pens%n", name, requiredPens );

      try {
        TimeUnit.MILLISECONDS.sleep ( random.nextInt ( 1000, 3000 ) );
      }
      catch ( InterruptedException e ) { Thread.currentThread().interrupt();
    }

      paintbox.releasePens ( requiredPens );
      System.out.printf ( "%s returned %d pens%n", name, requiredPens );

      try {
        TimeUnit.SECONDS.sleep ( random.nextInt ( 1, 5+1 ) );
      }
      catch ( InterruptedException e ) { Thread.currentThread().interrupt();
    }
    }
  }
}
```

The `run()` method runs indefinitely in theory unless the thread is terminated externally with an interrupt. The following happens in the body of the `while` loop:

1. A random number is calculated for the number of desired pins.
2. On the paintbox, `acquirePens(…)` is called to get this number of pens. A waiting situation may occur here if the desired number of pens is not available.
3. If the pens are available, `acquirePens(…)` returns and the requested number of pens are printed.
4. There is a wait because the child is drawing.
5. The pens are put back with `releasePens(…)`. Putting back never blocks for a long time.
6. It waits again, and a new loop cycle can begin.

Play Rock, Paper, Scissors—CyclicBarrier

The code is part of the `main(…)` method:
   com/tutego/exercise/thread/RockPaperScissorsHandGame.java

```
Queue<HandSign> handSigns = new ArrayBlockingQueue<>( 2 );
Runnable determineWinner = () -> {
  HandSign handSign1 = handSigns.poll();
  HandSign handSign2 = handSigns.poll();
  switch ( handSign1.beats ( handSign2 ) ) {
    case  0 -> System.out.printf ( "Tie, both players choose %s%n", handSign1 );
    case +1 -> System.out.printf ( "Player 1 wins with %s, player 2 loses with
%s%n",
                                    handSign1, handSign2 );
    case -1 -> System.out.printf ( "Player 2 wins with %s, player 1 loses with
%s%n",
                                    handSign2, handSign1 );
  }
};
```

```
CyclicBarrier barrier=new CyclicBarrier( 2, determineWinner );

Runnable playScissorsRockPaper=() -> {
  try {
    handSigns.add( HandSign.random() );
    barrier.await();
  }
  catch ( InterruptedException | BrokenBarrierException e ) { /* Ignore */ }
};

ScheduledExecutorService executor=Executors.newScheduledThreadPool( 2 );
executor.scheduleAtFixedRate( () -> {
  System.out.println( "Schnick, Schnack, Schnuck" );
  executor.execute( playScissorsRockPaper );
  executor.execute( playScissorsRockPaper );
}, 0, 1, TimeUnit.SECONDS );
```

In the proposed solution, we have two different Runnable types. One Runnable evaluates the winner, and the other Runnable executes the hand signal. The Runnable is implemented by lambda expressions and accesses a common data structure handSigns. Each player makes a random hand sign, places it in the Queue, and waits for the barrier to end.

The barrier itself is initialized with size 2 and initialized with the Runnable determineWinner, which is executed whenever it came to the second call of await() on the barrier. The determineWinner takes the two hand signs out of the queue, uses beats(...) to determine which player scored in which way, and prints a console message about the winner, loser, or tie.

The ScheduledExecutorService helps to replay the actual game every second and run the Runnable behind playScissorsRockPaper twice.

Find the Fastest Runner—CountDownLatch

The following code is in the main(...) method:
   com/tutego/exercise/thread/SprintRace.java

```
final int NUMBER_OF_ATHLETES=10;
CountDownLatch startLatch=new CountDownLatch( 1 );
CountDownLatch endLatch  =new CountDownLatch( NUMBER_OF_ATHLETES );

ConcurrentNavigableMap<Integer, String> records =
    new ConcurrentSkipListMap<>();

Runnable athlete=() -> {
  try {
    startLatch.await();
    int time=ThreadLocalRandom.current().nextInt( 1_000, 2_000 );
    TimeUnit.MILLISECONDS.sleep( time );
    records.put( time, Thread.currentThread().getName() );
    endLatch.countDown();
  }
  catch ( InterruptedException e ) { /* Ignore */ }
};

for ( int i=0; i<NUMBER_OF_ATHLETES; i++ )
  new Thread( athlete, "athlete-"+(i+1) ).start();
```

```
// Start the race
startLatch.countDown();

// Wait for race to end
endLatch.await();

records.forEach(
  (time, name) -> System.out.printf( "%s in %d ms%n", name, time )
);
```

The solution uses two CountDownLatch objects. The first startLatch we initialize with 1, and when multiple threads are started, they wait for this start CountDownLatch to become 0. The second CountDownLatch endLatch we initialize with 10, the number of athletes, and whenever an athlete reaches the finish line, the endLatch is decreased.

For sorting by run times, we resort to a sorted associative memory. Since the threads write concurrently to the data structure, the data structure must support this type of access. For this, the package java.util.concurrent offers various data structures. We use a ConcurrentSkipListMap, an associative memory that can handle concurrent writes. The class implements the interface ConcurrentNavigableMap.

The athletes are threads that are given a simple name via the constructor of the Thread class. After the threads are started, they all wait at the startLatch to reach 0. The call startLatch. countDown() fires the starting gun, and all the athlete threads start running. Each of the threads waits a random time, then writes itself to the data structure and decrements the counter in endLatch. The main program also waits with an endLatch.await() to unblock, and this is achieved by all athletes decrementing the counter so that it becomes 0. After the end of the run, forEach(...) iterates over the map and outputs the time along with the name.

Data Structures and Algorithms

5

Data structures store essential information in the application. They are organized via lists, sets, queues, and associative maps. In Java, the interfaces and classes around data structures are called *Collection API*. Since there are so many types to choose from, the purpose of this chapter is to bring order to the confusion and to illustrate the use of the corresponding collections through the exercises.

Prerequisites

- Be able to distinguish data structures, lists, sets, and associative memory.
- Know data types `List`, `ArrayList`, and `LinkedList`.
- Know data types `Set`, `HashSet`, and `TreeSet`.
- Know `Map`, `HashMap`, and `TreeMap` data types.
- Know the difference between queue and deque.
- Know how to create an order with `Comparator`.
- Know how to use and implement iterators.
- Be able to use data structures in a thread-safe way.
- Optional: Interest in the open-source library Guava for further data structures.

Data types used in this chapter:

- `java.util.Collection`
- `java.util.Collections`
- `java.util.Iterable`
- `java.util.List`
- `java.util.ArrayList`
- `java.util.LinkedList`
- `java.util.ListIterator`
- `java.util.Set`
- `java.util.HasSet`
- `java.util.TreeSet`
- `java.util.LinkedHashSet`
- `java.util.SortedSet`
- `java.util.Map`
- `java.util.HashMap`
- `java.util.TreeMap`
- `java.util.SortedMap`
- `java.util.WeakHashMap`
- `java.util.Properties`
- `java.util.Queue`
- `java.util.Deque`
- `java.util.BitSet`
- `java.util.concurrent.SynchronousQueue`
- `java.util.concurrent.ForkJoinPool`

DOI: 10.1201/9781003495550-6

THE TYPES OF THE COLLECTION API

The list of user types is long this time. However, the design follows a basic principle, so it is not so complicated after all:

- Interfaces describe the functionality of a data structure, "what is provided".
- Classes use different strategies to implement the specification from the interfaces; they represent the "*how* it is implemented".

As developers, we need to know interfaces and implementations, and to review, let's look again at the central types we'll encounter more often in this chapter:

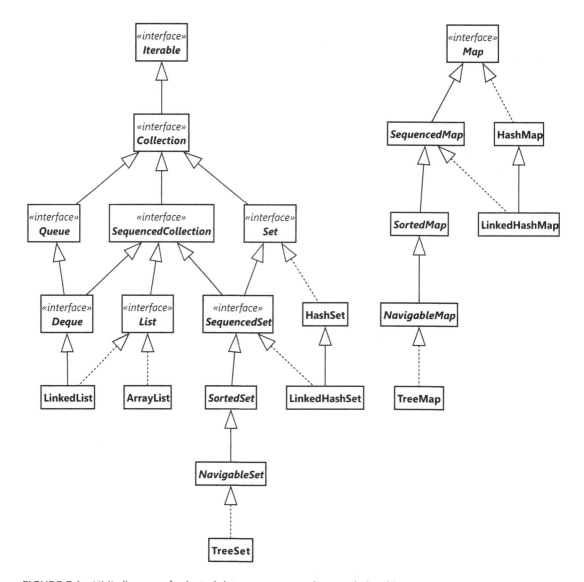

FIGURE 5.1   UML diagram of selected data structures and type relationships.

To note:

- `Iterable` is the most general interface, representing what can be traversed; `Iterable` provides `Iterator` instances. Not only data structures are `Iterable`.
- `Collection` is the top interface that really represents data structures. It specifies methods for adding elements to the collection or for deleting them.
- Under `Collection` are the actual abstractions, whether it is a list, set, or queue. Below are the implementations.
- Some operations are not with the data types themselves, but are outsourced to a class `Collections`. Similar applies to arrays, where there is also a utility class `Arrays`.

We want to build a decision tree for the classes and interfaces `java.util.Set`, `java.util.List`, `java.util.Map`, `java.util.HashSet`, `java.util.TreeSet`, `java.util.Hashtable`, `java.util.HashMap`, and `java.util.TreeMap`. The following considerations must be made in the selection process:

- Access via key.
- Duplicates allowed.
- Fast access.
- Sorted iteration.
- Thread safe.

If access is from a key to a value, this is generally an associative map, that is, an implementation of the `Map` interface. Implementations of `Map` are `HashMap`, `TreeMap`, and the outdated class `Hashtable`. However, lists are also special associative stores, where the index is an integer starting at 0 and ascending. Lists work quite well whenever the key is a small integer and there are few spaces. The association of arbitrary integers to objects does not work well with a list.

Duplicates are allowed in lists, but not in sets and associative stores. There are indeed requirements that a set should note how often an element occurs, but this must be implemented itself with an associative memory that associates the element with a counter.

All data structures allow fast access. The only question is what to ask for. A list cannot quickly answer whether an element is present or not because the list must be traversed from front to back to do so. With an associative store or set, this query is much faster because of the internal organization of the data. This test of existence can be answered even somewhat faster for data structures that use hashing internally than for data structures that keep elements sorted.

Lists can be sorted, and a traversal returns the elements in the sorted order. A `TreeSet` and a `TreeMap` are also sorted by criteria. The data structures with the hashing method have no user-defined order of sorting.

Data structures can be divided into three groups: Data structures since Java 1.0, data structures since Java 1.2, and data structures since Java 5. In the first Java version, the data structures `Vector`, `Hashtable`, `Dictionary`, and `Stack` were introduced. These data structures are all thread-safe, but they are no longer used today. In Java 1.2, the Collection API was introduced; all data structures are not thread safe. In Java 5, the new package `java.util.concurrent` has been introduced; all data structures in it are safe against concurrent changes.

Quiz: Search for StringBuilder ★

What is the output of the following program if it resided in a `main(...)` method of a class?

```
Collection<String> islands1 = new ArrayList<>();
islands1.add( "Galápagos" );
```

```
islands1.add( "Revillagigedo" );
islands1.add( "Clipperton" );
System.out.println( islands1.contains( "Clipperton" ) );

Collection<StringBuilder> islands2 = new ArrayList<>();
islands2.add( new StringBuilder( "Galápagos" ) );
islands2.add( new StringBuilder( "Revillagigedo" ) );
islands2.add( new StringBuilder( "Clipperton" ) );
System.out.println( islands2.contains( new StringBuilder( "Clipperton" ) ) );
```

How can the output be explained? Does it perhaps deviate from the presumed behavior? Could it be due to an important requirement that `String` fulfills, but not `StringBuilder`?

LISTS

For the exercises, let's start with the simplest data structure, lists. Lists are sequences of information where the order is maintained when appending new elements, and elements can occur multiple times. Even `null` is allowed as an element.

Singing and Cooking: Traverse Lists and Check Properties ★

Captain CiaoCiao is putting together a new crew. Everyone in the crew has a name and a profession:

```
record CrewMember( String name, Profession profession ) {
  enum Profession { CAPTAIN, NAVIGATOR, CARPENTER, COOK, MUSICIAN, DOCTOR }
}
```

For each crew, Captain CiaoCiao makes sure that there are as many cooks as musicians.
    Exercise:

- Write a method `areSameNumberOfCooksAndMusicians(List<CrewMember>)` that returns `true` if there are the same number of cooks as musicians, `false` otherwise.

Example:

```
CrewMember captain   = new CrewMember( "CiaoCiao", CrewMember.Profession.
CAPTAIN );
CrewMember cook1     = new CrewMember( "Remy", CrewMember.Profession.COOK );
CrewMember cook2     = new CrewMember( "The Witch Cook", CrewMember.Profession.
COOK );
CrewMember musician1 = new CrewMember( "Mahna Mahna", CrewMember.Profession.
MUSICIAN );
CrewMember musician2 = new CrewMember( "Rowlf", CrewMember.Profession.MUSICIAN );

List<CrewMember> crew1 = List.of( cook1, musician1 );
System.out.println( areSameNumberOfCooksAndMusicians( crew1 ) ); // true

List<CrewMember> crew2 = List.of( cook1, musician1, musician2, captain );
System.out.println( areSameNumberOfCooksAndMusicians( crew2 ) ); // false
```

```
List<CrewMember> crew3 = List.of( cook1, musician1, musician2, captain, cook2  );
System.out.println( areSameNumberOfCooksAndMusicians( crew3 ) ); // true
```

Filter Comments from Lists ★

Bonny Brain reads an old logbook of Captain Dipturus Dimwit, which repeatedly contains four entries:

1. Magnetic declination.[1]
2. Speed of water current.
3. Weather.
4. Comments and general observations.

Bonny Brain is searching for a specific comment in a list of strings. To do so, they need to delete the first, second, and third entries so that only the fourth entry, which contains the desired comment, remains. Task:

- Implement a method `void reduceToComments(List<String> lines)` that deletes each of the first, second, and third entries in the passed list, keeping only the fourth.

Examples:

- A1", "A2", "A3", "A4", "B1", "B2", "B3", "B4", "C1", "C2", "C3", "C4" → "A4", "B4", "C4".
- Empty list → nothing happens.
- "A1" → exception `Illegal size 1 of list, must be divisible by 4.`

Shorten Lists Because There Is No Downturn ★

For Captain CiaoCiao, things should only ever go up; when he reads sequences of numbers, they should only ever go up.

Exercise:

- Write a method `trimNonGrowingNumbers(List<Double> numbers)` that truncates the list when the next number is no longer greater than or equal to the previous one.
- Remember: the passed list must be mutable so that elements can be deleted.

Examples:

- If the list contains the numbers 1, 2, 3, 4, 5, the list stays that way.
- If the list contains the numbers 1, 2, 3, 2, 1, the sequence is shortened to 1, 2, 3.

Eating with Friends: Compare Elements, Find Commonalities ★

Captain CiaoCiao is planning a party on the mainland, and in a large circle, there should always be two guests sitting next to each other who have at least one thing in common. Guests are declared by the following type:

```
public record Guest(
    boolean likesToShoot,
    boolean likesToGamble,
    boolean likesBlackmail
) { }
```

Exercise:

- Create a method `int allGuestsHaveSimilarInterests(List<Guest> guests)`. This method should return -1 if each guest has a neighbor with at least one matching property. If not, it should return a non-negative result, representing the index of the first guest who does not share any property with their neighbors.
- The type `Guest` can be extended in any way.

Check Lists for the Same Order of Elements ★

Fat Donny Bone Spurs and Ally Al Lyons sneak into the Anonymous Buccaneers support group and are told to report to Captain CiaoCiao who is sitting to the right of whom in the conversation circle. Both try to remember. They do not necessarily start with the same person in their enumerations.
Task:

- Develop a method `boolean isSameCircle(List<String> names1, List<String> names2)`. This method should check if the names in both lists appear consecutively and in the same sequence. Assume that individuals are seated in a circular arrangement where the last person on the list is adjacent to the first person. Note that individual names may repeat in the list.

Examples:

- List 1: `Alexandre, Charles, Anne, Henry`. List 2: `Alexandre, Charles, Anne, Henry` → same
- List 1: `Anne, Henry, Alexandre, Charles`, List 2: `Alexandre, Charles, Anne, Henry` → same

- List 1: Alexandre, Charles, Anne, Henry. List 2: Alexandre, Charles, Henry, Anne → not the same
- List 1: Anne, Henry, Alexandre, Charles, List 2: Alexandre, William, Anne, Henry → not the same

And Now the Weather: Find Repeated Elements ★

Napoleon Nose chats with Bonny Brain about the weather, "We've had so many rainy days for the last few months, it's been bad for capering." Bonny Brain replies, "We haven't had that many rainy days in a row!". Who is right?

Given a list of weather data:

Rain, sun, rain, rain, hail, snow, storm, sun, sun, rain, rain, sun.

In the list, sun occurs three times in a row. That is what we want to know. Although rain occurs more often in the list overall, that is not relevant to the solution.

Task:

- Create a new record WeatherOccurrence for weather information:
  record WeatherOccurrence(String weather, int occurrences, int
  startIndex) { }.
- Implement a method WeatherOccurrence longestSequenceOfSameWeather(List
  <String> weather) that reveals:
  - What weather.
  - How many times it appears in the list directly after each other.
  - Where the longest list starts.
  - If weather occurs the same number of times in a row, the method is free to decide what it returns. Elements may be null.

Generate Receipt Output ★

A receipt contains entries and information such as quantity, product name, price, and total.
Program a receipt in this task.
Task:

- Create a new class `Receipt` for the receipt.
- A receipt consists of items of type `Item`. Create the class `Item` as a nested type in `Receipt`.
- Each `Item` has a name and a (gross) price stored in cents.
- `Receipt` should override `toString()` and return a formatted receipt.
  - Output all products and the total.
  - Items may be listed multiple times on the receipt and need to be consolidated. For instance, the list should not have two separate entries for nuts but should instead include a single entry like 2× nuts. The entries must have the same name and price for equivalence.
  - Use a locale you like in `NumberFormat.getCurrencyInstance(locale)` to format the currency.

Example:

- With the structure
  ```
  Receipt receipt = new Receipt();
  receipt.addItem( new Receipt.Item( "Peanuts", 222 ) );
  receipt.addItem( new Receipt.Item( "Lightsaber", 19999 ) );
  receipt.addItem( new Receipt.Item( "Peanuts", 222 ) );
  receipt.addItem( new Receipt.Item( "Log book", 1000 ) );
  receipt.addItem( new Receipt.Item( "Peanuts", 222 ) );
  System.out.println( receipt );
  ```
  is the output (the comma is used as a decimal separator):
  ```
  3×  Peanuts             2,22 €     6,66 €
  1×  Lightsaber        199,99 €   199,99 €
  1×  Logbook            10,00 €    10,00 €

  Sum: 216,65 €
  ```

Quiz: Arrays Decorated ★

Arrays are common in the API, and a conversion to the more convenient `List` happens regularly.
What is the result if we write the following in a Java program?

```
Arrays.asList( "One", "Two" ).add( "Three" );
```

Quiz: Searched and Not Found ★

What is the output if we have the following in a Java program?

```
int[] numbers1 = { 1, 2, 3 };
System.out.println( Arrays.asList( numbers1 ).contains( 1 ) );
Integer[] numbers = { 1, 2, 3 };
System.out.println( Arrays.asList( numbers ).contains( 1 ) );
System.out.println( Arrays.asList( 1, 2, 3 ).contains( 1 ) );
```

Everything Tastes Better with Cheese: Insert Elements into Lists ★

Captain CiaoCiao likes veggies, but when he does, he has to add lots of cheese.

Task:

- Write a method insertCheeseAroundVegetable(List) that gets a list of recipe ingredients and whenever vegetables appear in the list, adds the ingredient "cheese" right before or after it.
- The list must be modifiable.

Examples:

- Gnocchi, zucchini, peppers, cream, broth, milk, butter, onion, tomato, salt, bell pepper → gnocchi, zucchini, cheese, peppers, cheese, cream, broth, milk, butter, onion, cheese, tomato, cheese, salt, bell pepper.
- Cheese → Cheese

Use a fixed set of vegetables.

Quiz: With Nothing but Trouble ★

Given the following code, delete all empty strings in the list. Does the code do this?

```
List<String> names=new ArrayList<>();
Collections.addAll( names, "", "Sonny", "Crockett", "Burnett",
                    "Ricardo", "", "Rico", "Tubbs", "Ricardo", "Cooper", "" );

for ( String name : names )
  if ( "".equals( name ) )
    names.remove( name );
```

Search Elements with the Iterator and Find Covid Cough ★★

Bonny Brain runs to the port and looks for Covid Cough, who is stashing disinfectant in his ship. Each ship contains a list of passenger names. Ships are declared by the following small class:

```java
class Ship {
  private List<String> persons = new ArrayList<>();
  void addName( String name ) { persons.add( name ); }
  boolean contains( String name ) { return persons.contains( name ); }
  @Override public String toString() {
    return ""+persons;
  }
}
```

There are 100 ships at the port, stored in a `LinkedList<Ship>`. Covid Cough is hiding in an unknown ship, let's simulate that:

```java
final int NUMBER_OF_SHIPS = 100;

List<Ship> ships = new LinkedList<>();
for ( int i = 0; i < NUMBER_OF_SHIPS; i++ )

  ships.add( new Ship() );

ships.get( new Random().nextInt( ships.size() ) ).addName( "Covid Cough" );
```

Bonny Brain arrives at one of the many entrances to the harbor, and there are ships to her right and left:

```java
int index = new Random().nextInt( ships.size() );
ListIterator<Ship> iterator = ships.listIterator( index );
```

The only access to the ships is given by the `ListIterator`. Keep in mind that the `ListIterator` can only be used to go forward and backward, there is no random access!

Task:

- Visit the ships with the `ListIterator`, and find Covid Cough.
- Is there a strategy to find the person most efficiently? It is known how many ships there are in total, 100. Since the index is known where Bonny Brain enters the harbor, we also know how many ships are to the left and right of the entrance.

Move Elements, Play Musical Chairs ★

At a birthday party, the guests are playing *musical chairs*. People sit on chairs, and when the music starts playing, they get up and walk around the chairs. The names of the guests are in a list.
Task A:

- Create a new class `MusicalChairs`.
- Create a constructor `MusicalChairs(String... names)` that stores the names internally.
- Implement the method `toString()` which returns the names comma separated.
- Write a method `rotate(int distance)` that shifts the names in the list by the position `distance` to the right. The elements falling out to the right are pushed back into the left. The operation is *in place*, so the (internal) list itself is changed, and the method does not return anything.

Use a suitable method from `Collections` for the task.
   Example:

```
MusicalChairs musicalChairs =
    new MusicalChairs( "Laser", "Milka", "Popo", "Despot" );
musicalChairs.rotate( 2 );
System.out.println( musicalChairs ); // Popo, Despot, Laser, Milka
```

Task B:

- Write another method `void rotateAndRemoveLast(int distance)`, which first moves the list by `distance` positions to the right and then deletes the last element.
- Add a method `String play()` that calls `rotateAndRemoveLast(...)` in a loop until there is only one element left in the list; then the winner is determined, and it is returned as a string. The distance is random on each pass.

Consider the case where the list might be empty in the solution.

Programming a Question Game with Planets ★★

Captain CiaoCiao is accepting recruits, and to test their knowledge, he asks them the diameter of the planets in the solar system. He wants an interactive application for this, where a planet is randomly selected, and the recruits must know the diameter.
   The planets are predefined as an enumeration type:
   com/tutego/exercise/util/PlanetQuiz.java

```
enum Planet {
```

```
JUPITER( "Jupiter", 139_822 ), SATURN( "Saturn", 116_464 ),
URANUS( "Uranus", 50_724 ), NEPTUNE( "Neptune", 49_248 ),
EARTH( "Earth", 12_756 ), VENUS( "Venus,", 12_104 ),
MARS( "Mars", 6_780 ), MERCURY( "Mercury", 4_780 ),
PLUTO( "Pluto", 2_400 );

public final String name;
public final int    diameter; // km

Planet( String name, int diameter ) {
  this.name    = name;
  this.diameter = diameter;
}
}
```

Task:

- Program a console application that builds a random sequence of all planets in the first step. Consider how we can use the shuffle(...) method from java.util.Collections for this.
- Iterate over this random sequence of planets, and generate a console output that asks for the diameter of those planets. As a choice, the recruit should be shown four diameters in kilometers, where one diameter is the correct one and three diameters are from different planets.
- If the recruit enters the correct diameter, a message appears on the screen; if the wrong diameter is entered, the console output reports the correct diameter.

Example:

```
What is the diameter of planet Uranus (in km)?
49248 km
50724 km
12756 km
```

```
139822 km
50724
Correct!

What is the diameter of planet Pluto (in km)?
12104 km
4780 km
2400 km
12756 km
11111
Wrong! The diameter of Pluto is 2400 km.

What is the diameter of planet Jupiter (in km)?
139822 km
6780 km
2400 km
49248 km
…
```

SETS

Sets contain their elements only once. They can be unsorted or sorted. Java provides the `Set` interface for abstraction; two important implementations are `HashSet` and `TreeSet`.

A whole series of questions arise with sets:

1. Is the set empty?
2. Which elements are in the set?
3. Is an asked element in the set, yes or no?
4. Given two sets, do they both contain the same elements?
5. What does a new set look like when two sets are united?
6. Does the set completely contain another set, so is one set a subset of another?
7. What is the intersection of two sets, that is, what are the elements that occur in both sets?
8. What is the difference set, that is, if you delete elements from one set that are present in another set?

Some of these operations can be answered directly using the Set data type. For example, there are the methods `isEmpty()` or `contains(…)`. Set operations, in particular, are not very well-supported, and programmers sometimes have to take workarounds for them. For subsets, for example, there is the `Collections` method `disjoint(Collection<?>, Collection<?>)`, but it returns a `boolean` that says whether the two collections have no common element.

Let's answer some questions with tasks.

Form Subsets, Find Common Elements ★

Bonny Brain's daughter is dating Cora Corona, and they want to find out if they are compatible. So, they both write down what they like. It looks like this:

```
Set<String> hobbies1 = Set.of(
    "Candy making", "Camping", "Billiards", "Fishkeeping", "Eating",
```

```
      "Action figures", "Birdwatching", "Axe throwing" );
Set<String> hobbies2 = Set.of( "Axe throwing", "Candy making", "Camping",
  "Action figures", "Case modding", "Skiing", "Satellite watching" );
```

Task:

- What is the percentage of similarity between the two? Also, what are some methods we could use to answer this question?

 Look up methods in Set to see if they can be used to form subsets or intersections.

Quiz: Great Swords ★

The following program will compile. What is the program output?

```java
class Sword implements Comparable<Sword> {
  String name;

  public int compareTo( Sword other ) { return 0; }

  public boolean equals( Object other ) {
    throw new IllegalStateException();
  }

  public String toString() { return name; }

  public static void main( String[] args ) {
    Sword one = new Sword();
    Sword two = new Sword();
    one.name = "Khanda";
    two.name = "Kilij";
    Set<Sword> swords = new TreeSet<>();
```

```
    System.out.printf( "%s %s %s", swords.add( one ), swords.add( two ),
swords );
  }
}
```

Get All Words Contained in a Word ★★

Captain CiaoCiao intercepts a secret message, and the text consists of seemingly unrelated words. After some pondering, it occurs to him that there are other words in the words.

A program is to find out what valid words a given word contains. To find out what is a valid word, you can use a word list from the Internet, for example https://raw.githubusercontent.com/ullenboom/english-words/master/words_alpha.txt.
Task:

- Write a program with a static method Collection<String> wordList(String string, Collection<String> words) that generates all substring contained in string and returns exactly those words in a Collection that are valid words in the dictionary words and are at least three characters long.

Example for the English dictionary:

- wordList("wristwatches", words) → [wrist, wristwatch, wristwatches, rist, is, twa, twat, wat, watch, watches, tch, tche, che, hes]
- abibliophobia → [abib, bib, bibl, bibliophobia, pho, phobia, hob, obi, obia]

A file with words can be transformed into a data structure like this:

```
private static final String WORD_LIST_URL =
    "https://raw.githubusercontent.com/ullenboom/english-words/master/words_
alpha.txt";

private static Collection<String> readWords() throws IOException {
  URL url = URI.create(WORD_LIST_URL).toURL(); //    370.000 words
  Collection<String> words = new HashSet<>( 500_000 );
  // In Java 21:        … = HashSet.newHashSet( 400_000 );
  try ( InputStream is = url.openStream() ) {
    new Scanner( is ).forEachRemaining( s -> words.add( s.toLowerCase() ) );
  }
  return words;
}
```

Exclude Duplicate Elements with a UniqueIterator ★★

In other data structures, for example, lists and elements can occur more than once. Write a UniqueIterator that returns elements of a Collection only once. null never occurs as an element.

The generic types are declared as follows:

```
public class UniqueIterator<E> implements Iterator<E> {

  public UniqueIterator( Iterator<? extends E> iterator ) {
```

```
    // ...
  }

  // etc.
}
```

The constructor indicates that the new iterator gets an existing iterator as a parameter. So, a call could look like this:

```
List<String> names = …;
Iterator<String> UniqueIterator = new UniqueIterator( names.iterator( ) );
```

MAP KEYS TO VALUES

A hash table associates keys with values. In other programming languages, they are also called dictionaries. Java uses the Map interface to specify the operations for all implementations. Two important implementations are HashMap and TreeMap.

Convert Two-Dimensional Arrays to Map ★

Data types that inherit from Collection are relatively flexible in accepting data; for example, the elements of a List can be copied into a Set via addAll(Collection). Arrays can also be used directly as Collection with Arrays.asList(…).

The Map data type is less flexible; it is not possible to simply transfer arrays or other Collection collections into a Map.

Task:

- Write a method Map<String, String> convertToMap(String[][]) that converts a two-dimensional array into a java.util.Map.
- The first entry in the array should be the key, the second the value.
- The keys correctly implement hashCode() and equals(…).
- If later in the array the same key occurs again, the method will overwrite the earlier pair.
- Keys and values must not be null and must lead to an exception.

Example:

```
String[][] array = {
    { "red",   "#FF0000" },
    { "green", "#00FF00" },
    { "blue",  "#0000FF" }
};
Map<String, String> colorMap = convertToMap( array );
System.out.println( colorMap ); // {red=#FF0000, green=#00FF00, blue=#0000FF}
```

Convert Text to Morse Code and Vice Versa ★

Captain CiaoCiao needs to send a message to a distant island using Morse code. A Morse code message consists of short and long symbols, indicated by the characters . and -.

Copy the following definition into a new class `Morse`:

```
// A .-      N -.      0 -----
// B -...    O ---     1 .----
// C -.-.    P .--.    2 ..---
// D -..     Q --.-    3 ...—
// E .       R .-.     4 ....-
// F ..-.    S ...     5 .....
// G --.     T -       6 -....
// H ....    U ..-     7 --...
// I ..      V ...-     8 ---..
// J .---    W .--     9 ----.
// K -.-     X -..-
// L .-..    Y -.—
// M --      Z --..
```

Task:

- Create a new class `Morse`.
- Write two methods:

  - `String encode(String string)`. It accepts a string and converts it to Morse code. Each character of the string is to be output in the corresponding Morse code. Each block is to be separated by a space in the output. Unknown characters are skipped. Lowercase letters shall be evaluated like uppercase letters. There are two spaces between words.
  - `String decode(String string)`. Turns Morse code back into the original strings. The two spaces for word separators become single spaces again.

Remember Word Frequency with Associative Memory ★★

Girly Gossip listens in on the deck of a group, so she can tell Captain CiaoCiao later what is being discussed. What is important is what is often mentioned as a word or phrase.
Task:

- Write a method `List<String> importantGossip(String... words)` that returns, from a vararg of strings, exactly the five strings in a list that occur most frequently in the array passed.

Example:

```
String[] words = {
    "Baby Shark", "Corona", "Baby Yoda", "Corona", "Baby Yoda", "Tiger King",
    "David Bowie", "Kylie Jenner", "Kardashian", "Love Island",
"Bachelorette",
    "Baby Yoda", "Tiger King", "Billie Eilish", "Corona"
};
System.out.println( importantGossip( words ) );
```

outputs

```
[Baby Yoda, Corona, Tiger King, Baby Shark, Bachelorette.]
```

Keep in mind that it is not about the individual words like Baby or Yoda, but always about the whole string, for example, Baby Yoda or Baby Shark.

Read In and Read Out Colors ★★

Bonny Brain gets a new design for their flags, but the designers only speak gibberish:

```
For the background, let's use #89cff0 or #bcd4e6, and for the text, maybe
#fffaf0 or #f8f8ff.
```

She finds out that a specification like #RRGGBB stands for the red, green, blue (RGB for short) part of a color, coded in hexadecimal. Fortunately, there are "translation tables" like https://gist.githubusercontent.com/ullenboom/03a7ff2f742fe60752a975b1539d0273/raw/colors.csv, which contains lines like

```
amber,"Amber",#ffbf00,255,191,0
aqua,"Aqua",#0ff,0,255,255
blush,"Blush",#de5d83,222,93,131
wine,"Wine",#722f37,114,47,55
```

Occasionally, the file contains the color values only with three symbols, like in the example aqua with 0ff. In this case, the individual color values are doubled, so #RGB then becomes #RRGGBB. Task:

1. Create a new class Color for the representation of colors. Each color has a name (String name) and an RGB value (int rgb). Write—or generate via the IDE—the method toString(). Add further methods if that is useful.
2. Create a new class ColorNames.
   - Give the class an instance variable HashMap<Integer, Color> colorMap, so that ColorNames can internally remember all Color objects in a Map; the keys of the Map are the RGB values as integer, and the associated value is the corresponding Color object.
   - Copy the file https://gist.githubusercontent.com/ullenboom/03a7ff2f742fe60752a975b15 39d0273/raw/colors.csv locally to disk.
   - Create a constructor that reads the file. We can use Scanner for this, or read the file completely with Files.readAllLines(Paths.get("colors.csv")), which returns a List<String>.
   - Split each line of the CSV source, extract the color name (second column) and RGB value (third column). Tip: the color value can be converted to an integer using a Java method: Integer.decode("#722f37") returns 7483191. Remember that color names can be in the form #RGB and #RRGGBB.
   - Transfer the color name and integer value to Color objects, and place them in the Map.
   - Add a method decode(int rgb) that returns the associated Color object for an RGB value.

Example:

- mapper.decode(7483191) → Optional['Wine' is RGB #722F37]
- mapper.decode(7) → Optional.empty

Read in Names and Manage Lengths ★

Bonny Brain enjoys solving name crossword puzzles where each entry is a name. Sometimes she struggles to think of a name of a specific length—this is where software comes in handy!
Task:

1. The file https://gist.githubusercontent.com/ullenboom/c2a14035361627a5bae4dbc35bed56f2/raw/family-names.txt contains last names. Save the file on your file system.
2. To read the file, we can utilize either the `Scanner` class or the `Files` method `readAllLines(Path)`.
3. Sort the names into a `TreeMap<Integer, List<String>>`: the key is the length of the name, the list contains all names with the same length.
4. On the command line, list all names in ascending order of length.
5. Ask from the command line for a length and output all names of that length as long as the length is not 0 or negative.

Find Missing Characters ★★

Captain CiaoCiao has scammed the Dead Sea Scrolls (Cumexhopp scrolls) and no one has been able to decipher the text yet. He wants to make it! However, many characters are unreadable, while other characters are easily readable. It is also easy to see how many characters the word has.
Task:

- Create a new class with the `main(...)` method and copy the two lists into the program:
  ```
  List<String> words = Arrays.asList( "house", "mouse", "horn", "cannon" );
  List<String> missingLettersWords = Arrays.asList( "_ouse", "ho__", "ca__
  on", "gun", "__e__", "_____" );
  ```
- Match each word from `missingLettersWords` with all possible words from the dictionary `words` where the underscore symbolizes unknown characters.
- The length of the suggested words from the dictionary must be equal to the word length of the unreadable word.
- At least one character must be given.

Example:

- Possible screen output from the given lists:
  ```
  _ouse -> [mouse, house]
  ho__  -> [horn]
  ca__on -> [cannon]
  gun -> No results
  __e__ -> No results
  _____ -> No results
  ```

Calculate Number of Paths to the Three-Headed Monkey ★★

After a night of drinking in Manhattan, Captain CiaoCiao misses his three-headed monkey. He must have lost the stuffed animal somewhere along the way! But where could it be? His team has to walk all the streets from start to finish. The only thing Captain CiaoCiao can remember is that he didn't get across the diagonal.

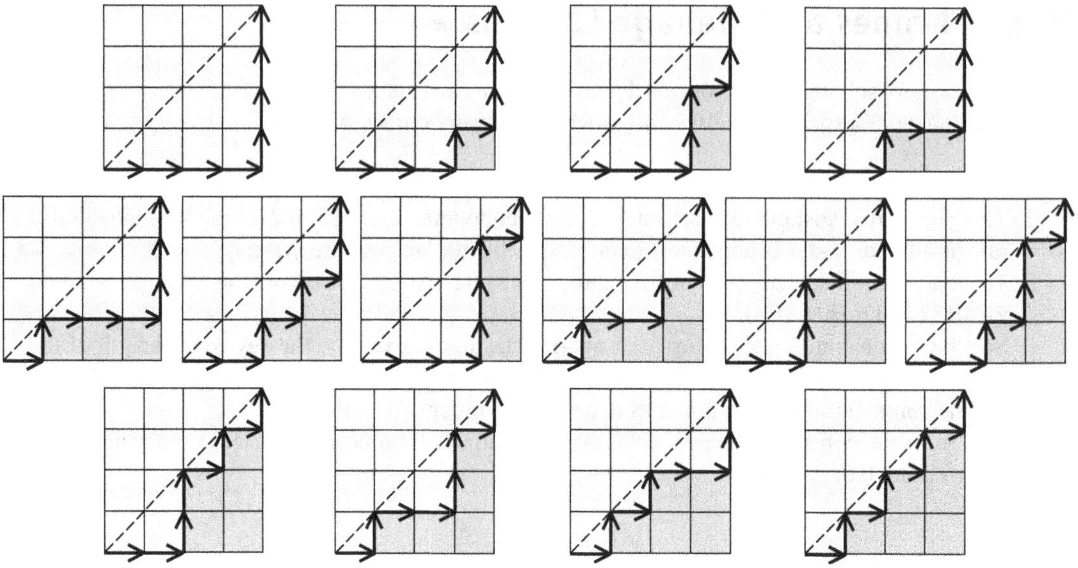

FIGURE 5.2 Possible routes from the start to the finish. (Source: Wikipedia.)

The image shows 4×4 street blocks and there are 14 possibilities. After some time of looking for, the crew finds the stuffed animal, they are lucky!

Captain CiaoCiao ponders: What if there were 5 or 10 blocks—wouldn't the number of paths then be much too large to search?

The answer to the question is provided by mathematics. What is being searched for here is a *monotonic path* for a square with $n \times n$ cells. The number of possible paths provides the *Catalan number*, which is calculated as follows:

$$C_n = (2n)! \, / \, (n+1)! \, n!$$

Task:

- Convert the formula by the method `BigInteger catalan(BigInteger n)`. Use your own internal method `BigInteger factorial(BigInteger n)` for the factorial calculation.
- Three factorials must be calculated in the formula: $n!$, $(n+1)!$ and $(2n)!$. It is $(n+1)!$ nothing else than $n! \times (n+1)$ is, so $n!$ has to be calculated twice; also on the way to the calculation of $(2n)!$ the intermediate result $(n+1)!$ arises. So many multiplications have to be done twice, so the products should be cached: resort to the data type `WeakHashMap` for this.
- Compare the times when we call the `catalan(…)` method twice with the same parameters. Use the following code as a template:

```
long start = System.nanoTime();
BigInteger catalan1000 = catalan( BigInteger.valueOf( 1000 ) );
long end = System.nanoTime();
System.out.println( catalan1000 );
System.out.println( TimeUnit.NANOSECONDS.toMillis( end - start ) );
```

Manage Holidays in a Sorted Associative Store ★

Elements in a `TreeMap` are automatically sorted. `TreeMap` implements `java.util.NavigableMap`, which `HashMap` does not. The order is either determined by an external `Comparator`, or the elements have a natural order.

From the API documentation, we see that `firstEntry()` and `lastEntry()` return the smallest and largest element, respectively. The return type is `Map.Entry<K,V>`.

Given a key `key`, the following methods return relative to that key:

- `ceiling*(K key)`: Returns a result that is *greater than or equal* to this key.
- `floor*(K key)`: Returns a result that is *less than or equal* to the given key.
- `lower*(K key)`: Returns a result that is *strictly less* than the given key.
- `higher*(K key)`: Returns a result that is *strictly greater* than the given key.

All methods return `null` if there is no answer to the question.

For subsets, the following methods are useful:

- `SortedMap<K,V> subMap(K fromKey, K toKey)`.
- `NavigableMap<K,V> subMap(K fromKey, boolean fromInclusive, K toKey, boolean toInclusive)`.

In the first case, `fromKey` is inclusive and `toKey` is exclusive; this corresponds to the usual convention of Java. The second method allows more precise control over whether the start or end element belongs.

Task:

- Build a sorted associative memory:
  ```
  NavigableMap<LocalDate, String> dates = new TreeMap<>( Map.of(
    LocalDate.of( 2024, Month.JANUARY, 1 ), "New Year's Day",
    ...
  ) );
  ```
  The type `<LocalDate, String>` means that a temporal type `LocalDate` should be associated with a string.
- The class `LocalDate` implements `Comparable`, which means that the elements have a natural order.
- Fill the data structure with some pairs for real or fictitious holidays.
- Answer the following questions using the appropriate methods of `NavigableMap`:
  - According to the data structure, what is the earliest and last holiday?
  - The Christmas vacation ends on the 6th of January. What is the first holiday after the Christmas vacation?
  - Which date values are in the Christmas vacation from December 23 to January 6 (date values inclusive)?
  - Delete all registered holidays that fall within the Christmas vacations from the data structure.

Quiz: Keys in a HashMap ★★

Consider what appears on the screen for the following program:

```
Map<Point, String> map = new HashMap<>();
Point p = new Point( 1, 2 );
map.put( p, p.toString() );
p.setLocation( 2, 1 );
System.out.println( map );
System.out.println( map.get( p ) );
```

```
p.setLocation( 1, 2 );
System.out.println( map.get( p ) );
```

What must be true for keys of an associative store?

Determine Commonality: Party Set and Souvenir ★

Bonny Brain plans a party, and all families contribute:

```
Set<String> gombonoGifts = new HashSet<>();
Collections.addAll( gombonoGifts, "Vodka", "BBQ Grill", "kneading soap" );

Set<String> banannaGifts = new HashSet<>();
Collections.addAll( banannaGifts, "Vodka", "drinking helmet" );

Set<String> cilimbiGifts = new HashSet<>();
Collections.addAll( cilimbiGifts,
                    "drinking helmet", "Money box", "Vodka", "water pistol" );

List<Set<String>> families =
    Arrays.asList( gombonoGifts, banannaGifts, cilimbiGifts );
```

Since Bonny Brain is a perfection strategist, she wants to know if things are brought multiple times. Task:

- Write a method `printMultipleGifts(List<Set<String>> families)` that outputs which things are brought how many times.
- What was brought more than once?

Example:

- Possible output for the upper assignments:
  ```
  {drinking helmet=2, kneading soap=1, water pistol=1, Money box=1, BBQ
  Grill=1, Vodka=3}
  drinking helmet
  Vodka
  ```

PROPERTIES

The class `Properties` is a special associative memory that associates only string with strings. The class not only represents a data structure but can also read and write files called *property files*. These are text files that are usually used for configuration. Key-value pairs are separated in the file by =. It is also possible to read and write the values in an XML format, but this is uncommon.

Develop Convenient Properties Decorator ★★

The `Properties` class contains key-value pairs, where the keys are always just strings. Possible conversions have to be done by developers themselves, which is inconvenient.

Task:

Write a class `PropertiesConfiguration` that decorates a `Properties` object. The most general method returns an `Optional` that is either filled or empty if the key does not exist:

- `Optional<String> getString(String key)`.

The advantage with the `Optional` is that alternatives for default values can easily be determined: `conf.getProperty("rank").orElse("Captain")`.

Other methods of `PropertiesConfiguration` are to perform conversions:

- `Optional<Boolean> getBoolean(String key)`.
- `OptionalLong getLong(String key)`.
- `OptionalDouble getDouble(String key)`.
- `Optional<BigInteger> getBigInteger(String key)`.

If there was no associated value to the key, the container is empty. If the conversion to an error fails, that also results in an empty container.

Example for the API:

```
Properties root = new Properties();
root.setProperty( "likes-rum", "true" );
root.setProperty( "age", "55" );
root.setProperty( "income", "123456789012" );
root.setProperty( "hobbies", "drinking, gambling\\, games, swearing
competitions" );
root.setProperty( "weakness_of_character", "" );
PropertiesConfiguration conf = new PropertiesConfiguration( root );
Optional<Boolean> maybeLikesRum = conf.getBoolean( "likes-rum" );
OptionalLong maybeAge = conf.getLong( "age" );
Optional<BigInteger> maybeIncome = conf.getBigInteger( "income" );

System.out.println( maybeLikesRum );        // Optional[true]
System.out.println( maybeAge );             // OptionalLong[55]
System.out.println( maybeIncome );          // Optional[123456789012]
```

Optional addition: query lists.

Advanced developers can implement the following method:

- `List<String> getList(String key)`. Returns a list of comma-separated strings. The comma itself can be masked out by `\,`.

Example:

```
List<String> hobbies = conf.getList( "hobbies" );
List<String> weaknessOfCharacter = conf.getList( "weakness_of_character" );

System.out.println( hobbies );              // [drinking, gambling, games,
swearing competitions]
System.out.println( hobbies.size() );       // 3
System.out.println( weaknessOfCharacter );  // []
```

Optional addition: store binary values

A `java.util.HashMap` can associate arbitrary types, for a `Properties` only strings can be associated with strings. If other data types, such as `byte` arrays, are to be stored, they must be converted to a string. A `byte[]` can be converted to an ASCII string in various ways, such as using BASE64 encoding; Java can do this using the class `Base64`.

Since `Properties` are read rather than written, the `get*(...)` methods were sufficient for us so far. With the following addition, two new methods are to be written, one for setting and one for querying:

- `void putBinary(String key, byte[] bytes)`.
- `Optional<byte[]> getBinary(String key)`.

An example of use:

```
conf.putBinary( "binary", new byte[]{ 0, 1, 127, (byte) 254, (byte) 255 } );
System.out.println( conf.getString( "binary" ) ); // Optional[AAF//v8=]
conf.getBinary( "binary" ).ifPresent( binary ->
  System.out.printf( "%d %d %d %d %d",
                     binary[0], binary[1], binary[2], binary[3], binary[4] )
);
```

STACK AND QUEUES

A general list in Java lets us access the elements by an index; we call such access also *random access* because we have the choice to ask for an element at any position. There are data structures that are much more restricted and can, for example, only insert or delete elements at the beginning or end. These include:

- Stack.
- Queues.

With a stack, you can only insert elements at one end and must remove the elements again at this end. The principle is also called *LIFO*: *last in, first out*. In contrast to this is the queue. With it, that is read out first, which was added also as first. The principle is called *FIFO*: *first in, first out*.

Pure stacks and queues do not exist in Java, only interfaces implemented by lists.

Program RPN Pocket Calculator ★

We usually write mathematical expressions in *infix notation*, where the operators are placed between the operands, such as 47 + 11. In principle, however, the operator can also stand in front of the operands, as in + 47 11, or behind them, as in 47 11 +.

The Hewlett-Packard pocket calculators had established a special input in the 1980s, the *Reverse Polish notation* (RPN). This is a postfix notation where the operators are placed after the values. The advantage for computers is that the precedence—point before line calculation—has already been resolved by users, simplifying program logic in the calculator. PostScript also uses this representation because mathematical expressions can be easily evaluated via a stack.[2]

We want to program a RPN calculator.

Task:

1. Write a program that first tokenizes a string like "12 34 23 + *". Hint: For splitting, you can use `split(...)` of `String` or a `Scanner`.
2. After splitting, the result is to be evaluated. Start with a fixed string for testing.

3. Read in a string from the command line so that we have a real RPN calculator.
4. What errors and problems need to be handled and caught? How should we handle errors?

BITSET

The class `BitSet` is a space-saving and performant alternative to `boolean` arrays. The data structure is useful when you need a mapping of an integer to a truth value. The data structure can quickly answer whether an index (a positive integer) is associated with `true` or `false`. If the number of bits becomes too large, or if there are large gaps, https://github.com/brettwooldridge/SparseBitSet is a good alternative.

Forget No Ship ★

Once a year, there is an exercise where 13 ships have to be boarded. Each of the ships is uniquely identified by a number from 10 to 22. Once the adventure is over, our trusty Bonny Brain receives a list of the ships that their crew boarded. It could be something like this:

• {10, 20, 21, 15, 16, 17, 18, 19, 11, 12, 13, 14, 22 }

Sometimes she gets lists where numbers are missing or appear twice:

• {10, 20, 21, 15, 16, 17, 18, 22 }
• {10, 20, 21, 10, 15, 16, 10 }

Such lists show Bonny Brain that ships were forgotten or repeatedly raided during the exercise. Since manual checking is inconvenient, software should do the job.

Task:

- Create a new class with a new static method `checkForCompletedCompetition(int...` `shipIds)`. Pass the IDs of the ships.
- Report which ships were raided multiple times. The amount is not significant.
- Report if a ship was not raided and which one it was.
- Write the program in such a way that no two nested loops are used. In other words, the runtime should not be quadratic.

Find Duplicate Entries and Solve the Animal Chaos ★

Captain CiaoCiao feeds the animals of his private zoo before going to bed. But being a bit tipsy from the rum, he forgets to close the gate. The next morning, Finian Fishbone and Fred Fritte notice that animals are missing. They quickly run to Captain CiaoCiao: "Some animals have escaped!" — "Scurvy baboon! Which ones?" asks the captain. The two ponder and record (writing is not their strong suit):

- 🐿🐢🐑🦋🐨
- 🐏🐘🐓😺🦋🐌

Captain CiaoCiao notes that both have poor memories, and only wants to have animals searched for that are named by both.

Task:

- Write a method `String sameSymbols(String, String)` that returns a string containing the common symbols. The order is not significant, all Unicode characters are possible.
- Since we have to iterate over all characters of the `string` and it contains "higher" Unicode characters, which are moved out by two `char`, the solution is to use `string.codePoints().` `forEach(consumer)`. This statement iterates over all characters of the String `string` and calls the passed `IntConsumer` for each character. This is an application of the Stream API, which we will look at in more detail in the next chapter.

Examples:

- `sameSymbols("🐿🐢🐑🦋🐨", "🐏🐘🐓😺🦋🐌") → "🐢🐑🦋"`.
- `sameSymbols("abcy", "bcd") → "bc"`.
- `sameSymbols("abc", "def") → ""`.

Since the result is urgent, implement the method so that the runtime is linear with the length of the strings, in computer science jargon: $O(N+M)$ if N and M are the lengths of the strings. All Unicode characters are allowed.

THREAD-SAFE DATA STRUCTURES

For the previous tasks around the data structures `ArrayList`, `LinkedList`, `HashSet`, `TreeSet`, etc. we never needed more than the main thread. In the following tasks, more threads and concurrent accesses come into play, and then we need to use thread-safe data structures. For the solutions, we want to use the data types from the package `java.util.concurrent`. The package contains different thread-safe data structures, which work correctly even with an arbitrary number of parallel accesses and have an excellent performance.

Loading Ship ★★

Captain CiaoCiao and the crew are getting ready for the next big adventure on Gazorpazorp Island. Five employees put crates and barrels on the loading ramp, and 10 employees stow the goods in the ship. There can be no more than five objects on the loading dock at a time.

Task:

- Create an `ArrayBlockingQueue<String>` of capacity 5 for the ramp.
- Create two different `Runnable` implementations `Loader` and `Unloader` which get a reference to the `ArrayBlockingQueue`.
  - The `Loader` puts strings on the ramp (random strings from a set of product names).
  - The `Unloader` shall take strings from the ramp and output them to the screen.
  - It takes `Loader` and `Unloader` randomly between 1 and 2 seconds for their work.
- Five threads shall be `Unloader` and 10 threads `Loader`.

There are different methods for adding and removing. The difference is important. Otherwise, program errors may occur:

TABLE 5.1   `BlockingQueue` methods for adding and removing elements

OPERATION	EXCEPTION	NULL RETURN	BLOCKED
insert	`add(e)`	`offer(e)`	`put(e)`
remove	`remove()`	`poll()`	`take()`

You can't deduce the semantics from the method names; you have to learn the difference. For our task, only one column, and these methods come into question.

Handle Important Messages First ★★

A `PriorityQueue` has an internal sorting so that the items with a higher priority move to the front. The priority comes from either the natural ordering of the elements implementing `Comparable` or an external `Comparator`. "Small" elements have a higher priority and move to the front of the `PriorityQueue`. At the end of the queue are the elements with the lowest priority. (This is the same as with vaccinations: Prioritization group 1 gets the stuff first).

Captain CiaoCiao gets work orders from various parties, but everything from Bonny Brain has top priority. Each work order from Bonny Brain contains the term of affection "Little Canon," which lets the captain know that it is time to spring into action immediately.
Task:

- Put the following record into the project:
```
record Message( String message, LocalDateTime timestamp ) {
  Message( String message ) {
    this( Objects.requireNonNull( message ), LocalDateTime.now() );
  }
  @Override public String toString() {
    return "'%s', %s".formatted(
      message, timestamp.format( DateTimeFormatter.ofPattern("mm:ss.
SSSSSSS") )
    );
  }
}
```
- `toString()` encloses the message in single quotes and displays only the minutes and seconds of the timestamp, because that is enough for a quick visual comparison of which message is younger or older.
- For `Message` implement a `Comparator` which creates an order so that messages with the term of endearment are »smaller« than messages without the term of affection, so that this can be evaluated as a higher priority later. If both messages contain a term of endearment or both messages do not contain a term of endearment, they are equally important.
- Extend the `Comparator` by another comparison logic, so that the timestamp is considered, and an earlier message is also processed earlier.
- Initialize the `PriorityQueue` with messages, and watch how messages with the term of endearment move forward in the queue.

Example:
  Assuming that `PriorityQueue<Message> tasks` is a correctly initialized data structure, the following program will produce the output shown:

```
tasks.add( new Message( "Treasure Hunt" ) );
System.out.println( "= "+tasks );

tasks.add( new Message( "Little Canon, Family Movie Night!" ) );
System.out.println( "= "+tasks );

tasks.add( new Message( "Build a pirate ship" ) );
System.out.println( "= "+tasks );

System.out.println( tasks.remove()+"\n"+"= "+tasks );
System.out.println( tasks.remove()+"\n"+"= "+tasks );
```

```
tasks.add( new Message( "Capture the Flag" ) );
System.out.println( "= "+tasks );

tasks.add( new Message( "Bury the treasure, Little Canon" ) );
System.out.println( "= "+tasks );

tasks.add( new Message( "Little Canon, make a treasure map" ) );
System.out.println( "= "+tasks );

for ( int i=0; i<4; i++ )
  System.out.println( tasks.remove()+"\n"+"= "+tasks );
```

The output is:

```
= ['Treasure Hunt', 44:20.8500129]
= ['Little Canon, Family Movie Night!', 44:20.8580242, 'Treasure Hunt',
44:20.8500129]
= ['Little Canon, Family Movie Night!', 44:20.8580242, 'Treasure Hunt',
44:20.8500129, 'Build a pirate ship', 44:20.8590231]
'Little Canon, Family Movie Night!', 44:20.8580242
= ['Treasure Hunt', 44:20.8500129, 'Build a pirate ship', 44:20.8590231]
'Treasure Hunt', 44:20.8500129
= ['Build a pirate ship', 44:20.8590231]
= ['Build a pirate ship', 44:20.8590231, 'Capture the Flag', 44:20.8665477]
= ['Bury the treasure, Little Canon', 44:20.8665477, 'Capture the Flag',
44:20.8665477, 'Build a pirate ship', 44:20.8590231]
= ['Bury the treasure, Little Canon', 44:20.8665477, 'Little Canon, make a
treasure map', 44:20.8665477, 'Build a pirate ship', 44:20.8590231, 'Capture
the Flag', 44:20.8665477]
'Bury the treasure, Little Canon', 44:20.8665477
= ['Little Canon, make a treasure map', 44:20.8665477, 'Capture the Flag',
44:20.8665477, 'Build a pirate ship', 44:20.8590231]
'Little Canon, make a treasure map', 44:20.8665477
= ['Build a pirate ship', 44:20.8590231, 'Capture the Flag', 44:20.8665477]
'Build a pirate ship', 44:20.8590231
= ['Capture the Flag', 44:20.8665477]
'Capture the Flag', 44:20.8665477
= []
```

If Used Up, Create a New One ★★★

The expression new BigInteger(1024, new SecureRandom()) generates a large random number of type BigInteger.
Task:

- Write a custom class SecureRandomBigIntegerIterator that implements Iterator and can return an infinite number of BigIntegers.
- Whenever the number is queried and used up, a background thread should automatically compute a new random number.

SUGGESTED SOLUTIONS

Quiz: Search for StringBuilder

The program returns the output

```
true
false
```

The explanation for this lies in the implementation of the contains(Object) method. It internally falls back to a method that returns the location of the element, but we can read from the current implementation of the Java library quite well what must be true for a search:

Excerpt from OpenJDK' implementation `java.lang.ArrayList`.

```java
int indexOfRange(Object o, int start, int end) {
    Object[] es = elementData;
    if (o == null) {
        for (int i = start; i < end; i++) {
            if (es[i] == null) {
                return i;
            }
        }
    } else {
        for (int i = start; i < end; i++) {
            if (o.equals(es[i])) {
                return i;
            }
        }
    }
    return -1;
}
```

The indexOfRange(...) method searches for the position of the object o, and first distinguishes whether to search for the null reference or a regular object. In our case, the object in the query is not null, so the equals(...) method is used, that is, a loop compares each element in the list with our value via the equals(...) method. Conversely, this means that the query will only work if we have also implemented a reasonable equals(...) method. And this is precisely the problem: the String class provides an equals(...) method, not the one from java.lang.Object, but an overridden method. The StringBuilder class, however, has no implementation of an equals(...) method, but inherits this method from the superclass Object. In the superclass, however, only a reference comparison is implemented, which means that the content is not relevant at all. However, since our StringBuilder objects in the list are always different, the reference comparison will never return true.

Singing and Cooking: Traverse Lists and Check Properties

There are different ways to solve the task. One variant is to remember the number of cooks in one variable and the number of musicians in another variable. Finally, the two variables are compared.

The proposed solution presents a different approach. It can be compared to a scale, where the quantity of two items needs to be identical on both sides to achieve balance. Surprisingly, the specific weight of each item is irrelevant as long as equilibrium is reached.

com/tutego/exercise/util/SameNumberOfCooksAndMusicians.java

```
public static boolean areSameNumberOfCooksAndMusicians( List<CrewMember>
crewMembers ) {
  int weight = 0;
  for ( CrewMember member : crewMembers ) {
    switch ( member.profession ) {
      case COOK     -> weight++;
      case MUSICIAN -> weight--;
    }
  }
  return weight == 0;
}
```

The solution variant implemented here loops over the list and counts up a variable `weight` if there is a cook, and counts down the variable if there is a musician in the list; of course, it could be the other way around. If the number of cooks and musicians is the same, `weight` will end up being 0.

The keyword `switch` can be used in another variant, as an expression:

com/tutego/exercise/util/SameNumberOfCooksAndMusicians.java

```
for ( CrewMember member : crewMembers ) {
  weight += switch ( member.profession ) {
    case COOK     -> +1;
    case MUSICIAN -> -1;
    default       ->  0;
  };
}
```

In this variant, we need to introduce a `default` branch. This creates one more line of code, and the notation is likely to be less attractive than the first notation or a variant with the conditional operator.

There is another way to solve the problem. It remains with the idea of creating a kind of scale, where some enumeration elements are transferred to +1 and the others to -1:

com/tutego/exercise/util/SameNumberOfCooksAndMusicians.java

```
int result = 0;
for ( CrewMember member : crewMembers ) {
  //                                          CAPTAIN -+
  //                                        NAVIGATOR -+ |
  //                                        CARPENTER -+ | |
  //                                             COOK -+ | | |
  //                                         MUSICIAN -+ | | | |
  //                                                   v v v v v
  int zeroOrOneOrTwo = ((1 << member.profession.ordinal()) & 0b1_1_0_0_0) / 8;
  int minusOneOrZeroOrPlusOne = (zeroOrOneOrTwo / 2) - (zeroOrOneOrTwo & 1);
  result += minusOneOrZeroOrPlusOne;
}
return result == 0;
```

This approach might cause head shaking at first sight, but it is good to have seen and understood this way once. Let's deduce the solution.

Given is an enumeration with various elements, which all have one position, the so-called ordinal number. `CrewMember.Profession.CAPTAIN.ordinal()` is 0, and `CrewMember.Profession. COOK.ordinal()` is 3. If we write `1 << x`, and x is between 0 and 5, we get 1 shifted left by x positions and padded with zeros on the right. In other words, we get in binary notation the numbers

- `0b000001` (`CAPTAIN`).
- `0b000010` (`NAVIGATOR`).
- `0b000100` (`CARPENTER`).
- `0b001000` (`COOK`).
- `0b010000` (`MUSICIAN`).
- `0b100000` (`DOCTOR`).

We are interested in `0b001000` (`COOK`) and `0b010000` (`MUSICIAN`). To test whether the third or fourth bit is set in a number, we combine this number with the bit pattern `0b11000`. If one of the two bits is set, the bit remains, all other bits are set to 0 by the AND operation with 0. In the end, because both bits cannot be set at the same time, we are left with 0 (no hit), `0b10000` (16), or `0b01000` (8). If we divide this value by 8 (or shift it three positions to the right), we get 0, 1, or 2.

If we want to use the principle of scales again, the numbers 1 and 2 do not help. We must bring either $1 \rightarrow -1$ and $2 \rightarrow +1$ or $1 \rightarrow +1$ and $2 \rightarrow -1$, and the 0 must remain 0. Of course, we could insert a condition statement, but we go to all the trouble to avoid an `if` statement. Let x be the number 0, 1, 2, then the expression `(x / 2) - (x & 1)` transforms exactly to the desired target, -1 and +1. We can add the expression and proceed in the same way as before.

Under normal circumstances, no one should program such solutions unless they are extremely performance critical and a profiler has shown that this variant is faster. Since we have here some mathematical operations—where /8, /2 are also cheap —, this should not be faster in the end than a small `if`. Condition statements are what people like to try to rewrite in micro-optimization, but if you don't know exactly what you're doing here, it ends up being more expensive.

Filter Comments from Lists

com/tutego/exercise/util/RetainComments.java

```java
public static void reduceToComments( List<String> lines ) {

  if ( lines.size() % 4 != 0 )
    throw new IllegalArgumentException(
        "Illegal size %d of list, must be divisible by 4".formatted(
            lines.size() ) );

  for ( int blockStart=lines.size() - 4; blockStart >= 0; blockStart -= 4 ) {
    // keep element at position blockStart+3
    lines.remove( blockStart+2 );
    lines.remove( blockStart+1 );
    lines.remove( blockStart+0 );
  }
}
```

For the algorithm to work correctly, the list length must be a multiple of 4. Therefore, the first condition statement checks if the length is divisible by 4; if not, there is an exception.

The following loop runs with an index `blockStart` in steps of four from back to front. The four sums `blockStart+0`, `blockStart+1`, `blockStart+2` and `blockStart+3` represent the index to the four elements of a block. `blockStart + 3` is to be kept, all other lines we delete via the `remove(..)` method. You always have to be a little careful with this method because it is overloaded.

- The one variant `remove(Object)` deletes an `equals(...)`-equal element from the list.
- The second `remove(int)` method deletes an entry at the given position.

When deleting elements, we go from the higher index toward the lower index. For lists (especially `ArrayList`), it is always reasonable to delete from the back, so that fewer elements have to be moved in memory. If we start at `blockStart + 0`, the element below the index is deleted, and all other elements move up. The solution would look like this:

```
lines.remove( blockStart );
lines.remove( blockStart );
lines.remove( blockStart );
```

An alternative solution is provided by a live view:

```
for ( int blockStart = lines.size() - 4; blockStart >= 0; blockStart -= 4 )
  lines.subList( blockStart, blockStart + 3 ).clear();
```

The `subList(...)` method returns a sublist and changes are live; if the sublist is erased with `clear()`, the elements in the underlying list are also removed. The solution approach can also be found in the following task.

Shorten Lists Because There Is No Downturn

com/tutego/exercise/util/TrimNonGrowingList.java

```
static void trimNonGrowingNumbers( List<Double> numbers ) {

  if ( numbers.size() < 2 )
    return;

  double previous = numbers.getFirst();
  for ( int i = 1; i < numbers.size(); i++ ) {
    double current = numbers.get( i );
    if ( current <= previous ) {
      numbers.subList( i, numbers.size() ).clear();
      break;
    }
    previous = current;
  }
}
```

At first glance, the task is simple: we run the list and see if the next element is larger. If this is not the case, we abort. Now, the peculiarity is the following: we do not remember the elements in a new list, but we have to modify the list that was passed to us. That means, from a point where the elements become smaller, we have to delete the passed list until the end.

However, such a method does not exist in the `List` interface. Therefore, we have to reprogram the functionality manually. There are two possible solutions:

- There is a remove(int) method to which we can pass an index so that an element can be deleted at that point. Sensibly, we start from right to left, calling the method until we have shortened the list.
- The second possibility takes advantage of a peculiarity of data structures that there are live views; the proposed solution also chooses this approach. The subList(...) method returns a view of the list, but this one is live, and changes to this sublist are applied to the original, i.e., written through. If we clear this sublist with clear(), all elements in the original list disappear as well.

Eating with Friends: Compare Elements, Find Commonalities

com/tutego/exercise/util/FriendsSittingTogether.java

```java
public record Guest(
    boolean likesToShoot,
    boolean likesToGamble,
    boolean likesBlackmail
) {
  public boolean hasDissimilarInterests( Guest other ) {
    return !(likesToShoot == other.likesToShoot ||
             likesToGamble == other.likesToGamble ||
             likesBlackmail == other.likesBlackmail);
  }
}

public static int allGuestsHaveSimilarInterests( List<Guest> guests ) {
  for ( int index=0; index<guests.size(); index++ ) {
    Guest guest=guests.get( index );
    Guest rightNeighbor=guests.get( (index+1) % guests.size() );
    if ( guest.hasDissimilarInterests( rightNeighbor ) )
      return index;
  }
  return -1;
}
```

We want to represent the guests as objects with three properties. This is done by the record Guest, which has an additional method hasDissimilarInterests(Guest); it compares itself with another Guest and checks if there are no common interests at all.

In the allGuestsHaveSimilarInterests(...) method, a loop runs all guests. In doing so, we get the guest and its right neighbor, where the last element in the list has no element behind it. With the remainder operator, we come back out at the front of the list, which means the last element is compared to the first element. This is correct because all the guests are in a circle, and they all have a neighbor.

In the loop, hasDissimilarInterests(...) determines if the two guests are without common interests. In this case, we return the index from our method. If the loop passes through all guests, and they all have one in common, the return is -1.

Check Lists for the Same Order of Elements

Let's look at two proposed solutions. Both of them work on the same basic principle that the original list is doubled or, in case of the query after the last element, it starts again from the first element.

If we double the list from the task, we see that the second list occurs in it:
"Alexandre", "Charles", **"Anne"**, **"Henry"**, **"Alexandre"**, **"Charles"**, "Anne", "Henry".

Suggested solution 1, copied lists

com/tutego/exercise/util/SameInTheCircle.java

```
List<String> names1 = Arrays.asList( "Alexandre", "Charles", "Anne", "Henry" );
List<String> names2 = Arrays.asList( "Anne", "Henry", "Alexandre", "Charles" );

ArrayList<String> duplicatedList = new ArrayList<>( names1 );
duplicatedList.addAll( names1 );
System.out.println( Collections.indexOfSubList( duplicatedList, names2 ) >= 0 );
```

For the first suggested solution, we copy all the names into a new list because we want to avoid destroying the original list, and maybe the list is even immutable. With the method addAll(…), we append to this copy the same elements from the source again. Thus, we have duplicated the first list. The method Collections.indexOfSubList(List<?> source, List<?> target) implements the test, and returns the position where the list target occurs in the list source. We do not get a truth value via the method, but directly the position, and we only need to check if this position is greater than or equal to 0. The method returns -1 if the second list is not present in the first list.

We must not work with containsAll(…) because the method does not check the order, but only checks if all elements of a second collection are present in the first collection, completely independent of the order, but the order is what matters.

The disadvantage of this solution is that we have to create a copy so that we can work with indexOfSubList(…). With a little trick, we can do without a copy.

Proposed solution 2, virtual duplicated list

What we need is a list that is virtually twice the size of the first one, and when accessing the element after the last element, starts again at the first element.

com/tutego/exercise/util/SameInTheCircle.java

```
private static <T> boolean isSameCircle( List<T> list1, List<T> list2 ) {

  if ( list1.size() != list2.size() )
    return false;

  AbstractList<Object> list1Duplicated = new AbstractList<>() {
    @Override public int size() {
      return list1.size() * 2;
    }

    @Override public Object get( int index ) {
      return list1.get( index % list1.size() );
    }
  };
  return Collections.indexOfSubList( list1Duplicated, list2 ) >= 0;
}
```

The method first checks whether the lists are the same size; this inquiry is also necessary for the first solution. Since isSameCircle(…) can in principle work with all objects and not only with strings, the method is declared as a static generic method. Only a valid implementation of equals(…) is required for the comparison.

The virtual list is implemented by a subclass of `AbstractList`. This base class is often used for list implementations to take over as much of the standard functionality as possible. We override two methods:

- The `size()` method returns twice as many elements as the original list.
- The method `get(int)` achieves by the remainder operator that if we go beyond the size with the index, it starts again at the beginning of the data structure.

This solution does not create a new list in memory, but it is virtual and duplicated for outsiders. Of course, the methods for modifying would not work at all, but `size()` and `get(…)` are enough to work with `indexOfSubList(…)` again.

And Now the Weather: Find Repeated Elements

com/tutego/exercise/util/WeatherOccurrences.java

```java
record WeatherOccurrence( String weather, int occurrences, int startIndex ) { }

static WeatherOccurrence longestSequenceOfSameWeather( List<String> weather )
{

  int localMaxOccurrences = 1;
  int localStartIndex    = 0;

  int globalMaxOccurrences = localMaxOccurrences;
  int globalStartIndex     = localStartIndex;

  String recurringElement = weather.getFirst();

  for ( int i = 1; i < weather.size(); i++ ) {
    String currentElement = weather.get( i );

    if ( Objects.equals( currentElement, recurringElement ) ) {
      localMaxOccurrences++;

      if ( localMaxOccurrences > globalMaxOccurrences ) {
        globalMaxOccurrences = localMaxOccurrences;
        globalStartIndex     = localStartIndex;
      }
    }
    else { // currentElement != recurringElement
      localStartIndex = i;
      localMaxOccurrences = 1;
      recurringElement = currentElement;
    }
  }

  return new WeatherOccurrence(
      weather.get( globalStartIndex ), globalMaxOccurrences, globalStartIndex );
}
```

To solve the problem, we need to consider two different sequences: a local longest sequence and a global longest sequence. Therefore, we need several variables in which to keep track of states. Two variables store the local maximum number of equal elements and the start index of this sequence; two other variables store the global maximum number of found elements and their position.

The program must answer whether an element occurs numerous times in a row. We initialize a variable `recurringElement` at the beginning with the first element and observe whether this element repeats itself. The actual loop can start at index 1. The body of the loop reads the element and compares it with `recurringElement` to see if there are sequences of `recurringElement`. The equivalence test is done by the static `equals(...)` method of the `Object` class because this has the advantage over calling `equals(...)` on the elements that `null` does not lead to a problem. If the element repeats, the `localMaxOccurrences` counter is incremented by 1, and a condition statement checks if the local number of the same occurring elements exceeds the global maximum. If it does, then the `if` block updates the `globalMaxOccurrences` and `globalStartIndex` variables. We don't need to remember the actual element itself because that only becomes relevant at the end, and then we can query the element because we know the position of the element in the data structure.

If a nonequal object appears in the list, the starting position is set to the index by the new sequence, the number of repeated elements is set to 1 and `recurringElement` is reinitialized for the rest of the sequence.

At the end of the loop, the parameterized constructor builds a `WeatherOccurrence` with the three desired states.

Generate Receipt Output

com/tutego/exercise/util/Receipt.java

```java
public class Receipt {
  public static class Item {
    public final String name;
    public final int centPrice;
    public final int occurrence;

    public Item( String name, int centPrice, int occurrence ) {
      if ( centPrice <= 0 )
        throw new IllegalArgumentException( "Price can not be <= 0" );
      if ( occurrence <= 0 )
        throw new IllegalArgumentException( "Occurrence can not be <= 0" );
      this.name = Objects.requireNonNull( name );
      this.centPrice = centPrice;
      this.occurrence = occurrence;
    }

    public Item( String name, int centPrice ) {
      this( name, centPrice, 1 );
    }

    public Item incrementOccurrence() {
      return new Item( name, centPrice, occurrence+1 );
    }

    @Override public boolean equals( Object other ) {
      return    other instanceof Item item
             && centPrice == item.centPrice && name.equals( item.name );
    }
```

```
    @Override public int hashCode() {
      return name.hashCode() * 31+centPrice;
    }
  }

  private final List<Item> items=new ArrayList<>();

  public void addItem( Item item ) {
    int maybeIndex=items.indexOf( item );

    if ( maybeIndex >=0 )
      items.set( maybeIndex, items.get( maybeIndex ).incrementOccurrence() );
    else
      items.add( item );
  }

  @Override public String toString() {
    NumberFormat currencyFormatter=NumberFormat.getCurrencyInstance( Locale.
GERMANY );
    StringBuilder result=new StringBuilder( 512 );
    int sum=0;

    for ( Item item : items ) {
      int itemPriceTotal=item.centPrice * item.occurrence;
      String line="%dx   %-20s%10s%10s%n".formatted(
                        item.occurrence, item.name,
                        currencyFormatter.format( item.centPrice / 100. ),
                        currencyFormatter.format( itemPriceTotal / 100. ) );
      result.append( line );
      sum += itemPriceTotal;
    }

    result.append( "\nSum: " )
          .append( currencyFormatter.format( sum / 100. ) )
          .append( "\n" );

    return result.toString();
  }
}
```

First, let's take a look at the Item class. There are two parameterized constructors:

- The first constructor initializes all three pieces of information—the name, the price, and the number of occurrences. In addition, the constructor checks the validity.
- The second constructor is a variant in which the number of occurrences is only one.

Since Item objects are immutable, the incrementOccurrence() method returns a new Item object with an incremented count. The Item class overrides two methods from Object: the equals(…) method and hashCode(). The compare method will become important later, as it allows us to search for Item objects in the data structure. occurrence is not considered, we will see why shortly.

The receipt itself consists of a collection of Item objects. With the method addItem(Item) we add a new Item to the receipt. We don't want to simply append the item, but do a reduction if an item with the same name and amount already exists, and then merge it. First, indexOf(…) searches for an equals(…) like Item in the list, so occurrence had to be ignored. If indexOf(…) finds an item, the result is >= 0, namely, the index of the found item. The following condition statement distinguishes:

- If the element was found, at the position the element is replaced by a new element where occurrence is increased by 1,
- If no equals(...)-equal Item was found in the list, it is appended at the end.

Finally, we come to the toString() method. It must go through all entries and output the product name, the quantity, the price, and the quantity multiplied by the price. We can implement price outputs in different ways; the solution chosen here uses the NumberFormat class to be able to support the currency symbol for different languages eventually. The object built with NumberFormat.getCurrencyInstance(Locale.GERMANY) then automatically places the Euro sign behind the number. It is also the task of the toString() method to calculate the sum, which can then be output at the end. When dividing by 100, it is important to make sure that it is not an integer division because otherwise, we will miss the decimal places. The configured NumberFormat automatically sets two decimal places and fills up with 0.

Quiz: Arrays Decorated

Result:

```
Exception in thread "main" java.lang.UnsupportedOperationException
```

asList(...) implements the design pattern *Adapter*, which matches two incompatible APIs. In this case, it adapts the array type with the square brackets for reading and writing and the length attribute to a java.util.List. The operations on the list are live and are written through to the array. No list is created as a copy. Since the length of arrays cannot change after construction, elements cannot be deleted or added. If you try, an UnsupportedOperationException is thrown. This can be seen quite well in the original implementation:

OpenJDK' implementation of java.util.Arrays

```java
public static <T> List<T> asList( T... a ) {
  return new ArrayList<>( a );
}

private static class ArrayList<E> extends AbstractList<E>
    implements RandomAccess, java.io.Serializable {

  private final E[] a;
  ArrayList( E[] array ) {
    a = Objects.requireNonNull( array );
  }

  @Override
  public int size() { return a.length; }

  @Override
  public E get( int index ) { return a[ index ]; }

  ...
}
```

From the OpenJDK's implementation of java.util.AbstractList

```java
public void add( int index, E element ) {
  throw new UnsupportedOperationException();
}
```

The method `asList(T...   a)` creates an instance of type `ArrayList`, where this does not refer to a `java.util.ArrayList`, but to a nested class in `Arrays`. It is easy to see that the read methods pass directly through to the array, but, for example, the `add(…)` method throws an `UnsupportedOperationException`.

Quiz: Searched and Not Found

The output is as follows:

```
false
true
true
```

The method used here is declared as follows:

```
public static <T> List<T> asList(T... a)
```

The parameter type is a vararg, which is an object array. In the first case, we pass an array of primitive integers to `asList(…)`, and primitive data types are not reference types addressed by a generic type variable. This means that the type T stands for the reference type `int[]`; consequently, the resulting list is of type `List<int[]>`, and the `contains(…)` method returns `false`.

Varargs don't actually exist within the JVM, they are just normal arrays. The key distinction is in the calling, where a series of arguments can be directly passed and grouped into an internal array. This offers two usage methods for vararg methods: passing numerous arguments, which are then assembled into an internal array, or directly passing an array. This is precisely the variant we use here. The wrapper type `Integer` is the type argument for the type variable T, creating a `List<Integer>`. The `contains(…)` methods finds the `1`, as it is converted to an `Integer` object through boxing, and the wrapper objects implement `equals(…)`.

In the third part, we use the variable argument list. First, the `int` elements are converted to `Integer` objects via boxing, then placed in the anonymous internal array and passed.

Everything Tastes Better with Cheese: Insert Elements into Lists

When making changes in data structures, we can basically go two ways: build a new data structure with the desired properties or modify the data structure itself. All typical data structures like `ArrayList`, `HashMap`, and `TreeSet` are modifiable, and so is this problem phrased, to insert elements into an existing data structure.

The assignment mentions a list, and elements in the list have a position. If something has to be introduced at a certain position, there are basically two possibilities: we can work with the index-oriented method `add(int index, E element)` or insert elements via a `ListIterator`. The index-oriented method has a disadvantage with a `LinkedList` because it does not provide fast `RandomAccess` to the elements via an index. Since the method has the general parameter type `List`, we have to adjust for every possible list, and we want to avoid having miserable performance with `LinkedList`. For our output, the `ListIterator` is perfect.

com/tutego/exercise/util/CheeseInserter.java

```
private static final Pattern vegetables = Pattern.compile(
    "zucchini|bell peppers?|onions?|tomat(?:o|oes)", Pattern.CASE_INSENSITIVE
);
```

```
public static void insertCheeseAroundVegetable( List<String> ingredients ) {
  for ( ListIterator<String> iterator=ingredients.listIterator();
        iterator.hasNext(); ) {
    String ingredient=iterator.next();
    if ( vegetables.matcher( ingredient ).matches() )
      // The new element is inserted before the implicit cursor
      iterator.add( "cheese" );
  }
}
```

The proposed solution gets the `ListIterator` from the list and runs over all elements as usual with a combination of `hasNext()` and `next()`. After taking the element, `matches(…)` asks if the element matches any of the predefined strings. So for this check, we use a regular expression that contains the different types of vegetables, even correctly with plural-s for selected types. If the string matches, `"cheese"` is inserted.

You can consider an iterator to be a cursor that stands between the elements. After a `next()`, the cursor is behind the element. The `add(…)` method inserts a new element just before the cursor's current position, or in other words, right after the element returned by `next()`. This means the cursor remains after the newly inserted element, so calling `next()` again will not return the newly added item `"cheese"`, but the next item in the sequence.

Quiz: With Nothing but Trouble

In a nutshell, no. There is an exception:

```
Exception in thread "main" java.util.ConcurrentModificationException
    at java.base/java.util.ArrayList$Itr.checkForComodification(ArrayList.
java:1012)
    at java.base/java.util.ArrayList$Itr.next(ArrayList.java:966)
```

The program looks innocent: the extended `for` loop iterates over the list, we remove an element in the list. At first glance, it is strange why removing elements leads to a `ConcurrentModificationException`, and what should be "concurrent" here? We do not work with threads!

"Concurrent" in our example is the iteration over the data structure and the "concurrent" deletion. Java recognizes when resuming the iterator that there has been a change to the data structure. In other words, the iterating and the removing are coupled by state. It works like this: an extended `for` loop does nothing but internally uses an `Iterator`. If we rewrite the program a bit, as it is in bytecode, we get the following:

```
for ( Iterator<String> iterator=names.iterator(); iterator.hasNext(); ) {
  String name=iterator.next();
  if ( "".equals( name ) )
    names.remove( name );

    System.out.println( names );
  }
}
```

The implementation of `List` and the `Iterator` has a state in which they remember the number of modifications. When the `Iterator` is created, it initializes once with the modification counter of the list, and when the list makes modifications, it increments its modification counter. Later, when the `Iterator` goes to the next element, it compares its stored modification counter with the modification counter of the list, and if there is an inequality, there is the exception. In the code, it looks like this:

OpenJDK's implementation of `java.util.AbstractList`

```java
class AbstractList {
  protected transient int modCount = 0;

  public Iterator<E> iterator() {
    return new itr();
  }

  private class Itr implements Iterator<E> {
    int expectedModCount = modCount;

    public E next() {
      checkForComodification();
      ...
    }

    final void checkForComodification() {
      if (modCount != expectedModCount)
        throw new ConcurrentModificationException();
    }
    ...
  }
  ...
}
```

The consequence is: we cannot make any change to the data structure inside the iteration loop. The expiration and deletion do not work this way, other solutions are needed for such tasks. A solution without a loop could look like this:

```java
names.removeIf( ""::equals );
```

`removeIf(…)` expects a predicate, and this very nice and compact method reference implements just such a predicate, testing whether the incoming object is `equals(…)`-equal to the empty string.

Search Elements with the Iterator and Find Covid Cough

We get an initialized `Iterator` and can only move left or right, not jump absolutely; restricted like a human. It is not easy to choose the right strategy because we could go by probabilities here or try to reduce the maximum `cost`.

Strategy 1: Suppose we have 100 ships, and Bonny Brain is standing next to the 90th ship. That is, there are 90 ships in one direction, and the probability that the one we are looking for is there is 90%. Still, there is a 10% chance that the ship we are looking for is not in that area, and then Bonny Brain would have to walk all the way back over the list to look at the rest afterward. So, in the worst case, $90+90+10=190$ ships would have to be visited.

Strategy 2: Bonny Brain knows if there are more ships on the left or right. The second strategy is to run the side with fewer ships first, then reduce the overall worst-case cost. For the 100 ship example, where Bonny Brain is on ship 90, this means $10+10+90=110$ visits maximum.

The proposed solution implements strategy 2:

com/tutego/exercise/util/FindCovidCough.java

```
if ( iterator.nextIndex() >= NUMBER_OF_SHIPS / 2 ) {
  if ( searchRight( iterator ) )
    System.out.println( "-> at ship "+iterator.previousIndex() );
  else if ( searchLeft( iterator ) )
    System.out.println( "-> <- at ship "+iterator.nextIndex() );
  else
    System.out.println( "Not found" );
}
else {
  if ( searchLeft( iterator ) )
    System.out.println( "<- at ship "+iterator.nextIndex() );
  else if ( searchRight( iterator ) )
    System.out.println( "<- -> at ship "+iterator.previousIndex() );
  else
    System.out.println( "Not found" );
}
```

The `Iterator` method `nextIndex()` returns the absolute position, we use it to compare whether Bonny Brain is in the right or left half. Our own method `searchRight(...)` runs through the entire right side using the `Iterator` and returns `true` if the searched item is found. If the method returns `false`, we have not found the searched person in the right half, but we have to run back from there and go all the way to the left. The search direction is indicated by the arrows in the output. If we reached the left side and `searchLeft(...)` returns the result `false`, then the searched person did not exist in the list at all! The second major `else` branch tests the other case, that Captain CiaoCiao is on the left side relative to the center and first runs entirely to the left.

    `searchRight(Iterator<Ship>)` and `searchLeft(ListIterator<Ship>)` are implemented like this:

    com/tutego/exercise/util/FindCovidCough.java

```
static final String COVID_COUGH = "Covid Cough";

private static boolean searchRight( Iterator<Ship> iterator ) {
  while ( iterator.hasNext() )
    if ( iterator.next().contains( COVID_COUGH ) )
      return true;
  return false;
}

private static boolean searchLeft( ListIterator<Ship> iterator ) {
  while ( iterator.hasPrevious() )
    if ( iterator.previous().contains( COVID_COUGH ) )
      return true;
  return false;
}
```

The method to search to the right does not need a `ListIterator` because the normal `Iterator` provides the two methods `hasNext()` and `next()` to traverse to the right and extract the next element. The method `searchLeft(...)` requires a `ListIterator` because we have to walk to the left with the methods `hasPrevious()` and `previous()`. A normal `Iterator` cannot run to the left or to the right arbitrarily. Only with the `ListIterator` we have the possibility to run multiple times over the data structure.

Move Elements, Play Musical Chairs

com/tutego/exercise/util/MusicalChairsGame.java

```java
class MusicalChairs {

  private final List<String> names;

  public MusicalChairs( String... names ) {
    if ( names.length == 0 )
      throw new IllegalArgumentException( "No names are given, but names must
not be empty" );
    this.names = new ArrayList<>( Arrays.asList( names ) );
  }

  public void rotate( int distance ) {
    Collections.rotate( names, distance );
  }

  public void rotateAndRemoveLast( int distance ) {
    if ( names.isEmpty() )
      throw new IllegalStateException( "Names is empty, no names to remove" );

    rotate( distance );
    names.removeLast();
  }

  public String play() {
    if ( names.isEmpty() )
      throw new IllegalStateException( "Names is empty, no names to play
with" );

    while ( names.size() > 1 ) {
      rotateAndRemoveLast( ThreadLocalRandom.current().nextInt() );
      System.out.println( names );
    }

    return names.getFirst();
  }

  @Override public String toString() {
    return String.join( ", ", names );
  }
}
```

The class MusicalChairs has an instance variable of type List, which contains the names. Although a vararg array is passed in the constructor, we are more flexible with lists if we want to use the rotate(...) method of the Collections class later. The constructor converts the array to a list and checks beforehand if the array contains any elements at all—otherwise, the constructor throws an exception. If the constructor was called with null, there is the usual NullPointerException.

About the three methods:

- Our rotate(...) method makes use of the Collections rotate(...) method. This method works *in place*, so it modifies the list. Our list is internal and not accessible from the outside.

- rotateAndRemoveLast(...) first performs the rotation and then deletes the last list element. But there is a possible error to report: if the game is played with multiple rounds, calling rotateAndRemoveLast(...) repeatedly may cause the list to become empty. This case is checked by the first if statement and throws an exception if the list is empty. If there is more than one element, we rotate the list and delete the last element from the list. An ArrayList has no dedicated method to delete the last element. If instead of ArrayList we would take a LinkedList, then there would be a method removeLast() from the interface Deque.
- The method play() is executing the game. Again, it must be true that the list must not be empty. The while loop executes the body until the number of elements in the list becomes 1. If there is more than one name in the list, the list is rotated and printed. After the loop passes, the list contains exactly one element. We fall back to the first element. Again, a List does not provide a special method to grab the first element. The situation is different for data structures that implement the Queue interface: here there is the remove() method.
- The toString() method falls back on the static method String.join(...) because this is the easiest way to create a comma-separated string with the elements.

Programming a Question Game with Planets

com/tutego/exercise/util/PlanetQuiz.java

```java
List<Planet> shuffledPlanets=new ArrayList<>( Arrays.asList
( Planet.values() ) );
Collections.shuffle( shuffledPlanets );

for ( Planet question : shuffledPlanets ) {
  System.out.printf( "What is the diameter of planet %s (in km)?%n",
                     question.name );

  List<Planet> misleadingPlanets=new ArrayList<>( Arrays.asList( Planet.
values() ) );
  misleadingPlanets.remove( question );
  Collections.shuffle( misleadingPlanets );

  List<Planet> choicePlanets=misleadingPlanets.subList( 0, 3 );
  choicePlanets.add( question );
  Collections.shuffle( choicePlanets );
  choicePlanets.forEach(
      planet -> System.out.println( planet.diameter+" km" )
  );
  if ( new Scanner( System.in ).nextInt() != question.diameter )
    System.out.printf( "Wrong! The diameter of %s is %d km.%n%n",
                       question.name, question.diameter );
  else
    System.out.printf( "Correct!%n%n" );
}
```

The proposed solution proceeds in several phases. In the first phase, a new List is built and then shuffled with the shuffle(..) method. Now we can iterate over these shuffled planets with the extended for loop and ask a question for each of these planets that needs to be answered.

The next step is to select three random planets to the known planet. It is important to keep in mind that the random selection does not include the queried planet again. Therefore, we build another list, remove the answer of the question; it is very convenient that the enumeration elements implement the `equals(Object)` method. Afterward we randomize this list, select three planets from this list, append the answer to the list, and randomize this list again. This guarantees that the answer is not always in the same position and that the three alternative answers are different.

What remains is the output on the screen and the query. If the planetary diameter is not correct, the solution is displayed.

Form Subsets, Find Common Elements

In the task, we are looking for the intersection set that cannot be formed directly with a single operation. There is no method in `Collections` or in `Set` or the implementation classes that returns a set with the elements from both sets. We, therefore, choose a workaround.

com/tutego/exercise/util/DatingCompatibility.java

```
Set<String> hobbies1 = Set.of(
    "Candy making", "Camping", "Billiards", "Fishkeeping", "Eating",
    "Action figures", "Birdwatching", "Axe throwing" );
Set<String> hobbies2 = Set.of( "Axe throwing", "Candy making", "Camping",
  "Action figures", "Case modding", "Skiing", "Satellite watching" );

Set<String> smallerSet, largerSet;
if ( hobbies1.size() < hobbies2.size() ) {
  smallerSet = hobbies1; largerSet = hobbies2;
} else {
  smallerSet = hobbies2; largerSet = hobbies1;
}

Set<String> intersection = new HashSet<>( smallerSet );
intersection.retainAll( largerSet );
System.out.println( intersection );

System.out.printf( "The hobbies of person 1 match those of person 2 by
%d%%.%n",
                   (intersection.size() * 100) / hobbies1.size() );
System.out.printf( "The hobbies of person 2 match those of person 1 by
%d%%.%n",
                   (intersection.size() * 100) / hobbies2.size() );
```

In the first step, we build a copy of one of the two sets. It does not matter which set we copy for its functionality; we take the smaller set, for a reason, and we will look at it shortly. The reason for the copy is that the following method modifies the set, and we definitely don't want to modify the incoming sets; possibly the sets passed into the method are also immutable, meaning exceptions would occur.

After building the copy, we call the `Set` method `boolean retainAll(Collection<?>)`. It modifies the object on which the method is called, leaving only those elements in its own set that are also present in the passed collection. This is effectively forming an intersection. Two things are interesting about the signature:

1. The parameter is not a set, but an arbitrary `Collection`. That is, we could also pass a list. If there are also elements in the list more than once, it wouldn't matter.
2. Moreover, in `retainAll(Collection<?>)`, the `<?>` is interesting that the type of the collection passed is irrelevant. Internally, the objects are compared using `equals(...)`.

The implementation of `retainAll(...)` is simple:

OpenJDK's implementation of `java.util.AbstractCollection`

```java
public boolean retainAll( Collection<?> c ) {
  Objects.requireNonNull( c );
  boolean modified = false;
  Iterator<E> it = iterator();
  while ( it.hasNext() ) {
    if ( !c.contains( it.next() ) ) {
      it.remove();
      modified = true;
    }
  }
  return modified;
}
```

The default implementation walks the own set with an `Iterator` and checks with `contains(...)` whether the element occurs in the passed collection. If so, the element is removed via the `Iterator`. If the passed `Collection` is a list, then the `contains(...)` method is on average more expensive than if the query is on a `TreeSet` or `HashSet`.

Knowing this, we come back to the fact that we copied the smaller of the two sets. This has two consequences:

1. First, copying small data structures is faster and more memory efficient than copying large collections.
2. Second, the OpenJDK implementation of `retainAll(...)` shows us that the iterator runs over its own set, meaning that if its own set is smaller, fewer elements are visited. One can counter that it is always necessary to test against a larger (or equally large) set, but if fewer queries are made overall, it is faster on average.

After forming the intersection, we set the size of the intersection with the number of hobbies the two people have, in correlation. If the two people have a different number of hobbies, the percentage match is not equal; it would be only if both partners specify an equal number of hobbies. The program output in our example is:

```
[Candy making, Axe throwing, Camping, Action figures]
The hobbies of person 1 match those of person 2 by 50%.
The hobbies of person 2 match those of person 1 by 57%.
```

Quiz: Great Swords

The output is

```
true false [Khanda]
```

There is no exception to this.

There are two possibilities for orderings in Java: either an object can compare among themselves, in which case classes implement the `Comparable` interface, or a `Comparator` is looking at two objects and decides what the order between the two objects is. In our example, the class implements the `Comparable` interface for a natural order, but the `compareTo(...)` method returns constant 0.

The implication would be that all objects would then be the same, regardless of what their name state. The assigned names are not included in the compare method at all.

When inserting elements into a Set, an element is only included if there is not already an equivalent element in the set. Usually, the data structures access the equals(...) method. TreeSet, which is a sorted set, is an exception because the implementation does not need the equals(...) method and can use compareTo(...) to read whether two objects are equivalent. Whether therefore a separate equals(...) method is implemented or throws an exception is not relevant because equals(...) is not called in the scenario.

The main(...) method outputs three things: twice the results of the add(...) method, and then the contents of the set via the toString() representation. The add(...) method of the set returns a boolean value whether an element has been added to the set. In the first case, a string is added, so the return is true. On the second call to the add(...) method, the TreeSet recognizes that, according to Comparable, the second string is equivalent to an already existing element of the set. Equal elements are not overwritten and replaced, but the element is discarded. Since nothing is added, the add(...) method returns false. In the toString() representation of the set, only the first inserted element appears.

Get All Words Contained in a Word

com/tutego/exercise/util/WordSequence.java

```java
private static final int MIN_WORD_LENGTH = 3;

private static Collection<String> substrings( String string ) {
  Collection<String> result = new ArrayList<>(
      (int)(string.length() * (string.length() - 3L) / 2 + 1)
  );
  for ( int startIndex = 0; startIndex < string.length(); startIndex++ )
    for ( int len = MIN_WORD_LENGTH;
          len <= string.length() - startIndex;
          len++ )
      result.add( string.substring( startIndex, startIndex + len ) );

  return result;
}

public static Collection<String> wordList( String string,
                                           Collection<String> words ) {
  Collection<String> result = new ArrayList<>();

  for ( String substring : substrings( string.toLowerCase() ) )
    if ( words.contains( substring ) )
      result.add( substring );

  return result;
}
```

Before we implement the wordList(...) method with dictionary access, we want to implement another method: substrings(String). The method returns a collection of all possible substrings. In essence, the method consists of two nested loops. The outer loop specifies the starting position, the inner loop generates all lengths starting from at least three characters, up to the maximum string length. The minimum size is determined by a constant, so it can be easily changed.

The results are built up in an internal list. The size of the list can be calculated. The strange type conversion has the reason that we blow up the value range when multiplying two large int values. The subtraction with 3L forces a conversion to long, and later the explicit type conversion changes the long back to an int.

Via the String method substring(...), a partial string is formed and added to the result set. As data structure, we choose an ArrayList because it is very space-saving and will be run sequentially from front to back later. In addition, we can determine the number of elements to be expected in advance, so that at runtime the internal array does not have to be enlarged.

The implementation of wordList(...) is short with the prework. Again, an ArrayList is built as a container and return, and in the loop, a word is placed in this container exactly when the word occurs in the passed dictionary.

Exclude Duplicate Elements with a UniqueIterator

The new iterator is a decorator around an existing iterator, from which the actual data originates. However, since the original iterator can repeatedly provide elements that have already been passed to us, we need to remember if elements have occurred before. For this task, a set is optimal. A data structure like a HashSet rapidly answers whether an element occurs in the set or not. So in principle we have to proceed in the solution in such a way that if we obtain an element in the new iterator, we have to ask the internal iterator in the background until a new element is delivered. This would be relatively simple in itself, but we must not forget the implementation of the hasNext() method. Therefore, we need to set up the implementation a little differently, and that's what this approach shows.

com/tutego/exercise/util/UniqueIteratorDemo.java

```java
class UniqueIterator<E> implements Iterator<E> {

  private final Iterator<? extends E> iterator;
  private final Set<E> hasSeenSet = new HashSet<>();
  private E next;

  public UniqueIterator( Iterator<? extends E> iterator ) {
    this.iterator = iterator;
    next = lookahead();
  }

  private E lookahead() {
    while ( iterator.hasNext() ) {
      E next = iterator.next();
      if ( ! hasSeenSet.contains( next ) )
        return next;
    }
    return null;
  }

  @Override
  public boolean hasNext() {
    return next != null;
  }

  @Override
  public E next() {
```

```
    E result = next;
    hasSeenSet.add( result );
    next = lookahead();
    return result;
  }
}
```

The constructor of the class takes the original `Iterator` and stores the reference in an internal instance variable. In addition, there are two other instance variables: one for the set of elements already seen, and the other referencing the next element. `next` will be `null` if the original `iterator` cannot supply any more elements. The constructor has a second task, to reference the first element. The focus here is on the `lookahead()` method.

The method `lookahead()` reaches the original `Iterator` and polls until there is an element that was not yet in the set of already seen elements. If the `Iterator` cannot return any more elements, the new `UniqueIterator` cannot return any elements either, and the method returns `null`. If the internal `Iterator` finds an element that does not yet occur in the set, `lookahead()` returns this element.

Let us summarize: when the constructor is called, the first element is queried immediately via the internal `iterator` and stored in the variable `next`. If `next` is equal to `null`, then there was no element in the underlying `Iterator`.

For an `Iterator`, two methods have to be overridden:

1. The implementation of `hasNext()` is accordingly simple: if `next` is not equal to `null`, then there is an element. The update is done by `next()`.
2. With the method `next()`, we first note the assignment of `next` in an intermediate variable `result`. If the method `next()` is called from outside, the result must be included in the set of elements already seen so that it is considered known for the next time. The instance variable `next` is updated with the `lookahead()` method for the next call to the `Iterator` methods. There may be a next element—in which case `next` will be nonzero—or there may be no element and `next` will be `null`. After updating the variable `next`, `result` will contain the previous value returned by the `next()` method.

So much for the algorithm. Iterators, like many other data types, are generic types. We also use this possibility. The class `UniqueIterator` has a type parameter E, which is inherited from the interface `Iterator`. This can be seen in the `next()` method, which returns something of type E. This type of variable becomes interesting in the constructor, which assumes an `Iterator<? extends E>`, thus not only expecting an `Iterator<E>`, but allowing more possibilities. `<? extends E>` expresses that the original iterator may contain subtypes of E. In other words: for example, if we declare a `UniqueIterator` with a type argument `Object`, then the internal underlying `Iterator` can return `String`, for example, because `String extends Object`.

Convert Two-Dimensional Arrays to Map

com/tutego/exercise/util/ConvertToMap.java

```java
public static Map<String, String> convertToMap( String[][] array ) {

  if ( array.length == 0 )
    return Collections.emptyMap();

  if ( array.length == 1 )
```

```
  return Collections.singletonMap( Objects.requireNonNull( array[ 0 ][ 0 ] ),
                        Objects.requireNonNull( array[ 0 ][ 1 ] ) );

Map<String, String> result =new HashMap<>( Math.max( array.length, 16 ) );

for ( String[] row : array )
  result.put( Objects.requireNonNull( row[ 0 ] ),
              Objects.requireNonNull( row[ 1 ] ) );

  return result;
}
```

Multidimensional arrays in Java are nothing more than arrays that reference other arrays. In a two-dimensional array, we have one main array, descriptive for the column, which references many small arrays for the rows.

Two peculiarities show up in the program code:

1. The optimization for empty arrays and arrays with only one key-value pair.
2. The check for null.

Arrays are objects in Java, so references come into play, which can be null. The first query on the length of the main array will throw a NullPointerException if null was passed to the method. If the row arrays do not exist and are null, access via array[index] will also throw a NullPointerException. Later calls to Objects.requireNonNull(…) will test at the elementary level to make sure they are not null; otherwise, the method will throw an exception.

Associative stores have a much larger memory footprint than, say, an array. For two special cases, we can reduce the memory requirement significantly, namely, when a Map contains no elements and when a Map contains only one key-value pair. The Collections class provides two special methods for building empty associative stores and those with only one pair: the emptyMap() and singletonMap(…) methods.

Only when there is more than one element, a HashMap is built; the capacity is pre-initialized with the number of rows of the array, but at least with 16. But what is the capacity? The capacity is a kind of buffer. A HashMap has a DEFAULT_LOAD_FACTOR that defaults to 75%; if new elements are added and the associative memory has reached 75% capacity, a so-called *rehashing* is performed. The HashMap is enlarged, all elements are reclassified. Of course, one wants to reduce this cost. If we give the initial capacity for 16 elements, the HashMap can directly hold 12 elements without rehashing. Knowing this, we could also work with array.length / 0.75 +1 and thus calculate the optimal size. But suppose we have a giant array, then multiplying by 1.3 leads to an overflow, the number becomes negative, and then there is an exception in the HashMap constructor. These are already very extreme special cases, but if we want to be outstanding software developers, we have to pay attention to such things. Starting from Java 19, we can use the HashMap.newHashMap(int) method to create a new, empty HashMap with a specified initial size. This map uses the default load factor of 0.75 and its initial capacity is generally sufficient to accommodate the expected number of mappings without resizing.

We can use a HashMap because the task says that equals(…) and hashCode() are implemented. We would have a problem if the two methods were not implemented correctly. Then the probability would be high that all entries of the array would be included in the associative memory anyway. If equals(…) and hashCode() were not overridden from the superclass Object, each nonidentical object would also not be equivalent to another object, and the hash code would most likely always be different so that the objects would have no connection to each other.

So, if the array contains more than one element, a HashMap is built, the array is expired, and the key-value pairs are added to the associative store.

There is a subtle difference in the return: for no or one element, the return is an immutable associative store. For more than two entries, we get back a mutable data structure.

Convert Text to Morse Code and Vice Versa

For the mapping of the characters to the Morse code, we can resort to an associative map. Since we need a conversion in two directions, two maps can be used: one Map associates the character with the Morse code, a second Map associates the Morse code with the character. In principle, the key-value pairs are the same, only the direction is different.

In essence, what we need is a *Bidirectional Map* (short: *BidiMap*). It stores both the key-value mapping and the value-key mapping. There is no implementation in Java in the Java SE library, but it is implemented simply:

com/tutego/exercise/util/MorseDemo.java

```java
class BidiMap<K, V> {
  private final Map<K, V> keyToValue = new HashMap<>();
  private final Map<V, K> valueToKey = new HashMap<>();

  void put( K key, V value ) {
    keyToValue.put( Objects.requireNonNull( key ),
                    Objects.requireNonNull( value ) );
    valueToKey.put( value, key );
  }

  Optional<V> getFromKey( K key ) {
    return Optional.ofNullable( keyToValue.get( key ) );
  }

  Optional<K> getFromValue( V value ) {
    return Optional.ofNullable( valueToKey.get( value ) );
  }
}
```

Each insert operation writes a pair into both associative memories. We would rather not accept null values, but they do not occur in our program anyway. If a query returns no value, the response is not null as in the Map method get(...), but Optional.empty(). Sorting the keys is not required, so we don't need a TreeMap, a HashMap is fine.

Let's get to the main program. The first step is to fill the BidiMap:

com/tutego/exercise/util/MorseDemo.java

```java
class Morse {
  private final BidiMap<Character, String> charToMorse = new BidiMap<>();

  Morse() {
    String encoded = "a.- b-... c-.- d-.. e. f...-. g--. h.... i.. j.--- k-. " +
                     "l.-.. m-- n-. o--- p.--. q--.- r.-. s... t- u..- v...- " +
                     "w.-- x-..- y-.-- z--.. 1.---- 2..--- 3...-- 4....- " +
                     "5..... 6-.... 7--... 8---.. 9----. 0-----";
    for ( String token : encoded.split( " " ) )
      charToMorse.put( token.charAt( 0 ), token.substring( 1 ) );
  }
```

To populate the BidiMap we could write lines like.

```java
bidiMap.put( 'a', ".-" );
bidiMap.put( 'b', "-..." );
```

However, this approach requires a lot of code. The proposed solution uses another way, a coding that a string consists of space-separated pairs, where in the pair the first symbol is for the key and the sequence after it are the Morse characters.

Let us come to encode(…) and decode(…):

com/tutego/exercise/util/MorseDemo.java

```java
public String encode( String string ) {
  StringJoiner result = new StringJoiner( " " );
  for ( int i = 0; i < string.length(); i++ ) {
    char c = string.charAt( i );
    if ( c == ' ' )
      result.add( "" );
    else
      charToMorse.getFromKey( Character.toLowerCase( c ) )
                 .ifPresent( result::add );
  }
  return result.toString();
}

public String decode( String string ) {
  StringBuilder result = new StringBuilder( string.length() / 4 );
  final String ONE_SPACE = " ", TWO_SPACES = "  ";
  for ( String word : string.split( TWO_SPACES ) ) {
    for ( String character : word.split( ONE_SPACE ) )
      Optional.of( character )
              .flatMap( charToMorse::getFromValue )
              .ifPresent( result::append );
    result.append( ' ' );
  }
  return result.toString();
}
}
```

The encode(String) method loops the string and converts it to Morse code. The result is built dynamically, which is actually a typical task of StringBuilder, but here a StringJoiner is used. This class is useful because, on the one hand, it is a dynamic data structure for strings, and on the other hand because it produces a result in which the individual substrings can be separated by a user-defined separator, in our case a space.

A simple for loop gets to each character. If the character is a space, we put a space string in the StringJoiner, resulting in two spaces in the output. Why? Because " " + "" + " " just gives " ". If no space is seen, we convert the character to a lowercase letter and then query the BidiMap. The getFromKey(…) method returns Optional.empty() if there is no corresponding Morse code for the character. In that case, there is nothing to do. Otherwise, we pass the Morse code to the StringJoiner.

The method decode(String) goes the opposite way. We get a long string of Morse code sequences that must be converted back to the original text. The result of the method is a string that is built dynamically using StringBuilder. We initialize it with a capacity and estimate how large the result will be; we estimate that it will be a quarter of the original size of the input string.

The Morse words are separated by two spaces, so the first thing we want to do is query the words. split(TWO_SPACES) will give us all the words. The split(…) method directly returns an array, which is fine for small results; for indeterminately large results it makes sense to work via an iterator, for example, via

```java
new Scanner( string ).useDelimiter( TWO_SPACES ).forEachRemaining( word -> … )
```

Alternatively, tokens can be run directly using the `hasNext()` and `next()` methods, something like this:

```
for ( var words=new Scanner(string).useDelimiter(TWO_SPACES); scanner.
hasNext(); ) {
  String word=words.next();
  ...
}
```

The letters and digits converted to Morse code are separated by spaces. Again we resort to `split(…)`, though a `Scanner` or `StringTokenizer` would also help. With the substring extracted, `getFrom-Value(…)` queries the `BidiMap`. The sequence of symbols might not exist and `getFromValue(…)` will then return `Optional.empty()`. With `Optional` we can express very well this cascade:

1. Build an `Optional` with the token, that will never be `null`.
2. Map the token to the entry. If the `Map` has no associated value, the `Optional` will be empty.
3. Append the associated value to the `StringBuilder` if there was an association.

Finally, we convert the `StringBuilder` into a `String` and return the result.

Remember Word Frequency with Associative Memory

com/tutego/exercise/util/ImportantGossip.java

```java
public static final int LIMIT=5;

private static Map<String, Integer> wordOccurrences( String... words ) {
  Map<String, Integer> wordOccurrences=new HashMap<>( words.length );
  for ( String word : words )
    wordOccurrences.merge( word, 1, Integer::sum );
  return wordOccurrences;
}

public static List<String> importantGossip( String... words ) {

  List<Entry<String, Integer>> wordOccurrenceList =
      new ArrayList<>( wordOccurrences( words ).entrySet() );

  Comparator<Entry<String, Integer>> wordOccurrenceComparator =
      Entry.<String,Integer>comparingByValue()
          .reversed()
          .thenComparing( Entry::getKey );

  wordOccurrenceList.sort( wordOccurrenceComparator );

  List<String> result=new ArrayList<>( LIMIT );
  for ( Entry<String, Integer> entry : wordOccurrenceList ) {
    result.add( entry.getKey() );
    if ( result.size() >= LIMIT )
      break;
  }

  return result;
}
```

The proposed solution consists of three steps: first, we want to count the frequency of all words in the text. In the second step, we sort by frequency. In the third step, we take the first five elements of the sorted data structure and prepare them for return.

Step 1: To make the solution more modular, `wordOccurrences(String... words)` helps us determine the occurences of strings. To count occurences, we use a `Map` that associates a `String` with an `Integer`, the occurency. A loop iterates over all words and adds them to the `Map`. To count up, we can use the convenient `merge(...)` method:

```
default V merge(K key, V value, BiFunction<? super V, ? super V, ?
  extends V> remappingFunction)
```

With it, we can either set an initial value (in our case, 1) for new keys, or call a `BiFunction` for existing keys that combines the old value with the merge value (also 1) and then writes it back. The combination is addition in our case.

Let's move on to the `importantGossip(...)` method.

Step 2: After calling `wordOccurrences(...)`, the `wordOccurrences` variable stores each word and its occurence as a `Map<String, Integer>`. The `Map` is not sorted, and even if we were to use `TreeMap`, we could only sort by keys, not by values. We need to copy the data into a different data structure that allows sorting by occurences. Here, two options come into consideration: a `List` that can be sorted later with `sort(Comparator)`, or a `TreeSet(Comparator)` that always keeps the elements sorted. The elements are tuples of the string and occurence. The `Map` method `entrySet()` is useful, which returns a `Set` of the key-value pairs of type `Map.Entry`. We can copy these `Map.Entry` objects into a new data structure and then sort them by occurences, which we get with `getValue()` from the `Map.Entry`.

To sort, we want to use a `List` that is more lightweight than a `TreeSet`. Therefore, a new changeable `ArrayList` is filled with the `Map.Entry` objects from `wordOccurrences(...)`.

The sorting is determined as usual by a `Comparator`; the variable `wordOccurrenceComparator` names the `Comparator`. This must take the occurence as the first criterion from the `Map.Entry` object, and if the occurence is equal, the lexicographic order of the words must be added as a comparison. The `Comparator` can be well built using the static and `default` methods. We have two options to start:

- `Entry.comparingByValue()`. The `Map.Entry` interface offers the static method that returns a `Comparator` that uses the natural order of the values; our key type is `Integer`, a natural order is given. (Otherwise, you can use `comparingByValue(Comparator<? super V>)`.).
- `Comparator.comparingInt(Map.Entry::getValue)`

Since Java generics cannot infer types in this case, it must be `Entry.<String,Integer>comparingByValue()`.

Since words with a higher occurence must come first and less frequent words last, we need to reverse the default order, which is done by `reversed()`. If an occurence occurs twice, we use `thenComparing(...)` to push the second `Comparator`, which uses the order of the words as the second criterion. This allows the list to be sorted.

Step 3: In the final step, the program must extract the first five elements from the sorted list. There are various ways to achieve this, and two approaches to fill the `List<String>` result with the results are:

1. An enhanced `for` loop that iterates through the sorted `List<Entry<String, Integer>>`, extracts the key (the word) from the `Map.Entry` object, and adds it to the target container `result`. The loop is terminated if `result` is already five elements long. If there are fewer than five words in the word list, the loop is terminated earlier, and not by the conditional statement.

2. We can reduce the wordOccurrenceList to a maximum of five elements already.[3] This
   eliminates the need for the conditional statement and break in the loop:

```
wordOccurrenceList = wordOccurrenceList.subList(
    0, Math.min( wordOccurrenceList.size(), LIMIT )
);
```

Read In and Read Out Colors

com/tutego/exercise/util/ColorNames.java

```java
public class ColorNames {
  public static class Color {
    private final String name;
    private final int rgb;

    private Color( String name, String rgb ) {
      this.name = Objects.requireNonNull( name );
      this.rgb  = decodeHexRgb( rgb );
    }

    public static int decodeHexRgb( String hexRgb ) {
      if ( ! hexRgb.startsWith( "#" ) )
        throw new IllegalArgumentException( "hex does not start with #" );
      if ( hexRgb.length() != 4 && hexRgb.length() != 7 )
        throw new IllegalArgumentException(
            hexRgb+" is not neither 4 (#RGB) nor 7 symbols (#RRGGBB) long" );

      if ( hexRgb.length() == 4 )
        hexRgb = "#"+hexRgb.charAt( 1 )+hexRgb.charAt( 1 )
                    +hexRgb.charAt( 2 )+hexRgb.charAt( 2 )
                    +hexRgb.charAt( 3 )+hexRgb.charAt( 3 );
      return Integer.decode( hexRgb );
    }

    @Override public String toString() {
      return "'%s' is RGB #%06X".formatted( name, rgb );
    }
  }

  private final HashMap<Integer, Color> colorMap = new HashMap<>();

  public ColorNames( String filename ) throws IOException {
    for ( String line : Files.readAllLines( Paths.get( filename ) ) ) {
      String[] tokens = line.split( "([\",])+" );
      Color color = new Color( tokens[ 1 ], tokens[ 2 ] );
      colorMap.put( color.rgb, color );
    }
  }

  public Optional<Color> decode( int rgb ) {
    return Optional.ofNullable( colorMap.get( rgb ) );
  }
}
```

In the suggested solution, the Color class is included as a nested static class in ColorNames. This dependency makes sense because Color objects are only relevant in the context of ColorNames. The Color object has the desired instance variables for the name and RGB value and provides a constructor that takes the name and RGB value. The instance variables are private, and so is the constructor—the outer class can still use the private constructor, a feature of Java visibility. The constructor takes the RGB value as a string, which means it must be decoded. For this, the Color class declares its own method. If the constructor was not private, we could have used a record instead of a class.

int decodeHexRgb(String) first checks the validity of the string. If it does not start with a #, the specification is false. Furthermore, if the string is not either four or seven characters long, that is an error, and an IllegalArgumentException follows. While the RGB values in the file are correct, this public method is for everyone to use, and incorrect strings should be noticed. If the string contains only four symbols, then it is the shorthand notation, and the red, green, and blue values are doubled. For the doubling, we resort to a simple concatenation that is easy to read. There are other possibilities, for example, with an argument index in the formatting string; one solution would be

```
"#%1$s%1$s%2$s%2$s%3$s%3$s".formatted(
    hexRgb.charAt( 1 ), hexRgb.charAt( 2 ), hexRgb.charAt( 3 ) );
```

Since Formatter also knows relative indexing, it could also read:

```
"#%1$s%<s%2$s%<s%3$s%<s".formatted( ... );
```

It should be obvious that simple concatenation is the best readable. Integer.decode(...) then returns the corresponding RGB value as an integer.

Also, ColorNames has a constructor, and this one takes the file name. Files.readAllLines(...) reads all lines of the file, and the extended for loop traverses them line by line. Each line is tokenized as a string with the split(...) method, and we access the second and third elements in the array—that is, index 1 and 2—and fill the constructor with them. We put the resulting Color object into the Map, where the RGB value as an integer is the key for the Color object associated with it.

The remaining method decode(String) queries the Map, and this may return null if there is no association between the RGB value and color. Since we want to avoid null as a return value, Optional. ofNullable(...) makes unknown RGB values become Optional.empty().

Read in Names and Manage Lengths

com/tutego/exercise/util/FamilyNamesByLength.java

```
SortedMap<Integer, List<String>> namesByLength = new TreeMap<>();

InputStream resource = FamilyNamesByLength.class.getResourceAsStream( "family-
names.txt" );
try ( Scanner scanner = new Scanner( resource ) ) {
  while ( scanner.hasNextLine() ) {
    String name = scanner.nextLine();
    namesByLength.computeIfAbsent( name.length(), __ -> new ArrayList<>() )
            .add( name );
  }
}

namesByLength.forEach(
    (len, names) -> System.out.println( len + " " + names )
);
```

```
for ( int len; (len=new Scanner( System.in ).nextInt())>0; ) {
  int finalLen=len;
  Optional.ofNullable( namesByLength.get( len ) )
          .ifPresentOrElse(
              System.out::println,
              () -> System.out.printf( "No words of length %d%n",
                                       finalLen ) );
}
```

The type `SortedMap<Integer, List<String>>` represents the association of an integer with a list. Before the strings can be added to the list, the list must be created. A program must proceed as follows:

1. It must check if there is already a list for the length, if so, the string can be appended.
2. If there is no entry in the `Map` for the length yet, a list must be associated with the length and the first word with the length must be added to this list.

In code, this can be expressed as follows:

```
if ( ! namesByLength.containsKey( line.length() ) )
  namesByLength.put( line.length(), new ArrayList<>() );

namesByLength.get( line.length() ).add( line );
```

It checks using `containsKey(…)` whether a list already exists for the string length, and if not, it creates a new `ArrayList` for that string length. The subsequent statement always succeeds in adding it with `put(…)`, as there is assured to be a list for this string length.

Since Java 8 we don't have to write this out manually but can use the default method `computeIfAbsent(…)`. The description is a bit complicated, easier is to understand the method at the source code:

OpenJDK's implementation of `java.util.Map`

```
default V computeIfAbsent( K key,
                           Function<? super K, ? extends V> mappingFunction )
{
  Objects.requireNonNull( mappingFunction );
  V v;
  if ( (v=get( key )) == null ) {
    V newValue;
    if ( (newValue=mappingFunction.apply( key )) != null ) {
      put( key, newValue );
      return newValue;
    }
  }

  return v;
}
```

First, the `get(…)` method is called, and there are two outputs:

1. If the value is not `null`, it is returned directly. For our case, this means that a list for the string length has already been built.
2. `get(…)` returns `null` for the case that there was no association. (We ignore the case where there might be `null` associated with a key). If there is no associated value, the passed function is called with the key. The function returns a value, and under the key the value is stored, at least if it is not `null`. In our case, the function creates a new `ArrayList`, and the name of the

key is unnecessary for this. Therefore, the program hides this identifier with two underscores
__. Question for readers: Instead of __ -> new ArrayList<>(), what is the argument
against the constructor reference ArrayList::new, which would also work?.[4]

computeIfAbsent(...) returns the list at the end in any case, and we can cascade add(...).

After the program has read the file line by line and filled the data structure, the Map method
forEach(BiConsumer) traverses all entries. Our BiConsumer gets the key and value and outputs
the pairs to the screen.

The last part of the program is in a loop that terminates only if the input is 0 or negative. The program asks for an integer for the word length. Then get(...) asks for the list, but the result could be null
if there is no list for the input. Optional.ofNullable(...) can wrap a possible null well into an
Optional because if there is no associated value to the key, Optional.isEmpty() is true. ifPre-
sentOrElse(...) is like a control statement: if the Optional contains a value, our Consumer prints
the list of names; if there is no associated value, a notice follows on the screen that no word of the desired
length exists. The trick with the assignment int finalLen=len is necessary because lambda expressions can only access final variables, but the counter len changes. The copy into an intermediate variable
solves the problem.

Find Missing Characters

The solution consists of two parts: first, we build a data structure that is optimal for us, and in the next
step we query the data structure.
com/tutego/exercise/util/FindMissingLetters.java

```
List<String> words=Arrays.asList( "house", "mouse", "horn", "cannon" );

Map<String, List<String>> map=new HashMap<>();

// Initialize the map
for ( String word : words ) {
  for ( int index=0; index<word.length(); index++ )
    map.computeIfAbsent( index+"-"+word.charAt( index ),
                    __ -> new ArrayList<>() ).add( word );
}
System.out.println(map);
```

The task can be solved with a wide variety of data structures and approaches. The version chosen here
does the following: it builds a Map<String, List<String>> in which the position of a letter is
associated with a list of words. Let us take house and mouse as an example. Both words have an o at
index 1. This association between index and letter is the key to associative memory. The program shall
transform the input house, mouse, horn, and cannon into the following map:

```
{0-m=[mouse], 2-n=[cannon], 1-o=[house, mouse, horn], 3-n=[horn, cannon],
1-a=[cannon], 5-n=[cannon], 4-o=[cannon], 0-c=[cannon], 2-r=[horn],
3-s=[house, mouse], 2-u=[house, mouse], 0-h=[house, horn], 4-e=[house,
mouse] }
```

To build the Map, an outer loop traverses all the words and then an inner loop over each letter of the
selected word. The pair from the index, a minus sign, and the position are put into the associative memory. Since the associative memory does not directly connect this key with the word, but the strings
come into a list, the list must be rebuilt whenever the first word is to be put into the list. For such tasks,

computeIfAbsent(K key, Function mappingFunction) is perfect; if there is no list associated under the key, yet, the mapping function is called and returns a new list which is then associated with the key. The result of the method computeIfAbsent(...) is the associated value, i.e., our list, where we can add the word.

In the second part, we can query the data structure and solve the problem with the unrecognized characters.

com/tutego/exercise/util/FindMissingLetters.java

```java
// Query the data structure
Consumer<String> letterFinder = word -> {
  Set<String> matches = null;
  for ( int index = 0; index < word.length(); index++ ) {
    // Skip unknown chars
    if ( word.charAt( index ) == '_' )
      continue;
    List<String> wordCandidates = map.get( index + "-" + word.charAt( index ) );
    // Exit loop if no known entry
    if ( wordCandidates == null ) {
      // Remove possible previous matches for correct console output
      matches = null;
      break;
    }
    // Build a copy and remove words that don't match with the length
    wordCandidates = new ArrayList<>( wordCandidates );
    wordCandidates.removeIf( s -> s.length() != word.length() );
    // Join matches from all known letters
    if ( matches == null )
      matches = new HashSet<>( wordCandidates );
    else
      matches.retainAll( wordCandidates );
  }
  System.out.println( word + " -> " +
                      (matches == null || matches.isEmpty() ?
                        "No results" : matches) );
};

List<String> missingLettersWords =
    Arrays.asList( "_ouse", "ho__", "ca__on", "gun", "__e__", "_____" );

missingLettersWords.forEach( letterFinder );
```

The Consumer is a kind of a subroutine that takes a word with underscores, queries the Map data structure, and prints the matching words on the screen. The matching words are stored in a set called matches. The algorithm works by first searching for all possible words that have the same character at the same position as the given word, adding them to the set, and then forming intersections with the added characters at the following positions. Initially, there may be numerous candidates with an h at the first position, for example, but the set becomes smaller and smaller as additional characters are added, such as an o at the second position.

A large main loop can be identified in the program. It runs the initial word from front to back, and all characters at the position 0, at the position 1, and so on are retrieved. Unknown characters are not helpful in recognition (but we can accept all words), so the program returns to the loop. If the character is not an underscore, we generate a key from the index, minus sign, and the character. With this key, we query the Map, and in the best case, we get a list of candidates. However, there may be no list for this key, that is, there is a character in the source word, but no match; there is no solution, the set of matches becomes null, and we can abort the loop.

Once we have found a list of matching words for the character, the program first creates a copy of the list and in the second step removes all words that do not have the same length as the source word. Now we have to create an intersection between the previous words and the new words under the `index` because the result must appear in both sets. If no words have been found before, `matches` is equal to `null`, and we build a new set with the current candidates. Only on the first hit, no intersection is built; if there were already results and `matches` was not `null`, `retainAll(...)` deletes from `matches` all words that do not also occur in `wordCandidates`.

At the end of the loop, we have iterated over all known characters and kept reducing the set of `matches`. A console output shows us the contents of the set or a message if the set is empty.

Calculate the Number of Paths to the Three-Headed Monkey

The data structure `WeakHashMap` used for the cache utilizes the so-called *weak references*. There are basically four types of references in Java:

- Strong references are the usual references we deal with as Java programmers in everyday life. The garbage collector would never clear these references.
- A `WeakReference` is a reference that is released when a garbage collector phase is running. It depends on the implementation of the JVM exactly when this is.
- With a `SoftReference` the JVM tries to keep the object alive until it is close to an `OutOfMemoryError`.
- With a `PhantomReference` we only get to know that the garbage collector has removed the object.

The `WeakHashMap` uses a `WeakReference` internally, so we have nothing to do with handling these references directly and cleaning up the bins. It is a usable data structure that keeps references as long as there is enough free memory, and then releases the objects when the garbage collector needs to make space. For our computation, this is a good choice because the `WeakHashMap` is filled when it is needed for the factorial computation—but the factorials do not need to be in memory for an unnecessarily long time and are cleared away again.

The `WeakHashMap` is a special Map, which means we can use all known methods.

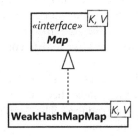

FIGURE 5.3   UML diagram of `WeakHashMap`, which implements `Map`.

com/tutego/exercise/util/CachedCatalan.java

```java
private static final Map<BigInteger, BigInteger> factorialCache =
    new WeakHashMap<>();

private static BigInteger factorial( BigInteger n ) {
  BigInteger maybeCachedValue = factorialCache.get( n );
```

```
  if ( maybeCachedValue != null )
    return maybeCachedValue;

  // n<2 ? 1 : n * factorial( n - 1 )
  BigInteger result = isLessThan( n, TWO )
                        ? ONE
                        : n.multiply( factorial( n.subtract( ONE ) ) );

  factorialCache.put( n, result );
  return result;
}

private static boolean isLessThan( BigInteger a, BigInteger b ) {
  return a.compareTo( b ) < 0;
}

public static BigInteger catalan( BigInteger n ) {
  // (2n)! / (n+1)!n!
  BigInteger numerator   = factorial( TWO.multiply( n ) );
  BigInteger denominator = factorial( n.add( ONE ) )
                              .multiply( factorial( n ) );
  return numerator.divide( denominator );
}
```

factorial(...) is the method that needs to access the cache. So, we first create an instance variable factorialCache for the internal cache that can hold BigInteger. The association is a mapping from *n* to *n*!; both types are BigInteger.

There are two main steps in using a cache:

1. When asked for a value, we first ask the cache if the value is contained. If it is in the cache, we are quickly done.
2. If the value is not in the cache, it is computed and cached. This takes time.

The method factorial(...) is implemented in the same way. The cache is queried, and maybe there is a result, perhaps not. We already know the response behavior of get(...) method of Map, which returns null if there is no associated value. This is the indicator for us whether we have a value in the cache or not. If the result is not equal to null, we have the BigInteger as a computed factorial in the cache and can return it directly. But if get(...) returns null, we have to compute the factorial and then put the result in the factorialCache and return it. For comparing whether one BigInteger is larger or smaller than another, there is no special method in BigInteger because BigInteger has a natural ordering, so it implements Comparable. However, the readability with compareTo(...) is not optimal; therefore, a separate method isLessThan(...) was introduced. The BigInteger constants ONE and TWO were imported statically, which shortens the code a bit.

An alternative implementation could use computeIfAbsent(...), but the code presented here is well understood and comprehensible.

The catalan(...) method performs the documented calculations and accesses factorial(...) three times. Many entries are already in the cache, so factorial(...) can serve many responses from the cache.

Manage Holidays in a Sorted Associative Store

com/tutego/exercise/util/Holidays.java

```
int year=2024;
NavigableMap<LocalDate, String> dates=new TreeMap<>( Map.of(
  LocalDate.of( year, Month.JANUARY, 1 ), "New Year's Day",
  LocalDate.of( year, Month.MARCH, 17 ), "Saint Patrick's Day",
  LocalDate.of( year, Month.APRIL, 1 ), "April Fools' Day",
  LocalDate.of( year, Month.APRIL, 22 ), "Earth Day",
  LocalDate.of( year, Month.MAY, 4 ), "Star Wars Day",
  LocalDate.of( year, Month.JUNE, 24 ), "Eid al-Fitr",
  LocalDate.of( year, Month.SEPTEMBER, 19 ), "International Talk Like a
Pirate Day",
  LocalDate.of( year, Month.SEPTEMBER, 21 ), "World Peace Day",
  LocalDate.of( year, Month.DECEMBER, 24 ), "Christmas Eve",
  LocalDate.of( year+1, Month.JANUARY, 1 ), "New Year's Day"
) );

System.out.println( dates.firstEntry() );
System.out.println( dates.lastEntry() );

LocalDate festiveSeasonStart=LocalDate.of( year, Month.DECEMBER, 23 );
LocalDate festiveSeasonEnd  =LocalDate.of( year+1, Month.JANUARY, 6 );

System.out.println( dates.higherEntry( festiveSeasonEnd ) );
SortedMap<LocalDate, String> festiveSeason =
    dates.subMap( festiveSeasonStart, true, festiveSeasonEnd, true );

System.out.printf( "%d festivals and holidays in range:%n", festiveSeason.
size() );
festiveSeason.forEach(
    (date, name) -> System.out.printf( "%s - %s%n", name, date )
);

festiveSeason.clear();

System.out.println( dates );
```

The proposed solution uses the described methods firstEntry(), lastEntry(), higherEntry(K) and subMap(K, boolean, K, boolean).

Different methods from the NavigableMap return so-called *views*. A view is not a copy of the data, but operations on this view always go to the underlying data structure. Thus, we can realize the deletion of the subarea via the clear() method on the view. Views are memory efficient and performant, but can lead to errors because you may accidentally modify the underlying data structure, but thought you were working on a copy. And it can lead to a problem if the underlying data structure is immutable, i.e., cannot be modified at all, but elements are inserted into the view, for example.

Quiz: Keys in a HashMap

The output of the program is as follows:

```
{java.awt.Point[x=2,y=1]=java.awt.Point[x=1,y=2]}
null
java.awt.Point[x=1,y=2]
```

The inserted key objects must be immutable, otherwise the dynamically computed hash code will change, and the objects will not be found.

Determine Commonality: Party Set and Souvenir

com/tutego/exercise/util/CommonGifts.java

```java
private static void printMultipleGifts( List<Set<String>> families ) {

  class Bag extends HashMap<String, Integer> {
    void add( String key ) { merge( key, 1, Integer::sum ); }
    // int getCount( String key ) { return getOrDefault( key, 0 ); }
  }

  Bag giftsToCounter = new Bag();

  for ( Set<String> gifts : families )
    for ( String gift : gifts )
      giftsToCounter.add( gift );

  System.out.println( giftsToCounter );

  giftsToCounter.forEach( (gift, counter) -> {
    if ( counter > 1 )
      System.out.println( gift );
  } );
}
```

We leave the counting and printing of the corresponding gifts to a method `printMultipleGifts(…)`. This method receives a list of quantities, representing the gifts each family brings. Counting the same things is a common task, but it cannot be done with a built-in data structure in Java. Therefore, we construct a small local class `Bag` that extends `HashMap`. This class `Bag` associates a string, the present, with the integer for the frequency. We give this small class a method so that we can externally increment the frequency for a key; internally, the associated value is incremented by 1. Here we resort to the `merge(…)` method provided by `Map`. If there is no value associated to a key yet, 1 is set, and if there was at least one value, 1 is added to the old value and the record is updated.

In our method, we then build an instance of `Bag`, iterate over all the sets of families with the gifts, then run all the gifts themselves and call the `add(…)` method for each gift.

If we want to know which gift occurred more than once, we can use the `forEach(…)` method of `Map` to iterate over all key-value pairs and ask if the counter surpassed 1, and in that case, output the gift.

Develop Convenient Properties Decorator

com/tutego/exercise/util/PropertiesConfiguration.java

```java
public class PropertiesConfiguration {
  private final Properties properties;

  public PropertiesConfiguration( Properties properties ) {
    this.properties = properties;
  }

  public Optional<String> getString( String key ) {
    return Optional.ofNullable( properties.getProperty( key ) );
  }
```

```java
public Optional<Boolean> getBoolean( String key ) {
   try { return getString( key ).map( Boolean::valueOf ); }
   catch ( Exception e ) { return Optional.empty(); }
}

public Optional<BigInteger> getBigInteger( String key ) {
   try { return getString( key ).map( BigInteger::new ); }
   catch ( Exception e ) { return Optional.empty(); }
}

public OptionalDouble getDouble( String key ) {
   try { return OptionalDouble.of( Double.parseDouble( properties.
getProperty( key ) ) ); }
   catch ( Exception e ) { return OptionalDouble.empty(); }
}

public OptionalLong getLong( String key ) {
   try { return OptionalLong.of( Long.parseLong( properties.getProperty( key
) ) ); }
   catch ( Exception e ) { return OptionalLong.empty(); }
}

public List<String> getList( String key ) {
   List<String> result = getString( key )
                          .map( s -> s.split( "\\s*(?<!\\\\),\\s*" ) )
                          .map( Arrays::asList )
                          .orElse( Collections.emptyList() );
   result.replaceAll( string -> string.replace( "\\,", "," ) );
   return result;
}

public void putBinary( String key, byte[] bytes ) {
   String base64 = Base64.getEncoder().encodeToString( bytes );
   properties.setProperty( key, base64 );
}

public Optional<byte[]> getBinary( String key ) {
   return getString( key )
           .map( base64 -> Base64.getDecoder().decode( base64 ) );
}
}
```

Our PropertiesConfiguration class has a constructor that accepts and stores the actual Properties. Our methods are more flexible than the methods provided by Properties, but our methods are internally based on the methods of the Properties class. That is, all the methods we provide rely in some way on the methods of the Properties class. In the center is the getProperty(String) method and once to set properties, we also use setProperty(…).

- Optional<String> getString(String): properties could exist or not; if we hit a property with the simple getProperty(String) method that does not exist, getProperty(…) returns null. While there is a getProperty(String key, String defaultValue) method, it does not prevent null from being returned and the caller must perform null handling. Java provides a nice way to express that a requested value does not exist with the Optional data type. Furthermore, Optional gives us a nice way to express alternatives, such as with the `Optional` methods `orElse(T other)` or `orElseGet(Supplier<? extends T> other)` or even `orElseThrow(Supplier<? extends X> exceptionSupplier)`.

- `Optional<Boolean>` `getBoolean(String)` and `Optional<BigInteger>` `getBigInteger(String)`: If we call `getString(…)` first, we can make use of the `Optional`-method `map(Function)` that converts a `String` to the data types `Boolean` and `BigInteger` and places them in a new `Optional` if the `Optional` has a present value. However, since the format might be wrong in the underlying `Properties` object, an exception might occur during the conversion. We catch this, and our methods return `Optional.empty()` in that case.

- `OptionalDouble` `getDouble(String)` and `OptionalLong` `getLong(String key)`: for the primitive types `double`, `long` there are special data types, namely, `OptionalDouble` and `OptionalLong`. The logic is similar.

- `List<String>` `getList(String)`: if we return a list, we use our own method `getString(…)` because it returns an `Optional`, to which we can directly set a `map(…)` to convert the individual entries, separated by a comma, into an array of strings. The next call to `map(…)` converts the array into a list. If the source `getString(…)` returns an `Optional.empty()`, `orElse(…)` will give us back an empty list. We had the convention that a comma must be masked out by \ and then is not considered a separator. The other strings now still contain \, instead of ,. We solve this by using the `List` method `replaceAll(…)`, which executes a function to replace each element.

- `void` `putBinary(String, byte[])`, `Optional<byte[]>` `getBinary(String)`: the previous methods were just convenient read methods. With `putBinary(…)` we have a method that encodes a `byte` array `Base64` and puts it into a `Properties` object. For the Base64 conversions, Java provides the class `Base64`. The `getEncoder()` and `getDecoder()` methods return objects for converting a `byte` array to a string and the string to a byte array. The conversion of a string to an array is handled by our `getBinary(…)` method. Again, our own `getString(…)` method returns an `optional`, and the `map(…)` method converts `String` to a `byte[]`.

Program RPN Pocket Calculator

com/tutego/exercise/util/RPN.java

```
String input = "160 50 30+/";
Queue<Integer> stack = Collections.asLifoQueue( new ArrayDeque<>() );

Pattern operatorPattern = Pattern.compile( "[+*/-]" );
Pattern numericPattern  = Pattern.compile( "\\d+" );
for ( String token : input.split( "\\s+" ) ) {
  Matcher operatorMatcher = operatorPattern.matcher( token );
  Matcher numericMatcher  = numericPattern.matcher( token );
  if ( numericMatcher.matches() )
    stack.add( Integer.parseInt( token ) );
  else if ( operatorMatcher.matches() ) {
    int operand2 = stack.remove();
    int operand1 = stack.remove();
    stack.add( switch ( token ) {
      case "+" -> operand1 + operand2;
      case "-" -> operand1 - operand2;
      case "*" -> operand1 * operand2;
      case "/" -> operand1 / operand2;
```

```
    default   -> throw new IllegalArgumentException( "Illegal operator
"+token+" found" );
    } );
  }
  else
    throw new IllegalArgumentException( "Unknown type "+token );
}
System.out.printf( "Result: %d", stack.remove() );
```

The RPN calculator works in two steps:

1. Decomposing the string into tokens.
2. Handling the tokens. Here, we make a difference as to whether the token is a number or a symbol.

The actual algorithm can be implemented in different ways. One approach would be to first collect all numbers on one stack and all operators on a second stack. Finally, the stack with the operators is processed together with the stack of values. We use a different approach with only one stack.

Java provides the data structure `java.util.Stack`, but this data structure belongs to the discarded types of Java 1.0, which should not be used anymore. Therefore, we use a LIFO queue, where `add(…)` appends something behind (Last In) and `remove(…)` takes something away from the queue (First Out).

If the token is the string representation of an integer, then we convert the string to an integer and put it on the stack. Furthermore, we use a regular expression to check if the token is a binary operator. With the order of the operators in the regular expression [+*/-], we have to take care that the character - is not between the symbols; otherwise, the minus stands for a range specification like a-z, which we don't want, of course.

If the token is an operator, we have to get two operands from the stack. It is important to take care to fetch the second operand from the stack first and then the first operand. Addition and multiplication are commutative, but subtraction and division are not. The `switch` expression with the modern arrow notation is performing the correct operation based on the token and puts the result back on the stack. Since the `switch` expression must be exhaustive, unfortunately, a `default` branch remains. This is unnecessary from the program logic because we checked the symbols before, but the compiler forces us to do so. An alternative notation would be a `switch` statement, then no `default` would be necessary. However, this solution also has an advantage: changes to the regex are noticeable if case blocks are not also adjusted.

Since a binary operation always consists of three symbols, only one number remains after the resolution. If we have processed all tokens from the input and the number of numbers and operators was balanced, there is only one number left at the end, the result. Readers may consider what errors could occur due to incorrect input values.

Forget No Ship

com/tutego/exercise/util/CompletedCompetition.java

```
static void checkForCompletedCompetition( int... shipIds ) {
  final int FIRST_SHIP_ID=10;
  final int LAST_SHIP_ID=22;
  BitSet shipsSeen=new BitSet( LAST_SHIP_ID - FIRST_SHIP_ID+1 );
  for ( int shipId : shipIds ) {
    if ( shipId<FIRST_SHIP_ID || shipId>LAST_SHIP_ID )
      throw new IllegalArgumentException( "Ship "+shipId+" is out of bounds" );
```

```
    boolean seenBefore = shipsSeen.get( shipId - FIRST_SHIP_ID );
    if ( seenBefore )
      System.out.printf( "Ship %d appears more than one.%n", shipId );
    else
      shipsSeen.set( shipId - FIRST_SHIP_ID );
  }

  for ( int i = FIRST_SHIP_ID; i <= LAST_SHIP_ID; i++ ) {
    if ( ! shipsSeen.get( i - FIRST_SHIP_ID ) )
      System.out.printf( "Ship %d is missing.%n", i );
  }
}
```

The data type BitSet is a kind of special data structure that can be used to associate a small integer value with a truth value. This is useful for the solution because we can map each ID of a ship to a truth value (bit set or not set) that tells us whether the ship was seen or not.

The first step is to build the BitSet itself. Since it is a good practice to specify the number of elements suspected when initializing, we do that. It is not too bad if this quantity is not precise, all dynamic data structures can adjust their internal capacity afterward.

The following extended for loop iterates over all IDs, tests the value ranges, and checks if the ID has already been seen. If it has, this is an error that is reported. If the ID has not been seen yet, a bit is set at the corresponding position in the BitSet.

Finally, a regular for loop runs over all IDs, and if the bit was not set, we know which ship ID was not seen.

The bits are shifted by the starting position 10. Of course, this is a tiny memory optimization—we could have left the first 10 bits unused.

Find Duplicate Entries and Solve the Animal Chaos

com/tutego/exercise/util/AnimalMissing.java

```
private static String sameSymbols( String string1, String string2 ) {
  BitSet bits = new BitSet( 1024 );

  string1.codePoints().forEach( character -> bits.set( character ) );
  int capacity = (int) ((long) string1.length() + string2.length()) / 2;
  StringBuilder result = new StringBuilder( capacity );
  string2.codePoints().forEach( character -> {
    if ( bits.get( character ) )
      result.appendCodePoint( character );
  } );

  return result.toString();
}
```

A task like this can be easily solved as follows: we take the first character of the first string and check if this character appears in the second string. If so, we note the character. Then we take the next character from the first string and test again if the character appears in the second string. However, the runtime would be quadratic because we would have to iterate over the second string from the beginning to the end repeatedly. If we want to avoid this, we need to approach the task differently.

The solution: we keep track of every occurred character in the first string. We could use a set, i.e., a Set<Character>, but an alternative solution is presented here. The BitSet is a special associative storage that associates an integer with a boolean. The integers should not be too large, as otherwise the BitSet will require more memory, but since our Unicode characters cannot be arbitrarily large, the memory requirement will also be manageable. We can easily calculate it. Unicode 15 has around 150,000 characters, so we need that many bits—150,000 bits / 8 = 18,750 bytes, which is less than 20 KiB, about as much as a tiny image.

The statement `string1.codePoints().forEach(…)` extracts each individual character of the first string. Each character is represented by a code point. The code point becomes an index, and at that position, we set a bit in the `BitSet` for marking. `codePoints()` returns an `IntStream`, a special data type that we will encounter more intensively in the next chapter.

For the second string, we proceed similarly. Here, too, we retrieve an `IntStream` of characters, but we do not set a bit. Instead, we ask if there is a bit set in the `BitSet` at the position of `character`. If so, the same character appears in the first and second strings. We want to remember the character in a `StringBuilder`. The `StringBuilder` size is estimated as the arithmetic mean of the lengths of `string1` and `string2`, and we must do the addition in the value range of the data type `long` to avoid risking overflow when adding two `int` numbers.

After the iteration, we convert the `StringBuilder` into a `String` and return it. The runtime is linear and dependent on the size of the two strings, as we only have to iterate over the first string once and then the second string once.

Loading Ship

The proposed solution consists of three parts: the declaration of the two records `Loader` and `Unloader` and the starting of the threads.

The data exchange is done by the `java.util.concurrent.BlockingQueue` implementation `ArrayBlockingQueue`. For our application, blocking is desired, so we use `put(…)` and `take()`.

com/tutego/exercise/thread/LoadingShips.java

```java
record Loader( BlockingQueue<String> ramp ) implements Runnable {
  @Override
  public void run() {
    var products = new ArrayList<>(
      List.of( "rum", "wine", "salami", "beer", "cheese", "comics" ) );
    while ( ! Thread.currentThread().isInterrupted() ) {
      try {
        Collections.shuffle( products );
        String product = products.getFirst() + ":" + UUID.randomUUID();
        ramp.put( product );
        System.out.printf( "Product with ID %s placed on the ramp%n", product
);
        MILLISECONDS.sleep( ThreadLocalRandom.current().nextInt(1000, 2000) );
      }
      catch ( InterruptedException e ) { Thread.currentThread().interrupt(); }
    }
  }
}
```

The `Loader` is a `Runnable` and has the desired constructor which takes a `BlockingQueue`, the data structure with which later the `Loader` and the `Unloader` exchange data. The `run()`- method contains a loop, which is always terminated, if an interrupt is sent from outside. This is not given in our case, but it corresponds to best practice.

In the body of the loop, a random product is selected and a product name with a random identifier is generated. This product is put on the ramp. The `put(…)` method blocks, because the ramp might already be full. If the thread comes back from `put(…)`, a product could be successfully put on the ramp. Finally, the thread delays execution a few milliseconds and continues repeating the loop.

com/tutego/exercise/thread/LoadingShips.java

```
record Unloader( BlockingQueue<String> ramp ) implements Runnable {
  @Override
  public void run() {
    while ( ! Thread.currentThread().isInterrupted() ) {
      try {
        String product = ramp.take();
        System.out.printf( "Product with ID %s taken off the ramp%n", product );
        MILLISECONDS.sleep( ThreadLocalRandom.current().nextInt(1000, 2000) );
      }
      catch ( InterruptedException e ) { Thread.currentThread().interrupt(); }
    }
  }
}
```

The record `Unloader` is similar in structure. The difference is only in the body of the `while` loop, where a product must be taken from the ramp. We use the `take()` method. It is possible that the `take()` method blocks because there is no product on the ramp. If the `take()` method returns, a product could be taken off the ramp and a screen output is made and the program flow is slightly delayed.

com/tutego/exercise/thread/LoadingShips.java

```
int RAMP_CAPACITY = 10;
BlockingQueue<String> ramp = new ArrayBlockingQueue<>( RAMP_CAPACITY );
ExecutorService executors = Executors.newCachedThreadPool();

for ( int i = 0; i < 5; i++ )   executors.execute( new Unloader( ramp ) );
for ( int i = 0; i < 10; i++ )  executors.execute( new Loader( ramp ) );
```

In the last part, the `ArrayBlockingQueue` is built, passed to the two instances of `Loader` and `Unloader`, and then the threads are started.

Handle Important Messages First

com/tutego/exercise/util/UrgentMessagesFirst.java

```
String KEYWORD = "Little Canon";
Comparator<Message> keywordComparator = ( msg1, msg2 ) -> {
  boolean msg1HasKeyword = msg1.message().contains( KEYWORD );
  boolean msg2HasKeyword = msg2.message().contains( KEYWORD );
  boolean bothMessagesHaveKeywordOrNot = msg1HasKeyword == msg2HasKeyword;
  return bothMessagesHaveKeywordOrNot ? 0 : msg1HasKeyword ? -1 : +1;
};
Comparator<Message> messageComparator =
    keywordComparator.thenComparing( Message::timestamp );
PriorityQueue<Message> tasks = new PriorityQueue<>( messageComparator );
```

The `keywordComparator` is at the heart of the solution. It takes the two messages from the message and checks for the presence of the term of affection. To make the code a bit clearer, the result of `contains(…)` is stored in two variables. Now there are four cases: both messages contain the term of affection, both messages do not contain it, or one of the two messages contains the searched word. If both contain the term or not, the `Comparator` returns 0, otherwise only one of the two messages contains the string. If the term of affection is contained in the first message, this message is smaller according to this `Comparator`, and the `Comparator` answers with a negative value. Otherwise, the term of affection must be present in the second message, and the `Comparator` responds with a positive value.

A `Comparator` downstream of the `keywordComparator` is necessary in case the `keyword-Comparator` returns 0. In this case, the time should be considered as a second criterion. An appended `thenComparing(…)` adds a `Comparator` which considers the timestamp. The order is correct because older messages carry a smaller timestamp.

The resulting `messageComparator` is passed to the constructor of `PriorityQueue`, and the data structure is initialized.

If Used Up, Create a New One

com/tutego/exercise/thread/SecureRandomBigIntegerIteratorDemo.java

```java
class SecureRandomBigIntegerIterator implements Iterator<BigInteger> {

  private final SynchronousQueue<BigInteger> channel =
      new SynchronousQueue<>();

  public SecureRandomBigIntegerIterator() {
    Runnable bigIntegerPutter = () -> {
      try {
        while ( true ) {
          BigInteger bigInteger = internalNext();
          System.out.printf( "> About to put number %s... into the queue%n",

                            bigInteger.toString().subSequence( 0, 20 ) );
          channel.put( bigInteger );
          System.out.println( "> Number was taken" );
        }
      }
      catch ( InterruptedException e ) { throw new IllegalStateException(e); }
    };
    ForkJoinPool.commonPool().submit( bigIntegerPutter );
  }

  private BigInteger internalNext() {
    return new BigInteger( 1024, new SecureRandom() );
  }

  @Override public boolean hasNext() {
    return true;
  }

  @Override public BigInteger next() {
    try {
      System.out.println( "< About to take a number" );
      BigInteger bigInteger = channel.take();
      System.out.println( "< Took a number out" );
      return bigInteger;
    }
    catch ( InterruptedException e ) { throw new IllegalStateException(e); }
  }
}
```

At the heart of the solution is the `SynchronousQueue` class. It differs significantly from a normal Queue and is essentially only used to pass an element from one thread to another. This is precisely the context in which we use `SynchronousQueue`.

Our class `SecureRandomBigIntegerIterator` implements the `Iterator` interface and can return infinitely large integers. The constructor of our class creates a `Runnable` and passes it to a pre-configured thread pool, the `ForkJoinPool.commonPool()`. Compared to a custom thread pool, the fork-join pool shuts down automatically when the application exits; however, this particular pool is not necessary for the solution.

The `Runnable` contains an infinite loop that immediately starts requesting an integer; the random `BigInteger` comes from the internal method. That is, even if the `next()` method on the `iterator` is not called at all, our implementation goes ahead and fills the `SynchronousQueue` with the `put(...)` method. In `put(...)`, the thread stays until the other party takes the element from the `SynchronousQueue`, then the thread continues with the infinite loop and the next number is determined.

The `next(...)` method of the `Iterator` instance takes the number from the `SynchronousQueue`, exactly for this case we have included this construction. With the `take()` method, the element is taken, which on the other side leads to the fact that again a new `BigInteger` is created and put into the queue. If there is always some time between the calls of the `next(...)` method, the thread in the background will have already calculated a new random number. That means, the `next(...)` method can immediately return a result and does not have to calculate the result first, because it was ready in the queue.

The methods `put(...)` and `take()` can throw an exception if they receive an interrupt. For this case, there is no special handling in the program, but only an `IllegalStateException`. It is a problem if the creator thread dies and the iterator waits forever for the element. With `poll(long timeout, TimeUnit unit)`, an alternative method is offered, where a maximum waiting time can be specified. In our case, this could mean: if we have no element in the queue after one second—the calculation never takes that long in life—we can assume that the thread has died.

NOTES

1 The Magnetic declination, aka Compass Course (CC), is the angle between a ship's path and compass north.
2 Linux users usually have `dc` installed and can play a bit with the RPN, a brief introduction is provided by https://en.wikipedia.org/wiki/Dc_(computer_program).
3 Interestingly, the `List` implementation `Vector` has a useful method `setSize(int)` that `ArrayList` does not have.
4 The constructor reference is for `ArrayList(int)`, i.e., the parameterized constructor, so an `ArrayList` is created with the capacity from the word length—things are not related at all.

Java Stream-API

6

The Stream API enables the step-by-step processing of data. After a source emits data, different steps follow that filter and transform data and reduce it to a result.

Although the term *Streams* can be ambiguous and may be mistaken for input/output streams, it is an essential feature of Java 8 that leverages other innovations in the Java SE library, including predefined functional interfaces and `Optional`. By combining Streams with lambda expressions and method references, developers can write concise code and configure processing steps declaratively in a novel way.

The first task in this assignment block makes use of the heroes we already met in the chapter about the class library. All the major terminal and intermediate operations are used for this collection of heroes. Different tasks follow, the solution of which shows the elegance of the Stream API.

Prerequisites

- Be able to build a stream.
- Be able to use terminal and intermediate operations.
- Be able to handle primitive streams.
- Be able to use lambda expressions practically.

Data types used in this chapter:

- `java.util.stream.Stream`
- `java.util.stream.IntStream`
- `java.util.stream.Collectors`
- `java.util.IntSummaryStatistics`
- `java.util.DoubleSummaryStatistics`
- `java.util.regex.Pattern`

REGULAR STREAMS WITH THEIR TERMINAL AND INTERMEDIATE OPERATIONS

For each stream, there are two mandatory steps and any number of optional steps in between:

1. Construction of the stream from a data source.
2. Optional processing steps called *intermediate operations*.
3. Final operation called *terminal operation*.

Hero Epic: Meet Stream API ★

In the chapter, "The Java Class Library", the class `Heroes` with heroes was introduced. This assignment is based on it.

Stream construction:

- For the following task items, always build a new `Stream` with the heroes, and then apply the terminal and intermediate operations according to the following pattern:

```
Heroes.ALL.stream().intermediate1(…).intermediate2(…).terminal()
```
Terminal operations:

1. Output all information about heroes in CSV format on the screen.
2. Ask if all heroes were introduced after 1900.
3. Ask if any female hero was introduced after 1950 (inclusive).
4. Which hero appears first?
5. Which hero is closest in the year of publication to 1960? Only one terminal operation should be used on the stream.
6. A `StringBuilder` is to be created that contains all years comma-separated. The result is to be created with a single terminal `Stream` method, with no intermediate operation in between. The order of the years in the string is not relevant.
7. Split the male and female heroes into two groups. The result shall be of type `Map<Sex, List<Hero>>`.
8. Form two partitions, with heroes introduced before and after 1970. The result shall be of type `Map<Boolean, List<Hero>>`.

Intermediate (nonterminal) operations:

1. How many female heroes are there in total?
2. Sort all heroes by release date, then output all heroes.
3. Go through the following steps:
    a. Create a comma-separated string with the names of all female heroes.
    b. In the `Hero` there is no setter because the `Hero` is immutable. But with the constructor, we can build new heroes. Convert the heroes to a list of anonymous heroes, where the plain name in parentheses is removed along with the parentheses themselves.
    c. Create an `int[]` with all years when heroes were introduced—without duplicate entries.
4. Go through `UNIVERSE` and not `ALL` to output the names of all the heroes.

Quiz: Double Output ★

If the following three lines are in the `main(…)` method and the program starts, what will the output be?

```
Stream<Integer> numbers = Stream.of( 1, 2, 3, 4, 5 );
numbers.peek( System.out::println );
numbers.forEach( System.out::println );
```

Get the Beloved Captain from a List ★

At the end of the year, the ship's crew votes for a new captain who they think will lead them to great riches. The person with the most votes wins.
Task:

- Given is an array of strings with names. Which name was mentioned how often? The names are not case-sensitive.

- Many people just call Captain CiaoCiao simply `CiaoCiao`, this should be equivalent to `Captain CiaoCiao`.

Example:

```
{"Anne", "Captain CiaoCiao", "Balico", "Charles", "Anne", "CiaoCiao",
"CiaoCiao", "Drake", "Anne", "Balico", "CiaoCiao" } → {charles=1, anne=3,
drake=1, ciaociao=4, balico=2}
```

Frame Pictures ★

Captain CiaoCiao has been chosen as the best captain, so the joy is great. He would like to have his picture framed.

Given is a multiline string, such as

```
             _____
 _.-':::::::::`.
\:::::::::::::::`.-._
 \:::''       `::::`-.`.
  \              `:::::`.\
   \               `-::::`:
    _____          `:::`.
    .|_.-'__`._        `:::\
   ,'`|:::|  )/`.        \:::
  /. -.`--'  : /.\       ::|
  `-,-'  _,'/| \|\\      |:|
  ,'`::.   |/>`;'\       |:|
  (_\ \:.:.:`((_));`.  ;:|
   \.:\ ::_:_:_`-','    `-:|
    `:\\|     SSt:
      )`__...---'
```

This is to be placed in a picture frame:

```
+-------------------------------+
|                               |
|                               |
|              _____          |
|  _.-':::::::::`.              |
| \:::::::::::::::`.-._         |
|  \:::''       `::::`-.`.      |
|   \              `:::::`.\    |
|    \               `-::::`:   |
|     _____          `:::`.  |
|     .|_.-'__`._        `:::\  |
|    ,'`|:::|  )/`.        \::: |
|   /. -.`--'  : /.\       ::|  |
|   `-,-'  _,'/| \|\\      |:|  |
|   ,'`::.   |/>`;'\       |:|  |
|   (_\ \:.:.:`((_));`.  ;:|   |
|    \.:\ ::_:_:_`-','    `-:|  |
|     `:\\|     SSt:           |
|       )`__...---'            |
|                               |
+-------------------------------+
```

Task:

- Write a frame(String) method that frames a multiline string. Use the String methods lines() and repeat(…).
  - The horizontal lines consist of -.
  - The vertical lines consist of |.
  - In the corners, there are plus signs +.
  - The spacing to the right and left of the frame is two spaces.
  - The inner space at the top and bottom is a blank line.
  - Line breaks are \n, but they should be relatively easy to change in the program.

Look and Say ★★

Captain CiaoCiao is daydreaming and writing on a piece of paper:

1

He sees the 1 and says to himself, "Oh, 1 times the 1!" He writes that down:

1 1

Now he sees two ones and can read it out like this:

2 1

"Arrr! That's a two and a one!" He writes it down:

1 2 1 1

He reads the numbers again and says:

1 1 1 2 2 1

Now the one even appears three times:

3 1 2 2 1 1

Captain CiaoCiao finds that the numbers get big quickly, though. He is curious to see if after a few passes only 1, 2, and 3 occur as digits.

Task:

- Create an infinite stream of look-and-say numbers using a `Stream.iterate(…)`.
- Limit the stream to 20 elements
- Output the numbers to the console; they can also be output compactly as a string like `111221`.

The task can be solved with a clever regular expression with a back-reference. However, this solution variant is sophisticated, and those who want to take this route can find more details at https://www. regular-expressions.info/backref.html.

What is asked here is the look-and-say sequence, which https://oeis.org/A005150 explains in more detail with many references.

Remove Duplicate Islands of Rare Earth Metals ★★★

The business with rare earth metals is particularly attractive to Bonny Brain. Their crew compiles a list of islands that are home to certain earth metals. The result goes into a text file that looks like this:

```
Balancar
Erbium
Benecia
Yttrium
Luria
Thulium
Kelva
Neodymium
Mudd
Europium
Tamaal
Erbium
Varala
Gadolinium
Luria
Thulium
```

One line contains the island, the next line contains the rare earth metals. However, different crew members may enter the same pairs in the text file. In the example, it is the pair `Luria` and `Thulium`.
Task:

- Write a program that deletes all duplicate line pairs from the text.
- The program must be flexible enough that the input can come from a `String`, `File`, `InputStream` or `Path`.
- The lines are always separated only with a \n. Moreover, the last line ends with a \n.

For the solution, the types `Pattern`, `Scanner`, and `MatchResult` as well as the `Scanner` method `findAll(..)` and further `Stream` methods are helpful.

Where Are the Sails? ★★

Bonny Brain needs a new high-performance sail for the ship. The clerks from materials management prepare a list of coordinates of suitable cloth manufacturers:

```
Point.Double[] targets={ // Latitude, Longitude
   new Point.Double( 44.7226698,  1.6716612 ),
   new Point.Double( 50.4677807, -1.5833018 ),
   new Point.Double( 44.7226698,  1.6716612 )
};
```

Task:

- In the list some coordinates occur twice, these can be ignored.
- At the end there should be a `Map<Point.Double, Integer>` with the coordinate and the distance in kilometers to the current location of Bonny Brain (40.2390577, 3.7138939).

An example output might look like this:

```
{Point2D.Double[50.4677807, -1.5833018]=1209, Point2D.Double[44.7226698,
1.6716612]=525}
```

The distance in kilometers is calculated using the Haversine formula like this:

```
private static int distance( double lat1, double lng1,
                             double lat2, double lng2 ) {
  double earthRadius=6371; // km
  double dLat=Math.toRadians( lat2 - lat1 );
  double dLng=Math.toRadians( lng2 - lng1 );
  double a=Math.sin( dLat / 2 ) * Math.sin( dLat / 2 ) +
      Math.cos( Math.toRadians( lat1 ) ) * Math.cos( Math.toRadians( lat2 ) ) *
          Math.sin( dLng / 2 ) * Math.sin( dLng / 2 );
  double d=2 * Math.atan2( Math.sqrt( a ), Math.sqrt( 1 - a ) );
  return (int) (earthRadius * d);
}
```

Buy the Most Popular Car ★★★

Captain CiaoCiao needs to increase his fleet, so he asks the crew what armored cars are recommended. He gets an array of model names of the following type:

```
String[] cars = {
  "Gurkha RPV", "Mercedes-Benz G 63 AMG", "BMW 750", "Toyota Land Cruiser",
  "Mercedes-Benz G 63 AMG", "Volkswagen T5", "BMW 750", "Gurkha RPV", "Dartz
Prombron",
  "Marauder", "Gurkha RPV" };
```

Task:

- Write a program that processes an array of model names and produces a Map<String, Long> at the end that associates the model names with the number of occurrences. This part of the task can be solved well with the Stream API.
- There should be no models named only once; only models named twice or more should appear in the data structure. For this part of the task, we can better do without the Stream API and use another variant.

An example output could look like this:

```
{Mercedes-Benz G 63 AMG=2, BMW 750=2, Gurkha RPV=3}
```

Modify the query so that all models are in a map, but the names are associated with false if there are fewer than two mentions. An output might look like this:

```
{Marauder=false, Dartz Prombron=false, Mercedes-Benz G 63 AMG=true, Toyota
Land Cruiser=false, Volkswagen T5=false, BMW 750=true, Gurkha RPV=true}
```

PRIMITIVE STREAMS

In addition to streams for objects, the Java standard library provides three special streams for primitive data types: IntStream, LongStream, and DoubleStream. Many methods are similar, important differences are ranges and special reductions, for example, to sum or average.

Detect NaN in an Array ★

Java supports three special values for the floating-point type double: Double.NaN, Double. NEGATIVE_INFINITY and Double.POSITIVE_INFINITY; corresponding constants exist for float in Float. For mathematical operations, it must be checked whether the result is valid and not a NaN. By the arithmetic operations like addition, subtraction, multiplication, and division NaN cannot be achieved, unless an operand is NaN, but various methods from the class Math return NaN as result in case of invalid input. For example, in the methods log(double a) or sqrt(double a), if the argument a is less than zero, the result is NaN.

Task:

- Write a method `containsNan(double[])` that returns `true` if the array contains a `NaN`, otherwise `false`.
- A single expression should suffice in the body of the method.

Example:

```
double[] numbers1 = { Math.sqrt( 2 ), Math.sqrt( 4 ) };
System.out.println( containsNan( numbers1 ) );          // false

double[] numbers2 = { Math.sqrt( 2 ), Math.sqrt( -4 ) };
System.out.println( containsNan( numbers2 ) );          // true
```

Generate Decades ★

A decade always represents a period of ten years, regardless of its start and end dates. Decades are typically grouped by their common tens' digit. The decade from 1990 to 1999 is known as the *0-to-9 decade*, starting on January 1, 1990, and ending on December 31, 1999. Another interpretation is the *1-to-0 decade*, where the counting of decades begins with a 1 in the one place. In this case, the 1990s would start on January 1, 1991, and end on December 31, 2000.
Task:

- Write a method `int[] decades(int start, int end)` that returns all decades from a start year to an end year as an array.
- The 0-to-9 decade is to be used.

Examples:

- `Arrays.toString( decades( 1890, 1920 ) ) → [1890, 1900, 1910, 1920]`
- `Arrays.toString( decades( 0, 10 ) ) → [0, 10]`
- `Arrays.toString( decades( 10, 10 ) ) → [10]`
- `Arrays.toString( decades( 10, -10 ) ) → []`

Generate Array with Constant Content via Stream ★

Task:

- Write a method `fillNewArray(int size, int value)`.

Example:

- `Arrays.toString( fillNewArray( 3, -1 ) ) → [-1, -1, -1]`

Draw Pyramids ★

Task:

- Create pyramids of the following shape from a clever combination of range(…), mapToObj(…) and forEach(…):

```
      /\
     /\/\
    /\/\/\
   /\/\/\/\
  /\/\/\/\/\
```

- Try to solve the task in just one statement, from building the pyramid to console output.
- The height should be configurable. The pyramid in the example is five lines high.

Teddies Labeled with Letters ★

In the aftermath of their latest raid, the pirates found themselves with a ton of loot that needed to be smuggled out of the country in inconspicuous crates. Their solution? Slap cute teddy bear designs on the boxes to distract anyone who might be snooping around. But to avoid any mix-ups, they decided to add a subtle letter identifier to each bear. Now, they needed to develop a program that could generate a series of printable teddy bear designs with the identifiers included.
Task:

- Given the following template for the teddy with a wildcard character #.

```
String teddy = """
     _       _      \s
    (c).-.(c)    \s
     / o_o \\    \s
    __\\( Y )/__  \s
   (_.-/'-'\\-._)\s
      || # ||    \s
    _.'  `-'  `._  \s
   (.-./`-'\\.-.)\s
    `-'       `-' \s""";
```

- Write a program, which converts a string into a sequence of consecutive teddies.

Example:

- For the input "MME" the following output should appear on the screen:

```
     _       _           _       _           _       _
    (c).-.(c)          (c).-.(c)          (c).-.(c)
     / o_o \            / o_o \            / o_o \
    __\( Y )/__        __\( Y )/__        __\( Y )/__
   (_.-/'-'\-._)      (_.-/'-'\-._)      (_.-/'-'\-._)
      || M ||            || M ||            || E ||
    _.'  `-'  `._      _.'  `-'  `._      _.'  `-'  `._
   (.-./`-'\.-.)      (.-./`-'\.-.)      (.-./`-'\.-.)
    `-'       `-'      `-'       `-'      `-'       `-'
```

Get the Letter Frequency of a String ★

One requirement for compression is to represent frequently occurring strings as short as possible. If, for example, 0 0 0 1 1 occurs in a file, then the following is stored later: four times a 0, then three times a 1. A compression algorithm tries to express the information about the numbers 0 and 1 in very few bits. It is helpful if it is known how often a symbol or a sequence occurs altogether, to be able to estimate whether compression of this sequence is worthwhile at all. A loop could be run over the input beforehand and count frequencies.

Task:

- The input is a string. Using clever stream concatenation, generate a new string containing each letter of the source string followed by the frequency of that letter in the given string.
- The pairs of letters and frequencies should be separated by a slash in the result string.
- Performance does not play a central role.

Examples:

- "eclectic" → "e2/c3/l1/e2/c3/t1/i1/c3"
- "cccc" → c4/c4/c4
- "" → ""

From 1 to 0, from 10 to 9 ★★

Bonny Brain wants to buy a new boat and sends Elaine to the marina to evaluate boats. Elaine writes her ratings from 1 to 10 in a row on a piece of paper, something like this:

```
102341024
```

The Bonny Brain gets the sequence of numbers, but is not happy with the order and the numbers. First, the numbers should be separated by a comma, and second, they should start at 0, not 1.

Task:

- Write a method `String decrementNumbers(Reader)` that reads a string of digits from an input source and converts it to a comma-separated string; all numbers should be decremented by 1. Anything that is not a digit should not be included in the result.

Examples:

- 102341024 → "9, 1, 2, 3, 9, 1, 3"
- -1 → "0"
- abc123xyz456 → "0, 1, 2, 3, 4, 5"

The Annual Octopus Contest ★★

The pirates around Bonny Brain and Captain CiaoCiao organized a contest to choose the most beautiful and intelligent octopus. Each octopus is assigned a number and is judged by the pirates. In the end, the octopus with the most mentions wins. Arrr, talk about a beauty pageant for tentacles!

Task:

- Given an `int` array with the identifiers of the octopuses. Write a program that determines the number from the array that occurs most often.

Example

- In the array
  ```
  int[] values = { 1, 1, 2, 3, 4, 2, 3, 2, 2, 1, 7, 3, 2, 2, 1 };
  ```
  2 is the winning octopus, since it was named most frequently.

Merge Three int Arrays ★

Shortly before the evaluation of the octopus competition, it turned out that the voting results for the smartest octopuses were not written down on one sheet of paper, but on three. Chaos erupts among the pirates and octopuses. The three lists must be merged into one list.
Task:

- A method is sought that merges three int arrays.
- There should be two overloaded methods:
  - `static int[] join(int[] numbers1, int[] numbers2, int[] numbers3)` and
  - `static int[] join(int[] numbers1, int[] numbers2, int[] numbers3, long maxSize)`
    The optional fourth parameter can be used to reduce the maximum number of elements in the result.

Examples:

```
int[] numbers1 = { 1, 2, 3 };
int[] numbers2 = { 1, 1, 2 };
int[] numbers3 = { 4, 3, 1, 2 };
int[] result1 = join( numbers1, numbers2, numbers3 );
int[] result2 = join( numbers1, numbers2, numbers3, 5 );
System.out.println( Arrays.toString( result1 ) ); // [1, 2, 3, 1, 1, 2, 4, 3, 1, 2]
System.out.println( Arrays.toString( result2 ) ); // [1, 2, 3, 1, 1]
```

Determine Winning Combinations ★★

Bonny Brain plans the next party and prepares a ring toss game. The first thing she does is set up different objects, such as these two:

▨ ▧

Then she puts two rings in the players' hands and lets them throw. If the ring goes over an object, that counts as a win. How many ways are there to win, and what are the possibilities? Taking the two objects ▨ ▧, it could be that a player "hits" ▨ or ▧, or both—▨ and ▧—no-hit is no win.
Task:

- Given a string of arbitrary characters from the Basic Multilingual Plane (BMP), i.e., U+0000 to U+D7FF and U+E000 to U+FFFF.
- Create a list of all the ways a player can win.

Example:

- ▨▩ → [▩, ▨, ▨▩], but not [▩, ▨, ▨▩, ▩▨].
- ■○▲ → [■○▲, ▲, ○, ■, ○▲, ■▲, ■○]
- MOON → [OO, MN, MO, MOON, MOO, MON, M, N, OON, ON, O]

STATISTICS

The streams `IntStream`, `LongStream`, and `DoubleStream` offers terminating methods such as `average()`, `count()`, `max()`, `min()`, and `sum()`. But if you need not just one, but several statistical pieces of information, you can gather various data in an `IntSummaryStatistics`, `LongSummaryStatistics`, or `DoubleSummaryStatistics`.

The Fastest and Slowest Paddlers ★

Bonny Brain hosts the annual "Venomous Paddle Open" paddling competition on party island X Æ A-12. In the end, the best, worst, and average times should be displayed as rounded integers. The results of the paddlers are represented by the following data type:

```
record Result( String name, double time ) { }
```

Task:

- Create a `Stream` of `Result` objects. Pre-assign some `Result` objects with selected values for testing.
- Output a small statistic of times in the end.

Example:
From the following stream ...

```
Stream<Result> stream=Stream.of(
      new Result( "Bareil Antos", 124.123 ), new Result( "Kimara Cretak",
434.22 ),
      new Result( "Keyla Detmer", 321.34 ), new Result( "Amanda Grayson",
143.99 ),
      new Result( "Mora Pol", 122.22 ), new Result( "Gen Rhys", 377.23 ) );
```

... the output may look like this:

```
count:   6
min:     122
max:     434
average: 254
```

Calculate Median ★★

The *SummaryStatistics types return the *arithmetic mean* with `getAverage()`. The arithmetic mean is calculated by dividing the sum of the given values by the number of values. There are many other mean values, such as the *geometric mean* or the *harmonic mean*.

Means are often used in statistics, but they have the problem of being more prone to outliers. Statistics frequently work with the *median*. The median is the central value, that is, the value that is "in the middle" of the sorted list. Numbers that are too small or too large are at the edge and are outliers and are not included in the median.

If the number of values is odd, then there is a natural middle.

- Example 1: In the list 9, 11, **11**, 11, 12, the median is 11. If the number of values is even, the median can be defined from the arithmetic mean of the two middle numbers.
- Example 2: In the list 10, **10, 12**, 12, the median is the arithmetic mean of the values 10 and 12, i.e., 11.

Task:

- Given is a `double[]` with measured values. Write a method `double median(double...` `values)` that calculates the median of the array values with even and odd numbers.
- Use a `DoubleStream` for the solution and consider whether `limit(...)` and `skip(...)` help.

Calculate Temperature Statistics and Draw Charts ★★★

Bonny Brain is skilled in numerical analysis, but her preference is for charts. Graphical representation of data is much simpler for her to comprehend compared to text-based formats.

She is given a chart with temperature data and would like to see at a glance when it is warmest and a vacation with the family is well possible.

Task:

- We are looking for a program that can process and display temperatures. More precisely:
  - Generate a list of random numbers that in the best case follow the temperature curve of the year, say in the form of a sine curve from 0 to π.
  - Generate random temperature values for several years, and store the years with the values in associative memory. Use the `Year` data type as a key for a `Map` sorted by years. Bonus: the number of days corresponds to the number of days in the year, so 365 or 366.
  - Write an ASCII (American Standard Code for Information Interchange) table with the temperatures of all years to the console.
  - Output the highest and lowest annual temperature of a year.
  - Output the highest, lowest, and average temperature for a month of a year.
  - Generate a file that aggregates and visualizes the 12 average temperatures of a month from one year. Take the following HTML document as a basis and fill the `data` array accordingly.

```
<!DOCTYPE html><html>
<head><meta charset="UTF-8"></head>
<body>
<canvas></canvas>
<script src="https://cdn.jsdelivr.net/npm/chart.js@3.3.2/dist/chart.min.
js"></script>
```

```
<script>
  const cfg={
    type: "bar",
    data: {
     labels:"Jan. Feb. Mar. Apr. May June July Aug. Sept. Oct. Nov.
Dec.".split(" "),
     datasets: [{
      label: "Average temperature",
      data: [11, 17, 21, 25, 27, 29, 29, 27, 25.6, 21.6, 17.5, 12.5],
     }]
    }
  };
  window.onload=() => new Chart(document.querySelector("canvas").
getContext("2d"), cfg);
</script>
</body></html>
```

SUGGESTED SOLUTIONS

Hero Epic: Meet Stream API

Terminal operation forEach(...)

As an abbreviation for Heroes.ALL, a helper variable is introduced in the following:

```
List<Hero> heroes=Heroes.ALL;
```

com/tutego/exercise/stream/LambdaHeroes.java

```
Consumer<Hero> csvPrinter =
   hero -> System.out.printf( "%s,%s,%s%n",
                               hero.name(), hero.sex(), hero.
yearFirstAppearance() );
heroes.stream().forEach( csvPrinter );
```

To run over all elements of a stream, the method forEach(...) can be used:

```
void forEach(Consumer<? super T> action).
```

This method expects a consumer of type Consumer. The method forEach(Consumer) calls the method apply(...) on the passed Consumer for each element, and in this way transmits the element in the stream to the Consumer. For the Consumer we declare a mapping that implements console output, pulling the three components from the Hero. For just traversing all elements, we don't need to fetch a Stream, an Iterable also provides forEach(...).

Terminal operation allMatch(...).

com/tutego/exercise/stream/LambdaHeroes.java

```
Predicate<Hero> isAppearanceAfter1900 =
    hero -> hero.yearFirstAppearance() >= 1900;
System.out.println( heroes.stream().allMatch( isAppearanceAfter1900 ) );
```

A Stream provides three methods that find out whether all or certain elements in the stream have a property or not: allMatch(...), anyMatch(...) and noneMatch(...). All methods are passed a Predicate to test the property. If we want to know whether all heroes were introduced after 1900, we use the allMatch(...) method. The allMatch(...) method walks over all elements of the stream and calls the Predicate method test(...). If this test always returns true, then all elements in the stream meet the correct criteria, and the overall response is true. If one of the tests returns false, then the final result is already false.

Terminal operation anyMatch(...)

com/tutego/exercise/stream/LambdaHeroes.java

```
Predicate<Hero> isFemale=hero -> hero.sex() == Sex.FEMALE;
Predicate<Hero> isAppearanceAfter1950 =
    hero -> hero.yearFirstAppearance() >= 1950;
System.out.println(
    heroes.stream().anyMatch( isFemale.and( isAppearanceAfter1950 ) )
);
```

The interface Predicate does have some default and static methods, including and(Predicate), or(Predicate), and negate(). If two criteria are supposed to be true at the same time, two predicates can be concatenated with the and(...) method and thus bound together to form a larger predicate. If we want to test whether some hero is female and was introduced after 1950, we can first build two single predicates and then link them. This approach is reasonable because, first, the predicates become smaller and easier to test, and second, they are easy to reuse.

Terminal operation min(...)

com/tutego/exercise/stream/LambdaHeroes.java

```
    Comparator<Hero> firstAppearanceComparator =
        Comparator.comparingInt( h -> h.yearFirstAppearance() );
//      Comparator.comparingInt( Hero::yearFirstAppearance );
    System.out.println( heroes.stream().min( firstAppearanceComparator ) );
```

A Stream provides min(...) and max(...) methods and can determine the largest and smallest element based on an ordering criterion:

* Optional<T> min(Comparator<? super T> comparator)
* Optional<T> max(Comparator<? super T> comparator)

The return of both methods is an Optional because it may be that the Stream is empty. The min(...) and max(...) methods expect a Comparator. If the hero/heroine is asked who was introduced first, the criteria are yearFirstAppearance. Comparator.comparingInt(...) helps to quickly build a Comparator, and the smaller the year, the smaller the objects. The min(...) method returns the answer according to the earliest hero.

Terminal operation reduce(...)

com/tutego/exercise/stream/LambdaHeroes.java

```
System.out.println( heroes.stream().reduce( ( hero1, hero2 ) -> {
  final int YEAR=1960;
  int diff1=Math.abs( YEAR - hero1.yearFirstAppearance() );
```

```
    int diff2 = Math.abs( YEAR - hero2.yearFirstAppearance() );
    return (diff1 < diff2) ? hero1 : hero2;
} ) );
```

For the question of which hero appeared first around 1960, we rely on the `reduce(...)` method, which favors exactly those heroes that are closer to the year 1960. `reduce(...)` is declared as follows:

```
Optional<T> reduce(BinaryOperator<T> accumulator)
```

In order to perform the operation, a `BinaryOperator` must be provided that takes two input elements and returns a single output element. In this particular implementation, the distance between the first and second heroes from the year 1960 is calculated, and the hero who is closer to the year 1960 is returned. In the event that both heroes are equidistant from 1960, the algorithm can arbitrarily select one of the two heroes.

In principle, another solution with a `Comparator` and the `min(...)` method of `Stream` is also possible, like this:

com/tutego/exercise/stream/LambdaHeroes.java

```
Optional<Hero> min = heroes.stream().min(
  Comparator.comparingInt( hero -> Math.abs(hero.yearFirstAppearance() - 1960) )
);
```

Terminal operation collect(Supplier, BiConsumer, BiConsumer)

com/tutego/exercise/stream/LambdaHeroes.java

```
StringBuilder collectedYears =
    heroes.stream().collect(
        StringBuilder::new,
        ( sb, hero ) -> sb.append( sb.isEmpty() ? "" : "," )
                          .append( hero.yearFirstAppearance() ),
        ( sb1, sb2 ) -> sb1.append( sb2.isEmpty() ? "" : ","+sb2 ) );
System.out.println( collectedYears );
```

If we want to end up with a `StringBuilder` with all values, we will not resort to the `reduce(...)` method, but to the `collect(...)` method. While `reduce(...)` always reduces two values to one, `collect(...)` looks at all elements and transfers them into another representation. The method is overloaded, but the variant of interest to us is the following:

```
R collect(Supplier<R> supplier,
          BiConsumer<R, ? super T> accumulator,
          BiConsumer<R, R> combiner).
```

The first argument is a producer of the result. Since in our case the result is a `StringBuilder`, the constructor reference `StringBuilder::new` produces this `Supplier`. The second parameter is a `BiConsumer` and puts the year of the hero into the `StringBuilder`. Special handling adds the comma between elements if necessary; the separator comes between elements exactly when the `StringBuilder` contains elements and is not empty. The last `BiConsumer` of `collect(...)` combines several `StringBuilders`, which may have been created by concurrent processing, into one `StringBuilder`. Although this is not necessary in our case, we want to implement this functionality as well.

Instead of passing the three arguments to the collect(...) method, it is also possible to build a Collector object that combines the Supplier and the two BiConsumer. This increases reusability and may look like this:

com/tutego/exercise/stream/LambdaHeroes.java

```
Collector<Hero, StringBuilder, StringBuilder> joiningComma = Collector.of(
    StringBuilder::new,
    ( sb, hero ) -> sb.append( sb.isEmpty() ? "" : "," )
        .append( hero.yearFirstAppearance() ),
    ( sb1, sb2 ) -> sb1.append( sb2.isEmpty() ? "" : ","+sb2 ) );
System.out.println( heroes.stream().collect( joiningComma ) );
```

Terminal operation collect(Collector) with groupingBy(...).

com/tutego/exercise/stream/LambdaHeroes.java

```
Map<Sex, List<Hero>> sexListMap =
    heroes.stream().collect( Collectors.groupingBy( hero -> hero.sex() ) );
System.out.println( sexListMap );
```

The second collect(...) method is parameterized as follows:

```
<R, A> R collect(Collector<? super T, A, R> collector).
```

A Collector is passed. The class Collectors declares numerous static methods for predefined Collector implementations. These include, for example, toList(), toSet(). A Collector is handy that can be used to group stream elements: Collectors.groupingBy(...):

```
<T, K> Collector<T, ?, Map<K, List<T>>
groupingBy(Function<? super T, ? extends K> classifier)
```

The generic type information is complex, but the method is simple: the job of the Function is to extract the keys for the resulting Map. All elements from the stream with the same key are associated as a list with the key in the Map.

Hence, if a Map of genders is desired, the function is hero -> hero.sex, and a Map<Sex, List<Hero>> is created, such that lists of heroes that are either male or female have lists attached under each of the two genders.

Terminal operation collect(Collector) with partitioningBy().

com/tutego/exercise/stream/LambdaHeroes.java

```
Predicate<Hero> isAppearanceAfter1970 =
    hero -> hero.yearFirstAppearance() >= 1970;
Map<Boolean, List<Hero>> beforeAndAfter1970Partition =
    heroes.stream()
        .collect( Collectors.partitioningBy( isAppearanceAfter1970 ) );
System.out.println( beforeAndAfter1970Partition );
```

The result of groupingBy(...) is always a Map with any number of keys. If the resulting set knows only two different parts, the method partitioningBy(...) can be used alternatively:

```
Collector<T, ?, Map<Boolean, List<T>> partitioningBy(Predicate<? super T>
predicate).
```

We pass a `Predicate` for a test, and those elements that pass this test go into the `Map` as keys under `Boolean.TRUE`, the others under `Boolean.FALSE`.

This answers the question of which heroes were introduced before and after 1970.

Intermediate operation filter(..)

com/tutego/exercise/stream/LambdaHeroes.java

```
System.out.println( heroes.stream()
                          .filter( hero -> hero.sex() == Sex.FEMALE )
                          .count() );
```

Perhaps the most important intermediate `Stream` method is `filter(…)`:

```
Stream<T> filter(Predicate<? super T> predicate);
```

All elements that satisfy the predicate are preserved in the stream. If the question is about female heroes, we write a predicate that extracts the gender of the hero and tests for `Sex.FEMALE`. A new `Stream` is created, but after filtering, the stream may contain fewer elements. The `count()` method returns the number of elements.

Intermediate operation sorted(...)

com/tutego/exercise/stream/LambdaHeroes.java

```
heroes.stream()
      .sorted( Comparator.comparingInt( hero -> hero.yearFirstAppearance() )
)
      .forEach( System.out::println );
```

Some methods of the `Stream` class are stateful. The operations cannot wait as long as possible with the evaluation (they are not *lazy*), but all elements of a stream must be read in so that operations like sorting or removing duplicate elements can be realized. If the hero stream is to be sorted by the time the heroes were introduced, we will first form a `Comparator` again with `Comparator.comparingInt(…)` and pass it to the `sorted(…)` method:

```
Stream<T> sorted(Comparator<? super T> comparator).
```

With `forEach(…)`, we consume the sorted stream and output all heroes on the screen.

Intermediate operation map(...) with Collectors.joining(...)

com/tutego/exercise/stream/LambdaHeroes.java

```
String femaleNames=heroes.stream()
                          .filter( hero -> hero.sex() == Sex.FEMALE )
                          .map( hero -> hero.name() )
                          .collect( Collectors.joining( ", " ) );
System.out.println( femaleNames );
```

Besides `filter(…)`, the `map(…)` method might be the second most important of the `stream` interface:

`<R> Stream<R> map(Function<? super T, ? extends R> mapper)`.

The `map(…)` method applies the `Function` to each element from the stream, and a new stream is created, possibly of a new type. Thus, we can also use the `map(…)` method to extract all hero names. After the desired filter operation, the name is extracted and then bound together via a special `Collector` to form a large `String` where the names are comma-separated.

Intermediate operation map(…) with toList()

com/tutego/exercise/stream/LambdaHeroes.java

```
Function<Hero, Hero> nameAnonymizer=hero ->
    new Hero( hero.name().replaceAll( "\\s*\\(.*\\)$", "" ),
              hero.sex(), hero.yearFirstAppearance() );
System.out.println( heroes.stream().map( nameAnonymizer ).toList() );
```

In the task, we want to remove the entries in round brackets. Again, we do this via the `map(…)` method and via a special function that replaces the heroes. The function gets a hero with a plain name and returns a new hero with everything in round brackets removed. Instead of the type `Function<Hero, Hero>` you can also use `UnaryOperator<Hero>`.

Processing chains of this kind could in principle modify objects and return the modified object, but it is cleaner to create new objects with the desired changes. Since `Hero` objects are immutable, we also need to build new `Hero` objects. We take the name, and use `replaceAll(…)` to replace everything in round brackets—and any sequence of spaces before it—with an empty string, thereby deleting that portion. This new name, along with the unchanged gender and year, is then passed to the constructor.. The newly created `Stream<Hero>` is transformed into a list by the `Stream` method `toList()`.

Intermediate operation mapToInt(…)

com/tutego/exercise/stream/LambdaHeroes.java

```
int[] years=heroes.stream()
    .mapToInt( hero -> hero.yearFirstAppearance() )
    .distinct()
    .toArray();
System.out.println( Arrays.toString( years ) );
```

In addition to the `map(…)` method, there are methods that return special primitive streams:

- `IntStream mapToInt(ToIntFunction<? super T> mapper)`
- `LongStream mapToLong(ToLongFunction<? super T> mapper)`
- `DoubleStream mapToDouble(ToDoubleFunction<? super T> mapper)`

These three special streams provide the `toArray()` method, which results in a primitive array at the end, rather than an array of objects. This is a good way to collect all the years in an array. Duplicate elements are removed by `distinct()`.

Intermediate operation flatMap(…)

com/tutego/exercise/stream/LambdaHeroes.java

```
Heroes.UNIVERSES.stream()
    .flatMap( Heroes.Universe::heroes )
    .map( hero -> hero.name() )
    .forEach( System.out::println );
```

The passed function of the method `map(…)` leads to a direct mapping. This does not create more elements, the elements are only exchanged. The situation is different with the `flatMap(…)` method:

```
<R> Stream<R> flatMap(Function<? super T, ? extends Stream<? extends R>>
mapper).
```

While `map(…)` is passed a `Function<? super T, ? extends R>`, `flatMap(…)` is passed a `Function<? super T, ? extends Stream<? extends R>>`; that is, for `flatMap(…)` the function must return a `Stream` for each element. `flatMap(…)` runs these substreams and puts the elements in the result stream. In other words, `flatMap(…)` returns a `Stream<…>` with the "sub-elements", while `map(…)` would instead return a `Stream<Stream<…>>`. `flatMap(…)` provides a way for the resulting stream to grow and become larger.

`Heroes.UNIVERSES` is a `List<Universe>`. If we query a stream, the result is a `Stream<Universe>`. A `Universe` has the methods `String name()` and `Stream<Hero> heroes()`. If we are interested in all `Hero` objects of the two universes, `flatMap( Heroes.Universe::heroes )` helps because this returns a `Stream<Hero>`. For comparison, `map(Heroes.Universe::heroes)` returns a `Stream<Stream<Hero>>`, we can't do anything with that.

Since only the names are relevant in the task, the additional `map(…)` results in a `stream<string>` and `forEach(…)` outputs the names.

Quiz: Double Output

If the program is executed, the exception occurs:

```
Exception in thread "main" java.lang.IllegalStateException: stream has
already been operated upon or closed
```

The intermediate operations of the stream objects return new stream objects, on which we must cascade to call the other methods. If the intention is that both streams start over via `peek(…)` and `forEach(…)`, the stream must also be rebuilt. Otherwise, it is not possible that `forEach(…)` to commence from the beginning of the stream numbers that were previously initiated by `peek(…)`.

Get the Beloved Captain from a List

com/tutego/exercise/stream/NameOccurrences.java

```
String[] names = {
    "Anne", "Captain CiaoCiao", "Balico", "Charles", "Anne", "CiaoCiao",
    "CiaoCiao", "Drake", "Anne", "Balico", "CiaoCiao" };
Map<String, Long> nameOccurrences =
    Arrays.stream( names )
```

```
.map( s -> "CiaoCiao".equalsIgnoreCase(s) ? "Captain CiaoCiao" : s )
.collect( Collectors.groupingBy( String::toLowerCase,
                                 Collectors.counting() ) );
System.out.println( nameOccurrences );
```

If we run the program, the output is:

```
{captain ciaociao=4, charles=1, anne=3, drake=1, balico=2}
```

The starting point is the array names with the names. `Arrays.stream(…)` gives us a `Stream` of strings, an alternative is `Stream.of(…)`. Since our captain can appear in different notations, we normalize the notations, and with the `map(…)` method, `Captain CiaoCiao` always appears in the `Stream` instead of `CiaoCiao`. Other strings are not transformed.

The actual aggregation and counting is done by a special `Collector`:

```
groupingBy( Function<? super T, ? extends K> classifier,
            Collector<? super T, A, D> downstream )
```

If we pass this `groupingBy(…)`-Collector to `collect(…)` we get a result of type `Map<K, D>` at the end.

All `groupingBy(…)`-collectors expect a classifier as the first argument. This determines the keys of the resulting associative memory. If we did not specify a second `Collector` for the `downstream`, a list would be associated with the key, but we do not need that—we are only interested in the number of elements associated with a key. A `Collector` to reduce to a `long` instead of a list is provided by `Collectors.counting()`. Internally, the `counting(…)` method is implemented as follows:

OpenJDK's implementation of counting(…)

```
public static <T> Collector<T, ?, Long> counting() {
  return summingLong(e -> 1L);
}
```

`counting()` returns a `Collector<T, ?, Long>`, that is, a collector that takes elements of type T and reduces them to a `Long`. From the code, we can see that this is also just a shortcut, and we might as well have written:

```
Collectors.groupingBy( String::toLowerCase, Collectors.summingLong( e -> 1L )
)
```

A function is passed to `summingLong(ToLongFunction)` that is called for each element in the stream. Due to the constant mapping `e -> 1L`, `summingLong(…)` only adds 1, and this is actually a waste of processing power.

`groupingBy(Function classifier, Collector downstream)` is also just a shortcut for `groupingBy(classifier, HashMap::new, downstream)`.

Frame Pictures

com/tutego/exercise/stream/FramePicture.java

```
private static String frame( String string ) {
  if ( string == null || string.isBlank() )
    throw new IllegalArgumentException("String to frame can't be null or
empty");
```

```
final String NEW_LINE = "\n";
int max = string.lines().mapToInt( String::length ).max().getAsInt();
String topBottomBorder = '+' + "-".repeat( max + 4 ) + '+' + NEW_LINE;
String emptyRow        = "|   " + " ".repeat( max ) + "   |" + NEW_LINE;

return
    string.lines()
          .map( s -> "|   " + s + " ".repeat( max - s.length() ) + "   |" )
          .collect( Collectors.joining(NEW_LINE,
                                       topBottomBorder + emptyRow,
                                       NEW_LINE + emptyRow + topBottomBorder) );
}
```

To draw the frame around the ASCII art, different sub-problems have to be solved. It starts with the question, how long is the longest line because that determines the width of the frame. The actual answer is provided by a single stream expression. If we map each string to the string length and determine the maximum from the stream of integers, we get our answer.

We do two things with this length: it helps generate the top and bottom horizontal frames, and it also pads shorter lines with spaces so that all lines are the same length later. The frame starts with a plus sign and is followed by minus signs, two more for each page than the longest string is long. There will be two more per side because that is the desired inner distance from the right and left margin. To generate the minus signs, we use `repeat(int)` from `String`. Aside from generating the upper and lower borders, it is also possible to generate a `String` for a free line that has strokes on the left and right edges with spaces in the middle. This free line can then be placed between the top and bottom lines.

After preparing the variables, the actual placing of the image in the frame is just a `Stream` expression. Again, we fetch a `Stream` of lines with the `lines()` method and use the `map(...)` method to transform each `String` from the ASCII image:

- Before the string from the image, the frame symbol and the spacing are set.
- Spaces are placed after the string so that the string always has the same width.
- Again some spacing and the frame symbol follow on the right side.

Finally, we collect all the lines and use a `Collector` for this, which we supply with three pieces of information:

1. How are the lines separated? With a line break.
2. What is the prefix of the whole string? It is the upper border followed by a blank line.
3. What is the suffix at the end of the frame? Again, the blank line and the bottom line for the frame.

Look and Say

The beauty of the solution is that, at its core, it consists of just a single statement. It is fascinating to see what possibilities the Stream API offers. Behind the solution, however, sits the `Pattern` class with a special regular expression.

com/tutego/exercise/stream/LookAndSay.java

```
Pattern sameSymbolsPattern = Pattern.compile( "(.)\\1*" );
Function<MatchResult, String> lengthAndSymbol =
    match -> match.group().length() + match.group( 1 );
```

```
Stream.iterate( "1", s -> sameSymbolsPattern.matcher( s )
                                    .replaceAll( lengthAndSymbol ) )
      .limit( 20 )
      .forEach( System.out::println );
```

Let's take the string 111221. Probably at first, you think of a counting loop, which sets the index always one position further and looks if the symbol has changed. But we can use regular expressions here. This sounds strange at first sight because what should be recognized here? The change from 1 to 2 to 1? No! A regular expression can help us to catch the symbol that repeats. We would write normal repetitions with the following regular expression:

```
.*
```

However, we would then have matched a sequence of arbitrary characters. But we need to express that the same character repeats multiple times. The character itself can be arbitrary. To achieve this, we can resort to a special feature of the regex engine implementation: the *back-reference*.

```
(.)\\1*
```

\1 is the back-reference that refers to the first group, that is, to (.). The dot matches one symbol in any case, and the back-reference matches any other number of identical symbols. We have to use * here and not +, because the symbol may occur only once, that is, the back-reference is not necessary.

The practical thing about sequences is that we only have to consider sequences of the same symbols. In this symbol, sequences are the two pieces of information we need: how many times did which symbol occur? If we find all places with the regular expression, we can replace the found places with the length of the string and the symbol. This is precisely what the proposed solution does.

In the first step, the intermediate variable sameSymbolsPattern stores the Pattern. This is always a good idea, if a program requires the same pattern several times. In the second step, we declare a variable lengthAndSymbol to map the MatchResult to a String. The string that contains the length of the symbol sequence is the first part and the repeating symbol is the second character of the string. Interestingly, only the lengths 1, 2, 3 occur, so it always remains with two characters that are concatenated. In principle, both variables are not necessary, but they make the following stream a bit shorter and more readable.

The static method Stream.iterator(...) needs a start value as the first argument. This is "1". It is followed by an UnaryOperator, a Function with the same type for input as for output. The operator is called with the last value of iterator(...), so at startup, it is "1", and can work its way up from there. In total, we limit the stream to 20 elements and output all elements to the screen in a terminal operation. At each step, the string grows by about 30%, so it's good to limit the number of iterations.

Remove Duplicate Islands of Rare Earth Metals

The task has two special features, so we can't just use

```
Arrays.stream( s.split( "\n" ) )
      .distinct()
      .collect( Collectors.joining("\n") )
```

- The input can not only originate from a String, but can also be given via a File, an InputStream or a Path.
- The input is not single line, but always consists of two lines.

However, both requirements do not change the approach of building a `Stream<String>` and having duplicate entries removed via `distinct()`. The central question is only: How do we get the different sources into one `Stream`, and how are two lines realized as one string in the stream?

To convert a string, with whatever separators, into a `Stream<String>`, the very flexible class `Scanner` can be used. `Scanner` objects can be initialized with different input sources, and these include the `String`, `File`, `InputStream`, and `Path` types required in the task.

com/tutego/exercise/stream/RemoveAllEqualPairs.java

```java
String lines =
    "Balancar\nErbium\n" +
    "Benecia\nYttrium\n" +
    "Luria\nThulium\n"+ // <-
    "Kelva\nNeodym\n" +
    "Mudd\nEuropium\n" +
    "Tamaal\nErbium\n" +
    "Varala\nGadolinium\n" +
    "Luria\nThulium\n";    // <-

// (?m)(^.*$\n?){2}
Pattern pattern = Pattern.compile( "(^.*$\n)"+ // A line
                                   "{2}",      // two lines
                                   Pattern.MULTILINE );
String s = new Scanner( lines )
                .findAll( pattern )
                .map( MatchResult::group )
                .distinct()
                .collect( Collectors.joining() );
System.out.println( s );
```

The `Scanner` is a tokenizer and can be used in different ways:

- The reading of tokens which are separated by white space.
- Reading of lines that are terminated by an end-of-line character.
- The reading of primitives.
- Reading of tokens using any regular expression which determines the separators.
- Reading tokens which match a regular expression.

These `next*()` methods do not help because they do not result in a `Stream`. The `Scanner` class has three methods that return a `Stream`:

- `Stream<MatchResult> findAll(String patString)`
- `Stream<MatchResult> findAll(Pattern pattern)`
- `Stream<String> tokens()`

The `findAll(…)` method is helpful in the task because it returns results from a `Match`. We just need to use the regular expression to determine what exactly we want to catch, and that is exactly two lines. The regular expression `"(^.*$\n){2}"` consists of four central components:

1. `^`: the match must start at the beginning of a line.
2. `$`: the match must occur at the end of a line.
   - `\n`: a new line follows a line.
3. `{2}`: This construction of a line and a new line occurs twice succeeding

so that the *boundary matchers* ^ and $ stand for a local line and not for the entire input, a flag `Pattern`. `MULTILINE` must be set. This variant is chosen by the proposed solution, but the flag can also be inserted directly into the regular expression, then one would write: `"(?m)(^.*$\n?){2}"`.

If this regex expression comes into the `findAll(…)` method, a `Stream<MatchResult>` is created. From the `MatchResult` objects in the stream, only the complete match returned by `group()` is relevant. Each group is a two-line string. `distinct()` removes all duplicate two-part strings, and finally a `collector` concatenates all these strings in the `stream` back into one big `String`.

Where Are the Sails?

In each case, a `Stream` must be built from `Point.Double` objects, and at the end, `Collectors.toMap(…)` creates the `Map`. There are two ways to reach the goal because the peculiarity is that the double elements become a problem when they are transferred as keys into a `Map` because in a `Map` the keys must appear only once.

The proposed solution presents two different variants. Variant 1:
com/tutego/exercise/stream/DistanceToNextStation.java

```
Function<Point.Double, Integer> distanceToCaptain =
    coordinate -> distance( coordinate.x, coordinate.y, 40.2390577, 3.7138939 );

Map<Point.Double, Integer> map =
    Arrays.stream( targets )
        .distinct()
        .collect( Collectors.toMap( Function.identity(), distanceToCaptain ) );
```

We can easily have duplicate elements removed with the `distinct()` method. Then `collect(…)` can use a `Collectors.toMap(…)` to transform the elements into a `Map`. Reminder:

```
Collector<T, ?, Map<K,U>> toMap(Function<? super T, ? extends K> keyMapper,
                                Function<? super T, ? extends U> valueMapper).
```

The first `Function` determines the keys, which in our case are the `Point.Double` objects in the `Stream`. `Function.identity()` is t -> t, so the elements in the stream are also immediately the keys. The second function calculates the distance to the captain, where our `Function<Point.Double, Integer>` internally falls back to `distance(…)`. Thus, `toMap(…)` establishes the association between the point and the distance.

If the `distinct()` method is missing, there are keys twice, and an exception `IllegalStateException: Duplicate key` follows.

But it also works without `distinct()`. Variant 2:
com/tutego/exercise/stream/DistanceToNextStation.java

```
map = Arrays.stream( targets )
            .collect( Collectors.toMap( Function.identity(),
                                        distanceToCaptain,
                                        (d,__) -> d ) );
```

The second approach uses a different `toMap(…)` method:

```
Collector<T, ?, Map<K,U>> toMap(Function<? super T, ? extends K> keyMapper,
                                Function<? super T, ? extends U> valueMapper,
                                BinaryOperator<U> mergeFunction)
```

The third argument is a `BinaryOperator` and the parameter name already reveals what it is about: `mergeFunction` is only called if keys occur multiple times and reduce the values to one result. Since in our case, the key-value pairs are always identical, we can simply drop a pair of coordinates and distance. This is handled by `(d,__) -> d`; the `BinaryOperator<Integer>` is passed two distances; the second value is ignored, and only the first distance is ever returned, since they are always the same.

Buy the Most Popular Car

The Stream API is a blessing for Java developers, but one should resist the temptation to write everything obsessively in a stream expression. This task is one of them. It is not very economical to invest 30 minutes in an unreadable stream expression when two other expressions also solve it in two minutes. Hence, the following suggested solution:

com/tutego/exercise/stream/PopularCar.java

```
Map<String, Long> map1 =
    Arrays.stream( cars )
        .collect( Collectors.groupingBy( Function.identity(),
                                         Collectors.counting() ) );

map1.entrySet().removeIf( stringLongEntry -> stringLongEntry.getValue()<2 );
```

The solution makes use of the `groupingBy(...)` method, which provides a function as a classifier, and a `Collector` for the associated elements. As a reminder:

```
Collector<T, ?, Map<K, D>> groupingBy(Function<? super T, ? extends
K> classifier,
                            Collector<? super T, A, D> downstream.
```

Our `Map<String, Long>` is formed via `Collectors.groupingBy(Function.identity(), Collectors.counting())`. The element in the stream forms the key, and the associated value is the number of occurrences of that value in the stream.

The `Map` method `entrySet()` returns a `Set<Entry<String, Long>>`, and the set does not contain a copy but is a live view of the data. It is possible to call `removeIf(Predicate<Entry<String, Long>>)`, and this method iterates over the whole set and deletes exactly those elements that satisfy the passed predicate. The predicate says to delete the entries that occur less than twice.

An alternative solution uses a separate `Collector`. It also no longer creates a `Map<String, Long>`, but a `Map<String, Boolean>`.

com/tutego/exercise/stream/PopularCar.java

```
Collector<Object, long[], Boolean> collector=Collector.of(
    // Supplier<A> supplier
    () -> new long[1],
    // BiConsumer<A,T> accumulator
    (array, string) -> array[0]++,
    // BinaryOperator<A> combiner
    (array1, array2 ) -> { array1[0] += array2[0]; return array1; },
    // Function<A,R> finisher
    array -> array[0]>1 );

Map<String, Boolean> map2 =
    Arrays.stream( cars ).collect( Collectors.groupingBy(Function.identity(),
                                          collector ) );
```

The second proposed solution also uses groupingBy(Function, Collector), but here the program does not use a predefined Collector, but writes its own for the return Map<String, Boolean>. Collector objects can be built using the following static factory method:

```
Collector<T, A, R> of (Supplier<A> supplier,
                 BiConsumer<A, T> accumulator,
                 BinaryOperator<A> combiner,
                 Function<A, R> finisher,
                 Characteristics... characteristics)
```

For the desired return type Map<String, Boolean> we are looking for a Collector that returns Boolean, so the parameterization must look like this: Collector<Object, *, Boolean>. The first type can remain Object because we do not access the strings. The type * does not occur in the stream and is an internal container, we use a long array to store the count; so the correct declaration is: Collector<Object, long[], Boolean>.

In the of (...) method, we pass the four necessary arguments; Characteristics is a vararg and irrelevant in our case.

1. The Supplier returns a long array with one entry only. The Collector remembers the number. The Collector has a state by which it can later decide whether String has occurred more than twice.
2. The BiConsumer gets the long array and the String, but only increments and does not access the String. Therefore, the type argument could also be Object and did not have to be String.
3. The BinaryOperator merges two long arrays. The operation is performed only on parallel streams.
4. The Function at the Collector maps the result to a boolean. Whenever the counter in the array exceeds 1, the result is true and thus forms the value associated with the string.

Detect NaN in an Array

com/tutego/exercise/stream/ArrayContainsNan.java

```java
public static boolean containsNan( double[] numbers ) {
  return DoubleStream.of( numbers ).anyMatch( Double::isNaN );
}
```

The terminal method anyMatch(*Predicate), available in both regular and primitive streams, effortlessly accomplishes this task. The method reference Double::isNaN is an abbreviation for value -> Double.isNaN(value).

Generate Decades

com/tutego/exercise/stream/DecadesArray.java

```java
public static int[] decades( int start, int end ) {
  return IntStream.rangeClosed( start / 10, end / 10 )
                  .map( x -> x * 10 )
                  .toArray();
}
```

The primitive streams `IntStream` and `LongStream` include two static `range*(…)` methods for creating a stream from integers:

IntStream

- `IntStream range(int startInclusive, int endExclusive)`
- `IntStream rangeClosed(int startInclusive, int endInclusive)`

LongStream

- `LongStream range(long startInclusive, long endExclusive)`
- `LongStream rangeClosed(long startInclusive, long endInclusive)`

The start and end value can be determined, also whether the end value belongs to the stream or not, but the step size is always 1. Since in the task, the end value belongs to the result, `rangeClosed(…)` is a good choice.

To solve the problem, we need to increase the step size from 1 to 10. This can be done by

1. Dividing the start and end value for `rangeClosed(…)` by 10, which results in a stream in steps of one.
2. Multiplying the elements by 10 in the next step via `map(…)`.

Since the target is an array and not an `IntStream`, `toArray()` returns the desired `int[]`.

Generate Array with Constant Content via Stream

com/tutego/exercise/stream/GenerateAndFillArray.java ·

```java
public static int[] fillNewArray( int size, int value ) {
  if ( size < 0 )
    throw new IllegalArgumentException( "size can not be negative" );

  return IntStream.range( 0, size ).map( __ -> value ).toArray();
}
```

In the first step, the method checks the validity of the parameters as usual. The size must not be negative, otherwise, an exception follows. The assignment of `value` does not have to be checked because the variable can be assigned with any value.

`IntStream.range(…)` generates the `IntStream` with `size` many elements. The fact that the stream generates the numbers from 0 to `size` is irrelevant in our case, we transfer all values to a fixed value. The identifier `_ _` expresses that the lambda parameter is unused. This creates a stream with only constant values. `toArray(…)` converts the stream into an array.

Teddies Labeled with Letters

com/tutego/exercise/stream/StreamPyramid.java

```java
String text = "MME";
String teddy = """
```

```
        _   _         \s
     (c).-.(c)     \s
      / o_o \\      \s
    _\\( Y )/__     \s
   (_.-/'-'\\-._)\s
     || %c ||       \s
   _.'  `-'  '._   \s
  (.-./`-'\\.-.)\s
   `-'        `-' \s""";
String teddies =
    teddy.lines()
         .map( line -> text.codePoints()
                           .mapToObj( line::formatted )
                           .collect( Collectors.joining() ) )
         .collect( Collectors.joining( "\n" ) );
System.out.println( teddies );
```

When solving the task, we have to keep the big picture in mind that we don't want the teddies to be one beneath the other, but side by side. To achieve this, we have to place the lines of the template several times behind each other, which necessitates an outer loop that runs over all the lines. We also need an inner loop that places the teddies next to each other.

The streams implement the loops. teddy.lines() builds a Stream<String> over all lines of the teddy bear. For each line, there is another stream over the number of characters in the text. The call to codePoints() returns an IntStream for the string. The primitive int elements of the stream are converted to a Stream<Object> with mapToObj(…), where the method reference is just a shortcut for (int c) -> line.formatted(c), so the int from the IntStream will go into the String format template exactly where %c is.

This gives us as many teddy bear lines as there are characters in text. The first collect(…) method concatenates each partial line into one big line string. Now the lines just need to be joined with a newline character to form the main string, this is done by the second call to collect(…).

Draw Pyramids

com/tutego/exercise/stream/StreamPyramid.java

```
static void printPyramid( int height ) {
  IntStream.rangeClosed( 1, height )
           .mapToObj( i -> " ".repeat( height - i ) + "/\\".repeat( i ) )
           .forEach( System.out::println );
}
```

The generated output has the peculiarity that there are always two characters /\ next to each other. In the first line, it is one pair, in the second line, it is two pairs, and so on. So, we have to create an IntStream that goes from 1 to the desired height. The spaces that have to be set in front are also dependent on this counter. For a generated stream from 1 to 5, the number of spaces is just 5 - i. The program is extracted into a method so that the height can be parameterized.

Get the Letter Frequency of a String

Classes implementing the CharSequence interface have two useful methods: chars() and code-Points(). They return an IntStream, where in the first method the stream consists of char characters expanded to an `int`, and in the second method they are equal to `int`. The difference primarily affects compound code points, for our case, we'll stick to the simple `chars()` method.

com/tutego/exercise/stream/LetterOccurrences.java

```
String input = "eclectic";
String output =
    input.chars()
        .mapToObj( c ->    (char) c + ""
                        + input.chars().filter(d -> d == c).count() )
        .collect( Collectors.joining( "/" ) );
System.out.println( output ); // e2/c3/l1/e2/c3/t1/i1/c3
```

The `IntStream` provides us with a stream containing each character. We now need to associate these characters with their respective frequencies in the input string. To count frequencies, we can repeatedly build an `IntStream` and use the filter method and `count()` to find out the number of characters in the stream. If we concatenate the character and this counter, in the next step, we have a `Stream<String>` in which each character has been mapped to this pair. Finally, these pairs must be put together with a slash. This can be done by a reduction with `Collectors.joining(...)`.

From 1 to 0, from 10 to 9

com/tutego/exercise/stream/DecrementNumbers.java

```
private static String decrementNumbers( Reader input ) {
  return new Scanner( input )
      .findAll( "10|[1-9]" )            // Stream<MatchResult>
      .map( MatchResult::group )        // Stream<String>
      .mapToInt( Integer::parseInt )    // IntStream
      .map( Math::decrementExact )      // IntStream
      .mapToObj( Integer::toString )    // Stream<String>
      .collect( Collectors.joining( ", " ) );
}
```

With a smartly chosen `Stream`, the task can be solved in a single expression. To get from start to finish, let's first look at the steps involved:

1. Split string into single numbers.
2. Reduce numbers.
3. Convert numbers concatenated into a string.

The first step is to recognize the numbers. Finding partial strings is the task of regular expressions. Regular expressions can be processed with the class `Pattern`, but this class does not help us with data streams. The second class that allows us to find strings that match regular expressions is `Scanner`. We can apply a `Scanner` directly to a `Reader`. The `Scanner` returns a `Stream<MatchResult>` of all matches with the `findAll(...)` method. The regular expression must recognize all possible occurring numbers, i.e., `10|9|8|...|1`. The or-connection can be abbreviated as `10|[1-9]`, but not as `[1-9]|10`.

The matches are returned as `MatchResult`, and we have to fall back from that to the main group with `group()`; that gives us a `String`. For summing, we use `mapToInt(...)` to convert the `String` to an integer first. This is done in `Integer.parseInt(...)`. It is perfect to use a method reference because `Integer.parseInt(...)` matches the signature of `Function`. Parse errors cannot occur because the regular expression only matches numbers.

The integer itself must be decremented by 1. We could write this as a lambda expression, but there is a suitable method that can also be accessed via a method reference: `Math.decrementExact(...)`; it does throw an `ArithmeticException` if we exceed the value range, but that does not occur in our case.

After decrementing the number, everything must be converted to a large string. This is done in two parts: in the first step, each integer is converted into a `string` by itself, then these strings are assembled into one long string using a special `collector`.

The Annual Octopus Contest

If we want to solve the task, we have to associate each occurring value with a numerator. This results in the following flow:

com/tutego/exercise/stream/OctopusContest.java

```
int[] values = { 1, 1, 2, 3, 4, 2, 3, 2, 2, 1, 7, 3, 2, 2, 1 };
OptionalInt winner =
  IntStream.of( values )                                        // IntStream
      .boxed()                                                  //
Stream<Integer>
      .collect( groupingBy( identity(), counting() ) )          //
Map<Integer,Long>
      .entrySet()                                               //
Set<Entry<Integer,Long>>
      .stream()                                                 //
Stream<Entry<Integer,Long>>
      .max( Comparator.comparingLong(Map.Entry::getValue) )  //
Optional<Entry<Integer,Long>>
      .map( Map.Entry::getKey )                                 //
Optional<Integer>
      .map( OptionalInt::of ).orElse( OptionalInt.empty() );// OptionalInt
System.out.println( winner );
```

- Since we want to use the Stream API for the task, it starts by creating a stream. First, an `IntStream` is generated from the array of primitive integers.
- Since the `IntStream` has no useful methods by which we can accomplish our task, a `Stream<Integer>` is generated from the `IntStream`, that is, the wrapper objects are generated from the primitive values.
- Regular streams allow grouping with the `collect(...)` method, and a special `Collector` that a `Map` is created at the end. The key is supposed to be the value in the stream, and the associated value is the frequency of occurrence. Both methods are imported statically, entirely it is called `Function.identity()` and `Collectors.counting()`. The result is a Map<integer, long>. With this, the main work is done.
- Now it is necessary to select the largest value from the associated value reflecting the frequencies. Keys and values are together in the `Map` and cannot be sorted by value. However, sets can already be sorted, so a Set<Map.Entry<Integer, Long>> is built.
- The `entrySet()` method returns a `Set`, but we cannot easily use it to determine the smallest or largest value. However, a `Stream` has this ability, so a Stream<Map.Entry<Integer, Long>> is built.
- Sorting the `Stream` is not necessary, only the largest associated value of the `Map.Entry` objects is needed. This can be obtained by the `max(...)` method with a special `Comparator`. The `Comparator` can be built using a key extractor, which extracts the value (not the key) from the `Map.Entry` object. The result is an object of type Optional<Map.Entry<Integer, Long>>.

- We need to move toward the result return, and an `Optional<Map.Entry<Integer, Long>>` doesn't help. We extract the key because we don't need the value, the number of ratings, for the result. The result is an `Optional<Integer>`. Since the array consists of primitive numbers, the return should not be a wrapper object.
- An `Optional<Integer>` should be transformed into an `OptionalInt`. The Java library does not provide a standard way to do this, so map (...) will hand the wrapper object to the static `OptionalInt.of(...)` method, resulting in an `OptionalInt`. But this is only created if the initial `Stream` contains elements. If not, the `Stream` was empty all along, and in that case, the return is an empty `OptionalInt`. This determines the winning octopus.

Merge Three int Arrays

To make our method `join(...)` a bit more flexible, there are two implementations. `join(int[] numbers1, int[] numbers2, int[] numbers3, int maxSize)` has an additional parameter `maxSize` which limits the number of elements of the resulting array.

com/tutego/exercise/stream/JoinIntArrays.java

```
public static final int MAX_ARRAY_LENGTH = Integer.MAX_VALUE - 8;

public static int[] join( int[] numbers1, int[] numbers2, int[] numbers3,
                          long maxSize ) {
  if ( maxSize > numbers1.length + numbers2.length + numbers3.length )
    throw new IllegalArgumentException(
        "The maximum number of elements exceeds the number of total elements" );

  if ( maxSize > MAX_ARRAY_LENGTH )
    throw new IllegalArgumentException( "Requested array size exceeds VM
limit" );

  return IntStream.concat( IntStream.of( numbers1 ),
                           IntStream.concat( IntStream.of( numbers2 ),
                                             IntStream.of( numbers3 ) ) )
              .limit( maxSize )
              .toArray();
}
public static int[] join( int[] numbers1, int[] numbers2, int[] numbers3 ) {
  return join( numbers1, numbers2, numbers3,
               (long) numbers1.length + numbers2.length + numbers3.length );
}
```

To make our method `join(...)` a bit more flexible, there are two implementations. `join(int[] numbers1, int[] numbers2, int[] numbers3, int maxSize)` has an additional parameter `maxSize` which limits the number of elements of the resulting array. Let's get started.

First, we run two tests.

1. The first test checks whether the desired maximum number of elements `maxSize` is achievable by three arrays at all. If there are fewer elements, there shall be an `IllegalArgumentException` with an error message.
2. As it stands now, arrays cannot get larger than `Integer.MAX _ VALUE - 8`, so there is a constant in the proposed solution.[1] Therefore, the second case distinction checks that the passed `maxSize` is not above the maximum size of Java arrays. Even if later `numbers1.length+numbers2.length>MAX _ ARRAY _ LENGTH` but `maxSize` is below `MAX _ ARRAY _ LENGTH`, `limit(maxSize)` of the `Stream` object keeps the later array within bounds.

There is no special method in Java to assemble arrays, but primitive streams come to the rescue. The `IntStream concat(IntStream a, IntStream b)` method concatenates two instances of `IntStream` into a new `IntStream`. Since our sources are `int[]` arrays, `IntStream.of(…)` returns the required `IntStream` instances. Since there is no parameterized `concat(…)` method with three arguments or a data structure, `concat(…)` must be nested, either by `concat(A, concat(B, C)` or `concat(concat(A, B), C)`. This is followed by pruning with `limit(…)` and in the end, `toArray()` creates the desired array.

The simpler method `join(…)` with three parameters calculates the total length and delegates to the method with four parameters. The array lengths are of type `int`, and we expand this to `long` so that the sum is `long`, we have no overflow, and then we can see that the sum is not greater than `MAX_ARRAY_LENGTH`.

Determine Winning Combinations

The algorithmic approach is the following: a method is declared that takes a string. From this string, the first character is deleted, and then the method is called recursively with the newly created string. Then the second character is deleted, and the method is again called recursively, and so on. The recursive method ends when the string has no more characters and is empty.

The method just described is in the solution `removeLetter(…)`:

com/tutego/exercise/stream/RemovingLetters.java

```java
private static void removeLetter( String word, Set<String> words ) {
  if ( word.isEmpty() )
    return;
  words.add( word );
  IntStream.range( 0, word.length() )
          .mapToObj( i -> new StringBuilder(word).deleteCharAt(i).toString()
)
          .forEach( substring -> removeLetter( substring, words ) );
}
public static Set<String> removeLetter( String word ) {
  Set<String> words = new HashSet<>();
  removeLetter( word, words );
  return words;
}
```

The resulting strings go into a set, and duplicate resulting strings fly out. Since the caller expects a set and should not pass an empty container into the method, there is a second public method `removeLetter(String)`. That method builds a `HashSet`, passes it along with the word to the private method `removeLetter(String, Set<String>)`, and returns the new set at the end.

The Fastest and Slowest Paddlers

The goal of the task is to create a `DoubleSummaryStatistics` object. This statistics object provides information about the number of elements considered, the minimum, maximum, and average. There are two ways to implement a statistics object.

com/tutego/exercise/stream/PaddleCompetition.java

```java
DoubleSummaryStatistics statistics =
    stream.mapToDouble( Result::time ).summaryStatistics();
System.out.printf( "count:   %d%n",   statistics.getCount() );
```

```
System.out.printf( "min:      %.0f%n", statistics.getMin() );
System.out.printf( "max:      %.0f%n", statistics.getMax() );
System.out.printf( "average: %.0f%n", statistics.getAverage() );
```

The first variant is to create a DoubleStream with the times from the Stream<Result> and then call summaryStatistics() on the DoubleStream.

The second possibility is to use directly a corresponding Collector:

com/tutego/exercise/stream/PaddleCompetition.java

```
DoubleSummaryStatistics statistics =
    stream.collect( Collectors.summarizingDouble( Result::time ) );
```

An extraction function can be supplied to Collectors.summarizingDouble(…) that extracts the time directly from the Stream<Result>; this saves the program an intermediate step.

Calculate Median

com/tutego/exercise/stream/DoubleStreamMedian.java

```
public static double median( double... values ) {
  if ( values.length< 1 )
    throw new IllegalArgumentException( "array contains no elements" );

  int skip = (values.length - 1) / 2;
  int limit = 2 - values.length % 2;
  return Arrays.stream( values ).sorted().skip( skip )
              .limit( limit ).average().getAsDouble();
}
```

As usual, we check the input, and if the array consists of no elements, there is an exception. Moreover, there is automatically an exception if values are equal to null.

When calculating the median, we have to navigate to the middle. Then we have to consider one element or two elements in the middle. If a DoubleStream is built and then sorted, skip(…) allows skipping a certain number of elements to get to the middle. limit(…) in the next step reduces the number of remaining elements in the stream to either one element (array had an odd number of elements) or two elements (array had an even number of elements). Finally, the chain averages the value, with nothing much to calculate for one value, but with two elements, the average() method gives us the arithmetic average. Since the method wants a floating-point number as the result, getAsDouble() returns that number, and that is valid since the stream has exactly one element. An alternative API design could have returned OptionDouble, thus accounting for the special case where the double array contains no elements.

The most exciting part is the calculation of the shift and the limit. For this, the program introduces two variables skip and limit, which are derived from the length of the input. Two examples:

The variables are initialized as follows:

TABLE 6.1 Examples for the assignment of limit and skip, the values in the middle of the list are shown in bold

LIST	SKIP	LIMIT
9, 11, **11**, 11, 12	2	1
10, **10**, **12**, 12	1	2

```
int skip = (values.length - 1) / 2;
int limit = 2 - values.length % 2;
```

Both variables depend on the length of the array. The center is the array length divided by two, which fits quite well for arrays with an odd number of elements, but a pure division by two leads to a problem for arrays with an even number of elements. Because in that case, we have to consider the two elements to the left of the center and the right of the center. (These elements even have a name and are called upper and lower median.) Therefore, if the length is decreased by one before dividing by two, we end up with an even number one element before the center. To clarify it:

TABLE 6.2 Examples for the calculation of `skip`, the values in the middle of the list are shown in bold

LIST	(VALUES.LENGTH - 1) / 2	(VALUES.LENGTH) / 2
9, 11, **11**, 11, 12	(5 − 1) / 2 = 2	5 / 2 = 2
10, **10, 12**, 12	(4 − 1) / 2 = 1	4 / 2 = 2

The limit must be 2 for an even number of elements in an array and 1 for an odd number of elements. `values.length % 2` returns 0 for an even number and 1 for an odd number. Consequently, the expression `2 - values.length % 2` returns `2 - 0 = 2` for an even number and `2 - 1` for an odd number, i.e., 1.

Calculate Temperature Statistics and Draw Charts

The task breaks down into several methods. A method `randomTemperaturesForYear(Year)` generates a random temperature for each day in the year. Another method `createRandomTemperatureMap()` calls `randomTemperaturesForYear(...)` five times. The output in the form of a small table on the command line is realized by another method `printTemperatureTable(...)`. Finally, the method `writeTemperatureHtmlFile(...)` writes the average values to a file.

Let's start with `randomTemperaturesForYear(Year)`.
com/tutego/exercise/stream/TemperatureYearChart.java

```
private static int[] randomTemperaturesForYear( Year year ) {
    int daysInYear = year.length();
    return IntStream.range( 0, daysInYear )
        .mapToDouble( value -> sin( value * PI / daysInYear ) ) // 0..1
        .map( value -> value * 20 ) // 0..20
        .map( value -> value + 10 ) // 10..30
        .mapToInt( value -> (int) (value + 3 * (random() - 0.5)) )
        .toArray();
}
private static SortedMap<Year, int[]> createRandomTemperatureMap() {
    UnaryOperator<Year> previousYear = year -> year.minusYears( 1 );
    return Stream
        .iterate( Year.now(), previousYear )
        .limit( 5 )
        .collect( toSortedMap( identity(),
                        TemperatureYearChart::randomTemperaturesForYear ) );
}
private static Collector<Year, ?, TreeMap<Year, int[]>>
toSortedMap( Function<Year, Year> keyMapper,
            Function<Year, int[]> valueMapper ) {
```

```
    return Collectors.toMap( keyMapper,
                             valueMapper,
                             (y1, y2) -> {throw new RuntimeException
("Duplicates");},
                             TreeMap::new );
}
```

The special data type Year is useful because it returns the number of days in the year via the length() method because not every year is 365 days long. With this number of days in the year, we can form an IntStream and then generate a random temperature for each day in the year. The average temperature distribution shows up in a curve: at the beginning and end of the year the temperature is low and in the middle of the year it is high. This is something we can express well using a sine function. Therefore, we transfer the integer with a function into a sine value. The beginning of the year at the first day corresponds to the sine of 0 and the end of the year at the last day results in the sine of π (Pi) thus again 0. In between is the sine hill. The sine values between 0 and 1 are small, the maximum of $\sin(\pi)$ is 1, so the values are multiplied by 20 in the next step and then taken plus 10 in the next step. The values are not random now, so the last mapping brings in some randomness so that the sine values fluctuate up and down a bit.

createRandomTemperatureMap() uses the randomTemperaturesForYear(...) method to build a Stream<Year> with five elements, starting at the current year and then moving forward one year at a time. The result is a SortedMap<Year, int[]> of the temperature values associated with each year. However, the method toMap(Function keyMapper, Function valueMapper) with two arguments should not be used because there is no prediction of the Map—internally, the OpenJDK uses a HashMap. In our case, a Map sorted by years is useful. Therefore, toMap(Function keyMapper, Function valueMapper, BinaryOperator mergeFunction, Supplier mapFactory) is used, so that explicitly the data come into a sorted TreeMap.

This can go into the output:

com/tutego/exercise/stream/TemperatureYearChart.java

```
private static void printTemperatureTable( SortedMap<Year,
                                           int[]> yearToTemperatures ) {
  yearToTemperatures.forEach( (year, temperatures) -> {
    String temperatureCells =
        Arrays.stream( temperatures )
              .mapToObj( temperature -> String.format( "%2d", temperature ) )
              .collect( Collectors.joining( " | ", "| ", " | " ) );
    System.out.println( "| "+year+" "+temperatureCells );
  } );
}
```

printTemperatureTable(...) takes care of printing the table for all the years passed in. The pass is an associative store that associates the years with the temperatures. The forEach(...) method goes over the data structure sorted by years and creates a string temperatureCells. To build the string, the first step is to turn the int array into an IntStream. Each temperature value is mapped to a string, with values less than 10 getting a preceding space so that the output is always two digits wide. The collector combines all the individual strings, and the result is temperatureCells. This string with the temperature values is printed, with the preceding years, on the screen.

Let's move on to the statistics:

com/tutego/exercise/stream/TemperatureYearChart.java

```
IntSummaryStatistics yearStatistics =
    Arrays.stream( yearToTemperatures.get( Year.now() ) ).summaryStatistics();
System.out.printf( "max: %d, min: %d%n",
                   yearStatistics.getMax(), yearStatistics.getMin() );
```

We have already used a few times the `Arrays.stream(…)` method, which is an alternative to `IntStream.of(…)` and creates an `IntStream` from an `int` array. The three primitive streams have a special method `summaryStatistics()` compared to the regular `Stream` objects, which provide a statistics object with information about the minimum, maximum, and average value. We can easily grab this information and output it.

A separate method `getStatistics(…)` retrieves these `IntSummaryStatistics` for one month of a year from the `Map`:

com/tutego/exercise/stream/TemperatureYearChart.java

```
private static IntSummaryStatistics getStatistics( YearMonth yearMonth,
                                                   int... temperatures ) {
  int start = yearMonth.atDay( 1 ).getDayOfYear();
  int end   = yearMonth.atEndOfMonth().getDayOfYear();
  return Arrays.stream( temperatures, start - 1, end ).summaryStatistics();
}
```

In the passed `int` array `temperatures`, all temperature values of the year are stored. If we want to calculate the statistics of a concrete month, we have to build a sub-array at the appropriate place. This can be solved well with `Arrays.stream(…)` because the start and end index in this array can be given. The question that arises with a year of approximately 365 days is: when does a month like March or December actually begin? The answer is provided by the `YearMonth` object. For the start value, we request with `atDay(1)` a new `YearMonth` object for the beginning of the month and get with `getDayOfYear()` the day in the year. We do the same for the last day of the month, using the `atEndOfMonth()` method to set the `YearMonth` object to the end of the month. We pass the start and end values to `Arrays.stream(…)`, where the month starts at 1, and we need to move the start value one position to the left. Furthermore, we do not move the end one position to the left because the value is exclusive and not inclusive.

The method can be called as follows:

com/tutego/exercise/stream/TemperatureYearChart.java

```
IntSummaryStatistics monthStatistics =
    getStatistics( YearMonth.of( 2020, SEPTEMBER ),
                   yearToTemperatures.get( Year.now() ) );
System.out.printf( "max: %d, min: %d, average: %.2f%n", monthStatistics.getMax(),
                   monthStatistics.getMin(), monthStatistics.getAverage() );
```

Finally, the method for writing to a file:

com/tutego/exercise/stream/TemperatureYearChart.java

```
  private static void writeTemperatureHtmlFile(
      Year year, Map<Year, int[]> yearToTemperatures, Path path )
        throws IOException {
    String template = """
<!DOCTYPE html><html>
 <head><meta charset="UTF-8"></head>
 <body>
 <canvas></canvas>
 <script src="https://cdn.jsdelivr.net/npm/chart.js@3.3.2/dist/chart.min.js">
 </script>
 <script>
   const cfg = {
     type: "bar",
```

```
      data: {
        labels:"Jan. Feb. Mar. Apr. May June July Aug. Sept. Oct. Nov.
Dec.".split(" "),
        datasets: [{
          label: "Average temperature",
          data: [%s],
        }]
      }
    };
    window.onload=()=>new Chart(document.querySelector("canvas").
getContext("2d"),cfg);
  </script>
  </body></html>""";
    String formattedTemperatures =
        IntStream.rangeClosed( JANUARY.getValue(), DECEMBER.getValue() )
          .mapToObj( Month::of )
          .map( month -> year.atMonth( month ) )
          .map( yearMonth->getStatistics(yearMonth,yearToTemperatures.
get(year)) )
          .map( IntSummaryStatistics::getAverage )
          .map( avgTemperature -> String.format( ENGLISH, "%.1f",
avgTemperature ) )
          .collect( Collectors.joining( "," ) );
    String html=String.format( template, formattedTemperatures );
    Files.writeString( path, html );
  }
```

The declaration of the HTML document takes up the largest area in the method. In one place it says
data: [%s], and this %s is a typical placeholder in the format string, so we can use the String.format(…) method later to insert the dynamically calculated values. The method proceeds as follows:

- rangeClosed(…) returns an IntStream with numbers from 1 to 12.
- mapToObj(…) transfers these numbers to Month objects.
- The year is passed to the writeTemperatureHtmlFile(…) method. The year.atMonth(month) expression associates the year with the month from the iteration and returns a new YearMonth object for mapping. The lambda expression month -> year.atMonth(month) could be abbreviated to year::atMonth, but the lambda expression is written out should be more readable.
- The resulting Stream<YearMonth> can be accessed using its own getStatistics(…) method on the IntSummaryStatistics; the result is of type Stream<IntSummaryStatistics>.
- From this IntSummaryStatistics we get the average value with the method reference, a Stream<Double> is created.
- Finally, we format this average value to create a string for one month.
- This is done for all months, and finally the strings are collected and comma-separated.

Finally, the string formattedTemperatures contains the result, which now has to be inserted into the HTML document. After creating the complete HTML document, write(…) creates the file.
writeTemperatureHtmlFile(…) can be used as follows:

com/tutego/exercise/stream/TemperatureYearChart.java

```
try {
  Path tempFile=Files.createTempFile( "temperatures", ".html" );
  writeTemperatureHtmlFile( Year.now(), yearToTemperatures, tempFile );
  Desktop.getDesktop().browse( tempFile.toUri() );
}
catch ( IOException e ) { e.printStackTrace(); }
```

NOTE

---

1 The OpenJDK declares a constant in the internal package jdk.internal.util: `public class ArraysSupport { public static final int MAX_ARRAY_LENGTH = Integer.MAX_VALUE - 8; … }`. Since the module jdk.internal.util is taboo for us, there is a copy of the constant in in the proposed solution.

Files, Directories, and File Access

7

Despite everything moving to the cloud and databases becoming all the rage, the good old file system is still relevant for storing and organizing important documents. Even tech-savvy folks like Captain Bonny Brain and Captain CiaoCiao still rely heavily on local storage. There are certain things that just shouldn't see the light of day, you know?

Prerequisites

- Know the `File` class, `Path` interface, and `Files` class in the basics.
- Be able to create temporary files.
- Have the capability to extract metafiles from both files and directories.
- Be able to list and filter directory contents.
- Read and write complete files.
- Know `RandomAccessFile`.

Data types used in this chapter:

- `java.io.File`
- `java.nio.file.Path`
- `java.nio.file.Paths`
- `java.nio.file.Files`
- `java.nio.file.DirectoryStream`
- `java.nio.file.FileVisitor`
- `java.io.RandomAccessFile`
- `java.awt.Desktop`

PATH AND FILES

As with so many things in Java, there is the "old" way and the "new" way when it comes to file processing. In many examples, you still see code with the types `java.io.File`, `FileInputStream`, `FileOutputStream`, `FileReader`, and `FileWriter`. These types are no longer up-to-date, so in this chapter we will deal exclusively with `Path` and `Files` because these types allow the use of virtual file systems, like a ZIP archive. `File` is now only required when actually dealing with files or directories of the local file system; examples would be opening files with the programs associated by the operating system or redirecting data streams from externally started programs.

DOI: 10.1201/9781003495550-8

Display Saying of the Day ★

Sometimes Captain CiaoCiao can't quite get motivated. A motivational or sense saying for the day brings the grumpy head to new thoughts. The task is to program an application that generates an HTML file with a saying and then opens the browser to display this text. The exercise can be solved with two methods of `java.nio.files.Files`.

Exercise:

- Create a temporary file ending with the file suffix `.html` using an appropriate `files` method.
- Write HTML code in the new temporary file, such as the following:
  ```
  <!DOCTYPE html><html><body>
  'The things we steal tell us who we are.'
  - Thomas of Tew
  </body></html>
  ```
- Find a method from the `java.awt.Desktop` class that opens the default browser and displays the HTML file as a result.

Merge Hiding Places ★

With certain `Files` methods, an entire file can be read and rewritten line by line in a single step.

Captain CiaoCiao collects potential hiding places in a large text file. But often he spontaneously thinks of more hiding places and quickly writes them into a new file. Now he takes his time and cleans up and merges everything; the small text files are to be merged with the large file. It is important that the order of the entries in the large file is not changed. Only the entries from the small files are included if they do not appear in the large file because it may be that the main file already contains the hiding places.

Exercise:

- Write a method `mergeFiles(Path main, Path... temp)` that opens the master file, adds all temporary contents, and then writes back the master file.

Create Copies of a File ★★

If you copy a file to the same folder in Windows Explorer, a copy is created. This copy automatically gets a new name. We are looking for a Java program that replicates this behavior.

Exercise:

- Write a Java method `cloneFile(Path path)` that creates copies of files, generating the file names systematically. Suppose `<name>` symbolizes the file name, then the first copy will be `Copy of <name>` and thereafter the file names should be `Copy (<number>) of <name>`.
- If you call the methods on directories or there are other errors, the method may throw an `IOException`.

Example:

- Suppose a file is called *Top Secret UFO Files.txt*. Then the new file names should look like this:
  - *Copy of Top Secret UFO Files.txt.*
  - *Copy (2) of from Top Secret UFO Files.txt.*
  - *Copy (3) of from Top Secret UFO Files.txt.*

Generate a Directory Listing ★

On the command line, the user can display directory contents and metadata, just as a file selection dialog displays files to the user.
Exercise:

- Using `Files` and the `newDirectoryStream(…)` method, write a program that lists the directory contents for the current directory.
- Call the `dir` program under DOS. Rebuild the output of the directory listing completely. The header and footer are not necessary.

Search for Large GIF Files ★

There's a mess on Bonny Brain's hard drive, partly because she stores all her images in exactly one directory. Now the pictures from the last treasure hunt are untraceable! All she remembers is that the images were saved in GIF (Graphics Interchange Format), and they were over 1024 pixels wide.
Exercise:

- Given is any directory. Search in this directory (not recursively!) for all images that are of type GIF and have a minimum width of 1024 pixels.

Access the following code to read the widths and perform GIF checking:

```java
private static final byte[] GIF87aGIF89a = "GIF87aGIF89a".getBytes();
private static boolean isGifAndWidthGreaterThan1024( Path entry ) {
  if ( ! Files.isRegularFile( entry ) || ! Files.isReadable( entry ) )
    return false;
  try ( RandomAccessFile raf = new RandomAccessFile( entry.toFile(), "r" ) ) {
    byte[] bytes = new byte[ 8 ];
    raf.read( bytes );
    if ( ! Arrays.equals( bytes, 0, 6, GIF87aGIF89a, 0, 6 ) &&
         ! Arrays.equals( bytes, 0, 6, GIF87aGIF89a, 6, 12 ) )
      return false;
    int width = bytes[ 6 ] + (bytes[ 7 ] << 8);
    return width > 1024;
  }
  catch ( IOException e ) {
    throw new UncheckedIOException( e );
  }
}
```

The method reads the first bytes and checks if the first six bytes match either the string GIF87a or GIF89a. In principle, this test can also be implemented with `! new String(bytes, 0, 6).matches("GIF87a|GIF89a")`, but that would cause some temporary objects in memory.
After the check, the program reads 2 bytes for the width and converts the bytes to a 16-bit integer.

Descend Directories Recursively and Find Empty Text Files ★

There is still a big mess on Bonny Brain's hard drive. For some inexplicable reason, it has many text files with 0 bytes.

Exercise:

- Using a `FileVisitor`, run recursively from a chosen starting directory through all subdirectories, looking for empty text files.
- Text files are files that have the file extension .*txt* (case-insensitive).
- If found, show the absolute path of the file on the console.

Develop Your Own Utility Library for File Filters ★★★

The `Files` class provides three static methods to query all entries in a directory:

- `newDirectoryStream(Path dir)`
- `newDirectoryStream(Path dir, String glob)`
- `newDirectoryStream(Path dir, DirectoryStream.Filter<? super Path> filter)`

The result is always a `DirectoryStream<Path>`. The first method does not filter the results, the second method allows a glob string such as *.txt, and the third method allows any filter.
   `java.nio.file.DirectoryStream.Filter<T>` is an interface that filters must implement. The method is `boolean accept(T entry)` and is like a predicate.
   The Java library declares the interface, but no implementation.
   Exercise:

- Write various implementations of `DirectoryStream.Filter` that can check files for
  - Attributes (like readable, writable).
  - The length.
  - The file extensions.
  - The filename via regular expressions.
  - Magic initial identifiers.

Ideally, the API allows all filters to be concatenated, something like this:

```
DirectoryStream.Filter<Path> filter =
    regularFile.and( readable )
              .and( largerThan( 100_000 ) )
              .and( magicNumber( 0x89, 'P', 'N', 'G' ) )
              .and( globMatches( "*.png" ) )
              .and( regexContains( "[-]" ) );
try ( var entries = Files.newDirectoryStream(dir,filter) ) {
  entries.forEach( System.out::println );
}
```

RANDOM ACCESS TO FILE CONTENTS

For files, an input/output stream can be obtained and read or written from beginning to end. Another API allows random access, i.e., a position pointer.

Output Last Line of a Text File ★★

Crew members write all actions in an electronic logbook, with new entries appended at the end. No entry is longer than 100 characters, the texts are written in UTF-8.

Now Captain CiaoCiao is interested in the last entry. What does a Java program look like if only the last line is to be read from a file? Since there are already plenty of entries in the log, it is not possible to read the file completely.

Exercise:

- Write a program that returns the last line of a text file.
- Find a solution that does not need unnecessary memory.

 Consider whether ([^\r\n]*)$ can be used in a meaningful way.

SUGGESTED SOLUTIONS

Display Saying of the Day

com/tutego/exercise/io/DailyWordsOfWisdom.java

```
try {
  String html = """
  <!DOCTYPE html><html><body>\
  >The things we steal tell us who we are.<\
   - Thomas von Tew</body></html>""";
  Path tmpPath = Files.createTempFile( "wisdom", ".html" );
  Files.writeString( tmpPath, html );
  Desktop.getDesktop().open( tmpPath.toFile() );
}
catch ( IOException e ) {
  System.err.println( "Couldn't write HTML file in temp folder or open file"
);
  e.printStackTrace();
}
```

In the proposed solution, we are dealing with three central statements. At the beginning, there is the creation of the file in the temporary directory. In the method `createTempFile(…)` we can specify a part of the name as well as a suffix, and we choose the extension `.html`, so that later the operating system can select the appropriate viewer via this file extension. It returns `createTempFile(…)` the generated `Path`, which we use to write the string into this file.

For writing a string, there is the method `writeString(Path path, CharSequence csq, OpenOption…  options)`. The class `String` implements `CharSequence`. The `OpenOption` parameter is not necessary in our particular case, as it would only be required if we needed to append to existing files.

`open(…)` is one of the few methods that require a `File` object. From the `Path` we generate a `File` object and use it to open the browser, which should be associated with rendering HTML files. Alternatively, for web pages, we can use `browse(URI)` and get the URI from the `path` via `toUri()`.

Merge Hiding Places

com/tutego/exercise/io/MergeFiles.java

```java
public static void mergeFiles( Path main, Path... temp ) throws IOException
{
  Iterable<Path> paths =
      Stream.concat( Stream.of( main ), Stream.of( temp ) )::iterator;
  Collection<String> words = new LinkedHashSet<>();
  for ( Path path : paths )
    try ( Stream<String> lines = Files.lines( path ) ) {
      lines.forEach( words::add );
    }
  Files.write( main, words );
}
```

For our task, the `LinkedHashSet` data structure is ideally suited because as a set, it contains elements only once, and it considers the order of the inserted elements. We only have to take care that the rows of the first file come first into the data structure, and then the rows of the remaining files.

For reading the lines and inserting them into the data structure, the first file should be treated in the same way as the rest of the files. But the unification is only possible by a workaround because the first data type in the parameter list is a single `Path` variable, and then follows a vararg, i.e., a `Path` array. The proposed solution first puts the first element into a `Stream` and combines that with a second stream of the elements in the vararg array; the result is a `Stream<Path>`. We only have to run this stream. In theory, `forEach(…)` can be used here, but there is a problem: input/output operations throw checked exceptions, and these do not get along with the lambda expressions. The `Stream` is therefore converted to an `Iterable` so that we can use the extended `for` loop. The `::iterator` method reference returns an expression of type `Iterable`; a neat trick, since `Stream` itself does not implement `Iterable`.

The extended `for` loop runs over the files, reads in all the lines, puts them into the data structure, and finally writes all the lines back to the first file.

Create Copies of a File

com/tutego/exercise/io/FileClone.java

```java
private static final String COPY_OF_FORMAT_STRING = "Copy of %s";
private static final String NUMBERED_COPY_OF_FORMAT_STRING = "Copy (%d) of %s";
public static void cloneFile( Path path ) throws IOException {
  if ( Files.isDirectory( path ) )
    throw new IllegalArgumentException(
        "Path has to be a file but was a directory" );
  Path parent   = path.getParent();
  Path filename = path.getFileName();
  Path copyPath = parent.resolve( COPY_OF_FORMAT_STRING.formatted( filename )
);
  for ( int i = 2; Files.exists( copyPath ); i++ )
    copyPath = parent.resolve( NUMBERED_COPY_OF_FORMAT_STRING.
formatted(i,filename) );
  Files.copy( path, copyPath );
}
```

The algorithm from the proposed solution proceeds by generating possible filenames in order and testing until a free filename is found. In round brackets, there is a counter starting at 2. There is no `Copy  (1)` of `<Name>`.

The method `cloneFile(Path  path)` starts with a query if a directory was passed as `path` accidentally, and raises an exception in that case; we cannot clone directories. If it is a file, we extract the directory of the file and the filename.

The first sample for a possible new filename starts with `Copy of` and does not yet contain a counter. We can test this filename for existence with `Files.exists(…)`. If the file exists, we have to continue with a counter. Therefore, we set this existence test as a condition in a `for` loop and use a counter variable `i`, which we initialize with 2 at the beginning to be able to represent the counter in round brackets. In the body of the loop, the variable `copyPath` is reassigned, always with the loop counter in round brackets. We run through the loop until we find a `copyPath` that does not exist. Then the loop terminates, and `Files.copy(…)` creates a copy of the file with the path specification of `copyPath`.

To make it easier to change the strings for different languages, they are extracted as constants.

Generate a Directory Listing

com/tutego/exercise/io/DosDir.java

```
private static final DateTimeFormatter ddMMyyyy_hhmm =
    DateTimeFormatter.ofPattern( "dd.MM.yyyy  hh:mm" );
static void listDirectory( Path dir ) throws IOException {
  try ( DirectoryStream<Path> entries = Files.newDirectoryStream( dir ) ) {
    for ( Path path : entries ) {
      Instant instant = Files.getLastModifiedTime( path ).toInstant();
      LocalDateTime dateTime = LocalDateTime.ofInstant( instant,
                                                  ZoneId.
systemDefault() );
      String formattedDateTime = dateTime.format( ddMMyyyy_hhmm );
      String dirLength = Files.isDirectory( path )
                  ? "<DIR>           "
                  : String.format( "%,14d", Files.size( path ) );
      String filename = path.getFileName().toString();
      System.out.printf( "%s    %s %s%n", formattedDateTime, dirLength,
filename );
    }
  }
}
```

To solve the task, different APIs come together. We need the class `Files`, the type `Path`, date/time calculations, and format strings.

Since the file operations can throw potential exceptions, but we cannot handle them, our method will pass possible exceptions to the caller. Nevertheless, a `try`-with-resources comes into play—the resource is the `DirectoryStream`. If you program quick and dirty, you will often see the `DirectoryStream` as an `Iterable`, located to the right of the colon of the extended `for` loop. But the `DirectoryStream` is a resource that needs to be closed. So, we find the extended `for` loop to loop through all entries in the directory in the next step.

The variable `path` now contains a path, which can stand for a file or a directory. In any case, we want to get the time of the last access. Although `Files.getLastModifiedTime(…)` returns the necessary `FileTime` object, the `toString()` method does not return anything appealing. Therefore, a little detour is necessary to get a nice output: first, the `FileTime` is converted to an `Instant`, which is then converted to a LocalDateTime, and this allows us to use a DateTimeFormatter with the pattern "dd.MM.yyyy hh:mm", for whose format we have introduced a separate constant.

We have the date and time, now the other segments follow. Depending on whether the path is a directory or a file, we have to set <DIR> or, in the case of a file, ask for the file length; String.format(…) brings the number of bytes to an appropriate length.

In the last step, we ask for the name of the file or directory and put everything together in one line. This line starts with the formatted date and time, then the indication if it is a directory, otherwise the file length, and finally the file name or directory name.

Search for Large GIF Files

For the solution we fall back on a Files method:

```
DirectoryStream<Path> newDirectoryStream(Path dir, DirectoryStream.Filter<?
super Path> filter).
```

For us, DirectoryStream.Filter<? super Path> filter is relevant because it can be used to implement a criterion for limiting the results. For context, let's look at the UML diagram:

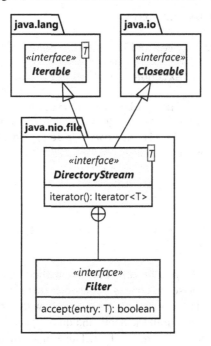

FIGURE 7.1   UML diagram of DirectoryStream and dependent types.

The Filter is a nested type of DirectoryStream. If we need to pass a filter, we need to implement the Filter interface and the accept(…) method. The implementation can be done by a class, by a lambda expression, or by a method reference. And "luckily" boolean isGifAndWidthGreaterThan1024(Path entry) matches boolean accept(Path entry), which suggests a method reference.

com/tutego/exercise/io/FindBigGifImages.java

```
Path directory = Paths.get( name );
```

```java
try {
  try ( DirectoryStream<Path> files =
            Files.newDirectoryStream( directory,
                                      FindBigGifImages::isGifAndWidthGreaterT
han1024 ) ) {
    files.forEach( System.out::println );
  }
}
catch ( IOException e ) {
  e.printStackTrace();
}
```

The Files.newDirectoryStream(…) method returns the DirectoryStream, which is AutoCloseable and must be closed again at the end. This is conveniently done by try-with-resources. The DirectoryStream is also an Iterable, so we can run it in an extended for loop or with a forEach(…) and an appropriate Consumer.

Descend Directories Recursively and Find Empty Text Files

com/tutego/exercise/io/EmptyFilesFinder.java

```java
public static void findEmptyTextFiles( Path base, Consumer<Path> callback )
    throws IOException {
  class PrintingFileVisitor extends SimpleFileVisitor<Path> {
    @Override
    public FileVisitResult visitFile( Path visitedFile,
                                      BasicFileAttributes fileAttributes ) {
      if ( visitedFile.toString().toLowerCase().endsWith( ".txt" )
          && fileAttributes.size() == 0L )
        callback.accept( visitedFile );
      return FileVisitResult.CONTINUE;
    }
  }
  Files.walkFileTree( base, new PrintingFileVisitor() );
}
```

The solution implements the findEmptyTextFiles(…) method with two parameters: the first one is used for the base directory, while the second one is a consumer that gets called whenever a path is found.

The static method Files.walkFileTree(…) recursively walks the file system from a directory to a desired depth. In our case, we do not limit the depth and do not provide any other options. The method must be passed as an implementation of FileVisitor. This is not a functional interface, but an interface with four methods. We could implement the interface ourselves, but the Java library provides a simple implementation with SimpleFileVisitor.

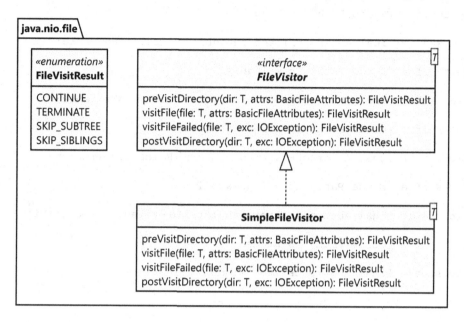

FIGURE 7.2 UML diagram of `FileVisitor`, the subclass `SimpleFileVisitor` and the enumeration `FileVisitResult` for the returns.

From this class, we make a subclass and override the `visitFile(...)` method relevant for us, which is called whenever `walkFileTree(...)` finds a file. Filter does not allow `walkFileTree(...)`, which is a pity because `newDirectoryStream(...)` allows filter. Consequently, we have to implement the criteria that the filename ends with `.txt` and is 0 bytes in size ourselves. Thankfully, `visitFile(...)` gives us

1. The path, so we can check if the filename ends in `.txt`.
2. The attributes, so we can test if the file is empty.

If both criteria are correct, we call the callback function and pass the path to the file. Then we want to continue the search in the directory, and for this the method returns `FileVisitResult.CONTINUE`.

Develop Your Own Utility Library for File Filters

com/tutego/exercise/io/FileFiltersDemo.java

```
class FileFilters {
  public interface AbstractFilter extends DirectoryStream.Filter<Path> {
    default AbstractFilter and( AbstractFilter other ) {
      return path -> accept( path ) && other.accept( path );
    }
    default AbstractFilter negate() {
      return path -> ! accept( path );
    }
    static AbstractFilter not( AbstractFilter target ) {
      return target.negate();
    }
  }
}
/**
```

```
   * Tests if a {@code Path} is readable.
   */
  public static final AbstractFilter readable = Files::isReadable;
  /**
   * Tests if a {@code Path} is writable.
   */
  public static final AbstractFilter writable = Files::isWritable;
  /**
   * Tests if a {@code Path} is a regular file.
   */
  public static final AbstractFilter directory = Files::isDirectory;
  /**
   * Tests if a {@code Path} is a regular file.
   */
  public static final AbstractFilter regularFile = Files::isRegularFile;
  /**
   * Tests if a {@code Path} is hidden.
   */
  public static final AbstractFilter hidden = Files::isHidden;
  /**
   * Tests if the file size of a {@code Path} is zero.
   */
  public static final AbstractFilter empty = path -> Files.size( path ) == 0L;
  /**
   * Tests if the file size of a {@code Path} is larger than the specified
size.
   */
  public static AbstractFilter largerThan( long size ) {
    return path -> Files.size( path ) > size;
  }
  /**
   * Tests if the file size of a {@code Path} is smaller than the specified
size.
   */
  public static AbstractFilter smallerThan( long size ) {
    return path -> Files.size( path ) < size;
  }
  /**
   * Tests if a {@code Path} is older than the specified {@code FileTime}.
   */
  public static AbstractFilter olderThan( FileTime other ) {
    return path -> Files.getLastModifiedTime( path ).compareTo( other ) > 0;
  }
  /**
   * Tests if a {@code Path} has a specified suffix, ignoring case, e.g.
".txt".
   */
  public static AbstractFilter suffix( String suffix, String... more ) {
    return path ->
        Stream.concat( Stream.of( suffix ), Stream.of( more ) )
            .anyMatch( aSuffix -> {
                String filename = path.toString();
                int suffixLen    = aSuffix.length();
                int suffixOffset = filename.length() - suffixLen;
                return filename.regionMatches( /* ignore case */ true,
```

```
                                        suffixOffset, suffix, 0,
suffixLen );
           } );
  }
  /**
   * Tests if the content of a {@code Path} starts with a specified sequence
of bytes.
   */
  public static AbstractFilter magicNumber( int... bytes ) {
    ByteBuffer byteBuffer = ByteBuffer.allocate( bytes.length );
    for ( int b : bytes ) byteBuffer.put( (byte) b );
    return magicNumber( byteBuffer.array() );
  }
  /**
   * Tests if the content of a {@code Path} starts with a specified sequence
of bytes.
   */
  public static AbstractFilter magicNumber( byte... bytes ) {
    return path -> {
      try ( InputStream in = Files.newInputStream( path ) ) {
        byte[] buffer = new byte[ bytes.length ];
        in.read( buffer );
        // If file is smaller than bytes.length, the result is false
        return Arrays.equals( bytes, buffer );
      }
    };
  }
  /**
   * Tests if a {@code Path} regexContains a specified regex.
   */
  public static AbstractFilter regexContains( String regex ) {
    return path -> Pattern.compile( regex ).matcher( path.toString()
).find();
  }
  /**
   * Tests if a filename of a {@code Path} matches a given glob string.
   */
  public static AbstractFilter globMatches( String glob ) {
    return path -> path.getFileSystem().getPathMatcher( "glob:"+glob )
                       .matches( path.getFileName() );
  }
```

The method Files.newDirectoryStream(…) allows recursive traversal of a directory tree. The method expects an implementation of the functional interface Filter and its accept(…) method as passing:

```
boolean accept(T entry) throws IOException
```

The interface has no additional default or static methods, and furthermore the type argument is always Path in our case, so a new interface AbstractFilter is to be created as a subtype of Filter with two additional default methods and one static method. The and(…) method associates two AbstractFilters with a logical AND, the negate() method negates the result of its own accept(…) method, and the static not(…) method returns a new AbstractFilter object, which also negates the result.

The `FileFilters` class declares various constants and methods. Whenever something has to be parameterized, a method is used; if no parameterization is necessary, a constant is sufficient. All following constants are of the data type `AbstractFilter` and the methods return `AbstractFilter`. The constants are initialized with a corresponding method from the `Files` class via the method reference.

Let's focus on the more exciting methods.

- `hasSuffix(…)` joins all possible file extensions to a `Stream` and then queries whether the path has one of the passed file extensions. This is done by first converting the path to a string and then using `regionMatches(…)` to check the suffix in a case-insensitive manner. Checking via `regionMatches(…)` is a bit more cluttered in code than working with `toLowerCase(…)` and `endsWith(…)`, but `regionMatches(…)` does not build temporary objects and is a little more performant.
- `magicNumber(byte...)` takes a variable number of bytes, throwing a `NullPointerException` if the parameter variable is `null`. Otherwise,
  1. An input stream is opened.
  2. Exactly as many bytes are read in as the parameter array is large.
  3. The two arrays are compared with `Arrays.equals(..)`. If the file is smaller than the passed number of bytes, then the `equals(…)` method will return `false` in any case, because the first thing the method checks is the same number of elements.
- `magicNumber(int...)` is the overloaded variant of `magicNumber(byte...)` because bytes in the parameter list are inflexible due to the value range –128 to +127; developers would have to write, for example:
  ```
  magicNumber( (byte) 0x89, (byte) 'P', (byte) 'N', (byte) 'G' )
  ```
  The `int`… data type is more convenient for callers; so it could be:
  ```
  magicNumber( 0x89, 'P', 'N', 'G' )
  ```
  Therefore, `magicNumber(int..)` converts the `int...` to a `byte[]` and delegates to the main method.
- `regexContains(…)` takes a regular expression, compiles it, then applies it to the path, and if the `find()` method returns `true`, matches the filename to the regular expression.
- `globMatches(…)` matches the filename against a glob string; these are simple expressions, like *.txt or ??-??-1976. `getPathMatcher(…)` returns a `PathMatcher` with the prefix `glob:` or `regex:`. The implementation of `regexContains(…)` does not fall back to a `PathMatcher` with regular expression because the `PathMatcher` tests for a full match, but in the solution a partial search is desired.

Output Last Line of a Text File

com/tutego/exercise/io/LastLine.java

```java
private static final int MAX_LINE_LENGTH = 100;
private static final int MAX_NUMBER_OF_BYTES_PER_UTF_8_CHAR = 4;
private static void printLastLine( String filename ) throws IOException {
  try ( RandomAccessFile file = new RandomAccessFile( filename, "r" ) ) {
    int blockSize = MAX_LINE_LENGTH * MAX_NUMBER_OF_BYTES_PER_UTF_8_CHAR;
    file.seek( file.length() - blockSize );
    byte[] bytes = new byte[ blockSize ];
    file.read( bytes );
    String string = new String( bytes, StandardCharsets.UTF_8 );
    Matcher matcher = Pattern.compile( "([^\\r\\n]*)$" ).matcher( string );
    if ( matcher.find() )
```

```
    System.out.println( matcher.group( 1 ) );
  }
}
```

The solution has two steps: First, a block is read at the end of the file, and then the last line is extracted from this block.

   To determine the correct block size, we multiply the maximum line length known from the task (100) by the maximum number of bytes expected per UTF-8 character; in UTF-8 encoding, a maximum of four characters can encode a symbol. The task becomes more difficult if the maximum line length is unknown, but the product `MAX_LINE_LENGTH * MAX_NUMBER_OF_BYTES_PER_UTF_8_CHAR` tells us that the last block of this size in the file also contains the last line.

   In the next step, we set the file pointer to the beginning of the last block. We read in a byte array and convert it to a string after UTF-8 encoding. If the last line does not have the maximum length, then the read block contains the remains of the previous line or lines with end-of-line characters as well as the last line. For extracting the last line, we can use `lastIndexOf`(...), but the regular expression `([^\r\\n]*)$` gives us the last line much nicer. The regular expression is composed as follows:

1. The dollar sign at the end signals the end of the input.
2. The group in round brackets represents what we want to extract.
3. In the character class `[^\r\n]` the little hat stands for the negation that we want all characters that are not end-of-line characters. `[^\r\n]*` with asterisk gives us a sequence of such non-line-end characters.

If there is a match, we output it. Otherwise, there is no output.

Input/Output Streams

8

In the previous chapter, as well as the chapter about exceptions, we have already dealt with the basic reading and writing of file contents. This chapter focuses on input and output streams and the continuous flow of data; it can be written to a destination or read from a source, passing through multiple filters. The nesting of Java's input/output streams is a good example of abstraction and flexibility that also helps a lot when modeling your filters.

Requirements

- Know type hierarchy of input/output classes.
- Be able to distinguish between character-oriented and byte-oriented classes.
- Understand decoration of streams.
- Be able to send stream data through filters.
- Be able to compress data.

Data types used in this chapter:

- `java.io.OutputStream`
- `java.io.InputStream`
- `java.io.Reader`
- `java.io.Writer`
- `java.nio.files.Files`
- `java.util.Scanner`
- `java.lang.Readable`
- `java.lang.Appendable`
- `java.io.IOException`
- `java.io.DataInputStream`
- `java.io.DataOutputStream`
- `java.io.FilterInputStream`
- `java.io.FilterOutputStream`
- `java.io.FilterReader`
- `java.io.FilterWriter`
- `java.io.DataInput`
- `java.io.DataOutput`
- `java.util.zip.GZIPOutputStream`
- `java.io.ByteArrayOutputStream`
- `java.io.InputStreamReader`
- `java.io.OutputStreamWriter`
- `java.io.PrintWriter`
- `java.lang.AutoCloseable`
- `java.io.BufferedOutputStream`
- `java.util.zip.CheckedOutputStream`
- `java.io.Serializable`

DOI: 10.1201/9781003495550-9

DIRECT DATA STREAMS

In Java, four different types are used: InputStream and OutputStream (byte-oriented reading and writing) and Reader and Writer (character-oriented reading and writing). We start with the exercises first with just those streams that directly write data to a resource or directly read from a resource.

Get the Number of Different Places (Read Files) ★

Captain CiaoCiao gets two text files, and they look very much the same at first glance. But he wants to know exactly if the two files match exactly or if there are differences.
Exercise:

- Write a method long distance(Path file1, Path file2) that returns the number of different characters. In computer science, this is called *Hamming distance.*
- It is assumed that the two files are the same length.

Example: A file contains the string

```
To Err is Human. To Arr is Pirate.
```

and another file contains the string

```
To Arr is Human. To Err is Pirate!
```

The distance is three as the three symbols do not align, referring to the Hamming distance.

Convert Python Program to Java (Write File) ★

In the chapter, "Imperative Language Concepts", we completed several exercises that write SVG output to the screen—now we want to write that output directly to HTML files. As a reminder, the following HTML contains an SVG with a rectangle of height and width 1 and x/y coordinates 10/10:

```
<!DOCTYPE html>
<html><body>
 <svg width="256" height="256">
  <rect x="10" y="10" width="1" height="1" style="fill:rgb(0,29,0);" />
 </svg>
</body></html>
```

In a book about computer-generated art, Captain CiaoCiao finds an illustration on the first few pages. The pattern is generated by a Python program:

```
import Image, ImageDraw

image = Image.new("RGB", (256, 256))
drawingTool = ImageDraw.Draw(image)
```

```
for x in range(256):
    for y in range(256):
        drawingTool.point((x, y), (0, x^y, 0))

del drawingTool
image.save("xorpic.png", "PNG")
```

The Python function point(...) gets the x-y coordinate and RGB color information, where the three arguments 0, x^y, and 0 represent the red, green, blue components, respectively.

Exercise:

- Since Captain CiaoCiao dislikes snakes, the Python program must be converted to a Java program.
- Instead of a PNG file, end up with an HTML file with an SVG block where each pixel is a 1×1 SVG rectangle.

Bonus: at the end, open the HTML file with the browser—the desktop class will help you here.

Generate Target Code (Write File) ★

From the post office, Captain CiaoCiao is getting more and more letters with pink barcodes. At first, he thinks of encoded love letters from Bonny Brain, but then he realizes that there is a so-called destination code on the envelope, which encodes the postal code.

The encoding of the numbers in dashes is as follows, where the underscore _ symbolizes the spacing by a space:

Exercise:

- Write a static method writeTargetCode(String, Writer) that writes a string of digits in the named encoding to a writer.
- There should be two spaces between the four symbols for a digit.

TABLE 8.1   Values and encodings

VALUE	ENCODING
0	| | | |
1	| | | _
2	| | _ |
3	| | _ _
4	| _ | |
5	| _ | _
6	| _ _ |
7	_ | _ |
8	_ | | |
9	_ | | _

Example:

- The string "023" is written to the file as \|\|\|\| \|\| \| \|\|.

Obtain a `Writer` from `Files` to be able to write in the files.

Convert File Contents to Lowercase (Read and Write File) ★

Text conversions from one format to another are common operations.
   Exercise:

- Open a text file, read each character, convert it to lowercase, and write it to a new file. Write a method that does this and call it `convertFileToLowercase(Path inPath, Path outPath)`.

Convert PPM Graphics to ASCII Grayscale ★★★

Generating pixel graphics is always a bit more complex because of the different formats. However, there is *PPM (Portable Pixel Map)*, a simple ASCII-based file format. The specification (http://netpbm.source-forge.net/doc/ppm.html) is rather simple, and a Java program can easily generate PPM images. A disadvantage under Windows, however, is that third-party programs are required for display, such as the free software GIMP (https://www.gimp.org/).
   The following example shows the basic structure of a PPM file:

```
P3
3 2
255
255    0    0
  0  255    0
  0    0  255
255  255    0
255  255  255
  0    0    0
```

There are various tokens separated by white space. We define the following rules:

- The first token is the identifier P3.
- It is followed by the width and height of the image.
- The maximum color value follows, we always assume 255.
- Red, green, and blue values follow for all pixels from the top left to bottom right.
- Height and width and the color values are always positive.

Exercise:

- Parse a PPM file and retrieve all color values.
- Convert each color value into its corresponding grayscale value.
- Transform every pixel in the image into an ASCII symbol by assigning each grayscale value between 0 and 255 to a corresponding ASCII character.
- Allow in the program the parameterization of the conversion of the RGB values to the grayscale value, so that the algorithm is interchangeable.
- Allow the parameterization of the conversion from the grayscale value to the ASCII character.

For conversion to grayscale value, the following interface and constant can be used:

```
public interface RgbToGray {
  RgbToGray DEFAULT = (r, g, b) -> (r+g+b) / 3;
  int toGray( int r, int g, int b );
}
```

Java provides a mapping from (int, int) to an int with the IntBinaryOperator, but there is no functional interface that has three parameters.

Although the average method for converting a color image to grayscale is efficient, it may not accurately reflect how humans perceive color. To create a more realistic grayscale image, it is necessary to take into account that people perceive colors differently. One popular method for doing this is the *luminosity method*, which takes into account the relative contributions of each color channel to perceived brightness. Specifically, the luminosity method assigns weights to each color channel (red, green, and blue) based on their perceived contribution to luminance, with red given a weight of 0.21, green given a weight of 0.72, and blue given a weight of 0.07. By combining these weighted color channel values, the luminosity method produces a grayscale image that more closely matches how people perceive the original color image.

The interface IntUnaryOperator can be used very well for mapping a grayscale value (int) to an ASCII character (char, expanded to int). A default converter may look like this:

```
public enum GrayToAscii implements IntUnaryOperator {
  DEFAULT;

  private final char[] ASCII_FOR_SHADE_OF_GRAY =
    // black=0, white=255
    "@MBENRWDFQASUbehGmLOYkqgnsozCuJcry1v7lit{}?j|()=~!-/<>\"^_';,:`.
  ".toCharArray();
  private final int CHARS_PER_RGB = 256 / ASCII_FOR_SHADE_OF_GRAY.length;
  @Override public int applyAsInt( int gray ) {
    return ASCII_FOR_SHADE_OF_GRAY[ gray / CHARS_PER_RGB ];
  }
}
```

The given string[1] is 64 characters long. Basically, this means black becomes @, and white becomes a space

Example:

- The result for upper PPM is:
kkk
? @

Split Files (Read and Write Files) ★★

On Anaa Atoll, the port software has been running on a Commodore *PC-30* for about 40 years. Bonny Brain has manipulated the computer successfully, but now the software needs an update, which must be installed via floppy disks. 3.5-inch HD floppy disks can store 1,474,560 bytes (1440 KiB) by default. The software update doesn't fit on a floppy disk, so software is needed to break up a large file into several small files in a "disk-compatible" manner.

Exercise:

- Write a program that is passed a file name on the command line and then splits that file into numerous smaller parts.

Example:

- The call looks like this:

```
$ java com.tutego.exercise.io.FileSplitter Hanjaab.bin
```

If the file *Hanjaab.bin* is 2440 KiB in size, then the Java program will turn it into the files *Hanjaab.bin.1* and *Hanjaab.bin.2* with sizes 1440 KiB and 1000 KiB.

NESTING STREAMS

Streams can be nested like Russian dolls; one stream is the actual resource in the core, and other streams are wrapped around it like a hull. Operations that go through the wrappers eventually go into the core.

Quiz: DataInputStream and DataOutputStream ★

DataInputStream and DataOutputStream are decorators that enhance a simple InputStream and OutputStream, respectively.

- How are the `java.io.DataInputStream` and `java.io.DataOutputStream` classes implemented? Look into the implementation, either through the IDE or online at https://github.com/openjdk/jdk/blob/master/src/java.base/share/classes/java/io/DataInputStream.java and https://github.com/openjdk/jdk/blob/master/src/java.base/share/classes/java/io/DataOutputStream.java.
- What is the purpose of the `java.io.FilterInputStream` and `java.io.FilterOutputStream`, respectively?

Compress Number Sequences with the GZIPOutputStream ★

`java.util.zip.GZIPOutputStream` is a special output stream that compresses data without loss. Exercise:

- Create a compressed file with numbers from 0 to $<N$ written to a `GZIPOutputStream` using `writeLong(...)`.
- Compare the file sizes for different N.
- At which N is compression worthwhile?

SERIALIZATION

Java uses *serialization* to allow object states to be written to a data stream, and then later to recreate the object from a data stream; this process is called *deserialization*.

To convert Java objects to a binary stream and vice versa, the classes `ObjectOutputStream` and `ObjectInputStream` are used; all object types to be serialized must be `Serializable`. We will use the types in the next exercises and see practical examples of serialization.

Both classes are typical decorators: when serializing, the `ObjectOutputStream` determines the data and writes the serialized byte sequences to the `OutputStream` specified in the constructor—when reading, it is the other way around, here the `ObjectInputStream` reads from a passed `InputStream`.

(De)serialize Data for Chat and Convert It to Text ★★

A chat program should be used to transmit Java objects. However, the chat program can only transmit ASCII characters. Therefore, the objects must not only be (de)serialized but also converted to or from text format.

Exercise:

- Write a method `String objectToBase64(Object)` that serializes an object, then compresses it with a `DeflaterOutputStream` and returns it Base64 encoded.
- Write a method `deserializeObjectFromBase64(String)` that will wrap a Base64 encoded string into a byte stream, unpack it with the `InflaterInputStream`, and use it as a source for deserialization.

 To convert binary data into a string and vice versa, the `Base64.Encoder` and `Base64.Decoder` and especially the `wrap(...)` method can help.

Quiz: Requirement for Serialization ★

If we form an object from the following class `Inputs`, can we serialize it using the `ObjectOutputStream`? Or what preconditions might not be met?

```
class Inputs {
  public static class Input {
    String input;
  }
  public List<Input> inputs = new ArrayList<>();
}
```

Save Last Inputs ★★

Bonny Brain regularly uses the STRING2UPPERCASE application, which at its core looks like this:

```
for ( String line; (line = new Scanner( System.in ).nextLine()) != null; )
  System.out.println( line.toUpperCase() );
```

But now every user input should be stored in the file system so that at startup the application displays the input made.

Exercise:

- Set the following container for all inputs in the project:

  ```
  class Inputs implements Serializable {
    public static class Input implements Serializable {
      String input;
    }
    public List<Input> inputs = new ArrayList<>();
  }
  ```

- Whenever a user input is made, it shall be included in an `Inputs` object.
- After each input, `Inputs` shall be serialized to a file.
- When the application restarts, all serialized values shall be displayed on the screen at the beginning. Exceptions due to nonexistent files or wrong file formats can be logged, but shall be ignored.
- In `Input` change the data type `String` of the instance variable `input` to the data type `CharSequence`. Restart the program. What happens during the deserialization of `inputs`? Are there any problems?
- Set in `Inputs` and `Input` the line

  ```
  private static final long serialVersionUID = 1;
  ```

- Restart the program and serialize new data.
- In `Input` add the line

  ```
  LocalDateTime localDateTime = LocalDateTime.now();
  ```

  for an additional instance variable. Restart the program: what happens or doesn't happen?

SUGGESTED SOLUTIONS

Get the Number of Different Places (Read Files)

com/tutego/exercise/io/HammingDistance.java

```java
public static long distance( Path file1, Path file2 ) throws IOException {

  long filesize1 = Files.size( file1 );
  long filesize2 = Files.size( file2 );

  if ( filesize1 != filesize2 )
    throw new IllegalStateException(
        "File size is not equal, but %d for %s and %d for %s".formatted(
            filesize1, file1, filesize2, file2 ) );

  long result = 0;

  try ( Reader input1 = Files.newBufferedReader( file1 );
        Reader input2 = Files.newBufferedReader( file2 ) ) {

    for ( int i = 0; i < filesize1; i++ )
      if ( input1.read() != input2.read() )
        result++;
  }

  return result;
}
```

One important requirement is equal file size. Therefore, the program first retrieves the file sizes, compares them, and if they do not match, an `IllegalStateException` follows. The error message is very precise and conveys which file has which size, so outsiders can easily understand the error.

Assuming successful completion of the previous step, we will proceed to construct two resources for the corresponding files. We call the `Files` method `newBufferedReader(…)` for a `Reader`. There are two reasons for this method: first, we want to process strings and not binary streams, hence the `Reader` and not an `InputStream`. Second, buffering is important for performance reasons, and `newBufferedReader(…)` returns a `Reader` with an internal buffer. Individual characters are read from the internal buffer, and there is no file system access for each character, which would be slow.

Since we already know the number of characters, a loop runs and asks for one symbol from each of the two streams. If the symbols do not match, we increment a counter, which we return at the end.

The `try`-with-resources closes the two streams again, even if there should be an error in processing. The method does not handle exceptions, but passes them on to the caller. Errors can occur when requesting the file size, opening the file, and reading the character.

Convert Python Program to Java (Write File)

com/tutego/exercise/io/XorFractal.java

```java
final String filename = "xorpic.html";
try {
   try ( Writer out = Files.newBufferedWriter( Paths.get( filename ) );
         PrintWriter printer = new PrintWriter( out ) ) {

      printer.println( "<!DOCTYPE html>" );
      printer.println( "<html><body><svg width=\"256\" height=\"256\">" );

      for ( int x = 0; x < 256; x++ )
        for ( int y = 0; y < 256; y++ )
          printer.printf(
              "<rect x=\"%d\" y=\"%d\" width=\"1\" " +
              "height=\"1\" style=\"fill:rgb(0,%d,0);\" />",
              x, y, x ^ y );

      printer.println( "</svg></body></html>" );
   }
   Desktop.getDesktop().open( new File( filename ) );
}
catch ( IOException e ) {
   e.printStackTrace();
}
}
```

The Java and Python languages are entirely unique, and the libraries vary as well. Therefore, there is little in common in the code, almost everything is different.

There are several ways to write files in Java. The common classes are: `FileOutputStream`, `FileWriter`, `PrintWriter`, and `Formatter`. Types based on `OutputStream` are omitted because we would rather not write bytes, but Unicode characters. Since format strings are quite useful, `FileWriter` is dropped, and `Formatter` is left out because it can only write formatted strings, but not just strings without format strings.

Since something can always go wrong with input/output, the Java methods throw exceptions that we have to handle. This is what the first `try` block takes care of. It catches every `IOException`.

Files are resources that need to be closed; therefore, the creation of the resource is also put into a try-with-resources block. This particular block does not have a `catch` branch because it is supposed to try-with-resources only to close the resource again at the end—any error handling is handled by the outer `try-catch` block.

First, we build a `BufferedWriter`, then we decorate it with a `PrintWriter` so that we also have a method for writing formatted strings.

The next step is to write the prologue of the HTML file. In the two nested loops, `printf(...)` writes the SVG rectangle to the data stream. The three values in Python are the color values for RGB, where the red and blue parts are 0, so they remain unused. The program writes only the green part, as XOR of the coordinates x and y. The value ranges of x and y are between 0 and 255, and this also happens to be the maximum value for the 8-bit RGB color values.

After passing through the two loops, the try-with-resources block closes the open stream. The fact that the two `try` blocks are so strangely nested at first sight is because after the end of a successful write, the file is to be opened with a browser. However, we have to consider two peculiarities: The try-with-resources must first write and close the file before we are allowed to reopen it for viewing. And, we are only allowed to open the file if it was written without errors. If there was an error while writing, then there must be no opening of the file. This logic converts these two nested write blocks.

Generate Target Code (Write File)

com/tutego/exercise/io/Zielcode.java

```
private static final String[] ZIELCODE = {
    "|||||",       // 0000 = 0
    "||| ",        // 0001 = 1
    "|| |",        // 0010 = 2
    "||  ",        // 0011 = 3
    "| ||",        // 0100 = 4
    "| | ",        // 0101 = 5
    "|  |",        // 0110 = 6
    "  | |",       // not 0111 = 7 but 1010 = 10
    " |||",        // 1000 = 8
    " || " };      // 1001 = 9

public static void writeZielcode( String string, Writer writer )
    throws IOException {
  for ( int i = 0; i < string.length(); i++ ) {
    int value = Character.getNumericValue( string.charAt( i ) );
    if ( value >= 0 && value <= 9 ) {
      writer.write( ZIELCODE[ value ] );
      if ( i != string.length() - 1 )
        writer.write( "  " );
    }
  }
}
```

To solve the task, we need to loop a `String` character by character and map the character to the symbol sequence. There are different approaches. For example, we could compare the digit to a `switch-case` and then write the corresponding string to the `writer`. Another solution offers a map, which we can build up beforehand with a composite of characters with the target code. The proposed solution shown here uses an array, where the entries correspond exactly to the corresponding target codes of this position.

A `switch-case` can make a case distinction directly on the `char`, but for an index on the array we need the numeric value; here `Character.getNumericValue(...)` helps. The big advantage of this method is that it works for all digits in all languages. A valid result is in the value range between 0 and 9, with this number, you can access the array and then write the value into the `writer`. If we have not yet reached the last digit in the input string, two spaces are written as separators.

The listing contains comments for the array, which show well that the dashes and spaces are in principle nothing else than a binary representation of the number. An anomaly is the number 7, which is not represented as the predictable bit pattern 0111, but with 1010, i.e., symbolically _ | _ |; 1010, however would be the bit pattern for the number 10. If | _ _ were to represent 7, too much white space would be involved, which could irritate readers—again, the underscore is symbolic of space.

If we interpret the number as a bit pattern, then a slightly different solution can be programmed that does not require an array:

com/tutego/exercise/io/Zielcode.java

```
String string = "0123456789";
```

```
for ( int i = 0; i < string.length(); i++ ) {
   BigInteger v = new BigInteger(
       string.charAt( i ) == '7' ? "10"
                           : string.substring( i, i+1 ) );
   System.out.print ( v.testBit ( 3 ) ? ' ' : '|' );
   System.out.print ( v.testBit ( 2 ) ? ' ' : '|' );
   System.out.print ( v.testBit ( 1 ) ? ' ' : '|' );
   System.out.print ( v.testBit ( 0 ) ? ' ' : '|' );
   System.out.print ( "   " );
}
```

As usual, we iterate through the string, initially checking for the presence of a 7 at each position. If found, we replace the digit with the string "10". If the digit is not a seven, we extract a string of length 1 containing only the current character using substring(…). The result in both cases is a string. This string is passed into the BigInteger constructor for initialization. BigInteger has a handy method testBit(…) which answers with true or false whether a bit is set at a position or not. To complete the task, we simply need to retrieve the values of bits 3, 2, 1, and 0, and based on these values, set either a space or a vertical bar. Although this differs from the task requirements, we will output the results directly onto the screen.

Convert File Contents to Lowercase (Read and Write File)

com/tutego/exercise/io/ConvertFileToLowercase.java

```
private static final int EOF = -1;

static void convertFileToLowercase( String source, String target )
     throws IOException {
  convertFileToLowercase( Paths.get( source ), Paths.get( target ) );
}

static void convertFileToLowercase( Path source, Path target )
     throws IOException {
  try ( BufferedReader reader = Files.newBufferedReader( source );
        BufferedWriter writer = Files.newBufferedWriter( target ) ) {
    for ( int c; (c = reader.read()) != EOF; )
      writer.write( Character.toLowerCase( (char) c ) );
  }
}
```

The proposed solution first declares a private static variable EOF, which we will use later because we run through the file character by character and -1 signals that there are no more characters in the stream.

The actual method convertFileToLowercase(…) is overloaded once with the parameter type String and once with the parameter type Path. The variant with the filenames creates Path objects and delegates to the actual conversion, to the second method.

Given a Path for the input file and a Path for the output file, we can use the Files methods to request a Reader and Writer. Both objects have the nice property that they buffer automatically, so character-by-character processing is much faster than if Reader and Writer were not buffered. When reading, BufferedReader first creates an 8 KiB buffer, which is then filled to the maximum. Reading of single characters takes place from this buffer first. When writing, the same applies: first all data are collected in an internal buffer and when the buffer is full, the `BufferedWriter` writes the data of the buffer into the output stream below.

The `for` loop declares a variable c for the character to be read. In the condition expression of the `for` loop, the program first reads a character and assigns the result to the variable c; in the next step, it compares with EOF. The loop runs as long as characters can be read. In the body of the loop, the character is converted to an uppercase letter and written to the `Writer`.

Convert PPM Graphics to ASCII Gray Scale

com/tutego/exercise/io/PPM.java

```java
class PPM {

  public interface RgbToGray {
    RgbToGray DEFAULT = (r, g, b) -> (r+g+b) / 3;
    int toGray( int r, int g, int b );
  }

  public enum GrayToAscii implements IntUnaryOperator {
    DEFAULT;

    // black = 0, white = 255
    private static final char[] ASCII_FOR_SHADE_OF_GRAY =
        "@MBENRWDFQASUbehGmLOYkqgnsozCuJcry1v7lit{}?j|()=~!-/<>\"^_';,:`. "
          .toCharArray();
    private static final int CHARS_PER_RGB =
        256 / ASCII_FOR_SHADE_OF_GRAY.length;
    @Override public int applyAsInt( int gray ) {
      return ASCII_FOR_SHADE_OF_GRAY[ gray / CHARS_PER_RGB ];
    }
  }

  private static final String MAGIC_NUMBER = "P3";

  private PPM() { }

  private static String nextStringOrThrow( Scanner scanner, String msg ) {
    if ( ! scanner.hasNext() )
      throw new IllegalStateException( msg );
    return scanner.next();
  }

  private static int nextIntOrThrow( Scanner scanner, String msg ) {
    if ( ! scanner.hasNextInt() )
      throw new IllegalStateException( msg );
    int number = scanner.nextInt();
    if ( number < 0 )
      throw new IllegalStateException( "Value has to be positive but was "
                                        + number );
    return number;
  }

  public static void renderP3PpmImage( Readable input, RgbToGray rgbToGray,
                                       IntUnaryOperator grayToAscii,
```

```
                              Appendable output )

    throws IOException {

  Scanner scanner = new Scanner( input );
  // Header P3
  String magicNumber = nextStringOrThrow( scanner,
                                 "End of file, missing header" );
  if ( ! magicNumber.equals( MAGIC_NUMBER ) )
     throw new IllegalStateException( "No P3 image file, but " + magicNumber );

  // Width and Height
  int width = nextIntOrThrow( scanner,
                         "End of file or wrong format for width" );
  int height = nextIntOrThrow( scanner,
                         "End of file or wrong format for height" );

  // Max color value
  int maxVal = nextIntOrThrow( scanner,
                         "End of file or wrong format for max value" );
  if ( maxVal != 255 )
     throw new IllegalStateException(
         "Only the maximum color value 255 is allowed but was " + maxVal );

  // Matrix
  for ( int y = 0; y < height; y++ ) {
    for ( int x = 0; x < width; x++ ) {
      int r = nextIntOrThrow( scanner,
                         "End of file or wrong format for red value" );
      int g = nextIntOrThrow( scanner,
                         "End of file or wrong format for green value" );
      int b = nextIntOrThrow( scanner,
                         "End of file or wrong format for blue value" );
      int gray = rgbToGray.toGray( r, g, b );
      output.append( (char) grayToAscii.applyAsInt( gray ) );
    }
    output.append( '\n' );
  }
}

public static void renderP3PpmImage( Readable input, Appendable output )
    throws IOException {
  renderP3PpmImage( input, RgbToGray.DEFAULT, GrayToAscii.DEFAULT, output );
}
```

Since the class has only static methods, a constructor is not necessary, and it is set privately. The class does not store any object states.

For retrieving consecutive tokens, the class Scanner is useful. Two kinds of errors can occur: data can be missing in the stream, or the data type is wrong. Two helper methods nextStringOrThrow(...) and nextIntOrThrow(...) simplify the reading of strings and integers, respectively, and raise an exception if there is no token in the stream. The method for reading integers also checks whether the number is incorrectly negative, and also throws an IllegalStateException in that case.

Accessible from the outside are the two overloaded methods renderP3PpmImage(...). Let's start with the entire method first, which has four parameters:

1. A Readable input.
2. A RgbToGray mapping for converting RGB values to grayscale values.
3. An IntUnaryOperator mapping for converting grayscale values to ASCII values.
4. An Appendable output destination for writing the resulting ASCII art.

It is possible for the method to throw an IOException due to the inherent risks of input/output operations, which may result in errors during reading and writing.

The Scanner is connected to the Readable, which is the source from which it can read data. We fetch a token and expect a special header, P3. This is the only use of the nextStringOrThrow(...) method.

After reading the header, the height and width must follow. They must not be negative; however, the assignment 0 will not lead to an error, we want to allow that. Afterward, the largest possible color value is read in, which according to our definition must always be 255. In principle, the standard allows arbitrary values, but we simplify this.

Once we have the height and width, we can write two nested loops, each reading the three color tones. In principle, one loop would also suffice, but the program may want to refer to the x/y coordinates of the points later. After reading the RGB values, the converter function is called, and the grayscale tone is created, which then becomes the ASCII character via the next mapping. The result from the IntUnaryOperator is an int, which we convert to a char and write to the output stream. At the end of the line, we write a new line.

The second method, renderP3PpmImage(...) accesses the default implementations of the two mappings. Users of the library can choose to use the default converters or pass in their own images.

Split Files (Read and Write Files)

com/tutego/exercise/io/FileSplitter.java

```java
private static final int EOF = -1;

private static void splitFile( Path source, int size ) throws IOException {
    Objects.requireNonNull( source );
    Objects.checkIndex( size, Integer.MAX_VALUE );

    try ( InputStream fis = Files.newInputStream( source ) ) {
        byte[] buffer = new byte[ size ];
        for ( int cnt = 1, remaining;
              (remaining = fis.read( buffer )) != EOF;
              cnt++ ) {
            Path path = Paths.get( source + "." + cnt );
            try ( OutputStream fos = Files.newOutputStream( path ) ) {
                fos.write( buffer, 0, remaining );
            }
        }
    }
}

public static void main( String[] args ) {

    if ( args.length == 0 ) {
        System.err.println( "You need to specify a file name to split the file." );
        return;
    }
```

```
  try {
    String filename = args[ 0 ];
    splitFile( Paths.get( filename ), 1_474_560 );
  }
  catch ( IOException e ) {
    System.err.println( e.getMessage() );
  }
}
```

If we later work via the read(...) method, it will return -1 if no new bytes can be read. For this, we introduce a constant EOF.

Our splitFile(...) method takes a path to the file and the size. The path could be null and the index negative. Although an exception would be thrown later because of this, we want to check the correctness beforehand. Here we turn to two static methods of the Objects class.

If there are input/output exceptions in the following, splitFile(...) does not catch them—what should also the handling look like?—but passes them upward. There may be exceptions when opening the file, reading the contents, and writing.

In the first step, we open the file for reading. Since the file is to be processed byte by byte, we obtain an InputStream. This is a resource that the program has to close at the end in any case, so try-with-resources is used. Splitting can be done in two different ways: one possibility would be to open an OutputStream, read bytes from the InputStream, and write them to the OutputStream; this would be very memory efficient. The other option is chosen here and saves some program code, but bears the risk of an OutOfMemoryError because the solution reads in an entire byte array in one go, and this array is as large as the passed size. However, with the intended size of a floppy disk, this is not to be expected, and reading into the buffer and writing directly gives a good performance.

The size of the array is the size byte. We use the array repeatedly in the loop. In the loop, we declare two variables, once a counter for a generated file extension and a variable remaining for the number of actually read bytes from the input stream. The actual reading is implemented in the condition part of the for loop, and after the reading, we get the variable remaining updated, which is either -1 or contains the number of bytes read.

In the body of the loop, the byte array is written to the file. Files.newOutputStream(...) returns an output stream. The first argument to the method is a generated Path object that takes the file name and appends a counter after the dot. Using the the OutputStream's method write(byte[], int, int), the populated portion of the array is written to the file. If the loop is run multiple times, the byte array is guaranteed to be filled by the second to last run. In the last pass, probably not size many bytes are read, so fewer bytes of the array must be written, it is always remaining <= size.

The main(...) method checks if an argument was passed on the command line, and if so, file-Split(...) is called with the argument. We write exceptions to the error output channel.

Quiz: DataInputStream and DataOutputStream

The classes FilterInputStream, FilterOutputStream, FilterReader, and FilterWriter are useful superclasses for custom filters. These classes provide dual benefits: firstly, they retain the encapsulated stream object in an instance variable; and secondly, they eliminate the need to reimplement every method from the InputStream, OutputStream, Reader or Writer from the ground up. To understand this in more detail, let's take a look at the implementation of FilterOutputStream:

OpenJDK's implementation of FilterOutputStream

```java
package java.io;

public class FilterOutputStream extends OutputStream {
    protected OutputStream out;
    // some fields omitted

    public FilterOutputStream(OutputStream out) {
        this.out = out;
    }

    @Override
    public void write(int b) throws IOException {
        out.write(b);
    }

    @Override
    public void write(byte b[]) throws IOException {
        write(b, 0, b.length);
    }

    @Override
    public void write(byte b[], int off, int len) throws IOException {
        if ((off | len | (b.length - (len+off)) | (off+len)) < 0)
            throw new IndexOutOfBoundsException();

        for (int i = 0 ; i < len ; i++) {
            write(b[off + i]);
        }
    }

    // flush() / close() omitted
}
```

The code highlights that only the write(int) method forward data to the underlying stream, whereas the other two write(…) methods are simply wrappers that invoke the write(int) method. Custom filters are only obligated to override the write(int) method. However, for optimal performance, it is advisable to implement the other methods as well, since writing entire byte arrays in a single operation is faster than performing individual write operations for each element in the array.

DataInputStream and DataOutputStream are special filter classes, as the UML diagram shows in more detail at method level for DataInputStream; in addition, they implement DataInput and DataOutput.

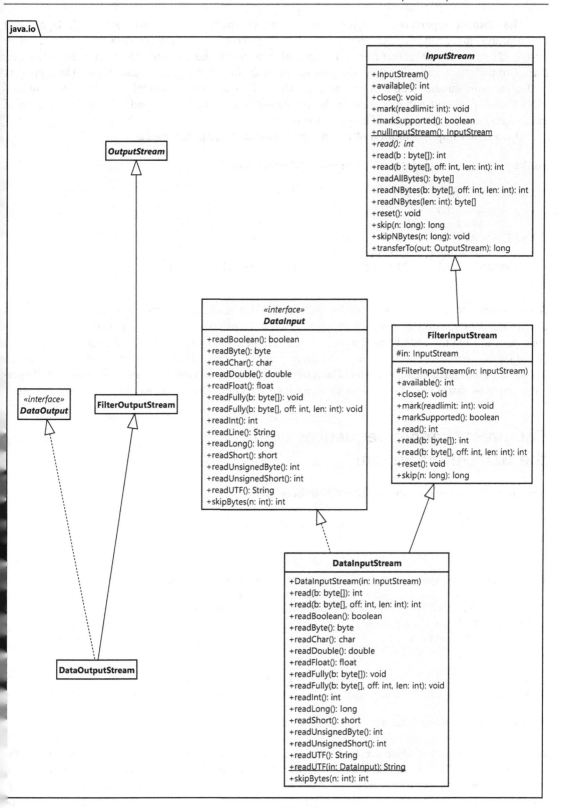

FIGURE 8.1   UML diagram.

The abstract superclasses `InputStream` and `OutputStream` work only with byte and byte arrays, just as the superclasses `Reader` and `Writer` handle only the data types char, char arrays, `String` or `CharBuffer`. The special feature of the classes `DataInputStream` and `DataOutputStream` is that they also provide methods for other primitive data types. Thus, integers or floating-point numbers can also be read and written. This is a typical example of a decorator that provides a more powerful API and goes for the simple methods in the background. The implementation of `readInt()` is a good example of how this works:

OpenJDK's implementation of `readInt()` from `DataInputStream`

```java
public final int readInt() throws IOException {
    int ch1 = in.read();
    int ch2 = in.read();
    int ch3 = in.read();
    int ch4 = in.read();
    if ((ch1 | ch2 | ch3 | ch4) < 0)
        throw new EOFException();
    return ((ch1 << 24) + (ch2 << 16) + (ch3 << 8) + (ch4 << 0));
}
```

A `DataInputStream` is a `FilterInputStream` that references in the protected variable in exactly the data stream that the `DataInputStream` wraps. To read an integer, four individual bytes must be read from the underlying resource. In the next step, the individual bytes must be positioned and added for the int. Very cleverly done is the query if one of the read(...) operations results in --1, which would mean the end of the data stream. The results from these operations are combined using an OR operation, ensuring that if any of the values were negative, the cumulative result would be negative as well..

Compress Number Sequences with the GZIPOutputStream

com/tutego/exercise/io/CompressLotOfNumbers.java

```java
Path tempFile = Files.createTempFile( "numbers", "bin.Z" );

final int n = 4;

try ( OutputStream     fos = Files.newOutputStream( tempFile );
      OutputStream     gos = new GZIPOutputStream( fos );
      DataOutputStream out = new DataOutputStream( gos ) ) {
  for ( int i = 0; i < n; i++ )
    out.writeLong( i );
}

System.out.println( "Uncompressed: " + n * Long.BYTES );
System.out.println( "Compressed:   " + Files.size( tempFile ) );

Files.delete( tempFile );
```

For example, we want to avoid creating a file in the current directory, but in the temp directory of the operating system. This should be deleted periodically, and therefore we try in Java to delete the temporary file again at the end of the program. After initializing the constant n, which we can easily change later, for example, we build up to three streams, which are nested. Since all these streams are of type

AutoCloseable, we use a `try` with resources. The nested streams are like nested rings: in the innermost ring is the output stream, which writes to files. Around it is a stream that compresses: everything written to the GZIPOutputStream is compressed and then written to the file stream. The last ring is the decorator, with a more powerful API. Therefore, the data type in the try-with-resources is no longer OutputStream, but DataOutputStream because it has the desired writeLong(long) method. DataOutputStream wraps around the compressing data stream. If we write something into the DataOutputStream, the data are passed to the GZIPOutputStream. The GZIPOutputStream passes the data to the output stream so that it is written.

In the loop, we write *n* numbers. In the end, we calculate how big the file would be if the data were not compressed. We don't need to create an actual file to do this; we can easily calculate the file size. To get the compressed size, we resort to the `Files.size(...)` method; another solution would have been to count the number of bytes flowing through the streams right away—but we didn't do that here.

The uncompressed size of the file would be 8,000,000 bytes, the compressed size of 2,129,303 bytes. Since the data are written as `long`, many bits are 0. Generated are the bit patterns (the last number stands for 999999, spaces separate the byte blocks):

```
00000000 00000000 00000000 00000000
00000000 00000000 00000000 00000001
..
00000000 00001111 01000010 00111110
00000000 00001111 01000010 00111111
```

The compressed file is about a quarter of the original size. Compression of this particular sequence is worthwhile for four or more `long` elements.

(De)serialize Data for Chat and Convert Them to Text

The solution consists of two parts: a method for mapping an object to a string, and a mapping of a string representation back to an object. Let's start with the mapping to a string:

com/tutego/exercise/io/ObjectBase64.java

```java
public static String serializeObjectToBase64( Object object ) {
  ByteArrayOutputStream baos = new ByteArrayOutputStream();

  try ( OutputStream b64os     = Base64.getEncoder().wrap( baos );
        OutputStream dos        = new DeflaterOutputStream( b64os );
        ObjectOutputStream oos = new ObjectOutputStream( dos ) ) {
    oos.writeObject( object );
  }
  catch ( IOException e ) {
    throw new IllegalStateException( e );
  }

  return baos.toString( StandardCharsets.US_ASCII );
```

The ObjectOutputStream writes the bytes to a DeflaterOutputStream, which compresses the bytes and then passes them on to an OutputStream of the Base64 class. The API is a bit unusual because normally the target is specified in the constructor of the classes; however, for the Base64 encoder and decoder, this is the wrap(...) method. The Base64 conversion writes to a ByteArrayOutputStream. To summarize: if writeObject(Object) writes to the ObjectOutputStream, the data go to the DeflaterOutputStream, then to the Base64 encoder, and finally to the ByteArrayOutputStream.

The mapping succeeds, or there is an exception, which is caught and terminates the processing as `IllegalStateException`, a runtime exception. If the `ByteArrayOutputStream` contains the data, `toString(...)` returns the result. The resulting strings consist of pure ASCII characters, so US _ ASCII encoding can be used.

The reverse step turns a string into an object.

com/tutego/exercise/io/ObjectBase64.java

```java
public static Object deserializeObjectFromBase64( String string ) {
  final byte[] bytes = string.getBytes( StandardCharsets.US_ASCII );

  try ( ByteArrayInputStream bis = new ByteArrayInputStream( bytes );
        InputStream b64is       = Base64.getDecoder().wrap( bis );
        InputStream iis         = new InflaterInputStream( b64is );
        ObjectInputStream ois   = new ObjectInputStream( iis ) ) {
    return ois.readObject();
  }
  catch ( IOException | ClassNotFoundException e ) {
    throw new IllegalStateException( e );
  }
}
```

We need to generate an `InputStream` from the `String` so that the `ObjectInputStream` class can be used. This is a bit of a problem because Java does not provide a natural way to use the `String` as a source for an `InputStream`. Open-source libraries such as Google Guava or Apache Commons have solutions here, for example, in the form of the Apache class `CharSequenceInputStream`. Java inherently offers only the other direction, for example with an `InputStreamReader`, which adapts an `InputStream` into a `Reader`, not lets a `Reader` be represented as an `InputStream`. Therefore, a `StringReader`, which is usually used when a string must appear as a `Reader`, does not help us either.

The chosen solution converts the string into a `byte` array. This is not satisfactory, since the input is run twice, once by the conversion and another time by reading from the stream. On the other hand, this should have little practical relevance, and the bit of extra memory is not a burden for our use case.

After converting to a `byte[]`, `ByteArrayInputStream` creates the desired `InputStream`. The input stream consisting of ASCII characters becomes a `byte` stream via the decoder of `Base64`. The `InflaterInputStream` unpacks the data, and finally the `ObjectInputStream` reconstructs the object via `readObject()`. The serialized stream contains an identifier in which the data type is to be reconstructed. This data type could in principle not exist on this virtual machine, which is why a `ClassNotFoundException` is thrown in this case. Just like a possible `IOException` we catch these checked exceptions and create an unchecked exception.

Quiz: Requirement for Serialization

An instance of `Inputs` cannot be serialized because `Inputs` and `Input` do not implement the `Serializable` interface. Correct would be:

```java
class Inputs implements Serializable {
  public static class Input implements Serializable {
    String input;
  }
  public List<Input> inputs = new ArrayList<>();
}
```

The mechanism for serialization traverses an object graph recursively, and all elements must be serializable. In our example:

1. Serialize `Inputs`. Is the class `Serializable`? Yes, then serialize the `ArrayList inputs`.
2. Serialize `ArrayList`. Is the class `Serializable`? Yes, then serialize internally the array of `inputs` entries.
3. Serialize `Input`. Is the class `Serializable`? Yes, then serialize the instance variable `String input`.
4. Serialize `String`. Is the class `Serializable`? Yes, then serialize the strings.

Primitive data types are serialized automatically, regardless of their visibility. However, static variables, including those marked as `transient`, are not serialized. Certain fundamental Java types, such as `String`, are inherently `Serializable`. Additionally, arrays and enumerations can also be serialized.

Save Last Inputs

The task consists of a series of statements, but one question needs to be asked and answered before presenting the proposed solution: What happens when an attribute data type changes and an object is to be deserialized on the data stream? The answer is:

```
java.io.InvalidClassException: com.tutego.exercise.net.Inputs$Input; local
class incompatible: stream classdesc serialVersionUID=-8691588030053894297,
local class serialVersionUID=6463495757449665144
```

There is an exception that reports an incompatible `serialVersionUID`. The background is the following: each class has an identifier, the *serial version UID*. This UID (*Unique Identifier*) is either statically fixed in the class, or it is dynamically calculated. Since an own UID is not available in the class from the task, the serializer calculates the UID similar to a hash code, only not from the allocations, but from the types. This happens on read and write; if an object is serialized, this UID is also written to the data stream. When reading, the deserializer checks whether the UID in the data stream matches the UID of the class. If there were structural changes, for example, the change of a data type, the dynamic UID changes. This is precisely what the exception indicates. The two values represent the UID from the data stream and the calculated UID of the changed class.

If structural changes are not supposed to lead to an exception, a UID must be set manually in the code. This brings us to the proposed solution.

com/tutego/exercise/io/InputHistory.java

```java
class Inputs implements Serializable {
  @Serial private static final long serialVersionUID=1;

  public static class Input implements Serializable {
    private static final long serialVersionUID=1;
    CharSequence input;
    LocalDateTime localDateTime=LocalDateTime.now();
  }

  public List<Input> inputs=new ArrayList<>();
```

`Inputs` and also the nested class `Input` both contain the private static `serialVersionUID`. The actual value assigned to this field is not significant. The `serialver` tool included with the JDK generates the same UID that is written to the data stream even if serialVersionUID is missing. If there is a serialVersionUID and in the data stream the UID matches that of the class, deserialization is more relaxed: unknown attributes in the data stream are ignored, and attributes where the data type has changed are also skipped.

CharSequence is an interface, and interfaces do not usually extend Serializable. Since type checking occurs at runtime and String implements the Serializable interface, there is no error. Nevertheless, String and CharSequence result in different UIDs.

The main program is embedded in the class InputHistory. The constructor of the class reads a file and deserializes the input. Another method, addAndSave(...), updates Inputs and serializes the result to a file. The main(...) method ties everything together.

com/tutego/exercise/io/InputHistory.java

```java
public class InputHistory {

  private final static Path FILENAME =
      Paths.get( System.getProperty( "java.io.tmpdir" ),
                 "String2Uppercase.ser" );

  private Inputs inputs;

  InputHistory() {
    try ( InputStream        is = Files.newInputStream( FILENAME );
          ObjectInputStream ois = new ObjectInputStream( is ) ) {
      inputs = (Inputs) ois.readObject();
      inputs.inputs.forEach( input -> System.out.println( input.input ) );
    }
    catch ( IOException | ClassNotFoundException e ) {
      inputs = new Inputs();
      e.printStackTrace();
    }
  }

  void addAndSave( String string ) {
    Inputs.Input newInput = new Inputs.Input();
    newInput.input = string;
    inputs.inputs.add( newInput );

    try ( OutputStream        os = Files.newOutputStream( FILENAME );
          ObjectOutputStream oos = new ObjectOutputStream( os ) ) {
      oos.writeObject( inputs );
    }
    catch ( IOException e ) {
      e.printStackTrace();
    }
  }

  public static void main( String[] args ) {
    InputHistory inputHistory = new InputHistory();
    for ( String line;
          (line = new Scanner( System.in ).nextLine()) != null; ) {
      inputHistory.addAndSave( line );
      System.out.println( line.toUpperCase() );
    }
  }
}
```

The class has two instance variables: the file name and a reference inputs to the inputs. The constructor opens an InputStream for the file and initializes the ObjectInputStream with it. readObject(...) starts deserialization, and if there is an exception, it is caught and a new Inputs object is built. If Inputs could be reconstructed, all strings are output via the forEach(...) method of the list.

The addAndSave(String) method creates a new Inputs object, sets the passed string into this object, and appends the new Inputs object to the inputs list. Then the list is serialized via the ObjectOutputStream. Errors should not occur unless there are file system problems.

The main(...) method creates an InputHistory object, which activates the constructor that deserializes the file. At the very first start, this file does not exist, an exception is thrown, but the program is not aborted. In the following, the file is created and grows by console input and saving. At the next program start, the deserialization should work and the last entered strings should appear on the screen.

NOTE

---

1 The string is a simplification of https://www.pouet.net/topic.php?which=8056&page=1.

Network Programming

9

Access to the network is as common nowadays, just like access to the local file system. Since Java 1.0 Java offers a network API for developing client–server applications. The Java library can establish encrypted connections and also bring support for the *Hypertext Transfer Protocol* (HTTP). The exercises in this chapter are about getting resources from a web server and developing a small client–server application with its protocol.

Prerequisites

- Know the URI and URL classes.
- Know input/output streams.
- Be able to read Internet resources.
- Be able to implement client and server with Socket and ServerSocket.

Data types used in this chapter:

- java.net.URL
- java.net.Socket
- java.net.ServerSocket
- javax.net.SocketFactory
- javax.net.ServerSocketFactory
- java.net.DatagramSocket

URL AND URLCONNECTION

In Java, the obvious class URL represents a URL and URI a URI. An HTTP connection can be opened via URL; internally this is handled by the class URLConnection.

Both classes are not very convenient for modern HTTP calls; only in Java 11, a new package java. net.http has been added with HttpClient in the core. Java enterprise frameworks have more solutions, and there are many alternatives in the open-source universe as well:

- Client API in Jakarta EE.
- RestClient in Spring.
- OkHttp.
- Apache HttpClient.
- Feign and Retrofit.

DOI: 10.1201/9781003495550-1

Download Remote Images via URL ★

The URL class provides a method that returns an InputStream so that the bytes of the resource can be read.

Captain CiaoCiao likes to relax with pictures of well-shaped ships on shiphub.com. He would like to have some pictures on his storage device so that he has something to daydream about on long voyages.
Task:

- For a given URL, write a program that downloads the resource and stores it on the local file system.
- The file name should be based on the URL.

Read Remote Text File from URL ★

The *Center for Systems Science and Engineering (CSSE)* at Johns Hopkins University publishes a CSV file of Covid disease data around the world every day at https://github.com/CSSEGISandData/COVID-19/tree/master/csse_covid_19_data/csse_covid_19_daily_reports. For March 1, 2021, the URL on the server is: https://raw.githubusercontent.com/CSSEGISandData/COVID-19/master/csse_covid_19_data/csse_covid_19_daily_reports/03-01-2021.csv.

The file starts with

```
FIPS,Admin2,Province_State,Country_Region,Last_Update,Lat,Long_,Confirmed,Dea
ths,Recovered,Active,Combined_Key,Incidence_Rate,Case-Fatality_Ratio
,,,Afghanistan,2020-10-22
04:24:27,33.93911,67.709953,40510,1501,33824,5185,Afghanistan,
104.06300129769207,3.7052579609972844
,,,Albania,2020-10-22 04:24:27,41.1533,20.1683,17948,462,10341,
7145,Albania,623.6708596844812,2.574102964118565
,,,Algeria,2020-10-22 04:24:27,28.0339,1.6596,55081,1880,38482,
14719,Algeria,125.60932701190256,3.4131551714747372
```

Task:

- Create a new class CoronaData with a new method String findByDateAndSearchTerm(LocalDate date, String search).
  - findByDateAndSearchTerm(...) should build a URL object with the date. Note that the filename has the order month, day, and year.
  - Open an input stream of the generated URL, read the stream line by line, and filter out all lines that do not contain the passed substring search.
  - The result is a string with all lines containing the search word, no need for a CSV parser.

Example:

- The call findByDateAndSearchTerm(LocalDate.of(2023, Month.MARCH, 9), "Miguel") returns from the remote CSV document all Corona numbers from the given day that contain "Miguel".
- Sample return:
  ```
  8113,San Miguel,Colorado,US,2020-10-22 04:24:27,
  38.00450883,-108.4020725,100,0,0,100,"San Miguel, Colorado,
  US",1222.643354933366,0.0
  ```

```
35047,San Miguel,New Mexico,US,2020-10-22 04:24:27,
35.48014807,-104.8163562,151,0,0,151,"San Miguel,
New Mexico, US",553.5799391428677,0.0
```

If the CORONA numbers go down, CSSE may stop publishing new documents. The old documents should stay.

HTTP CLIENT

Although URLConnection can be used to make an HTTP request, changing the HTTP method (GET, POST, PUT …) and setting headers, this is not comfortable. Therefore, the HTTP client was added in Java 11. With the new API, HTTP resources can be obtained more elegantly over the network. Moreover, the HTTP client supports HTTP/1.1 and HTTP/2 as well as synchronous and asynchronous programming models. In the next chapter on file formats, we will also return to the HTTP client in the exercises, since JSON or XML is often exchanged.

Top News from Hacker News ★★

Hacker News is a website with up-to-date discussions of technology trends. Articles can be accessed via a web service, and documentation can be found at https://github.com/HackerNews/API. Two endpoints are:

- https://hacker-news.firebaseio.com/v0/topstories.json: returns a JSON array with IDs of the most discussed articles.
- https://hacker-news.firebaseio.com/v0/item/24857356.json: returns a JSON object containing the message with ID 24857356.

Task:

- Create a new class HackerNews.
- Implement a new method long[] hackerNewsTopStories() which will
  - connect with the HTTP client to the endpoint https://hacker-news.firebaseio.com/v0/top-stories.json,
  - split the return from the JSON into long,
  - return all IDs as long[].
  - In case of an IO error, an empty array should be returned.
- Implement a new method String news(long id) that returns as a string the complete JSON document.

Example:

- The class with the two methods can be used like this:
  ```
  System.out.println( Arrays.toString( hackerNewsTopStories() ) );
  String newsInJson=news( 24857356 );
  System.out.println( newsInJson );
  ```

SOCKET AND SERVERSOCKET

Operating systems provide sockets for TCP/UDP communication; Java can use them via the classes

- `java.net.Socket` and `java.net.ServerSocket` for TCP and
- `java.net.DatagramSocket` for UDP.

Objects of `Socket` and `ServerSocket` are created via the constructor or even better via the factories `javax.net.SocketFactory` and `javax.net.ServerSocketFactory`; for UDP there is no factory.

Implement a Swear Server and a Client ★★

Bonny Brain is going to participate in the next swearing contest soon. She wants to prepare perfectly. A server should run an application that manages slurs, and clients can connect to this slur server and search for sentences.
Task:

- Write a server and client.
- Customize the server to accept multiple connections; use a thread pool.
- The thread pool should use a maximum number of threads to prevent denial-of-service (DOS) attacks. If the maximum number of concurrent connections is exhausted, a client must wait until another connection becomes available.

Example:

- After starting the server and client, an interaction may look like this:
```
sir
You, sir, are an oxygen thief!
an
You, sir, are an oxygen thief!
Stop trying to be a smart ass, you're just an ass.
```

Implement a Port Scanner ★★

Bonny Brain installs the new Ay! OS, but important analysis tools are missing. It needs a tool that detects and reports the occupied TCP/UDP ports.
Task:

- Write a program that tries to register a `ServerSocket` and `DatagramSocket` on all TCP/UDP ports from 0 to 49151; if it succeeds, the port is free. Otherwise, it is busy.
- Display the occupied ports on the console, and in addition, for the known ports, a description of the usual service that occupies that port.

Example:

- The output might look like this:

```
Protocol    Port        Service
TCP         135         EPMAP
UPD         137         NetBIOS Name Service
UPD         138         NetBIOS Datagram Service
TCP         139         NetBIOS Session Service
TCP         445         Microsoft-DS Active Directory
TCP         843         Adobe Flash
UPD         1900        Simple Service Discovery Protocol (SSDP)
UPD         3702        Web Services Dynamic Discovery
TCP         5040
UPD         5050
UPD         5353        Multicast DNS
UPD         5355        Link-Local Multicast Name Resolution (LLMNR)
TCP         5939
TCP         6463
TCP         6942
TCP         17500       Dropbox
UPD         17500       Dropbox
TCP         17600
TCP         27017       MongoDB
UPD         42420
```

A *network interface* connects computers via a computer network. In the following, we always assume a TCP/UDP interface. The network interface does not have to be physical, but can also be implemented in software. Like the loopback interface with the IP 127.0.0.1 (IPv4) or ::1 (IPv6). Typical network interfaces continue to exist for the LAN or WLAN. Operating system tools can display all network interfaces such as ipconfig /all under Windows or ip a under Linux. In Java, the network interfaces can be retrieved via java.net.NetworkInterface. Each network interface has its IP address.

To register a server socket there are two possibilities: either the service only accepts requests from a special local InetAddress or the service accepts requests from all local addresses. So, in principle it is possible to bind the same port several times on one network card, because on one network card any number of network interfaces can be configured because they have distinguishable IP addresses.

The solution of the task can perform a simple test and register the socket on all network interfaces; if this fails, a service was already active on one of the network interfaces. This is enough for us as a criterion that on some network interface the port is busy.

SUGGESTED SOLUTIONS

Download Remote Images via URL

com/tutego/exercise/net/ImageDownloader.java

```java
public static void downloadImage( URL url ) throws IOException {
  try ( InputStream inputStream = url.openStream() ) {
    String filename = url.toString().replaceAll( "[^a-zA-Z0-9_.-]",
                                                 "_" );
```

```
        Files.copy( inputStream, Paths.get( filename ),
                StandardCopyOption.REPLACE_EXISTING );
    }
}
```

The solution involves three steps.

1. The URL object returns an `InputStream` for the bytes of the resource with `openStream()`. Since you should close what you open, we put the opening of the stream in a `try`-with-resource block.
2. The name of the target file is derived from the URL. We have to be a bit careful with the file-name because not every character in the URL is always a valid character for a filename. The Wikipedia page https://en.wikipedia.org/wiki/Filename#Comparison_of_filename_limitations summarizes the special characters for some file systems. Furthermore, not all characters may appear in a URL, but even the simple path separator / will cause problems. Therefore, we replace all problematic characters. The regular expression `[^a-zA-Z0-9 _ .-]` chosen in the solution replaces all characters that are not letters, digits, _ , . or - with an underscore. This gives a safe filename for each file system. However, the URLs are not unique because, for example, the URLs `https://www.penisland.net/?;` and `https://www.penisland.net/?,` would become `http___www.penisland.net___`.
3. The second step elegantly uses the `copy(...)` method of the `Files` class. There are two of these: one for reading from a file and writing to an `OutputStream`, and one for reading all data from an `InputStream` and writing to a file—this is the version we use. All bytes are read from the `InputStream` and written to the new destination file. The third parameter at `copy(...)` is a vararg and stands for attributes: `StandardCopyOption.REPLACE_EXISTING` states, that existing files will be overwritten, otherwise there will be an exception at existing files.

Read Remote Text File from URL

om/tutego/exercise/net/CoronaData.java

```
private static final String URL_FORMAT_STRING =
    "https://raw.githubusercontent.com/CSSEGISandData/COVID-19/master/"
  + "csse_covid_19_data/csse_covid_19_daily_reports/%s.csv";

public static String findByDateAndSearchTerm( LocalDate date, String search )

  DateTimeFormatter MMddyyyy = DateTimeFormatter.ofPattern( "MM-dd-yyyy" );
  String url = URL_FORMAT_STRING.formatted( date.format( MMddyyyy ) );

  try ( var is =URI.create(url).toURL().openStream();
        var isr =new InputStreamReader(is, StandardCharsets.UTF_8);
        var br =new BufferedReader( isr ) ) {
    return br.lines()
            .filter( line -> line.contains( search ) )
            .collect( Collectors.joining( "\n" ) );
  }
  catch ( MalformedURLException e ) {
    System.err.println( "Malformed URL format of "+url );
  }
  catch ( IOException e ) {
    e.printStackTrace();
  }
  return "";
```

The first step is to build the URL. The URL contains the date, which we receive as a parameter. However, it is not possible to call toString() method directly on the LocalDate object because that returns a string according to the ISO 8601 notation; the smart *Center for Systems Science and Engineering* uses a different order when specifying the date segments. The program, therefore, builds up its own date formatting with the DateTimeFormatter by placing the month first, followed by the day, and then the year.

From this dynamically generated string, a URL object is built and the central method openStream() is called, which returns an InputStream. Since we want to read character by character, we convert this binary InputStream into a Reader. For line-by-line reading, the BufferedReader is well suited, in particular, the lines() method is handy, which returns a Stream<String>. Using a filter, we leave the lines in the stream that contain the search string, and finally concatenate all the lines into one big string, which we return.

Two possible exceptions are possible: the URL may be formed incorrectly, in which case there is a MalformedURLException, or there are connection errors or errors during the read. We catch these exceptions, print messages on the screen, and return an empty string since nothing was found even in the error case.

Top News from Hacker News

com/tutego/exercise/net/HackerNews.java

```java
private static final HttpClient client = HttpClient.newHttpClient();

public static long[] hackerNewsTopStories() {
  String url = "https://hacker-news.firebaseio.com/v0/topstories.json";
  HttpRequest request = HttpRequest
      .newBuilder( URI.create( url ) )
      .timeout( Duration.ofSeconds( 5 ) )
      .build();

  try {
    HttpResponse<InputStream> response =
        client.send( request, HttpResponse.BodyHandlers.ofInputStream() );
    var scanner = new Scanner( response.body() ).useDelimiter( "[,\\[\\]]" );
    return scanner.tokens().mapToLong( Long::parseLong ).toArray();
  }
  catch ( IOException | InterruptedException e ) {
    e.printStackTrace();
    return new long[ 0 ];
  }
}
```

com/tutego/exercise/net/HackerNews.java

```java
public static String news( long id ) {
  String url = "https://hacker-news.firebaseio.com/v0/item/" + id + ".json";
  HttpRequest request = HttpRequest
      .newBuilder( URI.create( url ) )
      .timeout( Duration.ofSeconds( 5 ) )
      .build();

  try {
    return client.send( request, HttpResponse.BodyHandlers.ofString() )
               .body();
  }
  catch ( IOException | InterruptedException e ) {
    e.printStackTrace();
```

```
    return "";
  }
}
```

For our example, we create a HttpClient as a class variable. Since our two methods are static, it is convenient to preconfigure the object. If object methods should access the HttpClient, and this still from several threads, then each thread should use its own HttpClient object.

The send(...) method has two parameters:

```
<T> HttpResponse<T> send(HttpRequest request,
                         HttpResponse.BodyHandler<T> responseBodyHandler)
    throws IOException, InterruptedException;
```

The first thing to do is to build and configure an HttpRequest for the individual request. This can be done with HttpRequest.newBuilder() and HttpRequest.newBuilder(URI); the second version saves the later call to uri(...). The timeout is optional and is set to 5 seconds by the program. The final build() method returns the HttpRequest object, which is executed by the HttpClient. This is the principle of the API: different HttpRequest calls run over the HttpClient once it is built and configured.

The second parameter of the send(...) method determines how the result should be fetched. For the following Scanner an InputStream is handy, which HttpResponse.BodyHandlers.ofInputStream() requests. From the HttpResponse<InputStream> response we read the content with body(), where the body is not the data for now, but just an InputStream of that data. This InputStream configures the Scanner. Encoding is not necessary in our case, because the JSON document consists of pure ASCII characters. However, the Scanner is configured with a delimiter that sees [and , and] as delimiters. The Scanner provides the useful method tokens() which gives us a stream of all tokens, in our case the numbers. mapToLong(...) converts any textual representation of a number into a LongStream, and toArray() returns all elements of the stream as an array. If there are any errors, they are caught, reported, and an empty array is returned.

The second method, news(long id), builds the HttpRequest with a concrete ID for a message. The implementation is a bit simpler because we don't need to parse the output, and HttpResponse.BodyHandlers.ofString() determines that a string is returned as the result.

JSON documents from web services will generally be converted to Java objects. We'll look at how to do this in the next chapter.

Implement a Swear Server and a Client

The server's job is to respond to incoming connections and pick out any insults that have a partial string.
com/tutego/exercise/net/SlangingMatchServer.java

```java
public class SlangingMatchServer {

  private static final int PORT = 10_000;

  public static void main( String[] args ) throws IOException {
    Executor executor = new ThreadPoolExecutor( 0, MAXIMUM_POOL_SIZE, 60,
TimeUnit.SECONDS, new SynchronousQueue<>() );
    try ( ServerSocket serverSocket =
              ServerSocketFactory.getDefault().createServerSocket( PORT ) ) {
      System.out.println( "Server running at port "+serverSocket.
getLocalPort() );

      while ( ! Thread.currentThread().isInterrupted() ) {
        Socket socket = serverSocket.accept();
```

```
          Thread.ofVirtual().start( () -> handleConnection( socket ) );
      }
    }
  }
  private static void handleConnection( Socket socket ) {
    try ( socket;
          Scanner requestReader =
              new Scanner( socket.getInputStream(), UTF_8 );
          PrintWriter responseWriter =
              new PrintWriter( socket.getOutputStream(),
                                  true, UTF_8 ) ) {
      String request = requestReader.nextLine();
      responseWriter.println( searchInsult( request ) );
    }
    catch ( IOException e ) {
      e.printStackTrace();
    }
  }

  private static String searchInsult( String search ) {
    return Stream.of( "You, sir, are an oxygen thief!",
                      "Stop trying to be a smart ass, you're just an ass.",
                      "Shock me, say something intelligent." )
             .filter( s -> s.toLowerCase().contains( search.toLowerCase()
) )
             .collect( Collectors.joining( "\n" ) );
  }
}
```

The main(...) method prepares a server socket on the predefined port 10,000, enters an infinite loop that can in principle be terminated with an interrupt, and waits for an incoming connection. The thread blocks at accept(), and the block does not unblock until there is an incoming client. In that case, a lightweight virtual thread will handle our handleCollection(...) method.

If accept() returns, the return is the client socket, and that becomes the argument of handle-Connection(...). We move the call to handleConnection(...) to a Runnable and that is passed to the virtual thread, and so executed in the background. While the thread handles the client server communication in the background, the infinite loop goes back to accept() to quickly serve the next interested party. At this point, we are not allowed to close the socket, so it must not say:

```
try ( Socket socket = serverSocket.accept() ) {
  executor.execute( () -> handleConnection( socket ) );
}
```

The processing is asynchronous! The close() from the try-with-resources would otherwise be right after sending via execute(...) and consequently the Socket would be closed quickly while handle-Connection(...) has just started communicating.

Let's have a look at handleConnection(...): a Socket is AutoCloseable, and the try-with-resources closes the Socket at the end. We have the unusual case here that we don't actually need to declare a new resource variable, but the abbreviated notation is only allowed since Java 9.

In communication, input and output streams are necessary. These are also resources to be closed via try-with resources. A string is read from the input stream, searched for the insulting word, and the result is written back. The protocol requires strings to go over the wire, so the InputStream and OutputStream are upgraded to character-oriented types. The Scanner can be built in the constructor with an InputStream and an encoding and can then read a line with nextLine(). We write the output to a PrintWriter; again, the constructor can accept the OutputStream and the encoding. The second argument true is important because it controls the flushing of the buffer on an end-of-line character. println (...) writes the result to the PrintWriter, the line feed signals the flushing of the buffer. The catch block ends the try-with-resources, and all resources are closed and the socket is returned to the operating system as a native resource.

The utility method searchInsult(...) checks if the search word is contained in the given strings, and concatenates all results with a newline.

The client has a similar logic, but of course, it doesn't have to listen for incoming connections, it establishes them.

com/tutego/exercise/net/SlangingMatchClient.java

```java
public class SlangingMatchClient {

  private static final String HOST = "localhost";
  private static final int    PORT = 10_000;

  public static void main( String[] args ) throws IOException {
    while ( true ) {
      String request = new Scanner( System.in ).nextLine();
      remoteSearchInsult( request );
    }
  }

  private static void remoteSearchInsult( String search ) throws IOException
  {
    try ( Socket socket = SocketFactory.getDefault().createSocket( HOST, PORT );
          PrintWriter requestWriter =
              new PrintWriter( socket.getOutputStream(), true,
                               StandardCharsets.UTF_8 );
          BufferedReader responseReader = new BufferedReader(
              new InputStreamReader( socket.getInputStream(),
                                     StandardCharsets.UTF_8 ) ) ) {
      requestWriter.println( search );
      System.out.println(
        responseReader.lines().collect( Collectors.joining( "\n" ) )
      );
    }
  }
}
```

The main(...) method contains an infinite loop, asks the user for a string, and passes it to remoteSearchInsult(String). The new method is responsible for communication with the server.

In the first step, the socket factory returns a socket object for localhost and the desired port. Sockets are native resources that must be returned to the operating system at the end; closing them is handled as usual by a try-with-resources block, which also closes the input/output streams.

Writing the string is again done by PrintWriter. The client uses a BufferedReader for reading, since it has the advantage of providing a stream of lines with the lines() method. The lines read in are joined with a Collector and printed. You cannot connect a Reader directly to an InputStream, so the InputStreamReader decorator is needed to enable the Reader API on an InputStream.

Implement a Port Scanner

The PortScanner class accesses its own Protocol enumeration, with TCP and UDP constants, a packet-visible object method isAvailable(int), the abstract helper method openSocket(int), and the static method serviceName(int).

com/tutego/exercise/net/PortScanner.java

```java
enum Protocol {
  TCP {
    @Override AutoCloseable openSocket( int port ) throws IOException {
      return ServerSocketFactory.getDefault().createServerSocket( port );
    }
  },
  UDP {
    @Override AutoCloseable openSocket( int port ) throws IOException {
      return new DatagramSocket( port );
    }
  };

  abstract AutoCloseable openSocket( int port ) throws IOException;

  boolean isAvailable( int port ) {
    try ( AutoCloseable __ = openSocket( port ) ) { return true; }
    catch ( Exception e ) { return false; }
  }

  private static final String COMPRESSED_SERVICE_NAMES = """
      7 Echo\n13 Daytime\n20 FTP\n21 FTP\n22 SSH\n23 Telnet\n25 SMTP
      53 DNS\n80 HTTP\n135 EPMAP\n137 NetBIOS Name Service
      138 NetBIOS Datagram Service\n139 NetBIOS Session Service
      445 Microsoft-DS Active Directory\n843 Adobe Flash
      1900 Simple Service Discovery Protocol (SSDP)
      3702 Web Services Dynamic Discovery\n5353 Multicast DNS
      5355 Link-Local Multicast Name Resolution (LLMNR)
      17500 Dropbox\n27017 MongoDB""";

  private static final Map<Integer, String> SERVICE_NAMES =
      COMPRESSED_SERVICE_NAMES
          .lines()
          .map( Scanner::new )
          .collect( Collectors.toMap( Scanner::nextInt, Scanner::nextLine ) );

  static String serviceName( int port ) {
    return SERVICE_NAMES.getOrDefault( port, "" );
  }
}
```

The Protocol enumeration type declares an abstract method openSocket(int) for opening the connection, since for TCP and UDP the code is different; the two enumeration elements implement the abstract method accordingly. In the case of TCP, the application builds a ServerSocket via the ServerSocketFactory or just a DatagramSocket via the constructor of DatagramSocket. Although ServerSocket and DatagramSocket are different types, both implement the AutoCloseable interface, and openSocket(int) also returns this type because only this type is relevant for isAvailable(int).

It is the task of isAvailable(int) to find out if the port is already in use. To do this, it calls openSocket(…), and if there was no exception, the port was free, and the connection can be closed right away; this is what try-with-resources on AutoCloseable takes care of.

serviceName(int) accesses a previously built Map. Inside the class, there is a constant COMPRESSED _ SERVICE _ NAMES, which could easily come from a file. The string contains the port number and, separated by spaces, a brief description, which in turn is terminated with a newline. Text

blocks save us the line break at the end of the line. A Stream expression prepares the Map by break-
ing the String into lines, this is where the lines() method is useful. The Stream then consists
of lines, which are passed into the constructor of the Scanner object, so that afterward nextInt()
returns the key for the Map and nextLine() the short description associated with the port number.
serviceName(int) can access this associative store SERVICE_NAMES and returns an empty string if
there is no description associated with the port number.

The main(…) method makes use of the methods of PortScanner:

com/tutego/exercise/net/PortScanner.java

```
final int MIN_SYSTEM_PORT    =    0;
//      final int MAX_SYSTEM_PORT    = 1023;
//      final int MIN_REGISTERED_PORT= 1024;
final int MAX_REGISTERED_PORT=49151;

System.out.println( "Protocol    Port         Service" );
for ( int port=MIN_SYSTEM_PORT; port <= MAX_REGISTERED_PORT; port++ ) {
   for ( Protocol protocol : Protocol.values() )
     if ( ! protocol.isAvailable( port ) )
       System.out.printf( "%s         %5d       %s%n",
                          protocol, port,      Protocol.serviceName( port ) );
}
```

First, we declare constants for the boundaries of the port ranges that our port scanner should run. They
represent the boundaries of the port ranges that our port scanner should run. In the code example, we
manage to use only two constants for the upper and lower limits because after MAX _ SYSTEM _ PORT
we continue with MIN _ REGISTERED _ PORT. We use a for loop to use all registered ports from 0
to 49151. Protocol.values() returns an array with the two enumeration elements TCP and UDP,
and if the isAvailable(…) method declared on the enumeration shows a blocked port, this prints the
console output.

Process XML, JSON, and Other Data Formats

10

Two important data formats for exchanging documents are XML and JSON (JavaScript Object Notation). XML is historically the older data type, we often find JSON nowadays in communication between a server and a JavaScript application. JSON documents are also popular for configuration files.

While Java SE provides different classes for reading and writing XML documents, JSON support is only available in Java Enterprise Edition or through complementary open-source libraries. Many of the tasks in this chapter, therefore, resort to external libraries.

Description languages form a significant category of document formats. They define the structure of the data. Among the most important formats are HTML, XML, JSON, and PDF.

Java does not provide support for other data formats, except for property files and the ability to process ZIP archives. This is especially true for CSV (Comma-separated values) files, PDFs, or Office documents. Fortunately, dozens of open-source libraries fill this gap, so you don't have to program this functionality yourself.

Prerequisites

- Know how to add Maven dependencies.
- Know StAX.
- Be able to write XML documents.
- Be able to create JAXB (Jakarta XML Binding) beans from XML schema files.
- Be able to use object XML mapping with Jakarta XML Binding.
- Basic understanding of Jakarta JSON libraries.
- Be able to read ZIP archives.

Data types used in this chapter:

- `javax.xml.stream.XMLOutputFactory`
- `javax.xml.stream.XMLStreamWriter`
- `javax.xml.stream.XMLStreamException`
- `javax.xml.stream.XMLInputFactory`
- `javax.xml.stream.XMLStreamReader`
- `jakarta.xml.bind.JAXB`

DOI: 10.1201/9781003495550-1

XML PROCESSING WITH JAVA

There are different Java APIs for handling XML documents. One way is to hold complete XML objects in memory; the other solution is similar to data streams. StAX is a pull API that allows elements to be actively pulled from the data stream and also written. The processing model is optimal for large documents that do not need to be completely in memory.

JAXB provides an easy way to convert Java objects to XML and XML back to Java objects later. Using annotations or external configuration files, the mapping can be precisely controlled.

Write XML File with Recipe ★

Captain CiaoCiao has so many recipes that he needs a database. He has several quotes for database management systems and wants to see if they can import all his recipes.

His recipes are in RecipeML format, an XML format that is loosely specified: http://www.formatdata. com/recipeml/. There is a large database at https://dsquirrel.tripod.com/recipeml/indexrecipes2.html. An example from "Key Gourmet":

```
?xml version="1.0" encoding="UTF-8"?>
recipeml version="0.5">
  <recipe>
    <head>
      <title>11 Minute Strawberry Jam</title>
      <categories>
        <cat>Canning</cat>
        <cat>Preserves</cat>
        <cat>Jams &amp; jell</cat>
      </categories>
      <yield>8</yield>
    </head>
    <ingredients>
```

```
      <ing>
        <amt>
          <qty>3</qty>
          <unit>cups</unit>
        </amt>
        <item>Strawberries</item>
      </ing>
      <ing>
        <amt>
          <qty>3</qty>
          <unit>cups</unit>
        </amt>
        <item>Sugar</item>
      </ing>
    </ingredients>
    <directions>
      <step>Put the strawberries in a pan.</step>
      <step>Add 1 cup of sugar.</step>
      <step>Bring to a boil and boil for 4 minutes.</step>
      <step>Add the second cup of sugar and boil again for 4 minutes.</step>
      <step>Then add the third cup of sugar and boil for 3 minutes.</step>
      <step>Remove from stove, cool, stir occasionally.</step>
      <step>Pour in jars and seal.</step>
    </directions>
  </recipe>
</recipeml>
```

Task:

- Write a program that outputs an XML document in RecipeML format.

Check If All Images Have an alt Attribute ★

Images in HTML documents should always have an alt attribute.
Task:

- Implement an XHTML checker that reports whether each img tag has an alt attribute set.
- Take as XHTML file, e.g., http://tutego.de/download/index.xhtml.

Writing Java Objects with JAXB ★

JAXB simplifies access to XML documents by allowing a convenient mapping from a Java object to an XML document and vice versa.

JAXB was included in the Standard Edition in Java 6 and removed in Java 11. We need a dependency

```
<dependency>
  <groupId>jakarta.xml.bind</groupId>
  <artifactId>jakarta.xml.bind-api</artifactId>
  <version>4.0.2</version>
</dependency>
<dependency>
  <groupId>org.glassfish.jaxb</groupId>
```

```
    <artifactId>jaxb-runtime</artifactId>
    <version>4.0.5</version>
    <scope>runtime</scope>
</dependency>
```

Task:

- Write JAXB beans so that we can generate the following XML:

```
<?xml version="1.0" encoding="UTF-8" standalone="yes"?>
<ingredients>
    <ing>
        <amt>
            <qty>3</qty>
            <unit>cups</unit>
        </amt>
        <item>Sugar</item>
    </ing>
    <ing>
        <amt>
            <qty>3</qty>
            <unit>cups</unit>
        </amt>
    </ing>
</ingredients>
```

- Creates the classes Ingredients, Ing, Amt.
- Give the classes corresponding instance variables; it is ok if these are public.
- Consider which annotation to use.

Read in Jokes and Laugh Heartily ★★

Bonny Brain is also laughing at simple jokes, which she can never have enough of. She finds the site https://sv443.net/jokeapi/v2/joke/Any?format=xml on the Internet, which always provides her with new jokes.

The format is XML, which is good for transporting data, but we are Java developers and want everything in objects! With JAXB we want to read the XML files and convert them into Java objects, so we can develop custom output later.

The first step is to automatically generate JAXB beans from an XML schema file. The schema for the joke page is as follows—don't worry, you don't have to understand it.

```
xs:schema attributeFormDefault="unqualified" elementFormDefault="qualified"
mlns:xs="http://www.w3.org/2001/XMLSchema">
  <xs:element name="data">
    <xs:complexType>
      <xs:sequence>
        <xs:element type="xs:string" name="category" />
        <xs:element type="xs:string" name="type" />
        <xs:element name="flags">
          <xs:complexType>
            <xs:sequence>
              <xs:element type="xs:boolean" name="nsfw" />
              <xs:element type="xs:boolean" name="religious" />
```

```
          <xs:element type="xs:boolean" name="political" />
          <xs:element type="xs:boolean" name="racist" />
          <xs:element type="xs:boolean" name="sexist" />
        </xs:sequence>
      </xs:complexType>
    </xs:element>
    <xs:element type="xs:string" name="setup" />
    <xs:element type="xs:string" name="delivery" />
    <xs:element type="xs:int" name="id" />
    <xs:element type="xs:string" name="error" />
  </xs:sequence>
  </xs:complexType>
  </xs:element>
</xs:schema>
```

The provider does not provide a schema, so it is generated from the XML using https://www.freeformatter.com/xsd-generator.html.

Task:

- Load the XML schema definition at http://tutego.de/download/jokes.xsd, and place the file in the Maven directory */src/main/resources*.
- Add the following element to the POM file:

```
<build>
<plugins>
  <plugin>
    <groupId>org.codehaus.mojo</groupId>
    <artifactId>jaxb2-maven-plugin</artifactId>
    <version>3.1.0</version>
    <executions>
      <execution>
        <id>xjc</id>
        <goals>
          <goal>xjc</goal>
        </goals>
      </execution>
    </executions>
    <configuration>
      <packageName>com.tutego.exercise.xml.joke</packageName>
      <sources>
        <source>src/main/resources/jokes.xsd</source>
      </sources>
      <generateEpisode>false</generateEpisode>
      <outputDirectory>${basedir}/src/main/java</outputDirectory>
      <clearOutputDir>false</clearOutputDir>
      <noGeneratedHeaderComments>true</noGeneratedHeaderComments>
      <locale>en</locale>
    </configuration>
  </plugin>
</plugins>
</build>
```

The plugin section includes org.codehaus.mojo:jaxb2-maven-plugin and configures it; all options are explained at https://www.mojohaus.org/jaxb2-maven-plugin/Documentation/v3.1.0/index.html.

- From the command line, launch mvn generate-sources. This will generate two classes in the com.tutego.exercise.xml.joke package:
  - Data.
  - ObjectFactory.
- Use JAXB to get a joke from the URL https://sv443.net/jokeapi/v2/joke/Any?format=xml and convert it to an object.

JSON

Java SE does not provide built-in support for JSON, but there are two standards from the Jakarta EE project that provide this support: *Jakarta JSON Processing (JSON-P)* (https://jakarta.ee/specifications/jsonp/) and *Jakarta JSON Binding (JSON-B)* (https://jakarta.ee/specifications/jsonb/). JSON-B allows for the mapping of Java objects to JSON and vice versa, while JSON-P provides APIs for processing JSON data. Another popular implementation is *Jackson* (https://github.com/FasterXML/jackson).

To use JSON-B, we need to add both the API and an implementation to our project's POM. The reference implementation, Yasson, is a good choice.

```
<dependency>
  <groupId>jakarta.json.bind</groupId>
  <artifactId>jakarta.json.bind-api</artifactId>
  <version>3.0.0</version>
</dependency>

<dependency>
  <groupId>org.eclipse</groupId>
  <artifactId>yasson</artifactId>
  <version>3.0.3</version>
  <scope>runtime</scope>
</dependency>
```

Hacker News JSON Exploit ★

The page Hacker News (https://news.ycombinator.com/) was briefly introduced in the chapter "Network Programming".

The URL https://hacker-news.firebaseio.com/v0/item/24857356.json returns a JSON object of the message with ID 24857356. The response looks (formatted and slightly shortened for the kids) like this:

```
"by":"luu",
"descendants":257,
"id":24857356,
"kids":[
    24858151,
    24857761,
    24858192,
    24858887
],
"score":353,
"time":1603370419,
```

```
    "title":"The physiological effects of slow breathing in the healthy
human",
    "type":"story",
    "url":"https://breathe.ersjournals.com/content/13/4/298"
}
```

With JSON-B this JSON can be converted into a Map:

```
Map map = JsonbBuilder.create().fromJson( source, Map.class );
```

The source can be a `String`, `Reader` or `InputStream`.
Task:

- Write a new method `Map<Object, Object> news(long id)` that, using JSON-B, obtains the JSON document at `"https://hacker-news.firebaseio.com/v0/item/"+id+".json"` and converts it to a Map and returns it.

Example:

- `news(24857356).get("title")` → "The physiological effects of slow breathing in the healthy human".
- `news(111111).get("title")` → null.

Read and Write Editor Configurations as JSON ★★

The developers are working on a new editor for Captain CiaoCiao, and the configurations should be saved in a JSON file.
Task:

- Write a class `Settings` so that the following configurations can be mapped:
  ```
  {
    "editor" : {
      "cursorStyle" : "line",
      "folding" : true,
      "fontFamily" : [ "Consolas, 'Courier New', monospace" ],
      "fontSize" : 22,
      "fontWeight" : "normal"
    },
    "workbench" : {
      "colorTheme" : "Default Dark+"
    },
    "terminal" : {
      "integrated.unicodeVersion" : "11"
    }
  }
  ```
- The JSON file gives a good indication of the data types:
  - cursorStyle is String, folding is boolean, and fontFamily is an array or List.
- If an attribute is not set, which means null, it should not be written.
- For terminal the contained key values are unknown, they shall be contained in a Map<String, String>.

HTML

HTML is an important markup language. The Java standard library does not provide support for HTML documents, except for what the `javax.swing.JEditorPane` can do, which is to render HTML 3.2 and a subset of CSS 1.0.

For Java programs to be able to write and read HTML documents correctly and validly, and to be able to read nodes, we have to turn to (open-source) libraries.

Load Wikipedia Images with jsoup ★★

The popular open-source library *jsoup* (https://jsoup.org/) loads the content of web pages and represents the content in a tree in memory.

Include the following dependency in the POM:

```
<dependency>
  <groupId>org.jsoup</groupId>
  <artifactId>jsoup</artifactId>
  <version>1.17.2</version>
</dependency>
```

Task:

* Study the examples at https://jsoup.org/cookbook/extracting-data/dom-navigation and https://jsoup.org/cookbook/extracting-data/selector-syntax.
* Retrieve from the main Wikipedia page all images and save them to your file system.

OFFICE DOCUMENTS

Microsoft Office continues to be at the top when it comes to word processing and spreadsheets. For many years, the binary file format has been well known, and there are Java libraries for reading and writing. Meanwhile, processing Microsoft Office documents has become much easier since the documents are, at their core, XML documents that are combined into a ZIP archive. Java support is excellent.

Generate Word Files with Screenshots ★★

Read the Wikipedia entry for POI: https://de.wikipedia.org/wiki/Apache_POI.
Task:

1. Add the following for Maven in the POM to include Apache POI and the necessary dependencies for DOCX:
   ```
   <dependency>
     <groupId>org.apache.poi</groupId>
     <artifactId>poi-ooxml</artifactId>
     <version>5.2.5</version>
   </dependency>
   ```

```
<dependency>
  <groupId>org.apache.commons</groupId>
  <artifactId>commons-compress</artifactId>
  <version>1.26.1</version>
</dependency>
```

2. Study the source code of SimpleImages.java.
3. Java allows you to capture screenshots, like this:

```
private static byte[] getScreenCapture() throws AWTException,
IOException {
  BufferedImage screenCapture = new Robot().createScreenCapture( SCREEN_
SIZE );
  ByteArrayOutputStream os = new ByteArrayOutputStream();
  ImageIO.write( screenCapture, "jpeg", os );
  return os.toByteArray();
}
```

4. Write a Java program that takes a screenshot every 5 seconds for 20 seconds and attaches the image to the Word document.

ARCHIVES

Files with metadata are collected in archives. A well-known and popular archive format is ZIP, which no only combines the data but also compresses it. Many archive formats can also store the files encrypted and store checksums so that errors in the transfer can be detected later.

Java offers two possibilities for compression: since Java 7, there is a ZIP file system provider, and already since Java 1.0, there are the classes `ZipFile` and `ZipEntry`.

Play Insect Sounds from ZIP Archive ★★

Bonny Brain likes to listen to the sounds of insects and uses the WAV collection of https://catalog.data. gov/dataset/bug-bytes-sound-library-stored-product-insect-pest-sounds, where various audio files are offered for download in a ZIP.

Task:

- Study the documentation at https://christian-schlichtherle.bitbucket.io/truezip/truezip-path/.
- Include two dependencies in the Maven POM:

```
<dependency>
  <groupId>en.schlichtherle.truezip</groupId>
  <artifactId>truezip-path</artifactId>
  <version>7.7.10</version>
</dependency>
<dependency>
  <groupId>en.schlichtherle.truezip</groupId>
  <artifactId>truezip-driver-zip</artifactId>
  <version>7.7.10</version>
</dependency>
```

- Download the ZIP with the insect sounds, but do not unpack it.
- Build a TPath object for the ZIP file.
- Transfer all filenames from the ZIP file into a list: `Files.newDirectoryStream(…)` helps here.
- Write an infinite loop, and
  - Select a random WAV file,
  - Open the random file with `Files.newInputStream(…)`, decorate it with a BufferedInputStream and open an `AudioSystem.getAudioInputStream(…)`. Play the WAV file and access the following code, where ais the AudioInputStream.

    ```
    Clip clip=AudioSystem.getClip();
    clip.open( ais );
    clip.start();
    TimeUnit.MICROSECONDS.sleep( clip.getMicrosecondLength()+50 );
    clip.close();
    ```
    In chapter "Exceptions", we had worked with the `javax.sound` API before.

SUGGESTED SOLUTIONS

Write XML File with Recipe

The proposed solution starts with two records for the data:
com/tutego/exercise/xml/RecipeMLwriterDemo.java

```
record Recipe(
    String head$title,
    List<String> head$categories,
    String head$yield,
    List<Ingredient> ingredients,
    List<String> directions) {

record Ingredient(
    String ing$amt$qty,
    String ing$amt$unit,
    String ing$item
) {}
```

A recipe is represented by the two types Recipe and Ingredient. Ingredient is a nested type, which expresses well the relationship between the two types Recipe and Ingredient. In principle, one could declare a separate record (or class) for each subelement, but this would be too much for the proposed solution. Therefore, the variable names with the dollar express the type hierarchy.

Before we start with our program, one observation: many elements are written, which entails many statements of the following type:

```
writer.writeStartElement( … );
…
writer.writeEndElement();
```

For this kind of problem, the execute-around pattern is useful. A thought experiment:

```
write.element( "my-tag", () -> {
  …
} );
```

We can pass the tag, a block representing the body, and at the end, we want to write the end tag. Since the Java library does not provide such a feature, the proposed solution introduces a separate helper class HierarchicalXmlWriter, a facade around the XMLStreamWriter:

com/tutego/exercise/xml/RecipeMLwriterDemo.java

```java
class HierarchicalXmlWriter implements AutoCloseable {

  private final OutputStream outputStream;

  interface XMLStreamWriterBlock {
    void write() throws XMLStreamException;
  }

  private final XMLStreamWriter writer;

  HierarchicalXmlWriter( OutputStream outputStream ) throws
XMLStreamException {
    this.outputStream = outputStream;
    XMLOutputFactory outputFactory = XMLOutputFactory.newFactory();
    this.writer = outputFactory.createXMLStreamWriter(
        outputStream, StandardCharsets.UTF_8.name() );
    writer.writeStartDocument( "utf-8", "1.0" );
  }

  @Override public void close() throws XMLStreamException, IOException {
    try {
      writer.writeEndDocument();
      writer.close();
    }
    finally {
      outputStream.close();
    }
  }

  void element( String tag, XMLStreamWriterBlock block ) throws
XMLStreamException {
    writer.writeStartElement( tag );
    block.write();
    writer.writeEndElement();
  }
```

```
  void string( String tag, String text ) throws XMLStreamException {
    element( tag, () -> writer.writeCharacters( text ) );
  }
}
```

The constructor takes the sink where the XML document will be written. The passed OutputStream is stored in an instance variable so that it can be closed later as a resource. Furthermore, the XMLStreamWriter is requested and saved via XMLOutputFactory so that the XMLStreamWriter can also be closed in close(). Finally, the constructor writes the XML prolog.

The XMLStreamWriterBlock is AutoCloseable, so that use as a resource in try-with-resources is possible. The close() method sets the end tag from the XML document, closes the XMLStreamWriter and the OutputStream. Important: The XMLStreamWriter does not independently pass the close() to the underlying resource, as is usually the case with input/output decorators. The OutputStream should also be closed if an exception occurs when calling the two XMLStreamWriter methods.

The first helper method element(String tag, XMLStreamWriterBlock block) sets the start tag, executes the block, and writes the end tag. The second helper method string(String tag, String string) writes the start tag, the text inside, and the end tag.

The main class RecipeMLwriterDemo can access HierarchicalXmlWriter and now build the XML blocks as desired:

com/tutego/exercise/xml/RecipeMLwriterDemo.java

```
var ingredient1 = new Recipe.Ingredient( "30", "cups", "fat" );
var ingredient2 = new Recipe.Ingredient( "1", "kg", "sugar" );
var recipe = new Recipe( "Fat Jam", List.of( "Canning", "Preserves" ), "8",
                         List.of( ingredient1, ingredient2 ),
                         List.of( "Start", "End" ) );
try ( var write = new HierarchicalXmlWriter( System.out ) ) {
  write.element( "recipe", () -> {
    write.element( "head", () -> {
      write.string( "title", recipe.head$title() );
      write.element( "categories", () -> {
        for ( String cat : recipe.head$categories() )
          write.string( "cat", cat );
      } );
      write.string( "yield", recipe.head$yield() );
    } );
    write.element( "ingredients", () -> {
      for ( Recipe.Ingredient ingredient : recipe.ingredients() ) {
        write.element( "ing", () -> {
          write.element( "ing", () -> {
            write.string( "qty", ingredient.ing$amt$qty() );
            write.string( "unit", ingredient.ing$amt$unit() );
          } );
          write.string( "item", ingredient.ing$item() );
        } );
      }
    } );
    write.element( "directions", () -> {
      for ( String step : recipe.directions() )
        write.string( "step", step );
    } );
  } );
```

```
catch ( XMLStreamException | IOException e ) {
  e.printStackTrace();
}
```

For those interested in RecipeML's XML schema: https://github.com/tranchis/xsd2thrift/blob/master/contrib/recipeml.xsd. However, the format has gone quiet.

Check If All Images Have an alt Attribute

com/tutego/exercise/xml/XhtmlHasImgTagWithAltAttribute.java

```
static void reportMissingAltElements( Path path ) {
  try ( InputStream is = Files.newInputStream( path ) ) {
    XMLInputFactory xmlInputFactory = XMLInputFactory.newInstance();
    xmlInputFactory.setProperty( XMLConstants.ACCESS_EXTERNAL_DTD, "" );
    xmlInputFactory.setProperty( XMLConstants.ACCESS_EXTERNAL_SCHEMA, "" );
    XMLStreamReader parser = xmlInputFactory.createXMLStreamReader( is );
    while ( parser.hasNext() ) {
      parser.next();
      boolean isStartElement =
          parser.getEventType() == XMLStreamConstants.START_ELEMENT;
      if ( isStartElement ) {
        boolean isImgTag = "img".equalsIgnoreCase( parser.getLocalName() );
        if ( isImgTag && !containsAltAttribute( parser ) )
          System.err.printf( "img does not contain alt attribute:%n%s%n",
                             parser.getLocation() );
      }
    }
  }
  catch ( IOException | XMLStreamException e ) {
    throw new RuntimeException( e );
  }
}

private static boolean containsAltAttribute( XMLStreamReader parser ) {
  return IntStream.range( 0, parser.getAttributeCount() )
      .mapToObj( parser::getAttributeLocalName )
      .anyMatch( "alt"::equalsIgnoreCase );
}
```

The Path object passed to the createXMLStreamReader(…) method is the basis for a InputStream, which we pass to createXMLStreamReader(…) to get an XMLStreamReader with this input stream. Unfortunately, to date (as of Java 21), an XMLStreamReader is not AutoCloseable so it cannot be closed in try-with-resources. However, this is not dramatic when reading; we close th InputStream of the file very well via a try-with-resources.

Passing the data through an XMLStreamReader always looks the same: hasNext() tells whethe there are still tokens in the data stream, and if so, fetches the next token with next(). This is similar t Scanner and Iterator. The call to next() changes the state of the XMLStreamReader elemen and getEventType() returns an integer to identify the incoming data. This can be e.g., the start of th document, a processing instruction, a comment, text, or even a start element. Instead of integers, we us constants, interface XMLStreamReader extends XMLStreamConstants. When an elemen starts, it could be an img element. So getLocalName() asks the parser for the element name and com pares it to img—case-insensitive. If this is true, we have found an img tag. Now the question is whethe

the `alt` attribute is also set. This is answered by our method `containsAltAttribute(…)`. If the img tag has no `alt` attribute, there is a message on the standard error channel and via `getLocation()` the exact location can also be identified and specified in the error message.

`containsAltAttribute(…)` gets the `XMLStreamReader` as parameter and runs all attributes from 0 to `getAttributeCount()`. If an attribute `alt` exists, regardless of the assignment, the method returns `true`, otherwise `false`.

Writing Java Objects with JAXB

com/tutego/exercise/xml/JaxbRecipeML.java

```
@XmlRootElement
class Ingredients {
   public Ing[] ing;
}

class Ing {
   public Amt amt;
   public String item;
}

class Amt {
   public int qty;
   public String unit;
}
```

com/tutego/exercise/xml/JaxbRecipeML.java

```
Ing ing1 = new Ing();
Amt amt1 = new Amt();
amt1.qty = 3;
amt1.unit = "cups";
ing1.amt = amt1;
ing1.item = "Strawberries";

Ing ing2 = new Ing();
Amt amt2 = new Amt();
amt2.qty = 3;
amt2.unit = „cups";
ing2.amt = amt2;
ing2.item = „Sugar";

Ingredients ingredients = new Ingredients();
ingredients.ing = new Ing[]{ ing1, ing2 };
JAXB.marshal( ingredients, System.out );
```

Working with JAXB is easy:

1. You write classes with a parameterless constructor and use either setters/getters or public instance variables for the data.
2. Builds an object graph and writes it with `JAXB.marshal(ingredients, System.out)` to an output stream, for example, to the console.

For compatibility reasons, the proposed solution sets the @XmlRootElement annotation to the root element Ingredients. This is no longer necessary for current JAXB implementations but is used for compatibility reasons so that the solution also works under Java 8, which contains a slightly older JAXB version (JAXB RI 2.2.8), currently 2.4.0.

Read in Jokes and Laugh Heartily

JAXB focuses on JavaBeans that use annotations to tell the JAXB framework how to map objects to XML or how to map XML to objects. We can write and annotate these JAXB beans manually, or we can have them generated from a schema. This variant was asked for in the task, and the generated class Data starts like this:

```
@XmlAccessorType(XmlAccessType.FIELD)
@XmlType(name = "", propOrder = {
    "category", "type", "flags", "setup", "delivery", "id", "error"
})
@XmlRootElement(name = "data")
public class Data {
    @XmlElement(required = true)
    protected String category;
    @XmlElement(required = true)
    protected String type;
    ...
}
```

To the client:
    com/tutego/exercise/xml/JaxbJokeReceiver.java

```
try {
  URL url = URI.create( "https://sv443.net/jokeapi/v2/joke/Any?format=xml"
).toURL();
  Data data = JAXB.unmarshal( url, Data.class );
  System.out.println( data.getSetup() );
  System.out.println( data.getDelivery() );
  System.out.printf( "Not Safe for Work? %s%n", data.getFlags().isNsfw() );
  System.out.printf( "Religious? %s%n", data.getFlags().isReligious() );
  System.out.printf( "Political? %s%n", data.getFlags().isPolitical() );
  System.out.printf( "Racist? %s%n", data.getFlags().isRacist() );
  System.out.printf( "Sexist? %s%n", data.getFlags().isSexist() );
}
catch ( MalformedURLException e ) {
  System.err.println( "malformed URL has occurred" );
  e.printStackTrace();
}
catch ( DataBindingException e ) {
  System.err.println( "failure in a JAXB operation" );
  e.printStackTrace();
}
```

JAXB.unmarshal(...) allows constructing Java objects from an XML stream from various data sources, including a URL. So if we build a URL object and put it on the endpoint of the joke, unmarshal(...) directly returns a Data object. The Data object then provides different getters, and th data can be read. Two exceptions can occur: the format of the URL could be invalid, which gives us a `MalformedURLException`, or the XML format cannot be mapped to the JavaBean, in which case the result is a `DataBindingException`.

Hacker News JSON Exploit

You can use the `Jsonb` object and the `fromJson(…)` method to read a JSON document into a `Map` of nested key-value pairs. Here are two suggested solutions:

com/tutego/exercise/json/HackerNewsJson.java

```java
@SuppressWarnings( "unchecked" )
public static Map<Object, Object> news( long id ) {
  String url = "https://hacker-news.firebaseio.com/v0/item/%d.json";

  try ( var in = URI.create(url.formatted(id) .toURL()).openStream();
        Jsonb jsonb = JsonbBuilder.create() ) {
    return jsonb.fromJson( in, Map.class );
  }
  catch ( Exception e ) {
    return Collections.emptyMap();
  }
}
```

In this solution, the `fromJson(…)` method takes an `InputStream` of an open network connection as the first parameter and the target type, which is `Map`, as the second parameter. The `Jsonb` object is an `AutoCloseable` and can be used with the `try`-with-resources block. The program catches exceptions and returns an empty `Map` if an exception is thrown. Since the `Class` object can only express the raw type `Map` but not the generics, implicit type conversion `Map<String, String>` is possible, but the compiler would give a notice; a `@SuppressWarnings("unchecked")` stops the compiler warning.

The bext solution uses the `HttpClient` API, which is more powerful than the `URL` class way in terms of configuring authenticator, thread pool, proxy, SSL context, and more.

com/tutego/exercise/json/HackerNewsJson.java

```java
@SuppressWarnings( "unchecked" )
public static Map<Object, Object> news( long id ) {
  HttpClient client = HttpClient.newHttpClient();

  String url = "https://hacker-news.firebaseio.com/v0/item/%d.json";
  HttpRequest request = HttpRequest
      .newBuilder( URI.create( url.formatted( id ) ) )
      .timeout( Duration.ofSeconds( 5 ) )
      .build();

  try ( InputStream body = client.send( request, ofInputStream() ).body();
        Jsonb jsonb = JsonbBuilder.create() ) {
    return jsonb.fromJson( body, Map.class );
  }

  catch ( Exception e ) {
    return Collections.emptyMap();
  }
}
```

The program creates the Jsonb object without any extras and falls back to a default configuration with HttpClient.newHttpClient(). The HttpRequest is set to the URL, and then a timeout is set. The result should be in a format that fromJson(…) can accept; here InputStream or String is suitable, for example. The InputStream is advantageous because it needs the least memory when reading.

Read and Write Editor Configurations as JSON

The JSON hierarchy is automatically derived from the fact that Settings references an Editor and a Workbench.

com/tutego/exercise/json/Settings.java

```
import java.util.*;

public class Settings {

  enum FontWeight {
    normal, bold
  }

  public static class Editor {
    public String cursorStyle = "line";
    public boolean folding = true;
    public List<String> fontFamily =
        Arrays.asList( "Consolas, 'Courier New', monospace" );
    public int fontSize = 14;
    public FontWeight fontWeight = FontWeight.normal;
  }

  public static class Workbench {
    public String colorTheme = "Default Dark+";
    public String iconTheme;
  }

  public Editor editor = new Editor();
  public Workbench workbench = new Workbench();
  public Map<String, String> terminal = new HashMap<>();
}
```

JSON-B directly accesses the instance variables and takes the lowercase identifiers for the JSON object. JSON-B will directly map lists to JSON arrays. Enumerations are also directly written and can be read back in. With Map<String, String> terminal arbitrary key-value pairs of strings can be used, which are not bound to special instance variables, but come into the associative memory.

com/tutego/exercise/json/EditorPreferences.java

```
public class EditorPreferences {

  private static final Path FILENAME = Paths.get(
      /*System.getProperty( "user.home" ),*/ ".editor-configuration.json" );

  private final Jsonb jsonb = JsonbBuilder.create(
      new JsonbConfig().setProperty( JsonbConfig.FORMATTING, true )
  );
```

```
private Settings settings = new Settings();

public Settings settings() {
  return settings;
}

public Settings load() {
  try ( var inputStream = Files.newInputStream( FILENAME ) ) {
    return settings = jsonb.fromJson( inputStream, Settings.class );
  }
  catch ( IOException e ) {
    return settings;
  }
}
public void save() {
  try ( var outputStream = Files.newOutputStream( FILENAME ) ) {
    jsonb.toJson( settings, outputStream );
  }
  catch ( IOException e ) {
    throw new IllegalStateException( e );
  }
}
}
```

EditorPreferences has a constructor that configures Jsonb[1]:

- The output should be formatted, because configuration files are made for users, so the file should not be as short as possible and save all spaces, but have breaks and inserts.

Internally, EditorPreferences creates a Settings object that reconstructs load() from the JSON file and writes the save() method. fromJson(...) and toJson(...) of the Jsonb object are responsible for the actual mapping.

The usage can be as follows:
com/tutego/exercise/json/EditorPreferencesDemo.java

```
EditorPreferences preferences = new EditorPreferences();
preferences.save();
Settings settings = preferences.load();
settings.editor.fontSize = 22;
settings.terminal.put( "integrated.unicodeVersion", "11" );
preferences.save();
```

Load Wikipedia Images with jsoup

com/tutego/exercise/net/WikipediaImageLoader.java

```
var url = "https://en.wikipedia.org/wiki/Main_Page";
var tempDir = Files.createTempDirectory( "wikipedia-images" );

var document = Jsoup.parse( URI.create(url).toURL(), 1000 /* ms */ );

for ( var imgElement : document.select( "img[src~=(?i)\\.(png|gif|jpg)]" ) ) {
  String imgUrl   = imgElement.absUrl( "src" );
  String filename = imgUrl.replaceAll( "[^a-zA-Z0-9_ .-]", "_" );
```

```
final int MAX_FILENAME_LENGTH = 128;
if ( filename.length() > MAX_FILENAME_LENGTH ) {
  String suffix = filename.substring( filename.length() - 4 );
  filename = filename.substring( 0, MAX_FILENAME_LENGTH - 4 ) + suffix;
}

try ( var imgStream = URI.create( imgUrl ).toURL().openStream() ) {
  Files.copy( imgStream, tempDir.resolve( filename ),
          StandardCopyOption.REPLACE_EXISTING );
}
}
System.out.println( "Successfully downloaded Wikipedia images to " + tempDir );
```

The class Jsoup has the static method parse(...), which can build the HTML document from different sources. In our case, we choose directly the URL object. When accessing the network, a timeout must be given to Jsoup, which we set to 1000 milliseconds. The parse(...) method returns an org.jsoup.nodes.Document object. There are two ways to access this Document and extract elements:

- DOM (Document Object Model) methods like getElementById(String   id) or child(int index).
- selector expressions as known from CSS.

The proposed solution works with the select(...) method. img[...] stands for all img tags, while src~= specifies via a regular expression what should be true for the src attribute, namely, that the strings match \.(png|gif|jpg), i.e., have the file extension .png, .gif or .jpg. The (?i) flag activates the search regardless of the case.

The result of the select(...) method is of type Elements, a subclass of ArrayList. A List is Iterable and can be conveniently traversed with an extended for loop. Each element in this list is of type Element. We could use the attr("src") call to get the set URL of the image, but more useful is the absUrl(...) method, which resolves the URL.

If we later download the images, then we can't directly use this URL as the filename because there are illegal symbols there that cause problems in the file system. The string method replaceAll(...) returns a new, cleaned-up string that we can use as a filename. Since the allowed length of the file name might be limited on the operating system, a block reduces the length to a maximum of 128 characters. The next step is to build a URL object and open an input stream to this image and copy it to the local file system via Files.copy(...); we have written the code before in the ImageDownloader task. However, this time we put the images in a temporary directory.

Generate Word Files with Screenshots

com/tutego/exercise/fileformat/ScreenCapturesInDocx.java

```
private static final int TOTAL_NUMBER_OF_SCREEN_CAPTURES  = 3;
private static final int DURATION_BETWEEN_SCREEN_CAPTURES = 5;
private static final Rectangle SCREEN_SIZE =
    new Rectangle( Toolkit.getDefaultToolkit().getScreenSize() );

private static byte[] getScreenCapture() throws AWTException, IOException {
  BufferedImage screenCapture = new Robot().createScreenCapture( SCREEN_SIZE );
  ByteArrayOutputStream os = new ByteArrayOutputStream();
  ImageIO.write( screenCapture, "jpeg", os );
  return os.toByteArray();
}
```

```
private static void appendImage( XWPFDocument doc, byte[] imageBytes )
    throws IOException, InvalidFormatException {
  XWPFRun paragraph=doc.createParagraph().createRun();
  paragraph.addPicture( new ByteArrayInputStream( imageBytes ),
                     Document.PICTURE_TYPE_JPEG,
                     UUID.randomUUID().toString(),
                     Units.toEMU( SCREEN_SIZE.width / 100. * 20 ),
                     Units.toEMU( SCREEN_SIZE.height / 100. * 20 ) );
  paragraph.addBreak();
}

public static void main( String[] args ) throws Exception {
  try ( XWPFDocument xwpfDocument=new XWPFDocument() ) {
    for ( int i=0; i<TOTAL_NUMBER_OF_SCREEN_CAPTURES; i++ ) {
      appendImage( xwpfDocument, getScreenCapture() );
      TimeUnit.SECONDS.sleep( DURATION_BETWEEN_SCREEN_CAPTURES );
    }

    Path tempFile=Files.createTempFile( "screen-captures", ".docx" );
    try ( OutputStream out=Files.newOutputStream( tempFile ) ) {
      xwpfDocument.write( out );
    }
    System.out.println( "Written to "+tempFile );
  }
}
```

The solution consists of three methods. The first method getScreenCapture() returns a byte[] with the screen content as JPEG. Java can do this via the Robot class, which is intended for automation. The Robot class can be used to move the cursor and send keystrokes.) The result of createScreenCapture(...) for the whole screen size is of type BufferedImage, an internal image format. To convert it to JPEG format, the program resorts to the ImageIO.write(...) method, which first writes the BufferedImage to a ByteArrayOutputStream and then converts it to a byte array and returns it.

The second method is appendImage(...); it appends an image to an existing XWPFDocument. Since each image is placed in its paragraph, a Paragraph is built first and then the image is added via addPicture(...). The method expects an input stream to the picture as well as a unique identifier, and size information. The image is scaled a bit.

The main method main(...) opens a new XWPFDocument, then takes a screen capture, appends it to the document, waits for a second, then takes another screen capture until the desired maximum number is reached. The document is only in memory so far. Files.createTempFile(...) creates a file in the temporary directory and writes the official document to this file.

Play Insect Sounds from ZIP Archive

com/tutego/exercise/io/TrueZipDemo.java

```
Path path=new TPath( filename );

List<Path> wavFiles=new ArrayList<>();
try ( DirectoryStream<Path> entries=Files.newDirectoryStream( path ) ) {
  entries.forEach( wavFiles::add );
}

while ( true ) {
```

```
int randomIndex = ThreadLocalRandom.current().nextInt( wavFiles.size() );
Path randomWavFile = wavFiles.get( randomIndex );
try ( InputStream fis = Files.newInputStream( randomWavFile );
      // for mark/reset support we need a BufferedInputStream
      BufferedInputStream bis = new BufferedInputStream( fis );
      AudioInputStream ais = AudioSystem.getAudioInputStream( bis ) ) {
  Clip clip = AudioSystem.getClip();
  clip.open( ais );
  clip.start();
  TimeUnit.MICROSECONDS.sleep( clip.getMicrosecondLength() + 50 );
  clip.close();
  }
}
```

The solution consists of the following parts:

1. Reading all audio files from the archive `filename`.
2. Selecting a random audio file.
3. Playing the audio file.

TrueZIP uses its own `Path` implementation `TPath` for its work. The constructor can be passed a `String`, `Path`, `URI`, or `File` object. If we use our ZIP file and have constructed `TPath`, `newDirectoryS-tream(..)` returns all directory contents, caching them in a list of `Path` objects.

The infinite loop starts and selects a random file from the list. An input stream is opened and then decorated with `BufferedInputStream`. This is necessary because the audio system requires a special feature on input streams, namely, that markers are supported. The input stream of TrueZIP does not support this, at least in the current version.

Thereafter, the `AudioInputStream` can be opened and the `Clip` can be played. The duration of the clip can be queried via `getMicrosecondLength(...)`, and this is how long we wait after starting playback. We add a small buffer of 50 microseconds on top. The clip is closed, and the next loop cycle follows.

NOTE

---

1 https://jakarta.ee/specifications/jsonb/3.0/apidocs/jakarta.json.bind/jakarta/json/bind/jsonbconfig

Database Access with JDBC

11

Java Database Connectivity (JDBC) provides access to various relational databases and enables the execution of SQL statements on a relational database management system (RDBMS). A JDBC driver implements the JDBC API. This chapter focuses on an example using the JDBC API to allow Captain CiaoCiao to store user information in a database for a pirate dating service.

Prerequisites

- Be able to build Maven project and add dependencies.
- Be able to install database management system.
- Be able to establish database connection.
- Be able to query and insert data.

Data types used in this chapter:

- `java.sql.DriverManager`
- `java.sql.Connection`
- `java.sql.SQLException`
- `java.sql.Statement`
- `java.sql.Statement`
- `java.sql.ResultSet`
- `java.sql.Date`
- `java.sql.ResultSetMetaData`

DATABASE MANAGEMENT SYSTEMS

Exercises with JDBC require a database management system, a database, and data. The exercises can be realized with any relational database management system because there are JDBC drivers for all major database management systems and the access always looks the same. The chapter uses the compact database management system H2.

There are graphical tools that display tables and simplify the execution of SQL queries. For IDEs there are often plugins; NetBeans has a SQL editor and IntelliJ Ultimate includes a database editor out of the box, for the free community edition there is https://plugins.jetbrains.com/plugin/1800-database-navigator, for example. For Eclipse there are different plugins, from the Eclipse Foundation itself the *Eclipse Data Tools Platform (DTP) Project* at https://www.eclipse.org/datatools/downloads.php.

DOI: 10.1201/9781003495550-12

Prepare H2 Database ★

H2 is such a compact program that the database management system, the JDBC driver, and a small admin interface are bundled together in a JAR (Java Archive).

Include the following dependency in the Maven POM:

```
<dependency>
  <groupId>com.h2database</groupId>
  <artifactId>h2</artifactId>
  <version>2.2.224</version>
  <scope>runtime</scope>
</dependency>
```

DATABASE QUERIES

Each database access runs through the following stages:

1. Starting the database access by establishing the connection.
2. Sending a statement.
3. Collecting the results.

Query All Registered JDBC Drivers ★

Java 6 introduced the *Service Provider API*, which can automatically execute code if it is on the classpath and listed in a special text file. JDBC drivers use the Service Provider API to automatically register with the DriverManager.

Task:

- Using the `DriverManager`, query all logged-in JDBC drivers, and output the class name to the screen.

Build Database and Execute SQL Script ★

Captain CiaoCiao wants to store information about pirates in a relational database. An initial draft results in storing a pirate's nickname, also email address, saber length, date of birth, and a brief description. After modeling the database, write an SQL script that builds the tables:

```sql
DROP ALL OBJECTS;

CREATE TABLE Pirate (
    id          IDENTITY,
    nickname    VARCHAR(255) UNIQUE NOT NULL,
    email       VARCHAR(255) UNIQUE NOT NULL,
    swordlength INT,
    birthdate   DATE,
    description VARCHAR(4096)
);
```

The first SQL statement deletes all entries in the database in H2. Then CREATE TABLE creates a new table with different columns and data types. Each pirate has a unique ID assigned by the database; we refer to *automatically generated keys*.

The SQL in the book follows a naming convention:

- SQL keywords are consistently capitalized.
- Table names are singular and start with a capital letter, just as class names in Java start with a capital letter.
- Table column names are lowercase.

A Java SE program uses the `DriverManager` to establish a connection using the `getConnection(...)` method. A JDBC URL contains details about the database and connection details, such as server and port. In the case of H2, the JDBC URL is simple if no server should be contacted but the RDBMS should be part of the own application:

```java
String jdbcUrl = "jdbc:h2:./pirates-dating";
try ( Connection connection = DriverManager.getConnection( jdbcUrl ) {
...
```

If the database `pirates-dating` does not exist, it will be created. `getConnection(...)` returns the connection afterward. Connections must always be closed. The `try`-with-resources handles the closing, as can be seen in the code above.

If the complete RDBMS runs as part of its application, this is called *embedded mode*. In embedded mode, a started Java application uses this database exclusively and multiple Java programs cannot connect to this database. Multiple connections are only possible with one database server. H2 can do this as well; those interested can learn the details from the H2 website: https://www.h2database.com/html/tutorial.html.

Task:

- Put a file *create-table.sql* in the *resources* directory of the Maven project. Copy the SQL script into the file.
- Create a new Java class, and load the SQL script from the classpath.
- Establish a connection to the database, and execute the loaded SQL script.

We can use a command-line tool to query the database at the end:

```
$ java -cp h2-2.2.222.jar org.h2.tools.Shell -url jdbc:h2:C:\path\to\your\
folder\pirates-dating

Welcome to H2 Shell 2.2.222 (2023-08-22)
Exit with Ctrl+C
Commands are case insensitive; SQL statements end with ';'
help or ?      Display this help
list           Toggle result list / stack trace mode
maxwidth       Set maximum column width (default is 100)
autocommit     Enable or disable autocommit
history        Show the last 20 statements
quit or exit   Close the connection and exit

sql> SHOW TABLES;
TABLE_NAME | TABLE_SCHEMA
PIRATE     | PUBLIC
(1 row, 15 ms)
sql> exit
Connection closed
```

Access the execute(...) method of Statement.

Insert Data into the Database ★

The database built so far does not contain any records. In the following three programs, data records shall be added. SQL offers the INSERT statement for inserting new rows. A new pirate can be inserted into the database with the following SQL:

```
INSERT INTO Pirate (nickname, email, swordlength, birthdate, description)
VALUES ('CiaoCiao', 'captain@goldenpirates.faith', 18, DATE '1955-11-07',
'Great guy')
```

The primary key id is explicitly absent from the statement because this column is automatically uniquely assigned.

Task:

- Establish a new connection to the database, create a Statement object, and send the INSERT INTO to the database with executeUpdate(...).
- A generated key can be supplied by a JDBC driver. To add a second pirate, you can output the generated key (which is a long) to the screen. When executeUpdate(...) is called, it returns an int. This indicates something about the executed statement, but what is it?

Insert Data into the Database in Batch Mode ★

If several SQL statements are to be executed, they can be collected in a *batch*. In the first step, all SQL statements are collected and then transmitted to the database in one batch. The JDBC driver does have to send each query over the network to the database.
Task:

- Create a new class and put the following array into the program:
```
String[] values = {
    "'anygo', 'amiga_anker@cutthroat.adult', 11, DATE '2000-05-21',
'Living the dream'",
    "'SweetSushi', 'muffin@berta.bar', 11, DATE '1952-04-03', 'Where are
all the bad boys?'",
    "'Liv Loops', 'whiletrue@deenagavis.camp', 16, DATE '1965-05-11',
'Great guy'" };
```

- From the data in the array, create SQL-INSERT statements, add them to the `Statement` with `addBatch(...)`, and submit the statements with `executeBatch()`.
- `executeBatch()` returns an `int[]`; what is inside?

Insert Data with Prepared Statements ★

The third way of inserting data is the most performant in practice. It makes use of a database feature, the *prepared statements*. Java supports this with the data type `PreparedStatement`. Here, first, an SQL statement with placeholders is sent to the database, and later the data are transmitted separately. This has two advantages: the volume of data in communication with the database is smaller, and the SQL statement is generally parsed and prepared by a database, so the execution is faster.
Task:

- Create a new class, and include the following declaration in the code:
```
List<String[]> data = Arrays.asList(
    new String[]{ "jacky overflow", "bullet@jennyblackbeard.red", "17",
                  "1976-12-17", "If love a crime" },
    new String[]{ "IvyIcon", "array.field@graceobool.cool", "12",
                  "1980-06-12", "U&I" },
    new String[]{ "Lulu De Sea", "arielle@dirtyanne.fail", "13",
                  "1983-11-24", "You can be my prince" }
);
```

- Create a prepared statement string with the following SQL statement:
```
String preparedSql = "INSERT INTO Pirate " +
                     "(nickname, email, swordlength, birthdate,
description) " +
                     "VALUES (?, ?, ?, ?, ?)";
```

- Loop over the list `data`, fill a `PreparedStatement`, and submit the data.
- All insert operations should be done in one large transactional block.

Request Data ★

Our recent program inserted new rows in the database; it's time to read them out!
Task:

- Send with `executeQuery(…)` a.
  SELECT nickname, swordlength, birthdate **FROM** Pirate
  to the database.
- Read the results, and output the nickname, sword length, and birthdate to the screen.

Interactive Scrolling through the ResultSet ★

For many databases, a `Statement` can be configured so that:

- The `ResultSet` can not only be read, but also modified, so that data can easily be written back to the database, and
- The cursor on the result set can not only be moved down with `next()`, but can also be arbitrarily positioned or set relatively upward.

Captain CiaoCiao wants to scroll through all the pirates of the databases in an interactive application.
Task:

- Initially, the application should display the number of records.
- The interactive application listens for console input. d (down) or n (next) shall fill the `ResultSet` with the next row, u (up) or p (previous) with the previous row. After the input, the call name of the pirate shall be output; no other details are asked.
- Consider that `next()` cannot jump after the last line and `previous()` cannot jump before the first line.

Pirate Repository ★★

Every major application relies on external data in some way. From the domain-driven design (DDD), there is the concept of a *repository*. A repository provides *CRUD operations*: create, read, update, and delete. The repository is an intermediary between the business logic and the data store. Java programs should only work with objects, and the repository maps the Java objects to the data store and, conversely, convert the native data in, for example, a relational database to Java objects. In the best case, the business logic has no idea whatsoever what format the Java objects are stored in.

To exchange objects between the business logic and the database, we want to use a custom Java record Pirate. (Before Java 16, you must use a class, and it can be immutable and have a parameterized constructor.) Objects that are mapped to relational databases, and have an ID, are called *Entity-Bean* in Java jargon. Entity Bean
com/tutego/exercise/jdbc/PirateRepositoryDemo.java

```
record Pirate(
    Long id,
    String nickname,
    String email,
    int swordLength,
```

```
    LocalDate birthdate,
    String description
) { }
```

The business logic retrieves or writes the data via the repository. Each of these operations is expressed by a method. Each repository looks a bit different because the business logic wants to retrieve or write back different information from or to the data store.

Task:

In modeling the application, it has been found that a `PirateRepository` is needed and must provide three methods:

- `List<Pirate> findAll()`: returns a list of all pirates in the database.
- `Optional<Pirate> findById(long id)`: returns a pirate using an ID or, if there is no pirate with the ID in the database, an `Optional.empty()`.
- `Pirate save(Pirate pirate)`: saves or updates a pirate. If the pirate does not have a primary key yet, which means id `== null`, a SQL `INSERT` shall be used to write the pirate to the database. If the pirate has a primary key, then the pirate has already been stored in the database before, and the `save(...)` method must use an SQL `UPDATE` to update it instead. The `save(...)` method responds with a `Pirate` object that always has the set key.

After a `PirateRepository` is developed, the following should be possible:

com/tutego/exercise/jdbc/PirateRepositoryDemo.java

```
PirateRepository pirates=new PirateRepository( "jdbc:h2:./pirates-dating" );
pirates.findAll().forEach( System.out::println );
System.out.println( pirates.findById( 1L ) );
System.out.println( pirates.findById( -1111L ) );
Pirate newPirate=new Pirate(
    null, "BachelorsDelight", "GoldenFleece@RoyalFortune.firm", 15,
    LocalDate.of( 1972, 8, 13 ), "Best Sea Clit" );
Pirate savedPirate=pirates.save( newPirate );
System.out.println( savedPirate );
Pirate updatedPirate=new Pirate(
    savedPirate.id(), savedPirate.nickname(), savedPirate.email(),
    savedPirate.swordLength()+1, savedPirate.birthdate(),
    savedPirate.description() );
pirates.save( updatedPirate );
pirates.findAll().forEach( System.out::println );
```

Query Column Metadata ★

Usually, in Java programs, the schema of a database is known, and queries can access all columns individually. However, there are queries and modeling where the number of columns is not known in advance. After a query, JDBC can request a `ResultSetMetaData`, which provides information about the total number of columns and data types of the individual columns.

Task:

- Write a method `List<Map<String, Object>> findAllPirates()`. The small `Map` objects in the list contain an association between the column name and the content of that column.
- Execute the SQL query `SELECT * FROM Pirate`.

SUGGESTED SOLUTIONS

Query All Registered JDBC Drivers

com/tutego/exercise/jdbc/DriverInfo.java

```
Collections.list( DriverManager.getDrivers() ).forEach(
    driver -> System.out.println( driver.getClass().getName() )
);
```

The static method `DriverManager.getDrivers()` returns an `Enumeration<Driver>`. Since we would rather not run the `Enumeration` manually, `Collections.list(…)` helps to put the elements into a list. Lists are `Iterable`, and so we can run over all the installed drivers concisely using a `Consumer` and output the class name.

The output will be:

```
org.h2.Driver
```

If at this point the output is empty, this is an error and the following programs will not work because the H2 driver is missing. In this case, the dependency should be checked again.

Build Database and Execute SQL Script

com/tutego/exercise/jdbc/CreateTable.java

```
final String filename = "create-table.sql";
String sql;
try ( var inputStream = CreateTable.class.getResourceAsStream(filename) ) {
  sql = new String( inputStream.readAllBytes(), StandardCharsets.UTF_8 );
}
catch ( Exception e ) { return; }

String jdbcUrl = "jdbc:h2:./pirates-dating";
try ( Connection connection = DriverManager.getConnection( jdbcUrl );
      Statement statement = connection.createStatement() ) {
  statement.execute( sql );
}
catch ( SQLException e ) { e.printStackTrace(); }
```

For Java to load the SQL file as a resource from the classpath, it is placed in the *src/main/resources* folder for any Maven project. Instead of putting the SQL file in the root directory, it can be put in the same directory as the class. In the proposed solution, the class is fully qualified com.tutego.exercise.jdbc CreateTable, which means *create-table.sql* is in the symmetric directory *src/main/resources/com tutego/exercise/jdbc/create-table.sql*.

Accessing resources from the classpath is accomplished with .class.getResourceAsStream(…), in our case we don't need to pay attention to the class loader; if Java programs otherwis load resources from the classpath, this may be relevant. When using getResourceAsStream(…) the program receives an InputStream or null if the resource is not found. If the file doesn't exist, NullPointerException will already be thrown. The program should handle this accordingly.

The InputStream class has a readAllBytes() method, and we can pass the bytes into the constructor of String so that we have the file contents.

After loading the SQL script, it can be executed. The database connection is established and a statement is requested. Statement objects provide the execute(String) method, which executes arbitrary SQL. The method is rarely used because usually, returns are relevant, like the number of changed rows or in the case of a SELECT the result.

The JDBC API reports errors via SQLException, a checked exception. In the proposed solution, the exception is caught, and errors are printed on the command line. Exception handling in JDBC is a bit more complicated because the SQLException object can contain other exceptions in a chain. In addition, SQLException objects contain a status code that documents the exact error. The following proposed solutions are somewhat simplified in that they do not have a catch block for handling SQLException; instead, the exceptions are passed up to the method caller with throws.

Insert Data into the Database

com/tutego/exercise/jdbc/InsertData.java

```java
String jdbcUrl = "jdbc:h2:./pirates-dating";
try ( Connection connection = DriverManager.getConnection( jdbcUrl );
      Statement  statement  = connection.createStatement() ) {

  String sql1 =
      "INSERT INTO Pirate " +
      "(nickname, email, swordlength, birthdate, description) " +
      "VALUES ('CiaoCiao', 'captain@goldenpirate.faith', 18, " +
      "DATE '1955-11-07', 'Great guy')";
  statement.executeUpdate( sql1 );

  String sql2 =
      "INSERT INTO Pirate " +
      "(nickname, email, swordlength, birthdate, description) " +
      "VALUES ('lolalilith', 'mefix@bumblebee.space', 12, " +
      "DATE '1973-07-20', 'I'm 99% perfect')";
  int rowCount = statement.executeUpdate( sql2, Statement.RETURN_GENERATED_KEYS );
  if ( rowCount != 1 )
    throw new IllegalStateException( "INSERT didn't return a row count of 1" );

  ResultSet generatedKeys = statement.getGeneratedKeys();
  if ( generatedKeys.next() )
    System.out.println( generatedKeys.getLong( 1 ) );
```

executeUpdate(…) is used whenever an SQL statement like INSERT, UPDATE, or DELETE is executed. The first variant of executeUpdate(…) gets the SQL string and executes it. In the second call to executeUpdate(…), the first argument is Statement.RETURN _ GENERATED _ KEYS which tells the database to pass the generated key along.

With the second executeUpdate(…), the program also remembers the return, which says something about the number of modified records; it is 0 if the SQL statement has no return. If the INSERT in our example inserts a new record, then the return value will be 1, which we can use as a confirmation.

The return is not the generated key. It can't be because keys can also be strings, for example, and the return type of executeUpdate(…) is always just int. The generated key is retrieved in a second statement, `getGeneratedKeys()`, via the `Statement` object. The method returns a `ResultSet`, as we will also see for `SELECT` statements later. The `next()` method determines if there is another row and fills the `ResultSet` with information, and the first column contains the generated primary key of type `long`. If `next()` returns `false`, there is no key to query.

Insert Data into the Database in Batch Mode

com/tutego/exercise/jdbc/BatchInsert.java

```
String jdbcUrl = "jdbc:h2:./pirates-dating";
try ( Connection connection = DriverManager.getConnection( jdbcUrl ) ) {
  connection.setAutoCommit( false );

  String sqlTemplate = "INSERT INTO Pirate " +
                   "(nickname, email, swordlength, birthdate,
description) " +
                   "VALUES (%s)";

  String[] values = {
       "'anygo', 'amiga_anker@cutthroat.adult', 11, "
       + "DATE '2000-05-21', 'Living the dream'",
       "'SweetSushi', 'muffin@berta.bar', 11, "
       + "DATE '1952-04-03', 'Where are all the bad boys?'",
       "'Liv Loops', 'whiletrue@deenagavis.camp', 16, "
       + "DATE '1965-05-11', 'Great guy'" };

  try ( Statement statement = connection.createStatement() ) {
    for ( String value : values )
      statement.addBatch( String.format( sqlTemplate, value ) );

    int[] updateCounts = statement.executeBatch();
    connection.commit();
    System.out.println( Arrays.toString( updateCounts ) );
  }
}
```

The variable `sqlTemplate` contains a formatting string into which arbitrary `VALUES` can be injected later. With an extended `for` loop, the program runs over the entries of the array and connects the SQL template to the data. The resulting string is passed to `addBatch(...)`. The `executeBatch(...)` method executes the collected SQL statements, and the return is an array containing exactly as many elements as SQL statements were executed in the batch. In the array, the cells contain the number of modified rows just as we have seen before with the `executeUpdate(...)` method.

The proposed solution does something else; it resets the *auto-commit mode*. By default, the JDBC driver puts each SQL statement it sends into its transactional block. For batch processing, it is undetermined whether the entire batch occurs in a transaction, parts of it, or each SQL statement. The Javadoc writes:

The commit behavior of `executeBatch` is always implementation-defined when an error occurs and auto-commit is true.

In the proposed solution, the batch should take place in a transaction. To accomplish this, the auto-commit mode must first be switched off. After submitting via `executeBatch()` the transaction is completed with `commit()`. If the transaction is successful and there is no exception, all statements are committed.

Insert Data with Prepared Statements

com/tutego/exercise/jdbc/PreparedInsert.java

```java
String preparedSql = "INSERT INTO Pirate " +
                    "(nickname, email, swordlength, birthdate, description) " +
                    "VALUES (?, ?, ?, ?, ?)";

String jdbcUrl = "jdbc:h2:./pirates-dating";
try ( Connection connection = DriverManager.getConnection( jdbcUrl );
      PreparedStatement stmt = connection.prepareStatement( preparedSql ) ) {

  connection.setAutoCommit( false );

  List<String[]> data = Arrays.asList(
      new String[]{ "jacky overflow", "bullet@jennyblackbeard.red", "17",
                    "1976-12-17", "If love a crime" },
      new String[]{ "IvyIcon", "array.field@graceobool.cool", "12",
                    "1980-06-12", "U&I" },
      new String[]{ "Lulu De Sea", "arielle@dirtyanne.fail", "13",
                    "1983-11-24", "You can be my prince" }
  );

  for ( String[] elements : data ) {
    stmt.setString( /* nickname    */ 1, elements[ 0 ] );
    stmt.setString( /* email       */ 2, elements[ 1 ] );
    stmt.setInt(    /* swordlength */ 3, Integer.parseInt( elements[ 2 ] ) );
    stmt.setDate(   /* birthdate   */ 4, Date.valueOf( elements[ 3 ] ) );
    stmt.setObject( /* description */ 5, elements[ 4 ] );
    stmt.executeUpdate();
  }

  connection.commit();
```

The procedure with a `PreparedStatement` is always the same: first, a `PreparedStatement` is built, which is always used in the following. The different set*(…) methods occupy the placeholders in the prepared SQL statement. Each ? is identified by an index starting at 1. For example, `setString(1, …)` assigns the pirate's call name to the first question mark. The order is exclusively that of the question marks and not that of the columns. In our SQL statement, the column `id` does not occur.

After filling each ? the prepared statement is sent with `executeUpdate()`. The automatically generated key can also be queried; we will return to this in a later task.

All operations are to be executed in a transactional block again, so the auto-commit mode is turned off again and at the end, the transaction is confirmed with `commit()`.

Request Data

com/tutego/exercise/jdbc/Select.java

```java
String sql = "SELECT nickname, swordlength, birthdate FROM Pirate";
String jdbcUrl = "jdbc:h2:./pirates-dating";
try ( Connection connection = DriverManager.getConnection( jdbcUrl );
      Statement statement = connection.createStatement();
      ResultSet resultSet = statement.executeQuery( sql ) ) {
```

```
while ( resultSet.next() ) {
  String nickname = resultSet.getString( /* nickname column */1 );
  int swordlength = resultSet.getInt( "swordlength" );
  Date birthdate = resultSet.getDate( "birthdate" );
  System.out.printf( "%-20s%-20s%10d%n",
    nickname,
    birthdate.toLocalDate().format(
       DateTimeFormatter.ofLocalizedDate(FormatStyle.LONG) ),
    swordlength );
  }
}
```

The execute*() methods of the Statement object return different result types. In the case of execute-
Query(...) the result is a ResultSet. The object allows access to the rows. A ResultSet will always
contain only the information about one row at a time. The method called next() sets a kind of cursor on
the next row of the result set and returns a boolean value with the information whether the next row could
be read or not. If next() returns true, the ResultSet contains the information about one row.

The content of a column can be read using two different approaches: with the column index, which in
SQL always starts at 1, or with the column name. There are also different get*(...) methods that convert
types. For all SQL data types, there are corresponding Java methods that give us the related Java type.
For example, the getString(...) method returns a String object for text columns. The JDBC driver
performs various conversions so that, for example, getString(...) works for any SQL column type. Java
has three own data types for SQL date and time values in the package java.sql: Date, Time (time)
and Timestamp (date and time). The data types allow converting to the data type of the Java Date-Time
API. It returns getDate(...) a java.sql.Date object that toLocalDate() converts to a known
LocalDate that can be formatted with the usual API.

Interactive Scrolling through the ResultSet

com/tutego/exercise/jdbc/ScrollableResultSet.java

```
int NICKNAME_COLUMN = 2;
String sql = "SELECT * FROM Pirate ORDER BY nickname";
String jdbcUrl = "jdbc:h2:./pirates-dating";
try ( Connection connection = DriverManager.getConnection( jdbcUrl );
      Statement   statement  = connection.createStatement(
                                 ResultSet.TYPE_SCROLL_SENSITIVE,
                                 ResultSet.CONCUR_READ_ONLY );
      ResultSet srs = statement.executeQuery( sql ) ) {

  if ( srs.last() )
    System.out.printf( "%d rows%n", srs.getRow() );

  srs.absolute( 1 );
  System.out.println( srs.getString( NICKNAME_COLUMN ) );

  for ( String input;
          ! (input = new Scanner( System.in ).next()).equals( "q" ); ) {
    switch ( input.toLowerCase() ) {
      case "u", "p" -> {
        if ( srs.isFirst() )
          System.out.println( "Already first" );
```

```
      else
        srs.previous();
    }
    case "d", "n" -> {
      if ( srs.isLast() )
        System.out.println( "Already last" );
      else
        srs.next();
    }
  }
  System.out.println( srs.getString( NICKNAME_COLUMN ) );
}
```

Before the ResultSet can be moved, the Statement object must be initialized correctly:

```
createStatement( ResultSet.TYPE_SCROLL_SENSITIVE,
                 ResultSet.CONCUR_READ_ONLY );
```

The Javadoc names the parameters resultSetType and resultSetConcurrency. The constants originate from ResultSet, and TYPE_SCROLL_SENSITIVE configures the request to be able to move the cursor freely in ResultSet. Not every database and database driver supports this feature, so an SQLFeatureNotSupportedException may be thrown.

If we succeed in building the Statement object, we can use the SELECT statement to build a ResultSet. Already, the first question about the total number of elements can be realized using the moving cursor. If we call last() of the ResultSet object, it sets the cursor to the last element. The getRow() method then returns the current row, in our case the number of records in the result set. A call to absolute(1) sets the cursor back to the first row. The ResultSet is always filled with the current data; thus, if we access the column for the call name, we get exactly the contents of the row on which the cursor is currently positioned.

For interactive use, the Scanner helps with console input. The loop is executed as long as the user does not press q (quit). In the case of u or p the user wants to move the cursor up. This is possible if the cursor is not already on the first line. This is checked by isFirst(). In the case of d or n, something similar is tested; the cursor can be moved to the next line with next() unless the cursor is already on the last line.

Pirate Repository

Before we start with the actual implementation, we should think about possible exceptions. Even though any SQL query should succeed, all queries via the JDBC API return checked inconvenient exceptions. Besides, a repository is supposed to hide the storage technology, and an SQLException does not come along very well. The chosen solution introduces a new class DataAccessException:

com/tutego/exercise/jdbc/PirateRepositoryDemo.java

```
class DataAccessException extends RuntimeException {
  public DataAccessException( Throwable cause ) { super( cause ); }
  public DataAccessException( String message ) { super( message ); }
}
```

DataAccessException is an unchecked exception that wraps every exception. Internally, our repository methods will catch an SQLException and convert it to a DataAccessException.

The `PirateRepository` is more extensive, so we will deal with the type declaration, constants, and constructor in the first part, and then with the individual methods in the next steps.

com/tutego/exercise/jdbc/PirateRepositoryDemo.java

```java
class PirateRepository {

  private static final String SQL_SELECT_ALL =
    "SELECT id, nickname, email, swordlength, birthdate, description " +
    "FROM Pirate";
  private static final String SQL_SELECT_BY_ID =
    "SELECT id, nickname, email, swordlength, birthdate, description " +
    "FROM Pirate WHERE id=?";
  private static final String SQL_INSERT =
    "INSERT INTO Pirate (nickname, email, swordlength, birthdate, description) " +
    "VALUES (?, ?, ?, ?, ?)";
  private static final String SQL_UPDATE =
    "UPDATE Pirate " +
    "SET nickname=?, email=?, swordlength=?, birthdate=?, description=? " +
    "WHERE id=?";

  private final String jdbcUrl;

  public PirateRepository( String jdbcUrl ) {
    this.jdbcUrl = jdbcUrl;
  }
  // ...
}
```

The `PirateRepository` class declares different constants for the SQL statements. We need one SQL statement each to query all pirates, to query a specific pirate with the given ID, to insert new pirates, and to update existing pirates. Only the first SQL statement to query all pirates does not use placeholders. Otherwise, the SQL strings will be used later in the `PreparedStatement`.

The program does not declare any constants for the columns; each index is documented in the code.

The constructor takes the JDBC URL and stores it in an attribute so that later the individual method can establish a new connection to this data source. If the identifier is invalid, there will be an exception later; `null` can be tested early.

We have already implemented the core of the individual methods in the previous tasks, so the JDBC API is not new.

For the first method `findAll()`:

com/tutego/exercise/jdbc/PirateRepositoryDemo.java

```java
public List<Pirate> findAll() {
  try ( Connection connection = DriverManager.getConnection( jdbcUrl );
        Statement   statement  = connection.createStatement();
        ResultSet   resultSet  = statement.executeQuery( SQL_SELECT_ALL ) ) {
    List<Pirate> result = new ArrayList<>();
    while ( resultSet.next() )
      result.add( mapRow( resultSet ) );
    return result;
  }
  catch ( SQLException e ) {
    throw new DataAccessException( e );
  }
}
```

After the Statement is built, all records are selected. The while loop goes over the result set and calls its own private method mapRow(...), which transfers a row in the ResultSet to a Pirate object. The result is placed in the list, and when the cursor reaches the end of the result, the list is returned.

com/tutego/exercise/jdbc/PirateRepositoryDemo.java

```
private static Pirate mapRow( ResultSet resultSet ) throws SQLException {
  return new Pirate( resultSet.getLong(    /* id */           1 ),
                     resultSet.getString( /* nickname */      2 ),
                     resultSet.getString( /* email */         3 ),
                     resultSet.getInt(    /* swordLength */ 4 ),
                     resultSet.getDate(   /* birthdate */    5 ).toLocalDate(),
                     resultSet.getString( /* description */ 6 ) );
}
```

mapRow(...) reads the columns with the known methods getLong(...), getString(...), getInt(...), and getDate(...) and transfers the assignments to the constructor of Pirate. The Pirate has nothing to do with the SQL data type Date, so toLocalDate() converts to a LocalDate object. Moving the ResultSet object is no part of the mapRow(...) duties.

The findById(...) method also uses mapRow(...):

com/tutego/exercise/jdbc/PirateRepositoryDemo.java

```
public Optional<Pirate> findById( long id ) {
  try ( Connection connection=DriverManager.getConnection( jdbcUrl );
        PreparedStatement stmt=connection.prepareStatement(SQL_SELECT_BY_ID) ) {
    stmt.setLong( 1, id );
    ResultSet resultSet = stmt.executeQuery();
    return resultSet.next() ? Optional.of( mapRow( resultSet ) )
                            : Optional.empty();
  }
  catch ( SQLException e ) {
    throw new DataAccessException( e );
  }
}
```

After building a PreparedStatement object, the SQL query is sent and the ResultSet is evaluated. There are two alternatives: the ResultSet could have exactly one result or none. If there is no result, then there was no pirate for the ID and the return is Optional.empty(). However, if next() returns true, mapRow(...) constructs a Pirate object from the ResultSet, which comes into the Optional and is returned.

The save(...) method needs to detect whether the record must be updated or written again based on an ID that has been set.

com/tutego/exercise/jdbc/PirateRepositoryDemo.java

```
public Pirate save( Pirate pirate ) {
  try ( Connection connection=DriverManager.getConnection( jdbcUrl ) ) {
    return pirate.id() == null ? saveInsert( connection, pirate )
                               : saveUpdate( connection, pirate );
  }
  catch ( SQLException e ) {
    throw new DataAccessException( e );
  }
}
```

```java
private Pirate saveInsert( Connection connection, Pirate pirate )
    throws SQLException {
  try ( PreparedStatement stmt = connection.prepareStatement(
                                    SQL_INSERT,
                                    Statement.RETURN_GENERATED_KEYS ) ) {
    stmt.setString( 1, pirate.nickname() );
    stmt.setString( 2, pirate.email() );
    stmt.setInt(    3, pirate.swordLength() );
    stmt.setDate(   4, Date.valueOf( pirate.birthdate() ) );
    stmt.setObject( 5, pirate.description() );
    stmt.executeUpdate();

    ResultSet keys = stmt.getGeneratedKeys();
    if ( keys.next() )
      return new Pirate( keys.getLong( 1 ),pirate.nickname(),
                    pirate.email(), pirate.swordLength(),
                    pirate.birthdate(), pirate.description() );
    throw new DataAccessException(
        "Could not retrieve auto-generated key for " +pirate );
  }
}

private Pirate saveUpdate( Connection connection, Pirate pirate )
    throws SQLException {
  try ( PreparedStatement stmt = connection.prepareStatement( SQL_UPDATE ) ) {
    stmt.setString( 1, pirate.nickname() );
    stmt.setString( 2, pirate.email() );
    stmt.setInt(    3, pirate.swordLength() );
    stmt.setDate(   4, Date.valueOf( pirate.birthdate() ) );
    stmt.setObject( 5, pirate.description() );
    stmt.setLong(   6, pirate.id() );// UPDATE Pirate SET...WHERE id=?
    stmt.executeUpdate();
    return pirate;
  }
}
```

The if statement checks exactly this case. If id == null, an internal method saveInsert(...) take
care of inserting a new record, otherwise saveUpdate(...) updates the row. Both methods return
Pirate object, which is also the return of save().

saveInsert(...) and saveUpdate(...) both work with PreparedStatement, where saveIn
sert(...) has to do a bit more work by asking for the generated key. Since Pirate objects are immutable
a new Pirate is created with the ID set. saveUpdate(...) returns the passed Pirate object.

Query Column Metadata

com/tutego/exercise/jdbc/QueryForListOfMaps.java

```java
public static List<Map<String, Object>> findAllPirates() throws SQLException
  String jdbcUrl = "jdbc:h2:./pirates-dating";
  try ( Connection connection = DriverManager.getConnection( jdbcUrl );
       Statement  statement  = connection.createStatement();
       ResultSet  resultSet  = statement.executeQuery( "SELECT * FROM Pirate"
) ) {
    ResultSetMetaData metaData = resultSet.getMetaData();
```

```
List<Map<String, Object>> result = new ArrayList<>();
while ( resultSet.next() ) {
    LinkedHashMap<String, Object> map = new LinkedHashMap<>();
    for ( int col = 1, columns = metaData.getColumnCount();
          col <= columns; col++ ) {
        String columnName = metaData.getColumnName( col );
        map.put( columnName, resultSet.getObject( col ) );
    }
    result.add( map );
}
return result;
}
```

After a query, the ResultSet method getMetaData() returns the metadata as a ResultSetMetaData object, and the number of columns in the result set is returned by getColumnCount(). Since a list is desired as the result, a container of type ArrayList is built. The ResultSet is iterated through as usual, and a LinkedHashMap is built as Map to preserve the order of the columns. A for loop goes through the columns one by one from 1 to getColumnCount(), reading the column assignment with the getObject(...) method and putting a new entry into the LinkedHashMap together with the column name. After a loop traversing all columns, the associative memory of one row contains all column mappings, and the Map is placed in the list. This is repeated for all rows, and at the end, there is a list of associative stores that findAllPirates() returns.

Operating System Access

12

Java developers often don't realize how much the Java libraries abstract from the operating system. A few examples: Java automatically sets the correct path separator (/ or \) for path entries, and automatically sets the operating system's usual end-of-line character for line breaks. When formatting for console input and when parsing console input, Java automatically falls back on the set language of the operating system.

Not only does the Java library use these properties internally, but they are accessible to all. The properties are hidden in various places, such as:

- In system properties.
- In platform MXBeans, like the `OperatingSystemMXBean` you get with `getSystemCpuLoad()`.
- In `java.net.NetworkInterface` for network cards and MAC address (media access control address).
- In `Toolkit` for screen resolution.
- In `GraphicsEnvironment` for the installed fonts.

If special information is missing, Java programs can call external native programs and interact with them, for example, to ask for more details. The tasks in this chapter focus on system properties and how to call external programs.

Prerequisites

- Know how to interact with the command line.
- Be able to evaluate environment variables.
- Be able to start external programs.

Data types used in this chapter:

- `java.lang.System`
- `java.util.Properties`
- `InputStream`
- `Process`
- `ProcessBuilder`

CONSOLE

Java programs are not just algorithms; they interact with us and with the operating system. Two of the first statements were `System.out.println(...)` and `new Scanner(System.in).next()`—a screen output and console input are typical interfaces between program and user.

DOI: 10.1201/9781003495550-1

System.out and System.err are of type PrintStream, System.in is of type InputStream. The class System has methods to redirect the three streams, for example, into files.

Colored Console Outputs ★

Even in the very earliest Java programs, we output text on the console. However, the text output on System.out and System.err shows the text once in black, then in red, so there are different colors.

In this task, we want to deal with the question of how we can write colored outputs ourselves. The solution behind this is that outputs write more than just text. There are special commands that change the color in the console, move the cursor, clear the screen, and so on. This is done by *ANSI (American National Standards Institute) escape sequences*; they start with a *control sequence introducer*, the string

\u001B[

and they end with the string

m

\u001B is the ESC character in the ASCII (American Standard Code for Information Interchange) alphabet, decimal 27.

In Java, escape sequences can easily be written to System.out or System.err, and there are libraries such as https://github.com/fusesource/jansi that simplify this via constants and methods. The only problem is that the different consoles do not necessarily recognize all escape sequences. By default, Windows' *cmd.exe*, for example, is unable to recognize any of them. However, support for some colors is common on other consoles:

- Black: \u001B[30m
- Red: \u001B[31m
- Green: \u001B[32m
- Yellow: \u001B[33m
- Blue: \u001B[34m
- Magenta: \u001B[35m
- Cyan: \u001B[36m
- White: \u001B[37m
- Reset: \u001B[0m

Suitable for decoration:

- bold: \u001B[1m.
- underlined: \u001B[4m.
- inverted: \u001B[7m.

Task:

- Create a new class AnsiColorHexDumper, and put the following constants in the class:

```
public static final String ANSI_RED    = "\u001B[31m";
public static final String ANSI_GREEN  = "\u001B[32m";
public static final String ANSI_BLUE   = "\u001B[34m";
public static final String ANSI_PURPLE = "\u001B[35m";
public static final String ANSI_CYAN   = "\u001B[36m";
public static final String ANSI_RESET  = "\u001B[0m";
```

- Write a new method `printColorfulHexDump(Path)` that reads the given file and prints it as a hexdump on the console. A hex dump is the output of a file in hexadecimal notation, i.e., sequences like 50 4B 03 04 14 00 06 00 08 00 written in columns.
- Extend the program so that colors indicate the occurrence of certain bytes in the file. For example, ASCII letters can appear in one color, but digits in another.

PROPERTIES

The term *properties* is used multiple times in Java. It stands for the JavaBean properties and for key-value pairs that can be used for configuration. When we talk about "properties" in this chapter, we always mean key-value pairs, especially the pairs that a `Properties` object manages.

Windows, Unix, or macOS? ★

The system properties contain a set of information, some of which is accessible via methods. The Javadoc lists the variables at https://docs.oracle.com/en/java/javase/21/docs/api/java.base/java/lang/System html#getProperties().
Task:

- Create a new enumeration type OS with the constants WINDOWS, MACOS, UNIX, UNKNOWN.
- Add a static method `current()` which reads the name of the operating system with `System.getProperty("os.name")` and returns the corresponding enumeration element as result.

Unify Command-Line Properties and Properties from Files ★

Properties can be set from the command line and can thus be introduced into a Java program from th outside.
Web servers run on different ports, usually 8080 in development mode.
Task:

- Write a program that can accept port information from different sources:
  - On the command line, the port can be specified with `--port=8000`.
  - If `--port` does not exist, an environment variable `port` should be evaluated, which can also be set on the command line with `-Dport=8020`.
  - If the environment variable does not exist, an assignment like `port=8888` is to be evaluated in an *application.properties* file.
  - If no specification is made at all, the port is set to 8080 by default.

  - Finally, output the port.
Example for three call variants:

```
$ java com.tutego.exercise.os.PortConfiguration
$ java com.tutego.exercise.os.PortConfiguration --port=8000
$ java -Dport=8020 com.tutego.exercise.os.PortConfiguration
```

EXECUTE EXTERNAL PROCESSES

As a platform-independent programming language, Java cannot offer everything, and so there are several ways to make requests to the host environment, to the operating system. One simple way is to call external programs, which is what is asked for in the next task.

Read the Battery Status via Windows Management Instrumentation ★★

Bonny Brain is playing a strategy game in her notebook. The next round will take 30 minutes, and since her notebook runs on battery power only, she wants to avoid having to abort the game if the battery is about to die. The following calls can be used on the command line on Windows to determine the percentage of runtime remaining and the number of minutes remaining estimated by that of the current load:

```
> wmic path win32_battery get EstimatedChargeRemaining
EstimatedChargeRemaining
90
> wmic path win32_battery get EstimatedRunTime
EstimatedRunTime
87
```

If the computer is not a laptop with a battery, the output is "No instances available." If the laptop is loaded, the result for EstimatedRunTime is 71582788 (hexadecimal 4444444). Microsoft provides details at https://docs.microsoft.com/en-us/windows/win32/cimwin32prov/win32-battery.
Task:

- In a Java program, start the Windows program wmic as an external process using ProcessBuilder. Read the result of EstimatedChargeRemaining and EstimatedRunTime.
- Consider that a laptop can be powered from the power grid or a desktop computer has no battery.

Microsoft's operating system provides an API *named Windows Management Instrumentation* (WMI) that can be used to read and, in some cases, change settings on a computer. WMI is comparable to JMX on the Java side. Because shell scripts often want to access this mapping for automation purposes, Microsoft has created a command-line interface *Windows Management Instrumentation Command-line* (WMIC).

A *WMI provider* provides information about CPU usage, motherboard, network, battery status, and much more. The following call gives a small overview:

```
wmic /?
```

SUGGESTED SOLUTIONS

Colored Console Outputs

com/tutego/exercise/os/AnsiColorHexDumper.java

```java
private static final int EOF = -1;
private static final int HEX_PER_LINE = 32;
private static void printColorfulHexDump( Path path ) throws IOException {
  try ( InputStream is = new BufferedInputStream(Files.newInputStream(path)) )
{
    for ( int i = 0, b; (b = is.read()) != EOF; i++ ) {
      String color = b == 0 ? ANSI_GREEN :
                     b == 0xFF ? ANSI_RED :
                     Character.isDigit( b ) ? ANSI_PURPLE :
                     Character.isLetter( b ) ? ANSI_BLUE :
                     b == ' ' ? ANSI_CYAN :
                     ANSI_RESET;
      System.out.printf( "%s%02X ", color, b );
      if ( i % HEX_PER_LINE == (HEX_PER_LINE - 1) )
        System.out.println();
    }
  }
}
```

Instead of reading the input in one go with `Files.readAllBytes(...)`, we open an input stream t then read byte by byte. The `for` loop declares two variables: a variable `i` controls the new line, whic should always be set after 32 hexadecimal characters, and the variable `b` contains the read byte. Th `InputStream` is read as long as the result is not unequal -1, i.e., bytes are still available.

In the body of the `for` loop, the read byte is tested and depending on the assignment, the variabl `color` is initialized with the ANSI escape sequence. If the byte does not fall into the five categories, th color is reset. Finally, the escape sequence is written together with the hexadecimal code and a newline i set after a maximum of 32 hexadecimal characters in one line.

Windows, Unix, or macOS?

com/tutego/exercise/os/OS.java

```java
public enum OS {
  WINDOWS,
  MACOS,
  UNIX,
  UNKNOWN;
  public static OS current() {
    String osName = System.getProperty( "os.name" );
    if ( osName == null ) return UNKNOWN;
    osName = osName.toLowerCase();
    return osName.contains( "windows" ) ? OS.WINDOWS :
           osName.contains( "mac" ) ? OS.MACOS :
```

```
osName.contains( "nix" ) || osName.contains( "nux" ) ? OS.UNIX :
UNKNOWN;
    }
}
```

The method current() reads the name of the operating system from the property os.name. If it is null, the answer is obvious. Otherwise, the method converts the name to lowercase for the comparisons and tests for various substrings in a cascade with condition operators. If no case distinction is caught, the name of the operating system is unknown.

Unify Command-Line Properties and Properties from Files

Since all parameters, no matter how presented, are strings, there is a separate method parseInt(String) that attempts to convert a string to a number:

com/tutego/exercise/os/PortConfiguration.java

```
private static final String PORT = "port";
private static final int DEFAULT_PORT = 8080;
private static OptionalInt parseInt( String value ) {
  try {
    return OptionalInt.of( Integer.parseInt( value ) );
  }
  catch ( NumberFormatException e ) {
    return OptionalInt.empty();
  }
}
```

The parseInt(String) method accesses Integer.parseInt(...) and catches the exceptions if the string cannot be converted to a number. Our method catches the exception and returns an OptionalInt.empty(), otherwise an OptionalInt with the parsed number.

Two more helper methods follow:

com/tutego/exercise/os/PortConfiguration.java

```
private static OptionalInt portFromCommandLine( String[] args ) {
  for ( String arg : args )
    if ( arg.startsWith( "--" + PORT + "=" ) )
      return parseInt( arg.substring( ("--" + PORT + "=").length() ) );
  return OptionalInt.empty();
}

private static OptionalInt portFromPropertyFile() {
  String filename = "/application.properties";
  try ( InputStream is = PortConfiguration.class.getResourceAsStream(filename) )
  {
    Properties properties = new Properties();
    properties.load( is );
    return parseInt( properties.getProperty( PORT ) );
  }
  catch ( IOException e ) { /* Ignore */ }
  return OptionalInt.empty();
}
```

portFromCommandLine(...) gets as a parameter the command-line arguments for evaluation. Since in principle multiple command-line arguments can be passed to the program, the method iterates through all console passes and examines whether `--port=` is present. If so, the method truncates the front part and returns the result of `parseInt(String)`. If the method finds nothing, the `OptionInt` is `empty()`.

`portFromPropertyFile(…)` evaluates the *application.properties* file in the classpath. File contents in the classpath are read in via the `Class` method `getResourceAsStream(…)` because that also supports resources packaged in a JAR archive. We first build an empty `Properties` object, then call the `load(…)` method, and pass the `InputStream`. If the file does not exist, the `InputStream` will be empty, which will throw an exception, but `catch` will catch it, as well as possible errors during loading. If the `Properties` object could be filled, we ask for the `port` property and convert it to an `OptionalInt` via our own method; if it is filled, we return the value.

The last method is `port(…)` ties everything together.

com/tutego/exercise/os/PortConfiguration.java

```
static int port( String[] args ) {
  // Step 1
  OptionalInt maybePort = portFromCommandLine( args );
  if ( maybePort.isPresent() )
    return maybePort.getAsInt();
  // Step 2
  OptionalInt maybePortProperty = parseInt( System.getProperty( PORT ) );
  if ( maybePortProperty.isPresent() )
    return maybePortProperty.getAsInt();
  // Step 3
  OptionalInt maybePortApplicationProperty = portFromPropertyFile();
  if ( maybePortApplicationProperty.isPresent() )
    return maybePortApplicationProperty.getAsInt();
  // Step 4
  return DEFAULT_PORT;
}
```

First, we test the command line. If there is a hit, we don't have to consider everything else, because passing on the command line has the highest priority.

If there is no exit from the first step, we continue with the second step. `System getProperty(String)` reads a system property, we pass the return in `parseInt(…)`. If the property does not exist, our `parseInt(…)` will return an `OptionalInt.empty()`. If there is an assignment, `port(…)` will return it.

If there was not the key with an associated value, we have to open the file and we are in step 3.

If there is no file or no port specification, comes the last step, step 4. We have no more options and return as default port 8080.

Read the Battery Status via Windows Management Instrumentation

com/tutego/exercise/os/WmicBattery.java

```
static OptionalInt wmicBattery( String name ) {
  try {
    String[] command = { "CMD", "/C",
                         "wmic", "path", "win32_battery", "get", name };
    Process process = new ProcessBuilder( command ).start();
    try ( InputStream is = process.getInputStream();
          Reader isr = new InputStreamReader( is );
          Stream<String> stream = new BufferedReader( isr ).lines() ) {
```

```
    return stream.map( String::trim )
                 .filter( s -> s.matches( "\\d+" ) )
                 .mapToInt( Integer::parseInt )
                 .findFirst();
  }
}
catch ( IOException e ) {
  Logger.getLogger( WmicBattery.class.getName() ).info( e.toString() );
  return OptionalInt.empty();
}
}
```

Since our program calls WMIC twice with different parameters, the proposed solution introduces a new method wmicBattery(…) that can be passed EstimatedChargeRemaining and EstimatedRunTime in our case. This works well because both queries always expect a numeric value.

wmicBattery(…) declares a new array and passes it to the constructor of ProcessBuilder so that the process can be started with start(). The return is the Process from which we get the output in the next step, which is our InputStream. We don't have to write anything into the process ourselves, so a separate OutputStream is not necessary. We also don't have to wait for the process to finish, which happens automatically.

There are different approaches to extract the relevant parts from the input stream. This proposed solution converts the InputStream into a BufferedReader so that the lines() method can be used, which returns a Stream of all lines. We first remove the white space at the beginning and end of each line, and then look only for lines that contain a number. This leaves either one line or no line. If a line contains a number, it is converted, resulting in an IntStream where findFirst() gives us an OptionalInt that is either empty if, for example, there is no number in the process output due to a missing battery, or otherwise contains the number. Possible errors during processing are caught and logged; the return is then an OptionalInt.empty().

In use, the method can be called as follows:

com/tutego/exercise/os/WmicBattery.java

```
wmicBattery( "EstimatedChargeRemaining" ).ifPresentOrElse(
    value -> System.out.printf( "Estimated charge remaining: %d %%%n", value

    () -> System.out.println( "No instances available." ) );
wmicBattery( "EstimatedRunTime" ).ifPresentOrElse(
    minutes -> System.out.printf(
        minutes == 0X4444444 ?
        "Charging" :
        "Estimated run time: %d:%02d h (%d minutes)%n",
        minutes / 60, minutes % 60,minutes ),
    () -> System.out.println( "No instances available." ) );
```

For EstimatedChargeRemaining, there is no value that needs special interpretation. If the OptionalInt is empty, a different operation should be performed than if the OptionalInt contains something. This is where the OptionalInt method ifPresentOrElse(IntConsumer action, Runnable emptyAction) is useful.

For EstimatedRunTime there is the special case that the battery is currently being charged and thus there is no estimate of the remaining time. The code tests this case and then returns a different string. Arguments are always passed to the printf(…) method, which is, of course, ignored in the charging case.

The output of the properties can quickly become confusing, like

```
> wmic diskdrive get
Availability BytesPerSector Capabilities CapabilityDescriptions Caption
CompressionMethod ConfigManagerErrorCode ConfigManagerUserConfig
CreationClassName DefaultBlockSize Description DeviceID ErrorCleared
ErrorDescription ErrorMethodology FirmwareRevision Index InstallDate
InterfaceType LastErrorCode Manufacturer MaxBlockSize MaxMediaSize
MediaLoaded MediaType MinBlockSize Model Name NeedsCleaning
NumberOfMediaSupported Partitions PNPDeviceID PowerManagementCapabilities
PowerManagementSupported SCSIBus SCSILogicalUnit SCSIPort SCSITargetId
SectorsPerTrack SerialNumber Signature Size Status StatusInfo
SystemCreationClassName SystemName TotalCylinders TotalHeads TotalSectors
TotalTracks TracksPerCylinder
512 {3, 4} {"Random Access", "Supports Writing"} SAMSUNG MZVLB1T0HALR-00000 0
FALSE Win32_DiskDrive Laufwerk \\.\PHYSICALDRIVE1 EXA7201Q 1 SCSI
(Standardlaufwerke) TRUE Fixed hard disk media SAMSUNG MZVLB1T0HALR-00000
\\.\PHYSICALDRIVE1 3 SCSI\DISK&VEN_NVME&PROD_SAMSUNG_
MZVLB1T0\5&1E3C5E74&0&000000 0 0 1 0 63 0025_3886_81B2_A1AD. 1024203640320 OK
Win32_ComputerSystem DESKTOP-0P7C7G7 124519 255 2000397735 31752345 255
512 {3, 4, 10} {"Random Access", "Supports Writing", "SMART Notification"}
WDC WD40EZRX-22SPEB0 0 FALSE Win32_DiskDrive Laufwerk \\.\PHYSICALDRIVE0
80.00A80 0 IDE (Standardlaufwerke) TRUE Fixed hard disk media WDC
WD40EZRX-22SPEB0 \\.\PHYSICALDRIVE0 1 SCSI\DISK&VEN_WDC&PROD_WD40EZRX-22SPEB0
\4&2D010F8D&0&000000 0 0 0 0 63 WD-WCC4E2SHPE5N 4000784417280 OK Win32_
ComputerSystem DESKTOP-0P7C7G7 486401 255 7814032065 124032255 255
```

shows. This is difficult to parse, which is why WMIC provides different output formats. At the end of the command, a /format:csv can be appended, which makes the output much easier to process.

```
wmic diskdrive get /format:csv
```

```
Node,Availability,BytesPerSector,Capabilities,CapabilityDescriptions,Caption,
CompressionMethod,ConfigManagerErrorCode,ConfigManagerUserConfig,CreationClas
sName,DefaultBlockSize,Description,DeviceID,ErrorCleared,ErrorDescription,Err
orMethodology,FirmwareRevision,Index,InstallDate,InterfaceType,LastErrorCode,
Manufacturer,MaxBlockSize,MaxMediaSize,MediaLoaded,MediaType,MinBlockSize,Mod
el,Name,NeedsCleaning,NumberOfMediaSupported,Partitions,PNPDeviceID,PowerMana
gementCapabilities,PowerManagementSupported,SCSIBus,SCSILogicalUnit,SCSIPort,
SCSITargetId,SectorsPerTrack,SerialNumber,Signature,Size,Status,StatusInfo,Sy
stemCreationClassName,SystemName,TotalCylinders,TotalHeads,TotalSectors,Total
Tracks,TracksPerCylinder
DESKTOP-0P7C7G7,,512,{3;4},{Random Access;Supports Writing},SAMSUNG
MZVLB1T0HALR-00000,,0,FALSE,Win32_DiskDrive,,Laufwerk,\\.\PHYSICALDRIVE1,,,,E
XA7201Q,1,,SCSI,,(Standardlaufwerke),,,TRUE,Fixed hard disk media,,SAMSUNG
MZVLB1T0HALR-00000,\\.\PHYSICALDRIVE1,,,3,SCSI\DISK&VEN_NVME&PROD_SAMSUNG_MZV
LB1T0\5&1E3C5E74&0&000000,,,0,0,1,0,63,0025_3886_81B2_
A1AD.,,1024203640320,OK,,Win32_ComputerSystem,DESKTOP-0P7
C7G7,124519,255,2000397735,31752345,255
DESKTOP-0P7C7G7,,512,{3;4;10},{Random Access;Supports Writing;SMART
Notification},WDC WD40EZRX-22SPEB0,,0,FALSE,Win32_DiskDrive,,Laufwerk,\\.\PHY
SICALDRIVE0,,,,80.00A80,0,,IDE,,(Standardlaufwerke),,,TRUE,Fixed hard disk
media,,WDC WD40EZRX-22SPEB0,\\.\PHYSICALDRIVE0,,,1,SCSI\DISK&VEN_WDC&PROD_WD4
0EZRX-22SPEB0\4&2D010F8D&0&000000,,,0,0,0,0,63, WD-WCC4E2SHPE5N,,400078441728
0,OK,,Win32_ComputerSystem,DESKTOP-0P7C7G7,486401,255,7814032065,124032255,25
```

The first line contains the column names, followed by the comma-separated values.

If only selected keys are requested, they are listed after get, for example:

```
> wmic diskdrive get Model,Size,SerialNumber /format:csv
Node,Model,SerialNumber,Size
DESKTOP-0P7C7G7,SAMSUNG MZVLB1T0HALR-00000,0025_3886_81B2_A1AD.,1024203640320
DESKTOP-0P7C7G7,WDC WD40EZRX-22SPEB0, WD-WCC4E2SHPE5N,4000784417280
```

Furthermore, /format:list is good to parse because it produces the property format known under Java, which is handy when there is a result. There are many other formats.

Reflection, Annotations, and JavaBeans

13

Reflection gives us the ability to look inside a running Java program. We can ask a class what properties it has, and later call methods on arbitrary objects and read and modify object or class variables. Many frameworks make use of the Reflection API, such as JPA (Jakarta Persistence API) for object-relational mapping or Jakarta XML Binding (JAXB) for mapping Java objects to XML structures. We will program some examples ourselves that would not be possible without Reflection.

Annotations are a kind of self-programmed modifiers. They allow us to enrich the source code with metadata that can later be read via reflection or another tool. Often we are just users of other people' annotations, but in this chapter, we will also practice how to write our own annotation types.

Prerequisites

- Know Class type.
- Be able to read type relationships at runtime.
- Be able to address object properties at runtime.
- Be able to read annotations.
- Be able to declare new annotation types.

Data types used in this chapter:

- java.lang.Class
- java.lang.reflect.Field
- java.lang.reflect.Method
- java.lang.reflect.Constructor
- java.lang.reflect.Modifier

REFLECTION API

The Reflection API can be used to examine arbitrary objects, and the following tasks use that to generate UML (Unified Modeling Language) diagrams of arbitrary data types. The tasks focus on practical applications; you can also do a lot of nonsense with the Reflection API, such as changing characters from immutable strings, but that's silly, and we would rather not do that.

DOI: 10.1201/9781003495550-1

Create UML Class Diagram with Inheritance Relationships ★

UML diagrams are very handy in documenting systems. Some UML diagrams can also be generated automatically by tools. We want to write such a tool from scratch. The starting point is an arbitrary class, which is examined by reflection. We can read all properties of this class and generate a UML diagram.

Since UML diagrams are graphical, the question naturally arises of how we can draw graphics in Java. We do not want to solve this problem, but use the description language *PlantUML* (https://plantuml.com/). PlantUML is for UML diagrams, what HTML is for web pages and SVG is for vector graphics. Example:

```
interface Serializable <<interface>>
Serializable <|-- ElectronicDevice
ElectronicDevice <|.. Radio
```

The arrows `--|>` or `<|--` are represented regularly, `..|>` or `<|..` are stippled.

PlantUML generates from these text documents a representation of the following type:

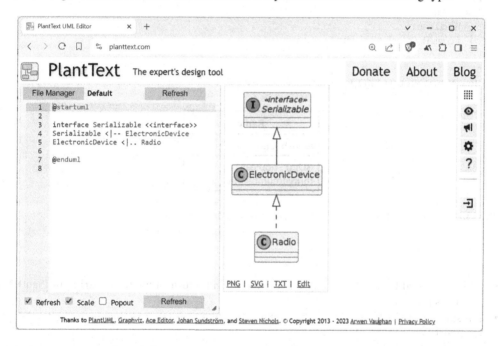

FIGURE 13.1   Representation of PlantUML Syntax as a Graphic on www.planttext.com.

PlantUML is open source, and you can install a command-line program that converts the textual description into a graph with the UML diagram. There are also websites like https://www.planttext.com that can display live UML diagrams.

Task:

- For any class, of which only the fully qualified name is given, generate a PlantUML diagram text, and output the text to the console.
  - The diagram should show the type and its base types (superclasses and implemented interfaces).
  - The diagram should also recursively list the types of the superclasses.

Example:

- For `Class.forName("java.awt.Point")`, the output might look like this:
```
Point2D <|-- Point
Object <|-- Point2D
interface Cloneable <<interface>>
Cloneable <|.. Point2D
interface Serializable <<interface>>
Serializable <|.. Point
hide members
```

Create UML Class Diagram with Properties ★

In PlantUML, not only type relationships—such as inheritance, implementation of interfaces and associations—can be described, but also object/static variables and methods:

```
class Radio {
isOn: Boolean
isOn() : Boolean
{static} format(number: int): String
}
```

The result will look something like this:

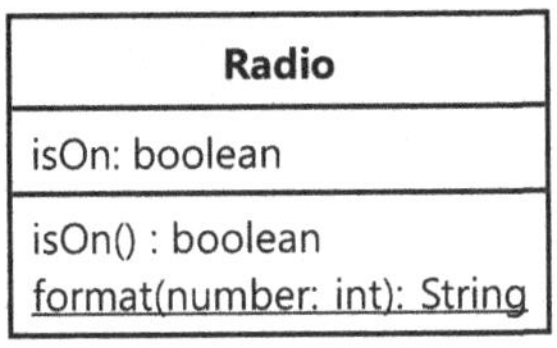

FIGURE 13.2   Representation of the PlantUML syntax as a graphic.

Task:

- Write a method that retrieves any `Class` object and returns a multi-line string in PlantUML syntax as the result.
- It is sufficient to include *only* the object/static variables, constructors, and methods, not the type relationships.

Example:

- For type `java.awt.Dimension` the output might look like this:
```
@startuml
class Dimension {
  +width: int
  +height: int
  - serialVersionUID: long
  +Dimension(arg0: Dimension)
  +Dimension()
  +Dimension(arg0: int, arg1: int)
  +equals(arg0: Object): Boolean
  +toString(): String
  +hashCode(): int
  +getSize(): Dimension
```

```
    - initIDs(): void
   +setSize(arg0: Dimension): void
   +setSize(arg0: double, arg1: double): void
   +setSize(arg0: int, arg1: int): void
   +getWidth(): double
   +getHeight(): double
 }
 @enduml
```

Generate CSV Files from List Entries ★★

In a CSV (comma-separated values) file, the entries are separated by comma or semicolon, it looks like this:

```
1;2;3
4;5;6
```

Task:

- Write a static method `writeAsCsv(List<?> objects, Appendable out)` that traverses all objects in the list, extracts all information via reflection, and then writes the results in CSV format to the given output stream.
- To extract, we can either call the public JavaBean getters (if we want to go via properties) or access the (internal) instance variables—the solution can use one of the two variants.

Example usage:

```
Point p = new Point( 1, 2 );
Point q = new Point( 3, 4 );
List<?> list = Arrays.asList( p, q );
Writer out = new StringWriter();
writeAsCsv( list, out );
System.out.println( out );
```

Bonus: if you use accesses to instance variables, the instance variables marked with the modifier `transient` should not be written.

ANNOTATIONS

Annotations allow us to introduce metadata into Java code that can later read—usually via Reflection. Annotations have become essential because many developers express configurations declaratively and leave the actual execution to the framework.

Create CSV Documents from Annotated Instance Variables ★★

Given a class with annotations:

```
@Csv
class Pirate {
  @CsvColumn String name;
  @CsvColumn String profession;
  @CsvColumn int height;
  @CsvColumn( format = "### €" ) double income;
  @CsvColumn( format = "###.00" ) Object weight;
  String secrets;
}
```

Task:

- Declare the annotation @Csv, which can only be set on type declarations.
- Declare the annotation @CsvColumn, which can only be set on instance variables.
- Allow a string attribute format at @CsvColumn, for a pattern that controls the formatting of the number using a DecimalFormat pattern.
- Create a class CsvWriter with a constructor that stores a Class object as a type-token and also a Writer, where the CSV rows will be written later. The class CsvWriter can be AutoCloseable.
- Create CsvWriter as a generic type CsvWriter<T>.
- Write two new methods.
  - void writeObject(T object): Write an object.
  - void write(Iterable<? extends T> iterable): Write multiple objects.
- The separator for the CSV columns is ';' by default, but should be able to be changed via a method delimiter(char).
- Consider what error cases may occur and report them as an unchecked exception.

Example usage:

```
Pirate p1 = new Pirate();
p1.name = "Hotzenplotz";
p1.profession = null;
p1.height = 192;
p1.income = 124234.3234;
p1.weight = 89.10;
p1.secrets = "kinky";

StringWriter writer = new StringWriter();
try ( CsvWriter<Pirate> csvWriter =
        new CsvWriter<>( Pirate.class, writer ).delimiter( ,,' ) ) {
  csvWriter.writeObject( p1 );
  csvWriter.writeObject( p1 );
}
System.out.println( writer );
```

SUGGESTED SOLUTIONS

Create UML Class Diagram with Inheritance Relationships

com/tutego/exercise/lang/reflect/PlantUmlTypeHierarchy.java

```java
public static void visitType( Class<?> clazz ) {

  if ( clazz.getSuperclass() != null ) {
    System.out.printf( "%s <|-- %s%n",
                       clazz.getSuperclass().getSimpleName(),
                       clazz.getSimpleName() );
    visitType( clazz.getSuperclass() );
  }

  for ( Class<?> interfaze : clazz.getInterfaces() ) {
    System.out.printf( "interface %s <<interface>>%n", interfaze.
getSimpleName() );
    System.out.printf( "%s <|.. %s%n",
                       interfaze.getSimpleName(),
                       clazz.getSimpleName() );
    visitType( interfaze );      }
}

 public static void main( String[] args ) throws ClassNotFoundException {
//   Class<?> clazz = Class.forName( "javax.swing.JButton" );
   Class<?> clazz = Class.forName( "java.awt.Point" );
   visitType( clazz );
   System.out.println( "hide members" );
}
```

At the heart of the solution is the custom method visitType(Class<?> clazz), which is called recursively. We don't have to care about the object/class variables, methods, and constructors, but only about the possible superclass and implemented interfaces.

The first case distinction takes care of the possible superclass. There can be at most one of these. On the Class object, we call getSuperclass() and get either null if we have already landed at java.lang.Object in the inheritance hierarchy, or just the superclass. If we have a superclass, the program generates an arrow.

And if we found a superclass, it will have a superclass again, so we call the visitType(…) method recursively.

The second part generates the arrows for the implemented interfaces. The extended for loop traverses all interfaces. If the class does not implement an interface, the loop is not executed. If there is an interface, we ask for the name as well as the name of our own class and generate the arrow. Since this interface can extend other interfaces, we again call visitType(…) recursively.

Create UML Class Diagram with Properties

om/tutego/exercise/lang/PlantUmlClassMembers.java

```java
private static String plantUml( Class<?> clazz ) {

 StringWriter result = new StringWriter( 1024 );
 PrintWriter body = new PrintWriter( result );
 body.printf( "@startuml%nclass %s {%n", clazz.getSimpleName() );

 for ( Field field : clazz.getDeclaredFields() ) {
   String visibility = formatUmlVisibility( field );
   String type = field.getType().getSimpleName();
   body.printf( "  %s %s: %s%n", visibility, field.getName(), type );
 }
```

```
for ( Constructor<?> method : clazz.getConstructors() ) {
  body.printf( "    %s %s(%s)%n",
                formatUmlVisibility( method ),
                clazz.getSimpleName(),
                formatParameters( method.getParameters() ) );
}

for ( Method method : clazz.getDeclaredMethods() ) {
  String visibility = formatUmlVisibility( method );
  String parameters = formatParameters( method.getParameters() );
  String returnType = method.getReturnType().getSimpleName();
  body.printf( "    %s %s(%s): %s%n",
                visibility, method.getName(), parameters, returnType );
}

  body.println( "}\n@enduml" );
  return result.toString();
}

private static String formatParameters( Parameter[] parameters ) {
  return Arrays.stream( parameters )
                .map( p -> p.getName() + ": " + p.getType().getSimpleName() )
                .collect( Collectors.joining( ", " ) );
}

private static String formatUmlVisibility( Member field ) {
  return Modifier.isPrivate( field.getModifiers() )    ? "-" :
         Modifier.isPublic( field.getModifiers() )     ? "+" :
         Modifier.isProtected( field.getModifiers() )  ? "#" :
         "~";
}
```

The focus is on the plantUml(Class) — method; it generates the text for the UML diagram for Class object. Since we need to build a string, we have several options. We could use the + operator t concatenate strings, or we could use the StringBuilder and use the append(...) methods. Howeve it would be handy if we could use a format string. Here we can use the PrintWriter class, which w already know in an API-like form from System.out. A PrintWriter offers us the nice print(... println(...), and printf(...) methods. A PrintWriter is an adapter that needs a target into which writes the generated string. We want to collect the result in a StringWriter.

Then we start to write the single segments of a UML diagram. First comes the class name, the we put in the object/class variables, then the constructors, and finally the methods. The Class obje provides us with the data via corresponding methods. There is one thing in common for the object/clas variables, constructors, and methods, and that is their visibility. This can be queried via the base typ Member. The own method formatUmlVisibility(Member) translates the modifier into a strin which we include in the PlantUML code for visibility.

Constructors and methods have another thing in common, a parameter list. Therefore, there is anoth method formatParameters(Parameter[]) which generates a string for PlantUML from an arra of parameter objects. It is an array because a method or constructor can have multiple parameters, an consequently, we need to ask for the name of each parameter, and the return type. This can be seen as step-by-step transformation, and this is where the Stream API is useful. First, we generate a Stream fro the array. In the next step, we transfer the Parameter object to a string. Here we proceed as follow the string consists of the name of the parameter, a colon, and a data type. After the map(...) operation, Stream<String> is created. This string is comma-separated to a large result and returned.

Generate CSV Files from List Entries

com/tutego/exercise/lang/reflect/ReflectionCsvExporter.java

```
public static void writeAsCsv( List<?> objects, Appendable out )
    throws IOException {
  for ( Object object : objects ) {
    String line =
        Arrays.stream( object.getClass().getFields() )
             .filter( f -> ! Modifier.isTransient( f.getModifiers() ) )
             .map( f -> accessField( f, object ) )
             .collect( Collectors.joining( ";" ) );
    out.append( line ).append( "\n" );
  }
}


private static String accessField( Field field, Object object ) {
  try {
    return field.get( object ).toString();
  }
  catch ( IllegalAccessException e ) {
    throw new RuntimeException( e );
  }
}
```

The solution consists of the desired method `writeAsCsv(List<?> objects, Appendable out)` and a helper method `accessField(…)`. Since we have a list of arbitrary elements, we must first traverse the list. This is where the extended `for` loop is useful.

When we consider each item from the list, we need to generate a line for each item. This sequence of operations, from an object to the CSV line, is realized by the Stream API. Taking an object as a starting point, we first query the `Class` object and then all object/class variables with `getFields()`. The result is an array that we want to enhance to a stream. The stream thus consists of `Field` objects, and since we do not want to consider transient fields, we use the filter method from the stream to leave only the object/class variables in the stream that are not transient.

In the next step, we need to read the instance variable. For this, we rely on a separate method. The reason is that lambda expressions and checked exceptions become syntactically cluttered because a checked exception must be caught within the lambda expression. However, the Reflection API uses checked exceptions frequently. The purpose of the custom method `String accessField(Field, Object)` is to read an instance variable for a given object, and convert it to a string. The method catches a possible checked exception and encapsulates it into an unchecked exception. The stream's terminal operation collects all partial strings and concatenates them with a semicolon. Finally, the line, including an end-of-line character, is written to the `writer`.

Create CSV Documents from Annotated Instance Variables

Two annotation types must be declared for the solution. The first type `Csv` is `@Target(ElementType.TYPE)` because it is only allowed to be at type declarations, and of course, this annotation must be read at runtime, so the `RetentionPolicy.RUNTIME`:

com/tutego/exercise/annotation/Csv.java

```java
import java.lang.annotation.ElementType;
import java.lang.annotation.Retention;
import java.lang.annotation.RetentionPolicy;
import java.lang.annotation.Target;

@Retention( RetentionPolicy.RUNTIME )
@Target( ElementType.TYPE )
public @interface Csv {
}
```

The second annotation type CsvColumn is only attached to class/instance variables, so @
Target(ElementType.FIELD). However, it is not possible to restrict the application to instance variables alone.

This annotation is also read at runtime. CsvColumn has a format attribute for the formatting
string, which is empty by default. We will not evaluate empty strings later.

com/tutego/exercise/annotation/CsvColumn.java

```java
import java.lang.annotation.ElementType;
import java.lang.annotation.Retention;
import java.lang.annotation.RetentionPolicy;
import java.lang.annotation.Target;

@Retention( RetentionPolicy.RUNTIME )
@Target( ElementType.FIELD )
public @interface CsvColumn {
  String format() default "";
}
```

Let's move on to the comprehensive CsvWriter:

com/tutego/exercise/annotation/CsvWriter.java

```java
public class CsvWriter<T> implements AutoCloseable {

  private final List<Field> fields;
  private final Class<?> clazz;
  private final Writer writer;
  private char delimiter=';';

  public CsvWriter( Class<T> clazz, Writer writer ) {
    if ( ! clazz.isAnnotationPresent( Csv.class ) )
      throw new IllegalArgumentException(
          "Given class is not annotated with @Csv" );

    fields=Arrays.stream( clazz.getDeclaredFields() )
                 .filter( field -> field.isAnnotationPresent( CsvColumn.class )
                 .toList();

    if ( fields.isEmpty() )
      throw new IllegalArgumentException(
          "Class does not contain any @CsvColumn" );
```

```java
    this.clazz =clazz;
    this.writer=Objects.requireNonNull( writer );
  }

public CsvWriter<T> delimiter( char delimiter ) {
    this.delimiter=delimiter;
    return this;
  }

public void write( Iterable<? extends T> iterable ) {
    iterable.forEach( this::writeObject );
  }

public void writeObject( T object ) {

  if ( ! clazz.isInstance( object ) )
    throw new IllegalArgumentException(
          "Argument is of type "+object.getClass().getSimpleName()
        +" but must be of type "+clazz.getSimpleName() );

  String line=fields.stream()
                    .map( field -> getFieldValue( object, field ) )
                    .collect( Collectors.joining(
                          Character.toString( delimiter ), "", "\n" ) );
  try {
    writer.write( line );
  }
  catch ( IOException e ) {
    throw new UncheckedIOException( e );
  }
}

private String getFieldValue( Object object, Field field ) {
  try {
    Object fieldValue=field.get( object );

    if ( fieldValue == null )
      return "";

    String format=field.getAnnotation( CsvColumn.class ).format();

    if ( format.isBlank() )
      return Objects.toString( fieldValue );
    if ( isNumericType( fieldValue ) )
      return new DecimalFormat( format ).format( fieldValue );

    throw new IllegalStateException( "Only numeric types can be formatted,
ut type was "
                                    +fieldValue.getClass().
etSimpleName() );
  }
  catch ( IllegalAccessException e ) {
    throw new RuntimeException( e );
  }
```

```
  }

  private static boolean isNumericType( Object value ) {
    return Stream.of( Integer.class, Long.class, Double.class,
                      BigInteger.class, BigDecimal.class )
              .anyMatch( clazz -> clazz.isInstance( value ) );
  }

  @Override public void close() {
    try {
      writer.close();
    }
    catch ( IOException e ) {
      throw new UncheckedIOException( e );
    }
  }
}
```

The constructor takes a `Class` object and a `Writer` and performs checks and preprocessing.

1. First, the constructor performs a test whether what is to be written later has the marking annotation `Csv`; if not, there is a runtime exception. This way, this test does not have to be repeated later when writing. Since the types will also always be the same when writing later, and reflection at runtime should be avoided for performance reasons, the constructor fetches the corresponding `Field` objects and stores them. Only the `Field` objects annotated with @ `CsvColumn` are placed in the internal list. If this list is empty, there is an exception because this would mean that there is nothing to write. Moreover, the constructor remembers the `Class` object for a later test because generics are just a trick of the compiler and at runtime wrong types could be foisted after all.

2. The `Writer` is stored internally, and as usual, an early test ensures that this `Writer` is not `null`. Our class implements `AutoCloseable`, and the implemented `close()` method closes the underlying `Writer`. Thus, `CsvWriter` can be used well in a `try`-with-resources block.

The delimiter, that is the CSV separator for the columns, can be reassigned by `delimiter(char)`. The method returns the current `CsvWriter`, so that calls cascade well in a fluent API way. Whether the delimiter is reasonable or not is not tested by the method. In principle, the delimiter could be a `'a'`, `'\n'`, or `'\u000'`.

`writeObject(T)` writes a single object that the `write(Iterable<? extends T>)` method can well access. The `forEach(...)` method provided by `Iterable` iterates over all the data and calls `writeObject(T)` on each element.

First, `writeObject(T)` performs a type check to see if the argument is type-compatible with the one declared in the constructor via the `Class` object. `clazz.isInstance(...)` is the dynamic variant of `instanceof`. If the type does not match, there is an exception. In the next step, the `Stream` walks overall `Field` elements, gets the value of the instance variable converted to a string for each `Field` with `getFieldValue(...)`, and finally assembles all strings with the delimiter for the CSV output. At the end of the line, there is a line break. The resulting string is written to `Writer` and a possible `IOException` is caught and translated into an unchecked exception. `getFieldValue(...)` is a separate method that hides the complexity for accessing and formatting numeric values.

The `getFieldValue(...)` method gets the object with the data and the `Field` object for the instance variable. The `Field` method `get(...)` returns the value stored in the instance variable. If it is `null`, then is nothing to write, and we return the empty string.

Now there are two possibilities: at the `CsvColumn` there is the `format` attribute with a formatting pattern or not.

- If there is no formatting pattern, or the format consists only of blanks, then the string representation of the value is returned.
- If there is a formatting pattern, `isNumericType(...)` checks whether the value in the attribute is numeric. This property could have been tested already in the constructor, but this would have a disadvantage: if the type is `Object` for example and there is a `Double` behind it at runtime, this is perfectly fine. Only at runtime, this can be tested. For a numeric attribute, the `format(...)` method of `DecimalFormat` returns the string representation. If a formatting pattern is given, but the type is not numeric, an `IllegalStateException` follows.

`DecimalFormat` can format different types automatically. The valid types are tested via the own method `isNumericType(...)`. These include `Integer`, `Long`, `Double`, `BigInteger`, and `BigDecimal`.

Epilogue

Kudos to those who persevered through the tasks, delved into the suggested solutions, and made it to the finish line. The journey may have been long, but now the groundwork for a prosperous Java career has been laid. But let's be real, this is just the beginning. The truly triumphant ones consistently follow these three steps:

1. Read books, study blog entries, watch learning videos.
2. Code, tinker, and scrutinize your own solutions with a critical eye.
3. Read and study other people's source code, recognize patterns, and learn new techniques.

In addition, there are websites and forums that regularly publish new tasks. A few free sites include:

CODE GOLF STACK EXCHANGE

"Code Golf Stack Exchange is a website for recreational programming competitions"—according to the official introduction. Some tasks are also solved in Java, many with very obscure programming languages invented just for compact notation (https://codegolf.stackexchange.com/questions).

PROJECT EULER

From the website: "Project Euler is a series of challenging math/programming problems that require more than mathematical insight to solve." Many of these problems come from mathematics, but developers must also use sophisticated algorithms to solve them (https://projecteuler.net/).

DAILY PROGRAMMER

Reddit calls itself the "front page of the Internet" and consists of a large collection of forums called "sub-reddits". One of these subreddits is Daily Programmer, which is all about challenging programmers of all skill levels with weekly programming challenges. There are varying levels of difficulty (https://www.reddit.com/r/dailyprogrammer/).

ROSETTA CODE

The charm of Rosetta Code is the diversity of programming languages. There are over 1,000 programming tasks and suggested solutions in more than 800 programming languages. We as Java developers can also learn from solutions of other programming languages; probably less from a dinosaur such as COBOL, but very much from functional programming languages (https://rosettacode.org/wiki/Rosetta_Code).

Some companies also use programming tasks as part of their recruitment process. This has given rise to a business model where commercial vendors offer closed-form tasks for applicants to complete, and the HR department and chief developers evaluate the proposed solutions and retrieve metrics.

Another development is *Competitive Programming*, where the goal is to develop solutions and points are awarded for successfully completing tasks, with the person with the most points declared the winner.

Printed in the United States
by Baker & Taylor Publisher Services